Issues in Managerial Finance

Second Edition

Edited by

Eugene F. Brigham
University of Florida

Ramon E. Johnson
University of Utah

The Dryden Press
Hinsdale, Illinois

The Dryden Press Series in Finance

Bradley
Administrative Financial Management
Fourth edition

Brigham
Financial Management
Second edition

Brigham
Fundamentals of Financial Management

Brigham and Johnson
Issues in Managerial Finance
Second edition

Fama and Miller
The Theory of Finance

Gitman
Personal Finance

Jessup
Innovations in Bank Management: Selected Readings

Kreps, Jr., and Wacht
Financial Administration

Lorie and Brealey
Modern Developments in Investment Management
Second edition

Myers
Modern Developments in Financial Management

Pappas and Brigham
Managerial Economics
Third edition

Reilly
Investment Analysis and Portfolio Management

Reilly
Readings and Issues in Investments

Robichek, Coleman, and Hempel
Management of Financial Institutions: Notes and Cases
Second edition

Weston and Brigham
Essentials of Managerial Finance
Fifth edition

Weston and Brigham
Managerial Finance
Sixth edition

Preface

This second edition of *Issues in Managerial Finance* was designed to help instructors in financial management go beyond the textbook treatment of various topics and achieve greater depth in some subjects, depending upon the instructor's discretion. There was an attempt in this second edition to provide more integrative concepts. The "Overview . . ." by Pogue and Lall is placed early, and "A Simultaneous Equation Model . . ." by Francis and Rowell is at the end of the book. Finally, a provocative piece, "Can the Corporation Survive?" by Jensen and Meckling raises some serious issues about the future of the corporate financial manager.

The book is designed primarily for use in the second undergraduate or beginning graduate course in financial management. However, depending on such factors as the backgrounds of the students, the duration of the course, and the orientation of the class, the appropriate usage will vary. The organization of the book roughly parallels that of most financial management texts, so there should be no difficulty in using it in conjunction with any of the standard texts.

The rigor and analytical complexity of the articles vary somewhat, reflecting partly the fact that financial management covers both institutional and quantitative topics. We have not made an effort to stress mathematics and statistics, but neither have we attempted to avoid them when they represent the best way of handling a given problem.

Articles were selected from numerous sources, but *Financial Management* is by far the most heavily represented. While it was our attempt to find recent articles, there were some, such as Altman's and Hertz's, which present the subject with such clarity and comprehension that nothing has replaced them. Further, although the CAPM appears to be under attack, the articles by Modigliani and Pogue were included because the model development was so excellent. The philosophical underpinnings of the CAPM are very important in financial management even though there may be caveats about attempting to use that model to estimate the cost of equity of a firm.

A brief introduction for each article, a set of questions at the end of each article, and in certain instances several problems which utilize the techniques described in the article have been provided. The introductions are designed to show how the article fits into the general perspective of financial management, while the end-of-article questions and problems are designed both to help students determine whether or not they really understand the article and to facilitate classroom discussion. Both the introductory paragraphs and the questions help to integrate the articles.

Financial management has continued to undergo significant changes in recent years, and, from every indication, the dynamic process will continue. It is stimulating to participate in these developments, and we sincerely hope that this second edition of *Issues in Managerial Finance* will contribute to the effective propagation of these ideas.

Gainesville, Florida
Salt Lake City, Utah
December 1978

Eugene F. Brigham
Ramon E. Johnson

Contents

I | An Overview of Finance: Analysis, Planning, and Control

1 Wilbur G. Lewellen*

Management and Ownership in the Large Firm

The study of financial management involves normative and descriptive concepts. Normative concepts refer to what management ought to do. Most of our normative theories and analytical methods have the objective of maximizing the value of shareholders' wealth; this is equivalent to maximizing the share price of the firm's stock. Regardless of what managers actually do, this normative objective is appropriate in framing theories and decision rules. It is of interest, however, to know something of the descriptive behavior of financial managers. For example, is there any reason to believe that managers actually would focus their efforts on the share price maximization objective?

In small firms in which the managers are the owners, it is easy to believe that they would act in the interest of their shareholders. However, in large firms, the management tends to be insulated from most shareholders, and they control the firm via the proxy mechanism. This has given rise to popular assertions that management would be interested in goals other than shareholder maximization—goals such as satisfactory profits, sales maximization, growth maximization, or job security maximization for managers. Professor Lewellen's study shows that the remuneration structure of top management of large firms is consistent with the general interest of shareholders, and, hence, with income or share price maximization.

The professionalization of American corporate management during this century continues to be one of the more remarked-upon features of our industrial society. We are reminded at regular intervals, both in the popular and in the

Source. Reprinted by permission from the *Journal of Finance*, May 1969, pp. 299–322. The author is professor of industrial management, Purdue University. Professor Lewellen reduced the size of his article by eliminating some of the technical aspects of how the study was performed. Accordingly, readers who desire a keener understanding of research details should refer to the original article.

* The research represented by this paper was supported in part by the National Bureau of Economic Research with funds supplied by the Life Insurance Association of America and the Rockefeller Brothers' Fund. Support was also provided by the Ford Foundation's grant for research in Business Finance to the Sloan School of Management at the Massachusetts Institute of Technology. The latter funds were drawn on while the author held a visiting appointment at M.I.T. during the 1966–67 academic year. The computations were performed at the computer centers of M.I.T. and Purdue University. The author is indebted to Professors Daniel M. Holland of M.I.T. and Robert W. Johnson of Purdue for a number of helpful comments on the manuscript. None of the foregoing individuals or organizations are, of course, to be held responsible for the opinions and conclusions presented.

scholarly press, that the era of the owner-manager has passed. The men who run the several hundred large firms which dominate our contemporary economy are said to be motivated no longer by the monetary rewards—and stirrings of pride—traditionally attendant upon proprietorship. Instead, they are pictured as something like the private sector's equivalent of civil servants: the secure employees of an immense organization who are apt to feel only an incidental identification with the interests and objectives of the organization's owners.

If accurate, certainly, this characterization is particularly unsettling where economic analysis is concerned. Most of our received doctrine in economics is predicated on the assumption that the productive units in the community seek some form of "profit maximization" in developing their activities. Unless the professional managers who nowadays administer the affairs of those units can be relied on to adopt a proprietary attitude and thereby pursue the indicated goal, the applicability of much of our theory becomes suspect. The likelihood that this suspicion is justified has, of course, received wide attention in the literature of business and economics. Two kinds of arguments can be observed.

On the one hand, behavioral scientists have pointed out that most men—including corporate executives—are strongly motivated by other than pecuniary considerations. Hence, the expressed profit objective of the firm and the possible eventual translation of higher profits into higher rates of executive pay is described as but one of many factors influencing managerial decisions. There will will be no attempt here to become involved in that aspect of the dialogue, much less to referee the accompanying discussion. On the other hand, even those writers who are content to emphasize monetary incentives—as we shall below—have come to the conclusion that the existing links between company success and executive earnings are too weak to be counted on as an encouragement to the right kind of efforts on behalf of a firm's shareholders by its management. Thus, even insofar as higher personal earnings are thought to be important to executives, the corporate system as presently constituted is said to lack the proper payoff mechanism to validate our normative economic models. The latter contention is the one with which the current paper takes issue.

THE PREVAILING VIEW

The evidence which has been offered in this regard concerns both the strength and the form of the empirical profit-compensation relationship. A quarter century ago, Berle and Means alerted us to the tendency for effective voting control of the country's large industrial enterprises to pass into the hands of management.[1] A recent study by Larner confirmed their predictions and concluded that the takeover is now virtually complete, i.e., that only about 30 of the

[1] A. Berle and G. C. Means, *The Modern Corporation and Private Property*, New York, Macmillan, 1934.

200 largest nonfinancial corporations in the United States can still be classified as truly "owner-controlled."[2] The implication is that, for all practical purposes, top management has become insulated from a meaningful performance review by stockholders—and that, in consequence, executive rewards are unlikely to be very sensitive to changes in company fortunes. On that basis, there might be good reason to wonder whether professional managers will concentrate on traditional entrepreneurial objectives in making their operating decisions.

The complementary view asserts that, even to the extent a firm's performance and its officers' earnings *are* related, the relationship is perverse. In particular, there is some indication that intercorporate differences in top executive salary and bonus scales are more closely associated with differences in the total annual sales of the firms in question than with differences in profit levels.[3] As a result, executives are characterized as being interested primarily in raising their firms' sales—subject perhaps to some vague requirement that the corresponding profit rates be "reasonable"—rather than as attempting to maximize profits per se.[4] In this manner, they are presumably following a course which will maximize their own income.

REBUTTAL

The intention here is not to deny the fact of management professionalization, to dispute the ability of top executives to exercise voting control of their firms via the proxy mechanism, or even at the moment to question the available statistical data on the empirical salaries-vs.-sales and salaries-vs.-profits relationships. Instead, the objective will be to present some new evidence about the economic circumstances of senior corporate executives which strongly suggests that the phenomena cited above are not in themselves sufficient either to (1) create a real difference between the pecuniary interests of management and stockholders, or (2) produce a set of managerial goals which conflict with profit maximization. The argument will be that, while ownership and management in the large firm are quite obviously separated nowadays, the possible undesirable consequences of the separation have been substantially overstated.

The basis for this heresy can be found in the neglect by previous writers of two key features of the corporate executive's relationship to his company. First,

---

[2] R. J. Larner, "Ownership and Control in the 200 Largest Nonfinancial Corporations, 1929 and 1963," *American Economic Review*, Volume LVI, No. 4 (September 1966), pp. 777–787.

[3] J. W. McGuire, J. S. Chiu, and A. O. Elbing, "Executive Incomes, Sales, and Profits," *American Economic Review*, Volume LII, No. 4 (September 1962), pp. 753–761; D. R. Roberts, *Executive Compensation*, New York, Free Press of Glencoe, 1959.

[4] W. J. Baumol, "On the Theory of Oligopoly," *Economica*, Volume XXV, No. 99 (August 1958), pp. 187–198; W. J. Baumol, "On the Theory of Expansion of the Firm," *American Economic Review*, Vol. LII, No. 5 (December 1962) pp. 1078–1087; R. Marris, *The Economic Theory of Managerial Capitalism*, New York, Free Press of Glencoe, 1964.

his compensation for services rendered does not consist solely of those direct cash payments called salary and bonus which are invariably used as measures of his earnings. In fact, the executive compensation package can be shown to have been weighted quite heavily in recent years towards "ownership" items— arrangements which utilize shares of the employer corporation's common stock as the compensation medium. Second, while it is true that there are now very few large companies in which management holds a majority or even a substantial minority of the outstanding stock, it is also true that the stockholdings which executives do have are very important in terms of their *personal* wealth positions. Thus, it turns out that the income these men enjoy each year from such items of remuneration as stock options, stock bonuses, and profit-sharing plans and from the dividends and capital gains occasioned by their stock holdings in their own companies bulks large in comparison with receipts from salaries, cash bonuses, and other fixed-dollar rewards. We therefore find that the ownership-management link is not so tenuous after all. In turn, the possiblity of a continuing close identification by executives with the interests and profit objectives of share-holders seems less preposterous than the conventional view suggests. That, in its simplest form, will be the position here.

Before examining the evidence, however, one important—if not very orig-inal—point should be emphasized: implicit in the discussion is the proposition that "profit maximization" and "share price maximization" for a firm are equiv-alent concepts. The latter is merely a more rigorous and more comprehensive restatement of the former in an environment where it is necessary to deal not only with the anticipated size of the elements in a stream of corporate earnings, but with their futurity and uncertainty as well. The theoretical literature of the last decade or so dealing with corporate investment and financing decisions has, of course, established this principle as the core of the normative decision-making process. Hence, the contention throughout the paper that (1) shareholders and management can be considered to share a common economic goal whenever management's income depends significantly on the market price behavior of the firm's shares, and (2) that this goal is consistent with that of optimizing the use of resources in the community in general. While the myriad nonpecuniary motives of individual managers are ignored by such an orientation, those matters are—as was indicated at the outset—topics for another discussion.

THE COMPENSATION DATA

The origins of the present paper lie in a recently-published empirical study of executive compensation practices conducted by the author for the National Bureau of Economic Research.[5] In that undertaking, a record was constructed

---

[5] W. G. Lewellen, *Executive Compensation in Large Industrial Corporations*, New York, National Bureau of Economic Research and Columbia University Press, 1968.

of the value to senior corporate executives of all the major items in their compensation packages: pension benefits, stock options, profit-sharing plans, and deferred-pay contracts as well as salaries and bonuses. The sample chosen consisted of the men who occupied the five-highest-paid positions every year between 1940 and 1963 in each of 50 of the nation's largest manufacturing firms. The list of companies was compiled from *Fortune* magazine's tabulation of the 500 largest industrials for fiscal 1963 and is presented in the Appendix.[6] By using the compensation reports required by the SEC to appear in each firm's annual proxy statement to shareholders, an analysis was performed of the rewards enjoyed by a total of 558 different executives. The resulting data encompass some 7800 man-years of compensation experience. Because the nature of the figures generated by that analysis are central to the data developed and the conclusions reached below, the procedures followed are worth outlining briefly. For a complete description, however, the reader is referred to the original study.[7]

The magnitude of the income accruing to an individual in a given year from his salary and bonus payments was easily determined simply by applying to the observed pre-tax figures the relevant personal income tax schedule for the year, along with an estimate of the deductions and exemptions the man might have been expected to claim. In the case of rewards having more complex taxation, timing, and contingency features, the following approach to valuation was adopted: for each deferred and contingent arrangement, a "current income equivalent" was constructed, defined to be the amount of additional current income—additional salary and bonus, if you will—which would be as valuable to the executive in question as the particular arrangement being considered. In effect, the hypothesis was that the most appropriate way to go about measuring on a common scale the compensation provided by the various supplements to direct cash payments was to calculate the size of the cash increments which, if *substituted* for those supplements, would leave the relevant executives as well off.

In connection with a pension plan, for example, the question was asked: "How much of an increase in annual after-tax salary would the prospective pension recipient require in order to be able to purchase with those funds an individual retirement annuity from an insurance company similar in form and equal in value to the benefits promised him under his company's retirement plan?" The necessary annual premium payments were taken to be the "after-tax current income equivalent" of the man's pension expectations. They measure the amount of additional cash income he would have needed during each year of his active working life to guarantee himself the same level of economic security in retirement that his pension was designed to provide. By similar reasoning,

---

[6] *Fortune*, Volume 70, No. 1 (July 1964), pp. 179–198. The 50 companies combined accounted for approximately one-fourth of the sales recorded by *all* U.S. manufacturers in 1963.

[7] Especially Chapters 2 through 6. For another study with a generally similar focus, see: L. R. Burgess, *Top Executive Pay Package*, New York, Free Press, 1963.

the current income equivalent of a deferred compensation agreement was specified to be a stream of equally valuable annual salary awards beginning at the time the agreement was made and continuing up to the executive's anticipated retirement age. Once a set of such indices had been developed for all the major components of the pay package, it became possible to make convenient and accurate statements about the absolute magnitude and relative importance of originally quite dissimilar rewards. The principle followed throughout was, of course, to define "equivalence" between a series of hypothetical increments to salary on the one hand and the benefits expected from a specific deferred or contingent arrangement on the other in terms of the *after-tax present values* of the two sets of payments. In most cases, a discount for mortality as well as futurity was called for in the calculations.

STOCK OWNERSHIP DATA

Executives' stockholdings in their own companies form the other half of the story. In addition to information on compensation, the SEC requires that corporations report annually in their proxy statements the number of shares of common stock each member of their board of directors owns. Since in practice most senior officers are also directors, it became evident while gathering the data for the compensation study that sizeable ownership positions were not unusual among top executives. In fact, the stockholdings observed were often sufficiently large as to suggest that the capital gains and dividends enjoyed therefrom might be as important to the individuals in question as their reported remuneration. That possibility prompted the current paper.

The approach was simply to go through the proxy statements a second time and record, for each executive who was included in the compensation sample, the amount of his company's stock he owned in every relevant year. The published figures cover those securities which are either directly or beneficially owned by the executive and his immediate family. Because the "immediate family" definition encompasses only the man's wife and any children living at home, the likelihood is that the resulting data somewhat understate the true extent of management's ownership involvement. Securities owned by married children and by other family members are excluded—and these can, of course, be quite substantial on occasion. The bias is worth noting, since it implies that a more comprehensive set of figures would necessarily reinforce the conclusions offered here.

COMPENSATION, 1940–1963

Tables 1 and 2 present the record of senior executive compensation from 1940 through 1963 for the 50 large manufacturing companies at issue. The numbers

TABLE 1.   *COMPENSATION OF HIGHEST-PAID EXECUTIVES (MEAN VALUES)*

YEAR	BEFORE-TAX SALARY AND BONUS	AFTER-TAX SALARY AND BONUS	OTHER AFTER-TAX COMPENSATION	TOTAL AFTER-TAX COMPENSATION
1940	$135,662	$76,382 (75)	$ 25,597 (25)	$101,979
1941	141,487	65,804 (72)	25,731 (28)	91,535
1942	134,827	49,627 (75)	16,333 (25)	65,960
1943	141,334	42,523 (75)	13,938 (25)	56,461
1944	137,407	41,795 (66)	21,872 (34)	63,667
1945	133,685	41,221 (67)	20,411 (33)	61,632
1946	130,751	48,569 (70)	20,474 (30)	69,043
1947	142,700	51,497 (66)	26,820 (34)	78,317
1948	153,978	75,201 (75)	24,553 (25)	99,754
1949	164,632	78,767 (75)	26,544 (25)	105,311
1950	167,645	79,595 (65)	43,195 (35)	122,790
1951	167,176	74,536 (68)	34,805 (32)	109,341
1952	173,284	71,894 (62)	44,763 (38)	116,657
1953	175,688	73,100 (55)	58,682 (45)	131,782
1954	177,562	78,353 (55)	65,117 (45)	143,470
1955	182,515	79,480 (37)	134,950 (63)	214,430
1956	190,523	81,347 (35)	154,327 (65)	235,674
1957	188,628	80,736 (36)	146,491 (64)	227,227
1958	190,554	80,985 (48)	87,822 (52)	168,807
1959	193,966	82,695 (39)	131,315 (61)	214,010
1960	186,370	80,733 (36)	144,120 (64)	224,853
1961	185,688	80,741 (39)	126,378 (61)	207,119
1962	182,631	79,539 (35)	148,693 (65)	228,232
1963	196,343	83,568 (44)	106,256 (56)	189,824
Average 1955–63	$188,580	$81,092 (38)	$131,150 (62)	$212,242

[Numbers in parentheses denote per cent of after-tax total each year]

represent mean values for the inviduals who occupied the five highest-paid positions in each company in each year. To minimize the range of tabulations required, the data are summarized in the form of two time series: one for the single highest-paid man in every firm and one for the five highest-paid men as a group. The latter figures were derived simply by dividing the total of the means obtained for the five separate positions by five.

Several features of the data deserve comment: First, the rates of growth in remuneration depicted are quite low. Between 1940 and 1963, after-tax salaries and bonuses grew at a compound annual rate of only $\frac{1}{4}$ of 1 per cent for top executives and at 1.2 per cent for the top five together.[8] The more interesting

---

[8] Similar calculations for executives ranked each year according to the size of their salaries and bonuses instead of their total compensation show essentially the same result.

TABLE 2. *AVERAGE COMPENSATION OF FIVE HIGHEST-PAID EXECUTIVES*
(MEAN VALUES)

YEAR	BEFORE-TAX SALARY AND BONUS	AFTER-TAX SALARY AND BONUS	OTHER AFTER-TAX COMPENSATION	TOTAL AFTER-TAX COMPENSATION
1940	$ 80,889	$50,847 (85)	$ 8,826 (15)	$ 59,673
1941	84,763	43,869 (77)	13,150 (23)	57,019
1942	86,382	36,445 (82)	8,100 (18)	44,545
1943	86,963	31,625 (81)	7,395 (19)	39,020
1944	85,772	31,493 (75)	10,227 (25)	41,720
1945	86,293	31,676 (76)	9,771 (24)	41,447
1946	91,977	38,072 (79)	9,847 (21)	47,919
1947	94,501	38,800 (78)	11,107 (22)	49,907
1948	102,847	55,536 (82)	11,891 (18)	67,427
1949	107,944	57,334 (81)	13,442 (19)	70,776
1950	115,737	60,183 (76)	18,812 (24)	78,995
1951	121,568	59,167 (76)	18,200 (24)	77,367
1952	125,557	56,893 (72)	22,658 (28)	79,551
1953	133,031	59,195 (69)	26,787 (31)	85,982
1954	136,906	64,243 (69)	29,024 (31)	93,267
1955	143,284	66,036 (53)	58,975 (47)	125,011
1956	150,390	68,009 (50)	68,356 (50)	136,365
1957	148,497	67,566 (51)	65,277 (49)	132,843
1958	141,700	65,894 (60)	43,051 (40)	108,945
1959	143,691	67,022 (51)	64,141 (49)	131,163
1960	140,664	66,056 (49)	67,408 (51)	133,464
1961	138,322	65,369 (50)	66,303 (50)	131,672
1962	143,257	67,207 (48)	72,038 (52)	139,245
1963	149,174	68,982 (57)	52,567 (43)	121,549
Average 1955–63	$144,331	$66,905 (52)	$62,012 (48)	$128,917

[Numbers in parentheses denote per cent of after-tax total each year]

total after-tax compensation averages[9] rose in both cases at a somewhat faster
3.3 per cent approximate annual rate,[10] but that figure is still rather unimpressive
by most common standards. Table 3 suggests a few such standards, based on
data compiled for the NBER study.[11] Clearly, corporate executives have not
done as well as other leading professional groups; they have been outdistanced
by the opposite end of the industrial organizational structure; the firms they
work for have grown much more rapidly in every important dimension; and

[9] Obtained by adding to the after-tax salary and bonus figures the ''after-tax current income equivalents'' of all other rewards.

[10] Computed using the recorded 1955–63 averages as the terminal values for the 24-year period.

[11] Lewellen, *op. cit.*, Chapter 9.

TABLE 3. COMPOUND ANNUAL RATES OF GROWTH, 1940–63

Professional Incomes, After Taxes:

1.	Physicians	5.2%
2.	Lawyers	3.9%
3.	Dentists	5.2%

Manufacturing Production Workers'
Spendable Weekly Earnings ... 5.5%

50 Sample Companies, Aggregate Data:

1.	Assets	7.0%
2.	Net Worth	6.8%
3.	Sales	9.1%
4.	Before-Tax Profits	9.1%
5.	After-Tax Profits	8.1%
6.	Equity Market Value	10.2%

Consumer Price Index ... 3.4%

price increases have completely cancelled any "real" income advances on their part.

A second phenomenon is the pronounced shift within the pay package away from direct salary and bonus payments and toward deferred and contingent rewards. In the early 1940's, salaries and bonuses accounted for some 75 to 80 per cent of total executive earnings. Since 1955, the figure has been in the range of 35 to 50 per cent. Apparently, the high progressive personal income tax rates on cash receipts, and the availability of alternative arrangements which are treated less severely by the fiscal authorities, have had an effect on compensation policies. Whatever the cause, it obviously is no longer meaningful to cast discussions of executives' rewards in terms of salary and bonus alone.

An outgrowth of this shift in emphasis is the increasing volatility of total remuneration. The data indicate that executives really have experienced no permanent pay increases since about 1955—but they have been subjected to fairly wide fluctuations in aggregate annual earnings. The reason, of course, lies in the fact that many of the newer deferred and contingent arrangements included in the pay package depend for their value on the market price behavior of the employer firm's stock. Year-to-year changes in market conditions consequently give rise to a sharp reaction in the total remuneration figures. Stock options are a particular source of instability. For purposes of drawing conclusions about longer-term movements in the level of executive earnings, therefore, the 1955–63 averages seem a better standard than the data for any single recent year. That attitude will be adopted in most of the subsequent discussions.

Our interest in executives' ownership connections suggests that a different sort of breakdown of aggregate remuneration than that shown in Tables 1 and 2 is in order. Table 4 presents the same historical record, but with the distinction

TABLE 4.   BREAKDOWN OF TOTAL AFTER-TAX COMPENSATION, 1940–63
(MEAN VALUES)

	TOP EXECUTIVES		TOP FIVE EXECUTIVES	
Year	Earnings From Fixed-Dollar Rewards	Earnings From Stock-Based Rewards	Earnings From Fixed-Dollar Rewards	Earnings From Stock-Based Rewards
1940	$ 98,755 (97)	$ 3,224 (3)	$56,904 (95)	$ 2,769 (5)
1941	88,776 (97)	2,759 (3)	54,757 (96)	2,262 (4)
1942	63,864 (97)	2,096 (3)	42,787 (96)	1,759 (4)
1943	54,467 (97)	1,994 (3)	37,486 (96)	1,534 (4)
1944	62,353 (98)	1,314 (2)	40,787 (98)	933 (2)
1945	60,682 (98)	950 (2)	40,780 (98)	667 (2)
1946	68,295 (99)	748 (1)	47,274 (99)	645 (1)
1947	77,693 (99)	624 (1)	49,306 (99)	601 (1)
1948	97,379 (98)	2,375 (2)	66,028 (98)	1,400 (2)
1949	99,450 (94)	5,861 (6)	68,202 (96)	2,575 (4)
1950	113,944 (93)	8,846 (7)	75,146 (95)	3,849 (5)
1951	99,317 (91)	10,024 (9)	72,843 (94)	4,524 (6)
1952	96,563 (83)	20,094 (17)	70,791 (89)	8,760 (11)
1953	102,072 (77)	29,710 (23)	74,242 (86)	11,740 (14)
1954	110,582 (77)	32,888 (23)	80,811 (87)	12,456 (13)
1955	130,450 (61)	83,980 (39)	90,332 (72)	34,679 (28)
1956	125,208 (53)	110,466 (47)	89,153 (65)	47,212 (35)
1957	127,552 (56)	99,675 (44)	90,023 (68)	42,820 (32)
1958	115,935 (69)	52,872 (31)	84,322 (77)	24,623 (23)
1959	121,837 (57)	92,173 (43)	85,779 (65)	45,383 (35)
1960	116,445 (52)	108,408 (48)	83,727 (63)	49,737 (37)
1961	111,100 (54)	96,019 (46)	81,657 (62)	50,015 (38)
1962	115,906 (51)	112,326 (49)	85,854 (62)	53,390 (38)
1963	107,596 (57)	82,228 (43)	84,357 (69)	37,191 (31)
Average 1955–63	$119,115 (56)	$ 93,127 (44)	$86,134 (67)	$42,783 (33)

[Numbers in parentheses denote per cent of after-tax total each year]

drawn this time between the income provided on the one hand by those pay arrangements which make use of the corporation's stock as the means of exchange and, on the other, by what might be called "fixed-dollar" rewards: salaries, cash bonuses, pensions, cash deferred compensation contracts, and the like.

A steady transformation of the pay package over the years is again evident. Stock-based rewards were virtually nonexistent a quarter century ago, but lately have supplied anywhere from 20 to 50 per cent of total after-tax senior executive earnings. This piece of information alone might well be enough to establish the presumption that executives should, purely as a matter of self-interest, conduct the affairs of their firms with the welfare of shareholders prominently in mind.

STOCK OWNERSHIP, 1940–1963

A much stronger case can be made when the stock ownership data are examined. Table 5 records the mean dollar values of the holdings by executives of their own companies' common stock for the period 1940 to 1963. As indicated earlier, the figures represent the product of January 1 market prices and January 1 stockholdings throughout.

TABLE 5. DOLLAR VALUE OF EXECUTIVE
STOCKHOLDINGS, 1940–63 (MEAN VALUES)

YEAR	TOP EXECUTIVES	TOP FIVE EXECUTIVES
1940	$ 682,502	$ 574,743
1941	544,599	482,267
1942	315,819	363,013
1943	333,339	392,891
1944	385,107	427,821
1945	776,553	492,254
1946	708,688	389,629
1947	511,150	238,310
1948	486,597	231,318
1949	421,314	201,886
1950	469,428	232,994
1951	720,040	321,783
1952	640,840	344,438
1953	687,144	383,363
1954	634,474	341,437
1955	1,131,830	522,320
1956	1,346,068	733,359
1957	989,553	962,243
1958	1,077,381	973,250
1959	1,523,092	1,461,881
1960	1,685,288	1,932,440
1961	2,050,280	1,879,604
1962	3,256,440	3,033,896
1963	2,624,557	2,365,847

The most striking feature of the resulting time series is unquestionably the sheer magnitude of the numbers tabulated. From 1960 on, the average stockholdings of the men in the sample have been in the range of $2 to $3 million per capita.[12] This suggests a degree of ownership involvement which would be difficult to characterize as inconsequential—and difficult to regard as unlikely to have a impact on executive decision-making. Clearly, the owner-manager relationship has not entirely disappeared from the large-scale business enterprise.

[12] The January 1, 1964, data would necessarily lend further support to this assertion, since stock prices recovered from the 1962 market break during 1963.

CAPITAL GAINS AND DIVIDENDS, 1940–1963

The personal economic consequences of that relationship are easily seen. Following the procedures outlined above, the before- and after-tax annual capital gains and dividends enjoyed by executives from their employer-company stockholdings were calculated. Tables 6 and 7 summarize the results. The "net" capital gains columns denote the mean values obtained by simply adding algebraically the gains experienced by the men in the sample at each position in every year. In these figures, the losses (profits) incurred by some executives necessarily offset a portion of the profits (losses) enjoyed by their contemporaries within each interval. The "absolute" gains columns present the means for the same data summed instead on an absolute basis. The latter figures therefore provide the better picture of the actual per capita changes in executives' wealth positions occasioned by their stockholdings, whether those changes are positive or negative for any given calendar year.[13]

TABLE 6. TOP EXECUTIVES' DIVIDENDS AND CAPITAL GAINS, 1940–63 (MEAN VALUES)

Year	NET CAPITAL GAINS Before-Tax	After-Tax	ABSOLUTE CAPITAL GAINS Before-Tax	After-Tax	DIVIDENDS Before-Tax	After-Tax
1940	$ − 72,006	$ − 61,205	$ 75,291	$ 63,997	$29,976	$17,749
1941	− 61,455	− 52,236	65,152	53,379	28,253	13,808
1942	41,617	35,374	69,849	59,371	16,658	6,101
1943	54,872	46,641	99,511	84,584	16,135	4,976
1944	72,792	61,873	74,061	62,951	17,911	5,511
1945	212,559	180,675	212,559	180,675	34,287	10,263
1946	− 84,011	− 71,409	100,057	85,048	23,669	9,280
1947	8,476	7,204	95,481	81,158	27,150	10,297
1948	7,139	6,068	39,586	33,648	30,589	15,870
1949	98,613	83,821	113,136	96,165	31,730	16,026
1950	148,628	126,333	160,524	136,445	37,602	18,880
1951	159,230	135,345	181,903	154,617	43,068	20,385
1952	57,569	48,933	92,765	78,850	31,675	13,913
1953	− 58,305	− 49,559	99,107	84,240	32,689	14,512
1954	368,532	313,252	368,532	313,252	38,665	18,080
1955	267,233	227,148	284,683	241,980	50,559	22,918
1956	158,906	135,070	244,543	207,861	50,799	23,234
1957	− 149,881	− 127,398	183,564	156,029	33,803	15,079
1958	458,493	389,719	459,454	390,535	40,919	18,100
1959	193,374	164,367	261,945	222,653	41,662	18,404
1960	− 119,204	− 101,323	400,462	340,392	43,292	19,287
1961	786,968	668,922	811,500	689,775	44,756	19,810
1962	− 885,513	− 752,686	926,982	787,934	56,780	23,825
1963	725,238	616,452	739,938	628,947	73,466	31,212

[13] Pursuant to an earlier discussion, the after-tax capital gains figures listed are just 85 per cent of the corresponding before-tax magnitudes.

TABLE 7.   TOP FIVE EXECUTIVES' DIVIDENDS AND CAPITAL GAINS, 1940–63
(MEAN VALUES)

Year	NET CAPITAL GAINS		ABSOLUTE CAPITAL GAINS		DIVIDENDS	
	Before-Tax	After-Tax	Before-Tax	After-Tax	Before-Tax	After-Tax
1940	$ − 74,851	$ − 63,623	$ 77,917	$ 66,229	$30,815	$17,639
1941	− 102,100	− 86,785	104,467	88,796	30,331	14,368
1942	73,838	62,762	95,118	80,850	20,490	7,820
1943	59,689	50,735	82,681	70,287	18,379	5,836
1944	75,313	64,016	76,952	65,409	21,742	6,781
1945	119,889	101,905	119,889	101,905	21,579	6,685
1946	− 47,537	− 40,406	63,702	54,146	13,343	5,326
1947	5,312	4,515	34,113	28,996	12,580	5,178
1948	− 3,417	− 2,904	18,173	15,447	14,035	7,656
1949	42,310	35,963	48,447	41,179	14,533	7,678
1950	67,403	57,292	74,243	63,106	18,598	9,567
1951	54,581	46,393	66,374	56,417	18,848	9,514
1952	40,839	34,713	54,936	46,695	18,151	8,506
1953	− 23,930	− 20,340	46,732	39,722	18,839	8,886
1954	209,798	178,328	209,798	178,328	20,644	10,012
1955	124,859	106,130	132,545	112,663	23,090	11,051
1956	97,976	83,279	148,443	126,176	27,728	13,294
1957	− 98,778	− 83,961	178,707	151,900	30,436	14,416
1958	451,948	384,155	456,111	387,694	33,823	16,417
1959	263,113	223,646	351,440	298,724	36,044	17,506
1960	− 122,066	− 103,756	466,927	396,887	41,210	20,602
1961	547,128	465,053	747,756	635,592	45,595	22,238
1962	− 630,360	− 535,806	786,985	668,937	65,924	˙30,640
1963	549,239	466,853	559,936	475,945	71,363	32,755

By almost any criterion, the record is impressive. Capital gains—and losses—have been running at an annual rate of about $600,000 before taxes since 1960, and dividends have averaged approximately $55,000 yearly. The stock market fluctuations and high corporate dividend payments of the last several years further suggest that, if the data were extended through 1968, similar orders of magnitude would emerge.

OWNERSHIP INCOME VS. COMPENSATION

The most telling comparison is presented in Tables 8 and 9, where the four major categories of income enjoyed by the men in the sample are combined. From this set of figures, the relative importance of those items of remuneration which are most commonly pointed to as the measure of a professional manager's earnings can readily be determined.

The last two columns in each table are the significant ones. Column #5 records the ratio of executives' annual after-tax "ownership income" from

TABLE 8.   TOP EXECUTIVES' OWNERSHIP INCOME AND COMPENSATION, 1940–63 (MEAN VALUES)

YEAR	(1) AFTER-TAX FIXED-DOLLAR REMUNERATION	(2) AFTER-TAX STOCK-BASED REMUNERATION	(3) AFTER-TAX DIVIDEND INCOME	(4) ABSOLUTE AFTER-TAX CAPITAL GAINS	(5) $\frac{[(3)+(4)]}{[(1)+(2)]}$	(6) $\frac{[(2)+(3)+(4)]}{(1)}$
1940	$ 98,755	$ 3,224	$17,749	$ 63,997	0.802	0.860
1941	88,776	2,759	13,808	55,379	0.756	0.810
1942	63,864	2,096	6,101	59,371	0.993	1.058
1943	54,467	1,994	4,976	84,584	1.586	1.681
1944	62,353	1,314	5,511	62,951	1.075	1.119
1945	60,682	950	10,263	180,675	3.098	3.162
1946	68,295	748	9,280	85,048	1.366	1.392
1947	77,693	624	10,297	81,158	1.168	1.185
1948	97,379	2,375	15,870	33,648	0.496	0.533
1949	99,450	5,861	16,026	96,165	1.065	1.187
1950	113,944	8,846	18,880	136,445	1.265	1.441
1951	99,317	10,024	20,385	154,617	1.601	1.863
1952	96,563	20,094	13,913	78,850	0.795	1.169
1953	102,072	29,710	14,512	84,240	0.749	1.259
1954	110,582	32,888	18,080	313,252	2.309	3.294
1955	130,450	83,980	22,918	241,980	1.235	2.674
1956	125,208	110,466	23,234	207,861	0.980	2.728
1957	127,552	99,675	15,079	156,029	0.753	2.123
1958	115,935	52,872	18,100	390,535	2.420	3.981
1959	121,837	92,173	18,404	222,653	1.126	2.735
1960	116,445	108,408	19,287	340,392	1.600	4.020
1961	111,100	96,019	19,810	689,775	3.425	7.251
1962	115,906	112,326	23,825	787,934	3.557	7.973
1963	107,596	82,228	31,212	628,947	3.478	6.900
Average 1955–63	$119,115	$ 93,127	$21,319	$407,345	2.020	4.381

TABLE 9. *TOP FIVE EXECUTIVES' OWNERSHIP INCOME AND COMPENSATION, 1940–63 (MEAN VALUES)*

YEAR	(1) AFTER-TAX FIXED-DOLLAR REMUNERATION	(2) AFTER-TAX STOCK-BASED REMUNERATION	(3) AFTER-TAX DIVIDEND INCOME	(4) ABSOLUTE AFTER-TAX CAPITAL GAINS	(5) $\frac{[(3)+(4)]}{[(1)+(2)]}$	(6) $\frac{[(2)+(3)+(4)]}{(1)}$
1940	$56,904	$ 2,769	$17,639	$ 66,229	1.405	1.523
1941	54,757	2,262	14,368	88,796	1.809	1.925
1942	42,787	1,759	7,820	80,850	1.991	2.113
1943	37,486	1,534	5,836	70,287	1.951	2.072
1944	40,787	933	6,781	65,409	1.730	1.793
1945	40,780	667	6,685	101,905	2.620	2.679
1946	47,274	645	5,326	54,146	1.241	1.272
1947	49,306	601	5,178	28,996	0.685	0.705
1948	66,028	1,400	7,656	15,447	0.343	0.371
1949	68,202	2,575	7,678	41,179	0.690	0.754
1950	75,146	3,849	9,567	63,106	0.920	1.018
1951	72,843	4,524	9,514	56,417	0.852	0.967
1952	70,791	8,760	8,506	46,695	0.694	0.904
1953	74,242	11,740	8,886	39,722	0.565	0.813
1954	80,811	12,456	10,012	178,328	2.019	2.485
1955	90,332	34,679	11,051	112,663	0.990	1.753
1956	89,153	47,212	13,294	126,176	1.023	2.094
1957	90,023	42,820	14,416	151,900	1.252	2.323
1958	84,322	24,623	16,417	387,694	3.709	5.084
1959	85,779	45,383	17,506	298,724	2.411	4.216
1960	83,727	49,737	20,602	396,887	3.128	5.580
1961	81,657	50,015	22,238	635,592	4.996	8.669
1962	85,854	53,390	30,640	668,937	5.024	8.770
1963	84,357	37,191	32,755	475,945	4.185	6.471
Average 1955–63	$86,134	$42,783	$19,980	$361,613	2.959	4.926

dividends and capital gains to their concurrent total annual after-tax compensation. Because the absolute capital gains figures are used in this comparison, the sum of the first four columns in the tables does not necessarily define executives' aggregate income each year. In fact, the aggregate in some years was negative since capital losses at times completely overwhelmed the compensation these men received as employees (see Tables 6 and 7). Column #4 therefore is most accurately characterized as a record of the mean annual changes in personal net worth experienced from price changes in employer-company stockholdings over the period studied.

Those changes, together with dividend receipts, have clearly come to dominate executives' economic circumstances. While in the 1940's and up to the mid-1950's, compensation and ownership income were about equally important, thereafter the balance shifted strongly toward the latter. Since 1955, the average annual increments to top executives' wealth resulting from their holdings of their firms' stock have been *twice* as great as the increments generated by their compensation. For the top five executives together the corresponding figure is *three* times.

But that comparison still understates the case. As we have seen, a sizeable fraction of total remuneration in recent years has itself been attributable to stock-based pay arrangements of one kind or another. Accordingly, a better index of what might be termed the relative "ownership dependence" of senior corporate executives is provided by column #6, which lists the ratio of the sum of their dividends, capital gains, and stock-based compensation to their traditional fixed-dollar rewards. Beginning with 1955, the first three items combined have been approximately *four* times as important as fixed-dollar earnings for top executives; for the top five men, *five* times as important. This situation should certainly lead to at least some identification by executives with shareholder interests—and to some concern with the often-expressed normative financial goal of share price maximization.[14]

DISPERSION OF THE DATA

There is, on the other hand, a possibility worth exploring that the data presented may not in fact fairly depict the relevant relationships. We have been dealing

---

[14] As noted above, the precise capital gains tax rate assumed in arriving at these figures has little effect on the conclusion that ownership income substantially outweighs fixed-dollar rewards. For example, if 25 per cent were used rather than the 15 per cent actually incorporated in Tables 8 and 9, the 1955–63 "absolute after-tax capital gains" average for top executives would be $359,422 and for the top five executives $319,070. These figures would produce ratios in column #6 for the same interval of 3.979 and 4.432, respectively, instead of 4.381 and 4.926. If a capital gains rate *lower* than 15 per cent were adopted, of course, an even greater role for ownership income than that shown in Tables 8 and 9 would emerge.

here exclusively with mean values for the sample as measures of a "typical" executive's experience. Should it turn out that a small number of individuals within the group have had extraordinarily large stockholdings during the period in question, those holdings will distort the averages. Given the presence in the sample of such firms as Firestone Tire, IBM, General Tire, DuPont, and several others with a family owner-manager history, the opportunity for distortion undoubtedly exists.

In order to guard against over-doing the argument, therefore, the standard deviations of the distribution of dollar value stockholdings for each executive position in each year were computed. All individuals whose holdings exceeded by 2σ or more the original means for their positions were then arbitrarily removed from the sample and a new set of time series constructed from the remaining observations. The effect was to eliminate an average of between two and three executives from each calculation, implying about a 6 per cent reduction in the original sample throughout.[15]

This 6 per cent did in fact strongly influence the record described above. The means shown in Table 5 are diminished by anywhere from one-third to one-half by the deletions. It remains true, however, that the revised stock-holding figures are in no sense trivial, averaging roughly $1 million per capita for each of the five executive positions over the last five years studied.[16]

The attendant ownership income also continues to bulk large in relation to compensation. When, for consistency, those executives whose total after-tax compensation exceeded by 2σ the compensation means for their positions were removed from the remuneration side of the equation, approximately a 6 per cent reduction in sample size again occurred but—because the extremes in remuneration were less pronounced than those in stock ownership—the compensation means suffered a rather smaller decline due to the deletions.[17] The new comparison between the two shows after-tax ownership income averaging about three fourths the size of total after-tax compensation in the 1940's and somewhat more than matching compensation since 1955. When stock-based rewards are moved to the other side of the comparison, however, the balance once more shifts noticeably in favor of ownership income. From 1955 through 1963, dividends, capital gains, and stock-connected pay items combined were approximately two and one-half times as large as fixed-dollar earnings at every level.

---

[15] In all cases, the μ minus 2σ limit was a negative number, and no executives were therefore excluded at the lower end of the various distributions.

[16] Interestingly, both the original and the revised data indicate that the rate of growth in the dollar value of executives' stockholdings between 1940 and 1963 was substantially below the 10.2 per cent compound annual rate associated with the aggregate equity market value of the 50 sample companies (Table 3). Table 5 suggests about a 6 per cent per annum rate for executives, and the revised figures a 4-to-5 per cent rate. The typical 1963 executive therefore owned approximately one-third as much of his firm's outstanding stock as his predecessor of a quarter century earlier.

[17] The *same* individuals, of course, were not necessarily removed from both sets of data.

CONCLUSIONS

This result suggests that, for purposes of the current discussion, the specific method of presentation employed and the particular figures thereby generated are not really matters worth belaboring further. The data outlined could be reworked and reorganized at length, and the same conclusions would inevitably emerge: the stockholdings of the senior executives of large publicly-held corporations are much more extensive than is commonly supposed; a considerable portion of their compensation is provided by devices that utilize the firm's stock as the means of payment; and the income attributable to both sources has come to far outweigh that supplied by traditional fixed-dollar rewards.

All these, of course, are happy phenomena from the viewpoint of the theorist. An executive who enjoys a $600,000 annual after-tax income, of which $500,000 is traceable to the market price appreciation in his company's shares and its dividend payments (Table 8) may not be so inclined to disregard the interests of its shareholders in making managerial decisions. He might even be sympathetic toward normative models which adopt share price maximization as their stated objective. While discretion prevents one from going so far as to coin phrases like "What's good for the executive is good for the company," the temptation is difficult to overcome. Certainly, the problem of possibly conflicting management-shareholder goals in the present industrial context would appear to be somewhat less of a concern than we have been led to believe. A separation of ownership and management *functions* clearly exists; it seems that a significant separation of their pecuniary interests does not. At the very least, the hope here is that the data presented enhances our understanding of the relevant environment, and offers some improved documentation of the income consequences and opportunities confronting the professional manager.

Appendix CORPORATIONS IN THE SAMPLE

Allied Chemical
American Can
American Cyanamid
American Metal Climax
American Tobacco
Anaconda
Bendix
Bethlehem Steel
Boeing
Borden

Caterpillar Tractor
Cities Service
Continental Can
Continental Oil
Douglas Aircraft
Dow Chemical
DuPont
Eastman Kodak
Firestone Tire
General Electric

General Foods   Phillips Petroleum
General Motors   Procter & Gamble
General Tire   RCA
B. F. Goodrich   Republic Steel
Goodyear Tire   Reynolds Tobacco
Gulf Oil   Shell Oil
Inland Steel   Sinclair Oil
IBM   Standard Oil (Indiana)
International Harvester   Swift
International Paper   Texaco
IT & T   Tidewater Oil
Jones & Laughlin Steel   United Aircraft
Lockheed Aircraft   U.S. Rubber
National Dairy Products   U.S. Steel
North American Aviation   Westinghouse Electric

QUESTIONS

1. Of what concern could it be that management controls large firms?
2. Under what kind of a remuneration structure would you expect management to seek to maximize sales?
3. Do you see any danger of sales maximization as the corporate goal? Explain.
4. From a normative perspective, what is the difficulty of the profit satisficing objective?
5. What items might be included in nonsalary compensation?
6. In 1963, what was the proportion of total after-tax compensation other than salary for the top executive and for the five highest-paid executives?
7. Describe the trend in the way executives in large firms have been compensated.
8. Comment on the average dollar amount of holdings of executives in their own firms.
9. Discuss the implications of Tables 8 and 9 in the Lewellen article.
10. The data used in this study were for the period 1940–1963. Had the study been extended out through 1976, how might this have affected the conclusions?

2 | Gerald A. Pogue and Kishore Lall

Corporate Finance: An Overview

This overview in corporate finance was designed by the authors to give students a feel for the theory they are beginning to study. Equally important is that this overview integrates the various facets of finance and provides some definitions early which will be helpful throughout a course of study.

It is important to study theory in financial management because it helps to establish what financial managers ought to do. Theory establishes relationships which the perceptive student and financial manager watch for and use in developing decision rules and helps the researcher design effective tests for which data can be used to support or reject hypotheses.

Theory is the fabric which makes a body out of what would otherwise be simply a collection of topics in finance. Theory, therefore, is necessary in building a basic body of knowledge.

INTRODUCTION

In the last two decades there has been a rapid evolution in the theory of corporate financial management. The objective of this article is to give a broad overview of some of the more important results. In particular, attention will be focused on answers to such basic questions as:

1. How should capital budgeting decisions be made?
2. What dividend policy should the firm follow?
3. How much debt should the firm have in its capital structure?
4. What is the cost of capital? How is it affected by project risk? By project debt capacity?

The intent is not to be rigorous but to provide the reader with a "feel" for the theory. The article primarily is aimed at readers with some prior knowledge of the field of finance.

The presentation begins with a description of why the maximization of the market value of the firm's equity is an appropriate objective for corporate

Source.   Reprinted by permission from *Sloan Management Review*, Spring 1974, Vol. 15, No. 3, pp. 19–38. Gerald Pogue is professor of finance at Baruch College, The City University of New York, and Kishore Lall is with First National Bank of Chicago.

decision making. This leads to the fundamental problem of security valuation: the determination of the market price of a firm's common stock. In connection with valuation, certain risk-return notions are introduced which are central to the valuation problem. Having determined how the market sets the price of a company's stock, the authors will show how this price is affected by changes in the firm's investment and financing decisions. Decision rules are indicated for the firm's investment and financing strategies such that behavior consistent with these rules leads to optimal financial results (that is, maximum market value). The relevance of a firm's dividend policy to its stock valuation and hence market value also will be discussed. A relatively new investment criterion (the adjusted present value rule) will be described, and the article will end with a brief summary of a long range financial planning model that incorporates the major ideas of modern financial theory in the format of a mathematical programming model.

THE OBJECTIVE OF THE FIRM

The existence of the business corporation is justified primarily on the grounds of economic efficiency. It is believed that a group of people acting collectively as an organization can perform with greater economic efficiency than each person acting separately. In this article, the authors view the business corporation essentially as an economic unit and write from that perspective. In a free enterprise economy the means of production are owned by private individuals. Given the assumption that the firm is primarily an economic unit, the objective of the firm is to maximize the net economic gain accruing to the owners of the firm, that is to maximize the net monetary gain to the firm's stockholders.[1] In order to derive operationally meaningful decision rules that are consistent with this objective, two cases are considered: the certainty case and the uncertainty case. The first assumes that all future cash flows of the firm are known exactly. This lays the groundwork for the second case where one more realistically assumes that the firm's future cash flows are uncertain.

Security Valuation: The Certainty World Case

The price of a share of a firm's common stock is equal to the present value of the future benefits of ownership. The benefits include dividends paid while the share is owned plus any capital gains obtained when the share is sold. For example assume the stockholder contemplated selling his share at the end of the year. The price at the beginning of the year P_0 will equal the present value

---

[1] All situations are ignored where there is a potential conflict between the bondholders and the shareholders of the firm. See Fama and Miller [2] Chapter 4 for a discussion of this.

of the annual (certain) dividend d_1 (assumed paid at year end) plus the year end selling price P_1:

$$P_0 = \frac{1}{1 + R} (d_1 + P_1) \tag{1a}$$

where R is the (certain) interest rate.

P_1 however similarly can be expressed in terms of d_2 and P_2, that is

$$P_1 = \frac{1}{1 + R} (d_2 + P_2). \tag{1b}$$

If P_1 in equation (1a) is replaced by equation (1b), then

$$P_0 = \frac{d_1}{1 + R} + \frac{d_2}{(1 + R)^2} + \frac{P_2}{(1 + R)^2}. \tag{1c}$$

Continuing in this fashion an expression can be obtained for P_0 in terms of the discounted sum of all future dividends:

$$P_0 = \sum_{t=1}^{t=\infty} \frac{d_t}{(1 + R)^t} \tag{1d}$$

where d_t = the (certain) future dividend payment per share at year end t.

The Greek letter Sigma (Σ) denotes the summation for all future periods, from period 1 to infinity (∞).

Since the market value of the firm's equity is identically equal to the number of shares outstanding multiplied by the price per share, an equivalent way of restating the above is to say the total market value of the firm's equity (MV_0) will equal the present discounted value of the total dividends paid.

$$MV_0 = \sum_{t=1}^{t=\infty} \frac{D_t}{(1 + R)^t} \tag{1e}$$

where D_t now stands for the total dividend payment by the firm at the end of year t.

A higher market value of the firm's equity implies increased wealth to the owners of the firm. Thus the decision rule which management should follow is to maximize the market value of the firm's equity or equivalently the price per share of the company's stock. Before describing the uncertainty world case it would be useful to digress for a moment and introduce some basic risk-return notions.[2]

Security Risk

The rate of return to a stockholder in holding a security for one period is given by the dividends received plus the capital gains incurred in that period divided by the initial market value of the security. In a world of uncertainty, one cannot be sure of the returns to be achieved in future periods. However the rate of return can be represented by a random variable with a probability distribution indicating the likelihood of occurrence of particular values. Figure 1 shows two examples of probability distributions. Instead of dealing directly with this general distribution, it is simpler in most cases to deal with just two parameters of the distribution that succinctly summarize its relevant features. The two parameters are the expected value and the standard deviation of return.

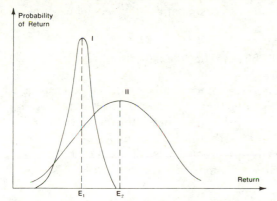

Figure 1.   Examples of Rate of Return Probability Distributions

The expected value represents the mean of the probability distribution. The expected return for distribution I in Figure 1 is E_1; the expected return for distribution II is E_2. The standard deviation indicates the "spread" of the distribution about the expected value. A distribution with a small standard deviation (a low spread, as distribution I in Figure 1) indicates a low degree of uncertainty in the value of the future return; a distribution with a large standard deviation (a high spread, as distribution II in Figure 1) indicates a higher degree of uncertainty.

When an event is termed as being risky, it is implied that the outcome of the

[2] See Fisher [3] for a complete discussion of the certainty world case.

event is not known with certainty. An event is said to be of low risk if the dispersion of possible outcomes about the expected value is small. Conversely a high risk event is one where the range of possible outcomes is large. It thus seems natural to associate the standard deviation of the probability distribution of a stock return with the risk of the stock. In this article the standard deviation of the distribution of possible future returns on a security is regarded as an appropriate quantitative measure of the total risk of the security.

Systematic Risk, Unsystematic Risk, and Diversification[3]

Much of the total risk (standard deviation of return) of a particular stock can be diversified away. When combined with other securities a portion of the variation of its return is smoothed or cancelled by complementary variations in the other securities. The nature of security risk can be better understood by dividing security return into two parts: one dependent (perfectly correlated) and a second independent (uncorrelated) of market return. The first component of return usually is referred to as "systematic," the second as "unsystematic" return. Thus,

Security Return = Systematic Return + Unsystematic Return.   (2)

Since the systematic return is perfectly correlated with the market return, it can be expressed as a factor, designated beta (β), times the market return, R_m. The beta factor is a "market sensitivity index," indicating how sensitive the security return is to changes in the market level. The unsystematic return, which is independent of market returns, usually is represented by a factor epsilon (ϵ). The return on a security, R, may be expressed as

$$R = \beta R_m + \epsilon. \qquad (3)$$

For example, if a security had a β factor of 2.0 (for example, an airline stock), then a 10 percent market return would generate a systematic return for the stock of 20 percent. The security return for the period would be the 20 percent plus the unsystematic component. The unsystematic return depends on factors unique to the company, such as labor difficulties or higher than expected sales.

If the returns on two securities are perfectly correlated with each other, then in some sense the two are identical except for a scale factor. Both have exactly the same risk-return characteristics and hence the same components of systematic and unsystematic risk. Clearly no diversification benefits can be

---

[3] The discussion on diversification follows Modigliani and Pogue [8].

gained by a combination of these two securities. Diversification only results from combining securities which have less than perfect correlation (dependence) among their returns. In this case the unsystematic risk of some securities cancels the unsystematic risk of others thereby causing a lowering in portfolio risk without a corresponding lowering in portfolio gain. The situation is depicted in Figure 2. The figure shows portfolio risk declining with an increasing number of holdings. The total risk of the portfolio consists of two parts: systematic or nondiversifiable risk and unsystematic risk. Unsystematic risk gradually is eliminated with increased numbers of holdings until portfolio risk is entirely systematic, that is, market related. The systematic risk is due to the fact that the return on nearly every security depends to some degree on the overall performance of the stock market. Investors are exposed to "market uncertainty" no matter how many stocks they hold. Consequently, the return on diversified portfolios is highly correlated with the market.

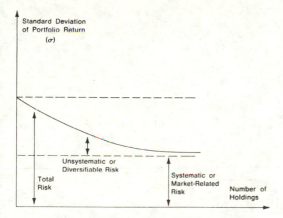

Figure 2.   Portfolio Risk and the Number of Holdings

Although in principle one would have to construct a portfolio of all the stocks in the market to obtain complete diversification, in practice the inclusion of about twenty securities which are not highly correlated with each other will assure a high degree of risk diversification. In all the following sections, it is assumed that an individual purchasing a given security either holds or is about to hold a well diversified portfolio. The only risk of consequence to him is the security's systematic risk. Changes in the portfolio composition merely reflect a shift in the degree of systematic risk that the individual is willing to bear.[4]

---

[4] According to modern capital market theory, the only risky portfolio that an individual should hold is the (fully diversified) market portfolio. An individual wishing to bear less risk than the

The Relationship between Expected Return and Risk

Since much of the total risk of a security can be eliminated by simply holding
the stock in a portfolio, there is no economic requirement for the return earned
to be in line with the total risk. Instead a security's expected return should be
related to that portion of security risk that cannot be diversified by portfolio
combination. It is a result of modern capital market theory that the equilibrium relationship between a security's systematic risk and its expected rate of
return is linear as illustrated in Figure 3. In equilibrium all securities will lie
along the line which is called the security market line. It easily can be shown
that the portfolio consisting of any two securities which plot along the security
market line itself plots along the security market line. Thus in equilibrium all
portfolios of all sizes also will plot along the security market line. This should
not be totally surprising. A security and a portfolio are both financial assets
yielding uncertain returns and can be characterized by the two parameters of
expected value and standard deviation.

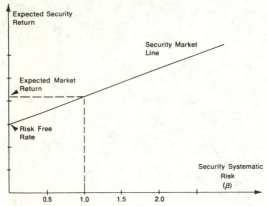

Figure 3.   Relationship between Expected Return and
Systematic Risk

Risk Aversion

A hypothesis that is crucial to the development of the modern theory of
finance is the notion that in a world of uncertainty individuals are risk averse in

---

market invests part of his funds in the market and part in the purchase of riskless bonds yielding
the risk free rate. An individual wishing to bear greater risk than the market invests his own funds
plus additional funds borrowed at the risk free rate in the market portfolio. The exact proportion
of the amount of funds invested in the market and the amount lent or borrowed at the risk free rate
will depend on the degree of (systematic) risk that the individual is willing to bear. Finally, it
should be noted that for a diversified portfolio, the terms risk, total risk, and systematic risk are all
equivalent. See Sharpe [13] for a more complete discussion.

their decision making. This means that increasing increments of compensation (expected return) are required for investors to bear increasing increments of risk. In a market populated with risk averse investors, greater expected returns can be achieved only at the cost of bearing greater systematic risk. The concepts of the previous pages now can be used to discuss security valuation in a world of uncertainty.

Security Valuation: The Uncertainty World Case

The firm is considered to be a going concern which expects to make future dividend payments. However, unlike the hypothetical certainty world case the magnitude of these dividend payments is no longer known with certainty. If the firm were in a very stable industry (such as the utility industry), the uncertainty regarding the future dividend stream would be relatively small. Conversely, a firm in a risky industry (such as the high technology electronics industry) would have a dividend stream with a high degree of uncertainty. As a firm becomes increasingly risky, the greater is the variation and hence uncertainty attached to a given dividend payment. Since it has been assumed that people are risk averse in their decision making, the market will demand increasing rates of return if it is to be induced to invest in increasingly risky stocks. The criterion for the management of the firm is to maximize the market value of the firm's equity. Market value now is obtained by discounting the future stream of expected dividends at a discount rate that reflects and compensates for the uncertainty (systematic risk) associated with the dividend stream. In symbols,

$$MV_0 = \sum_{t=1}^{t=\infty} \frac{\bar{D}_t}{(1 + k)^t} \tag{4}$$

where MV_0 = current market value of the firm's equity
$\bar{D}_t$ = the expected total dividend payment at the end of year t
k   = the appropriate discount rate.

(As discussed above, the value of k would be expected to increase as the systematic risk of the stock increased.)[5] Note the similarity between equations (1e) and (4).[6]

[5] See Solomon [14] for a fuller discussion of the uncertainty world case.

[6] Note that the capital gains are not considered explicitly. If the number of periods considered is finite, then assume that the firm is liquidated at the end of the last time period and a lump-sum dividend payment is made to the firm's stockholders. If the firm is treated as a going concern, then the capital gain in any period is merely a reflection of greater anticipated dividends in the future. The consideration of the firm's expected dividend stream is thus sufficient in determining the market value of the firm's equity.

THE FIRM'S INVESTMENT STRATEGY

The purpose of this section is to derive a decision rule (the net present value rule) for an all equity financed firm such that investment behavior consistent with this rule always will increase the market value of the firm and hence the price per share of the company's stock. The all equity assumption then will be relaxed to show how the introduction of debt leads to a simple modification of the net present value rule. This implied interaction between a firm's investment and financing decision will be examined further. Throughout the article it will be assumed that the firm can obtain all funds required from the capital markets; this is equivalent to saying that the firm is not subject to capital rationing.

The Net Present Value (NPV) Rule

Suppose the firm is faced with the opportunity of investing funds in a given project.[7] For simplicity, initially assume that the investment involves a certain initial outlay (I) to be followed by a stream of future cash inflows (C_t, where $t = 1, \ldots, T$). Assume that the uncertainty associated with future cash flows can be determined by the management. The expected value and the uncertainty of the future cash inflows together with the initial outlay provide the necessary information for management to make the correct decision regarding the acceptance or rejection of the given project.

The investment criterion which the management should use is a simple cost benefit analysis. The cost of the project is straightforward. In the example stated above, it is simply the magnitude of the certain initial outlay (I). The benefits C_t ($t = 1, \ldots, T$), however, are spread over time. If they are known with complete certainty, they simply would be discounted back to the present at the risk free rate. For an uncertain stream the present value of the benefits is computed by discounting the expected cash flows at the rate which corresponds to the project's systematic risk. If the present value of the benefits is greater than the present value of the cost of the project, then the market value of the firm will increase by the difference between the two terms, with a corresponding rise in share price. The difference between the discounted benefits and the cost of a project is called the net present value of the project. That is,

Net Present Value = Present Value Benefits − Present Value Costs

$$= \sum_{t=1}^{t=\infty} \frac{C_t}{(1 + k)^t} - I. \tag{5}$$

---

[7] It is assumed that the acceptance of the project does not change the risk characteristics of the firm. This assumption is dropped later on when the notion of the cost of capital and the adjusted present value rule are explained.

Note the similarity between equation (5) and the security valuation formulas which were derived earlier.

Investing in only those projects which have a positive NPV will increase the market value of the firm, the expected increase in market value being equal to the net present value of the project. Another way of seeing this is to note that a project with a positive net present value is earning a rate of return that is greater than that required by the shareholders on opportunities of similar risk. This extra rate of return causes the market value of the firm to rise until the return on project market value is equal to the required rate (the increment in market value being equal to the NPV of the project).

Risk Independence

Given the net present value criterion for estimating the value of a given project, how should one value a given collection of projects which are held by a firm? The solution to this multi-project valuation problem was proposed by Professor Stewart C. Myers.[8] Assuming no physical dependencies among project cash flows (that is, economies or diseconomies of scale), the value of a set of projects (NPV) is simply the sum of the values of the individual projects:

$$NPV = \sum_{j=1}^{j=N} NPV_j \qquad (6)$$

where NPV_j = the net present value of project j
N = the number of projects.

The market value of the firm can be viewed simply as the summation of the values of the individual projects. The firm can be viewed as a "mutual fund" of projects, the value of the total fund simply being the summation of the project values. The significance of the risk independence argument is that the market value of a project should not depend on the firm which undertakes it (assuming of course the absence of physical dependencies). Thus the firm's investment decision is independent of the risk characteristics of the firm's present asset structure. This is the meaning of the term risk independence.

Corporate Diversification and Mergers and Acquisitions

It would be appropriate at this stage to consider the motivation behind corporate diversification. A corporation typically diversifies in order to reduce the riskiness of its future cash flows and dividends. It achieves this objective by investing in new projects or acquiring already existing firms whose returns have a low degree of correlation with the cash flows of the

[8] See Myers [9].

firm's present assets. However, as described in the previous section, the risk independence concept implies that the market value of the new firm will simply equal the sum of values of the component firms (in the absence of physical dependencies). No gain in aggregate market value can be anticipated. Corporate diversification, while often attractive to corporate management, may lead to no benefits for the stockholders.[9] The shareholder easily can achieve any desired degree of portfolio diversification by selecting a portfolio of securities that he feels to be appropriate. Additionally, corporate diversification reduces the number of diversification options open to investors and may lead to a reduction rather than an increase in aggregate market price.

THE DIVIDEND DECISION

So far the discussion has ignored the various sources of funds which a corporation can tap to obtain financial resources for its investment projects. A firm wishing to retain an all equity capital structure has only two basic sources. It either can utilize its retained earnings, both current and future, or it can issue new equity in the capital markets. Since varying the amount of retained earnings reinvested in the firm varies the amount of dividends that the firm can pay to its stockholders, it is important to try and discern what relationship if any exists between the market value of the firm and its dividend policy. Professors Miller and Modigliani (hereafter MM) demonstrated that if (1) dividends and capital gains are taxed at the same rate; (2) all transaction costs are ignored; (3) the investment strategy of the firm remains unchanged; and (4) there are no information effects associated with current dividends; then dividend policy should not affect current stock price.[10] Any decreases in future dividends used to repurchase stock or increases in dividends resulting from new stock issues will only result in exactly offsetting changes in future share price. Current stock price remains invariant to changes in dividend policy.

As some of MM's conditions are relaxed, it would appear that if anything stockholders would prefer less dividends rather than more. First, stock issues usually are accompanied by fairly large issuing costs whereas retained earnings have no such costs associated with them. The implication is that the firm should use retained earnings instead of issuing stock whenever possible.

---

[9] The preceding analysis is not applicable if a corporation diversifies for reasons of synergy or to acquire undervalued companies. In the former case the project in question is not physically independent of the other projects of the firm. In the latter case the firm is taking advantage of market imperfections; this is contrary to the perfect market assumptions of the article.

[10] If the investment strategy of the firm is not held constant then clearly a decrease (or increase) in the funding of a profitable investment by raising (lowering) the dividend payment will decrease (increase) the market value of the firm. See [5] for MM's original paper.

Second, the differential tax treatment of dividends and capital gains should make stockholders prefer one dollar of capital gains to an equivalent amount in dividends.

Informational Content of Dividends

The management of a firm typically has much wider access than its shareholders to information regarding the firm's future opportunities. It therefore uses certain financial variables to signal its expectations of the firm's future state to the market. The dividend payment of the firm is such an indicator. Changes in dividends are based on economic grounds but are subject to the constraint that the informational content inherent in a change of dividend policy is not misleading. Consequently, a firm at times will choose the more expensive alternative of issuing new stock rather than decreasing its dividend payment and giving a false signal to the market.

A similar situation often holds in the firm's investment strategy. A firm at times may not undertake profitable investment opportunities (that is, projects with a positive NPV) if the acceptance of the project will have an adverse short run impact on the firm's earnings per share.

THE FIRM'S FINANCING DECISION

The preceding discussion has been restricted to firms with all equity capital structures. It is now time to relax this assumption and to see what effect if any the issuance of debt may have on the market value of the firm's equity. The possible existence of an optimal capital structure for the firm will be investigated. The concepts of business versus financial risk and the cost of capital will be introduced first. The discussion is based on the assumption that the investment strategy of the firm remains fixed. The assumption of a fixed investment strategy implies that equity must be retired in order to introduce more debt into the firm's capital structure.

Business versus Financial Risk

Business risk is the common term used to denote the risk of an all equity financed firm. If, however, the firm introduces debt in its capital structure, the uncertainty associated with the equity returns is increased. This is because the equity earnings are now subordinate to the fixed interest payments. Since the interest payments are known with relative certainty, the aggregate returns to the firm's stockholders will have the same total risk (standard deviation) as in the all equity case. However, this risk now is spread over a smaller equity base. The total risk per share will increase. The increment in total risk per share is termed the stock's financial risk, and it increases with the amount of debt issued by the firm. It is possible to show that an increase in a stock's financial risk also increases the systematic risk of the stock. The concept of risk aversion introduced earlier implies that stockholders will bear this additional systematic risk only if they are suitably compensated. The term leverage often is used to indicate the presence of debt in a firm's capital structure. A highly leveraged firm is one with a high proportion of debt relative to equity.

The required rate of return on the stock of a leveraged firm will be an increasing function of the degree of leverage of the firm's capital structure. The required return is called the "cost of capital." The cost of capital usually is denoted using the Greek letter rho (ρ); the cost of capital for a project j is denoted by ρ_j.

The Cost of Capital

The cost of capital for an investment is the rate of return that investors could earn elsewhere on investments of equivalent risk. It is the minimum return the project must earn to make it acceptable to the investors (when the project's NPV = 0). The greater the (systematic) risk of the project the greater will be the cost of capital. Projects yielding returns greater than the cost of capital (those with a positive NPV) will increase the market value of the firm and should be accepted.

If a project is all equity financed, the cost of capital is equal to the rate of return that shareholders would demand if the project were separately financed.[11] If the project is partially debt financed, the cost of capital (ρ_j) will be a weighted average of the cost of equity and debt capital. In the case of projects which are perpetuities, the weights will be the relative market value proportions of the debt and equity used in financing the project. That is,

$$\rho_j = i_j \left(\frac{D_j}{V_j}\right) + k_j \left(\frac{E_j}{V_j}\right) \tag{7}$$

where i_j = after tax cost of debt capital for the project
D_j = market value of debt supported by the project
k_j = cost of equity capital for the project
E_j = market value of equity in the project
V_j = market value of the project
$\quad$ = $E_j + D_j$.

By a process of aggregation the cost of capital for the overall firm (ρ) is a weighted average of the costs for the individual projects. In the case where all

---

[11] This relates back to the risk independence concept defined earlier.

the projects are perpetuities, the weights are the relative market values of the projects:

$$\rho = \sum_{j=1}^{j=N} \rho_j \left(\frac{V_j}{V_T}\right) \tag{8}$$

where V_T is the sum of V_1 through V_N (N = the number of projects comprising the firm).

The overall cost of capital ρ in the perpetuity case is also a weighted average of the aggregate debt and equity costs. That is,

$$\rho = i_T \left(\frac{D_T}{V_T}\right) + k_T \left(\frac{E_T}{V_T}\right) \tag{9}$$

where the parameters are defined for equation (7) but for the total firm rather than a single project.

Changes in the Firm's Capital Structure

MM were also among the first to analyze the capital structure problem rigorously.[12] They considered the effect of a change in the firm's capital structure on the market value of the firm, first in a hypothetical world with no corporate taxes and then in a world which taxes corporate profits and allows for the tax deductibility of debt interest payments. Their analysis, known as the MM propositions for the no tax and tax world respectively, now will be described. In both cases it is assumed that the investment strategy of the firm remains fixed; that the capital markets are perfect in the sense that transactions costs can be ignored; that the same financing opportunities exist for both private and corporate entities; and that reorganization (resulting from bankruptcy) is a costless affair (more on this later).

The MM Proposition in a No Tax World

MM's first proposition in the no tax world is that the market value of a firm is independent of the relative amounts of debt and equity in the firm's capital structure. The market value of the firm is determined solely by the magnitude and riskiness of the cash flows generated by the firm's capital assets. The firm's debt to equity ratio merely indicates how this stream of future returns will be divided between the bondholders and stockholders. It is the magnitude and riskiness of the total return stream and not its mode of partitioning between the debt and equity holders that determines the market value of the

---

[12] See MM [6] and [7].

firm. Consequently, the weighted average cost of capital in the firm is independent of leverage as well.

The result at first seems paradoxical. Is not the cost of debt capital "cheaper" than the cost of equity capital in the sense that the minimum required rate of return demanded by bondholders (the interest rate) is usually less than the minimum required rate of return demanded by stockholders? If so, will not the inclusion of more cheap debt in the firm's capital structure lower the firm's weighted average cost of capital? MM's reply is as follows: It is true that the rate of return demanded by a company's bondholders is less than that demanded by its stockholders. However, an increase in the degree of financial leverage of the firm raises the systematic risk which the stockholders have to bear. Being risk averse individuals the stockholders will accept this situation only if there is a corresponding increase in the expected rate of return on their equity. MM assert that the increase in the cost of equity capital will be such as to exactly offset the effect of acquiring cheaper debt. Similarly decreasing the amount of cheap debt will not increase the cost of capital as the reduction in the degree of financial leverage of the firm will cause an exactly offsetting decrease in the required rate of return on the firm's equity. It is thus meaningless to speak of debt as being "cheaper" than equity.

The so-called "traditionalists" would disagree. They would assert that the introduction of debt into a firm's capital structure initially will cause an increase in the stockholders' required rate of return that is less than that predicted by MM. At high debt equity ratios the increase in stockholders' required return will be greater than that predicted by MM. Even in a world with no corporate taxes, the graph of the cost of capital of the firm against the amount of debt outstanding will be "U" shaped. At the optimal degree of financial leverage the firm will have its lowest cost of capital and its highest market value.

To summarize, the weighted average cost of capital ρ is invariant to changes in the firm's capital structure. It is determined solely by the risk characteristics of the firm's investments. A further consequence of the above is that in the no tax world a project's cost of capital is independent of the mix of debt and equity funds used in its financing.

The MM Proposition in a World with Corporate Taxes

In a world which taxes corporate profits and allows for the tax deductibility of debt interest payments, MM assert that the value of a firm increases proportionally with the amount of debt outstanding in the firm's capital structure.

In the no tax world, any increase in the interest payments to the firm's bondholders causes an exactly equal decrease in the dividends available for the stockholders. This is no longer true in a world with corporate taxation. An increase in the degree of financial leverage of the firm results in an increase in aggregate distributions, due to the tax shield associated with interest payments. Given a 50 percent tax rate the corporation only pays 50 percent of the interest payments and the government pays the rest. The total returns available for stockholders increases, and the market value of the firm rises. According to the above analysis, the increase in market value should be exactly equal to the present value of the tax savings generated by maintaining the extra debt.

If the additional debt is to be maintained perpetually, it can be shown that the present value of the tax savings is equal to the corporate tax rate multiplied by the extra amount of debt outstanding. MM's proposition in the tax world can be succinctly stated as:

$$V_D = V_0 + TD \tag{10}$$

where V_D = market value of the leveraged firm (debt plus equity)

$\quad\quad V_0$ = market value of the firm with no debt in its capital structure—that is, the all equity value of the firm

$\quad\quad T$ = the corporate tax rate and

$\quad\quad D$ = total amount of perpetual debt outstanding.

The MM Proposition and Bankruptcy Costs

Taken at face value, MM's proposition in a world with corporate taxes clearly implies that the optimal capital structure for a firm should be 100 percent debt or at least 99 percent debt since a corporation must have a minimal equity participation. Few if any corporations are found to use such large amounts of debt. The reason for this apparently glaring discrepancy between "theory" and "practice" is that the assumption has been that the costs associated with bankruptcy and reorganization are zero. In the real world, however, large costs are involved in bankruptcy proceedings. Moreover, if the firm is in a very dire state but not yet bankrupt it may make suboptimal decisions in order to ward off the threat of bankruptcy. It is the summation of these explicit costs and other implicit costs that is loosely termed "bankruptcy costs." The implication is that a graph of market value against the amount of debt issued by the firm will have an upside down "U" shape, as illustrated in Figure 4.

In the range AB (Figure 4), bankruptcy costs are negligible and the value of the firm increases linearly with the amount of debt issued in accordance with the MM proposition. The possibility of bankruptcy begins to have an increasing negative consequence from point B onwards. An optimal market value is reached at C. After C the expected costs associated with additional amounts of debt outweigh the benefits associated with the present value of the additional tax savings, and the market value of the firm begins to decline. Thus there does exist an optimal capital structure for the firm.

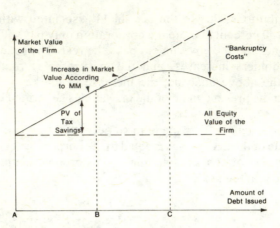

Figure 4.   Effect of Debt on Market Value

Again the "traditionalists" would state that for moderate amounts of debt the present value of the tax savings understates the true increase in market value of the firm. Empirical evidence to date has not been able to satisfactorily resolve the debate between MM and the "traditionalists." The degree of financial leverage at the optimum will vary from industry to industry and is largely dependent on the business risk of the firm. Firms with low business risk (public utilities) can support substantial amounts of debt (60-70 percent of market value), while firms with high business risk (machine tool manufacturers) can support only much lower debt ratios (20-30 percent of market value).

THE ADJUSTED PRESENT VALUE METHOD

To this point the discussion of the NPV rule for capital budgeting has assumed either the projects were totally equity financed (in which case the discount rate is the all equity rate) or, if partially debt financed, the projects were perpetuities (in which case the discount rate is the market weighted average of the costs of debt and equity financing defined by equation [7]). The MM result, however, allows one to compute present values for debt financed projects without the perpetuity restriction. The extended NPV rate called the "Adjusted Present Value Rule" was developed by Professor Stewart C. Myers.[13]
. As shown by MM, the present value of a project in the perpetuity case is the present value of the project cash flows discounted at the all equity rate plus the

[13] See Myers [10]. MM laid the groundwork by establishing their valuation formula $V_D = V_0 + TD$ in [6] and [7].

present value of the tax savings associated with the project's contingent debt financing. This result can be generalized to the non perpetuity case:

The 'adjusted' net	NPV of project	Net present
present value (APV) =	computed at the +	value of
	all equity rate	contingent financing

$$= \sum_{t=1}^{t=T} \frac{\bar{C}_t}{(1 + \rho_0)^t} + \sum_{t=1}^{T} \frac{TS_t}{(1 + i)^t} \tag{11}$$

where $\bar{C}_t$ = after tax cash flow from project in period t
ρ_0 = cost of capital of the project if it were all equity financed
TS_t = tax savings in period t
i = interest rate on debt
T = time horizon of the project.

(The tax shield on the debt has the same risk as the debt itself, and hence the appropriate discount rate in computing its present value is the debt interest rate.)

It also is known that the present value of the project is equal to the project cash flows discounted at the overall project cost of capital. That is,

$$NPV = \sum_{t=1}^{t=T} \frac{\bar{C}_t}{(1 + \rho_j)^t} \tag{12}$$

where ρ_j = the overall project cost of capital.

The overall cost of capital ρ_j is difficult to compute for projects which are not perpetuities. It may be necessary to first compute the APV for the project from equation (11) in order to solve for the value of ρ_j in equation (12) which produces a NPV equal to the APV. In general, the overall cost of capital is not an operational concept.

In the case of projects that are perpetuities, MM demonstrated that if the project makes a permanent contribution to the firm's debt capacity then the correct value of ρ_j is given by

$$\rho_j = \rho_0 \left(1 - T\frac{D}{V} \right) \tag{13}$$

where ρ_j = the overall project cost of capital
ρ_0 = the cost of capital if the project were all equity financed
T = the corporate tax rate
D = the market value of debt supported by the project
V = the total market value of the project ($V = D + E$).

As long as the MM assumptions hold, there is a simple decision rule regarding the acceptance or rejection of perpetuity projects that can support debt. One simply calculates the net present value of the project cash flows discounted at the project cost of capital ρ_j given by equation (13) and accepts the project only if the NPV as given by equation (12) (with $T = \infty$) is positive.

Note that ρ_j is a decreasing function of the proportion of debt used in the project's financing and is always less than or equal to ρ_0. This is because the project's debt financing is equivalent to accepting a contingent project which, for "moderate" amounts of debt, has a positive net present value—see equation (10). Debt financing reduces the required return which the project must earn by itself; the project's cost of capital decreases as D increases.

The APV rule takes explicit consideration of the interaction between a firm's investment and financing decision and gives the correct decision rule regarding the firm's investment strategy. The rule shows explicitly that the firm which uses debt financing will be able to accept more projects than the all equity financed firm.

INTEGRATION: THE MYERS POGUE MODEL
FOR FINANCIAL MANAGEMENT

As described above, the theory of financial management now includes detailed considerations of investment and financing decisions, dividend policy, and most other aspects of corporate finance.

However, as discussed by Myers and Pogue,

> . . . there is a clear tendency to isolate these decisions in order to analyze them. To take a simple example, consider the capital budgeting rules which depend on an exogenous weighted average cost of capital. These must assume that the firm's financing decision is taken as given or is independent of the investment decision, even though neither theory nor practical considerations support such a separation.
>
> Financial management really requires simultaneous consideration of the investment, financing, and dividend options facing the firm. In this paper an outline is presented of LONGER, a financial planning model based on mixed integer linear programming. The model is based on recent advances in capital market theory, but at the same time it recognizes certain additional considerations that are manifestly important to the financial manager.[14]

Without getting into detail, the main features of the Myers Pogue approach can be stated in the following terms:

---

[14] See Myers and Pogue [11], page 1.

The linear programming model follows from two propositions of modern capital theory, namely:

(1) That the risk characteristics of a capital investment opportunity can be evaluated independently of the risk characteristics of the firm's existing assets or other opportunities.

(2) The Modigliani-Miller result that the total market value of the firm is equal to its unleveraged value plus the present value of taxes saved due to debt financing.

Thus, the firm is assumed to choose that combination of investment and financing options that maximize the total market value of the firm, specified according to the two axioms. The major constraints are a debt limit (specified as a function of the value and risk characteristics of the firm's assets and new investment) and a requirement that planned sources and uses of funds are equal. In addition, there are constraints on liquidity, and investment choices (due to mutually exclusive or contingent options), etc.[15]

Other modifications to the objective function of the model include taking into account the transaction costs of planned equity issues, attaching a tax penalty to dividend payments and attaching further penalties when target growth rates for dividends and reported earnings are not met.

Although other optimization models have been proposed for financial planning, the Myers Pogue model is the first to incorporate the major results of modern capital market theory and to take into explicit consideration most of the issues and interactions that have been raised in this article.[16] Models of this type clearly are going to play an icreasingly important role in the formulation of corporate financial plans.

SUMMARY

In this article a broad outline has been given of the major recent results in the theory of corporate finance. It was demonstrated that the maximization of the market value of a firm's equity is an appropriate objective for the firm. This led to an investigation of the valuation effects of various investment and financing strategies of the firm. The capital budgeting rule (the NPV rule) was obtained for a project that is all equity financed, and the appropriate risk measure of the project was shown to be the project's systematic risk. The notion of the cost of capital was explained, and this together with the MM propositions on capital structure allowed the derivation of the correct capital budgeting rule for projects which are partially debt financed (the APV rule). The MM proposi-

---

[15] See Myers and Pogue [11], page 2.

[16] See Carleton [1] and Hamilton and Moses [4].

tion regarding the irrelevance of a firm's dividend policy was discussed. This has been only an introduction to the field, and the interested reader is encouraged to consult the many in-depth expositions which are now available.[17]

REFERENCES

1. Carleton, W. T. "An Analytical Model for Long Range Financial Planning." *The Journal of Finance* 25 (1970): 291–315.
2. Fama, E. F., and Miller, M. H. *The Theory of Finance*. New York: Holt, Rinehart and Winston, 1972.
3. Fisher, I. *The Theory of Interest*. New York: Augustus M. Kelley, 1965. Reprinted from the 1930 edition.
4. Hamilton, W., and Moses, M. "An Optimization Model for Corporate Financial Planning." *Operations Research* 21 (1973): 677–692.
5. Miller, M. H., and Modigliani, F. "Dividend Policy, Growth and the Valuation of Shares." *Journal of Business* 24 (1961): 411–433.
6. Modigliani, F., and Miller, M. H. "The Cost of Capital, Corporation Finance and the Theory of Investment." *American Economic Review* 48 (1958): 261–297.
7. ———. "Corporate Income Taxes and the Cost of Capital: A Correction." *American Economic Review* 53 (1963): 433–443.
8. Modigliani, F., and Pogue, G. A. "An Introduction to Risk and Return Concepts and Evidence." *Financial Analysts Journal*, in press.
9. Myers, S. C. "Procedures for Capital Budgeting under Uncertainty." *Industrial Management Review*, Spring 1968, pp. 1–29.
10. ———. "Interactions of Corporate Financing and Investment Decisions—Implications for Capital Budgeting." *Journal of Finance*, in press.
11. Myers, S. C., and Pogue, G. A. "A Programming Approach to Corporate Financial Management." *Journal of Finance*, in press.
12. Robichek, A. A., and Myers, S. C. *Optimal Financing Decisions*. Englewood Cliffs, N. J.: Prentice-Hall, 1965.
13. Sharpe, W. F. *Portfolio Theory and Capital Markets*. New York: McGraw-Hill, 1970.
14. Solomon, E. *The Theory of Financial Management*. New York: Columbia University Press, 1963.
15. Van Horne, J. C. *Financial Management and Policy*. Englewood Cliffs, N. J.: Prentice-Hall, 1971.
16. Weston, J. F., and Brigham, E. F. *Managerial Finance*. New York: Holt, Rinehart and Winston, 1971.

---

[17] See for example Van Horne [15] or Weston and Brigham [16]. [6] and [7] are the original MM papers on capital structure, and [10] is the formulation of the APV rule by Myers. Modigliani and Pogue [8] provide a basic introduction to modern capital market theory. See Sharpe [13] for a more complete discussion.

QUESTIONS

1. In what way does the subject of security valuation apply in financial management?
2. Show why the present value of a common stock is the present value of all future dividends the stock will pay.
3. Explain why a stock whose returns are highly variable is considered more risky than one whose returns are not so variable.
4. Describe how the diversification effect can eliminate unsystematic risk.
5. Define β.
6. What evidence do you see in the structure of security yields which indicates that investors are risk averse? Explain.
7. Distinguish between business risk and financial risk.

3 | *Edward I. Altman**

Financial Ratios, Discriminant Analysis, and the Prediction of Corporate Bankruptcy

This paper evaluates the analytical quality of ratio analysis for its potential as a tool in predicting corporate bankruptcy. Professor Altman was one of the first to use multiple discriminant analysis in financial management. The approach uses various ratios as the variables in a discriminant function to categorize borrowers into two groups–those who did and those who did not go bankrupt.

Similar methodology has subsequently been used in the analysis of granting bank loans, trade credit, consumer loans, and issuance of credit cards. Many of these have been proprietary studies for individual companies, and they are not available in the published media.

Academicians seem to be moving toward the elimination of ratio analysis as an analytical technique in assessing the performance of the business enterprise. Theorists downgrade arbitrary rules of thumb, such as company ratio comparisons, widely used by practitioners. Since attacks on the relevance of ratio analysis emanate from many esteemed members of the scholarly world, does

Source. Reprinted by permission from the *Journal of Finance*, September 1968, pp. 589–609. The author is professor of finance, New York University.

* The author acknowledges the helpful suggestions and comments of Keith V. Smith, Edward F. Renshaw, Lawrence S. Ritter and the *Journal*'s reviewer. The research was conducted while under a Regents Fellowship at the University of California, Los Angeles.

this mean that ratio analysis is limited to the world of "nuts and bolts"? Or, has the significance of such an approach been unattractively garbed and therefore unfairly handicapped? Can we bridge the gap, rather than sever the link, between traditional ratio "analysis" and the more rigorous statistical techniques which have become popular among academicians in recent years?

The purpose of this paper is to attempt an assessment of this issue—the quality of ratio analysis as an analytical technique. The prediction of corporate bankruptcy is used as an illustrative case.[1] Specifically, a set of financial and economic ratios will be investigated in a bankruptcy prediction context wherein a multiple discriminant statistical methodology is employed. The data used in the study are limited to manufacturing corporations.

A brief review of the development of traditional ratio analysis as a technique for investigating corporate performance is presented in section I. In section II the shortcomings of this approach are discussed and multiple discriminant analysis is introduced with the emphasis centering on its compatibility with ratio analysis in a bankruptcy prediction context. The discriminant model is developed in section III, where an initial sample of sixty-six firms is utilized to establish a function which best discriminates between companies in two mutually exclusive groups: bankrupt and non-bankrupt firms. Section IV reviews empirical results obtained from the initial sample and several secondary samples, the latter being selected to examine the reliability of the discriminant model as a predictive technique. In section V the model's adaptability to practical decision-making situations and its potential benefits in a variety of situations are suggested. The final section summarizes the findings and conclusions of the study, and assesses the role and significance of traditional ratio analysis within a modern analytical context.

I.   TRADITIONAL RATIO ANALYSIS

The detection of company operating and financial difficulties is a subject which has been particularly susceptible to financial ratio analysis. Prior to the development of quantitative measures of company performance, agencies were established to supply a qualitative type of information assessing the credit-worthiness of particular merchants.[2] Formal aggregate studies concerned with portents of

---

[1] In this study the term bankruptcy will, except where otherwise noted, refer to those firms that are legally bankrupt and either placed in receivership or have been granted the right to reorganize under the provisions of the National Bankruptcy Act.

[2] For instance, the forerunner of well known Dun & Bradstreet, Inc. was organized in 1849 in Cincinnati, Ohio, in order to provide independent credit investigations. For an interesting and informative discussion on the development of credit agencies and financial measures of company performance see Roy A. Foulke, *Practical Financial Statement Analysis*, 5th Ed., (New York, McGraw-Hill, 1961).

business failure were evident in the 1930's. A study at that time[3] and several later ones concluded that failing firms exhibit significantly different ratio measurements than continuing entities.[4] In addition, another study was concerned with ratios of large asset-size corporations that experienced difficulties in meeting their fixed indebtedness obligations.[5] A recent study involved the analysis of financial ratios in a bankruptcy-prediction context.[6] This latter work compared a list of ratios individually for failed firms and a matched sample of non-failed firms. Observed evidence for five years prior to failure was cited as conclusive that ratio analysis can be useful in the prediction of failure.

The aforementioned studies imply a definite potential of ratios as predictors of bankruptcy. In general, ratios measuring profitability, liquidity, and solvency prevailed as the most significant indicators. The order of their importance is not clear since almost every study cited a different ratio as being the most effective indication of impending problems.

II. MULTIPLE DISCRIMINANT ANALYSIS

The previous section cited several studies devoted to the analysis of a firm's condition prior to financial difficulties. Although these works established certain important generalizations regarding the performance and trends of particular measurements, the adaptation of their results for assessing bankruptcy potential of firms, both theoretically and practically, is questionable.[7] In almost every case, the methodology was essentially univariate in nature and emphasis was placed on individual signals of impending problems.[8] Ratio analysis presented in this fashion is susceptible to faulty interpretation and is potentially confusing. For instance, a firm with a poor profitability and/or solvency record may be

---

[3] R. F. Smith and A. H. Winakor, *Changes in the Financial Structure of Unsuccessful Corporations.* (University of Illinois: Bureau of Business Research, 1935).

[4] For instance, a comprehensive study covering over 900 firms compared discontinuing firms with continuing ones, see C. Merwin, *Financing Small Corporations* (New York: Bureau of Economic Research, 1942).

[5] W. B. Hickman, *Corporate Bond Quality and Investor Experience* (Princeton, N.J.: Princeton University Press, 1958).

[6] W. H. Beaver, "Financial Ratios as Predictors of Failure," *Empirical Research in Accounting, Selected Studies, 1966* (Institute of Professional Accounting, January, 1967), pp. 71–111. Also a recent attempt was made to weight ratios arbitrarily, see M. Tamari, "Financial Ratios as a Means of Forecasting Bankruptcy," *Management International Review*, Vol. 4 (1966), pp. 15–21.

[7] At this point bankruptcy is used in its most general sense, meaning simply business failure.

[8] Exceptions to this generalization were noted in works where there was an attempt to emphasize the importance of a group of ratios as an indication of overall performance. For instance, Foulke, *op. cit.*, chapters XIV and XV, and A. Wall and R. W. Duning, *Ratio Analysis of Financial Statements*, (New York: Harper and Row, 1928), p. 159.

regarded as a potential bankrupt. However, because of its above average liquidity, the situation may not be considered serious. The potential ambiguity as to the relative performance of several firms is clearly evident. The crux of the shortcomings inherent in any univariate analysis lies therein. An appropriate extension of the previously cited studies, therefore, is to build upon their findings and to combine several measures into a meaningful predictive model. In so doing, the highlights of ratio analysis as an analytical technique will be emphasized rather than downgraded. The question becomes, which ratios are most important in detecting bankruptcy potential, what weights should be attached to those selected ratios, and how should the weights be objectively established.

After careful consideration of the nature of the problem and of the purpose of the paper, a multiple discriminant analysis (MDA) was chosen as the appropriate statistical technique. Although not as popular as regression analysis, MDA has been utilized in a variety of disciplines since its first application in the 1930's.[9] During those earlier years MDA was used mainly in the biological and behavioral sciences.[10] More recently this method had been applied successfully to financial problems such as consumer credit evaluation[11] and investment classification. For instance in the latter area, Walter utilized a MDA model to classify high and low price earnings ratio firms,[12] and Smith applied the technique in the classification of firms into standard investment categories.[13]

MDA is a statistical technique used to classify an observation into one of several *a priori* groupings dependent upon the observation's individual characteristics. It is used primarily to classify and/or make predictions in problems where the dependent variable appears in qualitative form, e.g., male or female, bankrupt or non-bankrupt. Therefore, the first step is to establish explicit group classifications. The number of original groups can be two or more.

After the groups are established, data are collected for the objects in the groups; MDA then attempts to derive a linear combination of these characteristics which "best" discriminates between the groups. If a particular object, for

---

[9] R. A. Fisher, "The Use of Multiple Measurements in Taxonomic Problems," *Annals of Eugenics*, No. 7 (September, 1936), pp. 179–188.

[10] For a comprehensive review of studies using MDA see W. G. Cochran, "On the Performance of the Linear Discriminant Function," *Technometrics*, vol. 6 (May, 1964), pp. 179–190.

[11] The pioneering work utilizing MDA in a financial context was performed by Durand in evaluating the credit worthiness of used car loan applicants, see D. D. Durand, *Risk Elements in Consumer Installment Financing*, Studies in Consumer Installment Financing (New York: National Bureau of Economic Research, 1941), pp. 105–142. More recently, Myers and Forgy analyzed several techniques, including MDA, in the evaluation of good and bad installment loans, see H. Myers and E. W. Forgy, "Development of Numerical Credit Evaluation Systems," *Journal of American Statistical Association*, vol. 50 (September, 1963), pp. 797–806.

[12] J. E. Walter, "A Discriminant Function for Earnings Price Ratios of Large Industrial Corporations," *Review of Economics and Statistics*, vol. XLI (February, 1959), pp. 44–52.

[13] K. V. Smith, *Classification of Investment Securities Using MDA*, Institute Paper #101 (Purdue University, Institute for Research in the Behavioral, Economic, and Management Sciences, 1965).

instance a corporation, has characteristics (financial ratios) which can be quantified for all of the companies in the analysis, the MDA determines a set of discriminant coefficients. When these coefficients are applied to the actual ratio, a basis for classification into one of the mutually exclusive groupings exists. The MDA technique has the advantage of considering an entire profile of characteristics common to the relevant firms, as well as the interaction of these properties. A univariate study, on the other hand, can only consider the measurements used for group assignments one at a time.

Another advantage of MDA is the reduction of the analyst's space dimensionality, i.e., from the number of different independent variables to $G - 1$ dimension(s), where G equals the number of original *a priori* groups.[14] This paper is concerned with two groups, consisting of bankrupt firms on the one hand, and of non-bankrupt firms on the other. Therefore, the analysis is transformed into its simplest form: one dimension. The discriminant function of the form $Z = v_1 x_1 + v_2 x_2 + \cdots + v_n x_n$ transforms individual variable values to a single discriminant score or Z value which is then used to classify the object

where $v_1, v_2, \ldots, v_n$ = Discriminant coefficients

$x_1, x_2, \ldots, x_n$ = Independent variables.

The MDA computes the discriminant coefficients, v_j, while the independent variables x_j are the actual values

where $j = 1, 2, \ldots, n$.

When utilizing a comprehensive list of financial ratios in assessing a firm's bankruptcy potential there is reason to believe that some of the measurements will have a high degree of correlation or collinearity with each other. While this aspect necessitates careful selection of the predictive variables (ratios), it also has the advantage of yielding a model with a relatively small number of selected measurements which has the potential of conveying a great deal of information. This information might very well indicate differences between groups but whether or not these differences are significant and meaningful is a more important aspect of the analysis. To be sure, there are differences between bankrupt firms and healthy ones; but are these differences of a magnitude to facilitate the development of an accurate prediction model?

---

[14] For a formulation of the mathematical computations involved in MDA, see J. G. Bryan, "The Generalized Discriminant Function, Mathematical Foundation & Computational Routine," *Harvard Educational Review*, vol. XXI, no. 2 (Spring, 1951), pp. 90–95, and C. R. Rao, *Advanced Statistical Methods in Biometric Research* (New York: John Wiley & Sons, Inc., 1952).

Perhaps the primary advantage of MDA in dealing with classification problems is the potential of analyzing the entire variable profile of the object simultaneously rather than sequentially examining its individual characteristics. Just as linear and integer programming have improved upon traditional techniques in capital budgeting[15] the MDA approach to traditional ratio analysis has the potential to reformulate the problem correctly. Specifically, combinations of ratios can be analyzed together in order to remove possible ambiguities and misclassifications observed in earlier traditional studies.

Given the above descriptive qualitites, the MDA technique was selected as most appropriate for the bankruptcy study. A carefully devised and interpreted multiple regression analysis methodology conceivably could have been used in this two group case.

III. DEVELOPMENT OF THE MODEL

Sample Selection

The initial sample is composed of sixty-six corporations with thirty-three firms in each of the two groups. The bankrupt group (1) are manufacturers that filed a bankruptcy petition under Chapter X of the National Bankruptcy Act during the period 1946–1965.[16] The mean asset size of these firms is $6.4 million, with a range of between $0.7 million and $25.9 million. Recognizing that this group is not completely homogeneous, due to industry and size differences, a careful selection of non-bankrupt firms was attempted. Group 2 consisted of a paired sample of manufacturing firms chosen on a stratified random basis. The firms are stratified by industry and by size, with the asset size range restricted to between $1–$25 million.[17] Firms in Group 2 were still in existence in 1966. Also, the data collected are from the same years as those compiled for the bankrupt firms. For the initial sample test, the data are derived from financial statements one reporting period prior to bankruptcy.[18]

---

[15] H. M. Weingartner, *Mathematical Programming and the Analysis of Capital Budgeting, Budgeting Problems,* (Englewood Cliffs, New Jersey: Prentice-Hall, 1963).

[16] The choice of a twenty year period is not the best procedure since average ratios do shift over time. Ideally we would prefer to examine a list of ratios in time period *t* in order to make predictions about other firms in the following period (*t* + 1). Unfortunately it was not possible to do this because of data limitations. However, the number of bankruptcies were approximately evenly distributed over the twenty year period in both the original and the secondary samples.

[17] The mean asset size of the firms in Group 2 ($9.6 million) was slightly greater than that of Group 1, but matching exact asset size of the two groups seemed unnecessary.

[18] The data was derived from Moody's Industrial Manuals and selected Annual Reports. The average lead time of the financial statements was approximately seven and one-half months prior to bankruptcy.

An important issue is to determine the asset-size group to be sampled. The decision to eliminate both the small firms (under \$1 million in total assets) and the very large companies from the initial sample essentially is due to the asset range of the firms in Group 1. In addition, the incidence of bankruptcy in the large asset-size firm is quite rare today while the absence of comprehensive data negated the representation of small firms. A frequent argument is that financial ratios, by their very nature, have the effect of deflating statistics by size, and therefore a good deal of the size effect is eliminated. To choose Group 1 firms in a restricted size range is not feasible, while selecting firms for Group 2 at random seemed unwise. However, subsequent tests to the original sample do not use size as a means of stratification.[19]

After the initial groups are defined and firms selected, balance sheet and income statement data are collected. Because of the large number of variables found to be significant indicators of corporate problems in past studies, a list of twenty-two potentially helpful variables (ratios) is compiled for evaluation. The variables are classified into five standard ratio categories, including liquidity, profitability, leverage, solvency, and activity ratios. The ratios are chosen on the basis of their (1) popularity in the literature,[20] (2) potential relevancy to the study, and a few "new" ratios initiated in this paper.

From the original list of variables, five variables are selected as doing the best overall job together in the prediction of corporate bankruptcy.[21] In order to arrive at a final profile of variables the following procedures are utilized: (1) Observation of the statistical significance of various alternative functions including determination of the relative contributions of each independent variable; (2) evaluation of inter-correlations between the relevant variables; (3) observation of the predictive accuracy of the various profiles; and (4) judgment of the analyst.

The variable profile finally established did not contain the most significant variables, amongst the twenty-two original ones, measured independently. This would not necessarily improve upon the univariate, traditional analysis described earlier. The contribution of the entire profile is evaluated, and since this process is essentially iterative, there is no claim regarding the optimality of the resulting discriminant function. The function, however, does the best job among the alternatives which include numerous computer runs analyzing different ratio-profiles. The final discriminant function is as follows:

---

[19] One of these tests included only firms that experienced operating losses (secondary sample of non-bankrupt firms).

[20] The Beaver study (cited earlier) concluded that the cash flow to debt ratio was the best single ratio predictor. This ratio was not considered here because of the lack of consistent appearance of precise depreciation data. The results obtained, however (see section IV), are superior to the results Beaver attained with his single best ratio, see Beaver, *op. cit.*, p. 89.

[21] The MDA computer program used in this study was developed by W. Cooley and P. Lohnes. The data are organized in a blocked format; the bankrupt firms' data first followed by the non-bankrupt firms'.

(I) $$Z = .012X_1 + .014X_2 + .033X_3 + .006X_4 + .999X_5$$

where X_1 = Working capital/Total assets

X_2 = Retained earnings/Total assets

X_3 = Earnings before interest and taxes/Total assets

X_4 = Market value equity/Book value of total debt

X_5 = Sales/Total assets

Z = Overall Index.

X_1—Working Capital/Total Assets

The Working capital/Total assets ratio, frequently found in studies of corporate problems, is a measure of the net liquid assets of the firm relative to the total capitalization. Working capital is defined as the difference between current assets and current liabilities. Liquidity and size characteristics are explicitly considered. Ordinarily, a firm experiencing consistent operating losses will have shrinking current assets in relation to total assets. Of the three liquidity ratios evaluated, this one proved to be the most valuable.[22] Inclusion of this variable is consistent with the Merwin study which rated the net working capital to total asset ratio as the best indicator of ultimate discontinuance.[23]

X_2—Retained Earnings/Total Assets[24]

This measure of cumulative profitability over time was cited earlier as one of the "new" ratios. The age of a firm is implicitly considered in this ratio. For example, a relatively young firm will probably show a low RE/TA ratio because it has not had time to build up its cumulative profits. Therefore, it may be argued that the young firm is somewhat discriminated against in this analysis, and its chance of being classified as bankrupt is relatively higher than another, older firm, *ceteris paribus*. But, this is precisely the situation in the real world. The incidence of failure is much higher in a firm's earlier years.[25]

[22] The other two liquidity ratios were the current ratio and the quick ratio. The Working capital/Total assets ratio showed greater statistical significance both on a univariate and multivariate basis.

[23] Merwin, *op. cit.*, p. 99.

[24] Retained Earnings is the account which reports the total amount of reinvested earnings and/or losses of a firm over its entire life. The account is also referred to as Earned Surplus. It should be noted that the Retained Earnings account is subject to manipulation via corporate quasi-reorganizations and stock dividend declarations. While these occurrences are not evident in this study it is conceivable that a bias would be created by a substantial reorganization or stock dividend.

[25] In 1965, over 50 per cent of all manufacturing firms that failed did so in the first five years of their existence. Over 31 per cent failed within three years. Statistics taken from *The Failure Record, Through 1965* (New York: Dun & Bradstreet, Inc., 1966), p. 10.

X_3—Earnings Before Interest and Taxes/Total Assets

This ratio is calculated by dividing the total assets of a firm into its earnings before interest and tax reductions. In essence, it is a measure of the true productivity of the firm's assets, abstracting from any tax or leverage factors. Since a firm's ultimate existence is based on the earning power of its assets, this ratio appears to be particularly appropriate for studies dealing with corporate failure. Furthermore, insolvency in a bankruptcy sense occurs when the total liabilities exceed a fair valuation of the firm's assets with value determined by the earning power of the assets.

X_4—Market Value of Equity/Book Value of Total Debt

Equity is measured by the combined market value of all shares of stock, preferred and common, while debt includes both current and long-term. The measure shows how much the firm's assets can decline in value (measured by market value of equity plus debt) before the liabilities exceed the assets and the firm becomes insolvent. For example, a company with a market value of its equity of $1,000 and debt of $500 could experience a two-thirds drop in asset value before insolvency. However, the same firm with $250 in equity will be insolvent if its drop is only one-third in value. This ratio adds a market value dimension which other failure studies did not consider.[26] It also appears to be a more effective predictor of bankruptcy than a similar, more commonly used ratio: Net worth/Total debt (book values).

X_5—Sales/Total Assets

The capital-turnover ratio is a standard financial ratio illustrating the sales generating ability of the firm's assets. It is one measure of management's capability in dealing with competitive conditions. This final ratio is quite important because, as indicated below, it is the least significant ratio on an individual basis. In fact, based on the statistical significance measure, it would not have appeared at all. However, because of its unique relationship to other variables in the model, the Sales/Total assets ratio ranks second in its contribution to the overall discriminating ability of the model.

To test the individual discriminating ability of the variables, an "F" test is performed. This test relates the difference between the average values of the ratios in each group to the variability (or spread) of values of the ratios within

---

[26] The reciprocal of X_4 is the familiar Debt/Equity ratio often used as a measure of financial leverage. X_4 is a slightly modified version of one of the variables used effectively by Fisher in a study of corporate bond interest rate differentials, see Lawrence Fisher, "Determinants of Risk Premiums on Corporate Bonds," *Journal of Political Economy*, LXVII, No. 3 (June, 1959), pp. 217–237.

each group. Variable means one financial statement prior to bankruptcy and the resulting "F" statistics are presented in Table 1.

TABLE 1.   VARIABLE MEANS AND TEST OF SIGNIFICANCE

VARIABLE	BANKRUPT GROUP MEAN	NON-BANKRUPT GROUP MEAN	F RATIO
	$n = 33$	$n = 33$	
X_1	$- 6.1\%$	41.4%	32.60*
X_2	-62.6%	35.5%	58.86*
X_3	-31.8%	15.3%	26.56*
X_4	40.1%	247.7%	33.26*
X_5	150.0%	190.0%	2.84

* Significant at the .001 level.

$F_{1.60}(.001) = 12.00$
$F_{1.60}(.01) = 7.00$
$F_{1.60}(.05) = 4.00$

Variables X_1 through X_4 are all significant at the .001 level, indicating extremely significant differences in these variables between groups. Variable X_5 does not show a significant difference between groups and the reason for its inclusion in the variable profile is not apparent as yet. On a strictly univariate level, all of the ratios indicate higher values for the non-bankrupt firms. Also, the discriminant coefficients of equation (I) display positive signs, which is what one would expect. Therefore, the greater a firm's bankruptcy potential, the lower its discriminant score.

One useful technique in arriving at the final variable profile is to determine the relative contribution of each variable to the total discriminating power of the function, and the interaction between them. The relevant statistic is observed as a scaled vector which is computed by multiplying corresponding elements by the square roots of the diagonal elements of the variance-covariance matrix.[27] Since the actual variable measurement units are not all comparable to each other, simple observation of the discriminant coefficients is misleading. The adjusted coefficients shown in Table 2 enable us to evaluate each variable's contribution on a relative basis.

The scaled vectors indicate that the large contributors to group separation of the discriminant function are X_3, X_5, and X_4, respectively. The profitability ratio contributes the most, which is not surprising if one considers that the incidence of bankruptcy in a firm that is earning a profit is almost nil. What is

[27] For example, the square root of the appropriate variance-covariance figure (standard deviation) for X_1 is approximately 275 and when multiplied by the variable's coefficient (.012) yields a scaled vector of 3.29.

surprising, however, is the second highest contribution of X_5 (Sales/Total assets). Recalling that this ratio was insignificant on a univariate basis, the multivariate context is responsible for illuminating the importance of X_5.[28] A probable reason for this unexpected result is the high negative correlation $(-.78)$ we observe between X_3 and X_5 in the bankruptcy group. The negative correlation is also evident in subsequent bankrupt group samples.

TABLE 2. RELATIVE CONTRIBUTION
OF THE VARIABLES

VARIABLE	SCALED VECTOR	RANKING
X_1	3.29	5
X_2	6.04	4
X_3	9.89	1
X_4	7.42	3
X_5	8.41	2

In a recent evaluation of the discriminant function, Cochran concluded that most correlations between variables in past studies were positive and that, by and large, negative correlations are more helpful than positive correlations in adding new information to the function.[29] The logic behind the high negative correlation in the bankrupt group is that as firms suffer losses and deteriorate toward failure, their assets are not replaced as much as in healthier times, and also the cumulative losses have further reduced the asset size through debits to Retained Earnings. The asset size reduction apparently dominates any sales movements.

A different argument, but one not necessarily inconsistent with the above, concerns a similar ratio to X_5, Net Sales to Tangible Net Worth. If the latter ratio is excessive the firm is often referred to as a poor credit risk due to insufficient capital to support sales. Companies with moderate or even below average sales generating lower (low asset turnover, X_5) might very well possess an extremely high Net Sales/Net Worth ratio if the Net Worth has been reduced substantially due to cumulative operating losses. This ratio, and other net worth ratios, are not considered in the paper because of computational and interpretive difficulties arising when negative net worth totals are present.

It is clear that four of the five variables display significant differences between groups, but the importance of MDA is its ability to separate groups using multivariate measures. A test to determine the overall discriminating power of

[28] For an excellent discussion of how a seemingly insignificant variable on a univariate basis can supply important information in a multivariate context see W. W. Cooley and P. R. Lohnes *Multivariate Procedures for the Behavioral Sciences* (New York: John Wiley and Sons, Inc., 1962), p. 121.

[29] Cochran, *op. cit.*, p. 182.

the model is the common F-value which is the ratio of the sums-of-squares between-groups to the within-groups sums-of-squares. When this ratio of the form,

$$\lambda = \frac{\sum\limits_{g=1}^{G} N_g [\bar{y}_g - \bar{y}]^2}{\sum\limits_{g=1}^{G} \sum\limits_{p=1}^{N_g} [y_{pg} - \bar{y}_g]^2},$$

where G = Number of groups

g = Group g, $g = 1 \cdots G$

N_g = Number of firms in group g

y_{pg} = Firm p in group g, $p = 1 \cdots N_g$

$\bar{y}_g$ = Group mean (centroid)

$\bar{y}$ = Overall sample mean,

is maximized, it has the effect of spreading the means (centroids) of the G groups apart and, simultaneously, reducing dispersion of the individual points (firm Z values, y_{pg}) about their respective group means. Logically, this test (commonly called the "F" test) is appropriate because one of the objectives of the MDA is to identify and to utilize those variables which best discriminate *between* groups and which are most similar *within* groups.

The group means, or centroids, of the original two-group sample of the form

$$\bar{y}_g = \frac{1}{N_g} \sum\limits_{p=1}^{N_g} y_{pg}$$

are

Group 1 $= -0.29$ $F = 20.7$
Group 2 $= +5.02$ $F_{5, 60} (.01) = 3.34.$

The significance test therefore *rejects* the null hypothesis that the observations come from the same population. With the conclusion that *a priori* groups are significantly different, further discriminatory analysis is possible.

Once the values of the discriminant coefficients are estimated, it is possible to calculate discriminant scores for each observation in the sample, or any firm, and to assign the observations to one of the groups based on this score. The essence of the procedure is to compare the profile of an individual firm with that of the alternative groupings. In this manner the firm is assigned to the group it most closely resembles. The comparisons are measured by a chi-square value and assignments are made based upon the relative proximity of the firm's score to the various group centroids.

IV. EMPIRICAL RESULTS

At the outset, it might be helpful to illustrate the format for presenting the result. In the multi-group case, results are shown in a classification chart or "accuracy-matrix." The chart is set up as follows:

	PREDICTED GROUP MEMBERSHIP	
ACTUAL GROUP MEMBERSHIP	Bankrupt	Non-Bankrupt
Bankrupt	H	M_1
Non-Bankrupt	M_2	H

The actual group membership is equivalent to the *a priori* groupings and the model attempts to classify correctly these firms. At this stage, the model is basically explanatory. When new companies are classified, the nature of the model is predictive.

The H's stand for correct classifications (Hits) and the M's stand for mis-classifications (Misses). M_1 represents a Type I error and M_2 a Type II error. The sum of the diagonal elements equals the total correct "hits," and when divided into the total number of firms classified (sixty-six in the case of the initial sample), yields the measure of success of the MDA in classifying firms, that is, the per cent of firms correctly classified. This percentage is analogous to the coefficient of determination (R^2) in regression analysis, which measures the per cent of the variation of the dependent variable explained by the independent variables.

The final criterion used to establish the best model was to observe its accuracy in predicting bankruptcy. A series of six tests were performed.

(1) Initial Sample (Group 1)

The initial sample of 33 firms in each of the two groups is examined using data one financial statement prior to bankruptcy. Since the discriminant coefficients and the group distributions are derived from this sample, a high degree of successful classification is expected. This should occur because the firms are classified using a discriminant function which, in fact, is based upon the individual measurements of these same firms. The classification matrix for the initial sample is as follows:

	PREDICTED	
ACTUAL	Group 1	Group 2
Group 1	31	2
Group 2	1	32

	NUMBER CORRECT	PER CENT CORRECT	PER CENT ERROR	n
TYPE I	31	94	6	33
TYPE II	32	97	3	33
TOTAL	63	95	5	66

The model is extremely accurate in classifying 95 per cent of the total sample correctly. The *Type I error* proved to be only 6 per cent, while the *Type II error* was even better at 3 per cent. The results, therefore, are encouraging, but the obvious upward bias should be kept in mind and further validation techniques are appropriate.

(2) Results Two Years Prior to Bankruptcy

The second test is made to observe the discriminating ability of the model for firms using data from two years prior to bankruptcy. The two year period is an exaggeration since the average lead time for the correctly classified firms is approximately twenty months with two firms having a thirteen month lead. The results are:

	PREDICTED	
	Group 1 (Bankrupt)	Group 2 (Non-Bankrupt)
Group 1	23	9
Group 2	2	31

	NUMBER CORRECT	PER CENT CORRECT	PER CENT ERROR	n
TYPE I	23	72	28	32
TYPE II	31	94	6	33
TOTAL	54	83	17	65

The reduction in the accuracy of group classification is understandable because impending bankruptcy is more remote and the indications are less clear. Nevertheless, 72 per cent correct assignment is evidence that bankruptcy can be predicted two years prior to the event. The Type II error is slightly larger (6 per cent vs. 3 per cent) in this test but still is extremely accurate. Further tests will be applied below to determine the accuracy of predicting bankruptcy as much as five years prior to the actual event.

(3) Potential Bias and Validation Techniques

When the firms used to determine the discriminant coefficients are re-classified, the resulting accuracy is biased upward by (a) sampling errors in the original sample and (b) search bias. The latter bias is inherent in the process of reducing the original set of variables (twenty-two) to the best variable profile (five). The possibility of bias due to intensive searching is inherent in any empirical study. While a subset of variables is effective in the initial sample, there is no guarantee that it will be effective for the population in general.

The importance of secondary sample testing cannot be over-emphasized and it appears appropriate to apply these measures at this stage. A method suggested by Frank *et al.*[30] for testing the extent of the aforementioned search bias was applied to the initial sample. The essence of this test is to estimate parameters for the model using only a subset of the original sample, and then to classify the remainder of the sample based on the parameters established. A simple t-test is then applied to test the significance of the results.

Five different replications of the suggested method of choosing subsets (sixteen firms) of the original sample are tested, with results listed in Table 3.[31]

TABLE 3. ACCURACY OF CLASSIFYING
A SECONDARY SAMPLE

REPLICATION	PER CENT OF CORRECT CLASSIFICATIONS	VALUE OF t
1	91.2	4.8*
2	91.2	4.8*
3	97.0	5.5*
4	97.0	4.5*
5	91.2	4.8*
Average	93.5	5.1*
Total number of observations per replication 34		

* Significant at the .001 level.

$$t = \frac{\text{proportion correct} - .5}{\sqrt{\frac{.5(1 - .5)}{n}}}$$

[30] R. E. Frank, W. F. Massy, and G. D. Morrison, "Bias in Multiple Discriminant Analysis," *Journal of Marketing Research*, vol. 2 (August 1965), pp. 250–258.

[31] The five replications included (1) random sampling (2) choosing every other firm starting with firm number one, (3) starting with firm number two, (4) choosing firms 1–16, and (5) firms 17–32.

The test results reject the hypothesis that there is no difference between the groups and substantiate that the model does, in fact, possess discriminating power on observations other than those used to establish the parameters of the model. Therefore, any search bias does not appear significant.

(4) Secondary Sample of Bankrupt Firms

In order to test the model rigorously for both bankrupt and non-bankrupt firms two new samples are introduced. The first contains a new sample of twenty-five bankrupt firms whose asset-size range is the same as that of the initial bankrupt group. Using the parameters established in the discriminant model to classify firms in this secondary sample, the predictive accuracy for this sample as of one statement prior to bankruptcy is:

			PREDICTED		
			Bankrupt		Non-Bankrupt
BANKRUPT GROUP (ACTUAL)			24		1
		Number Correct	Per cent Correct	Per cent Error	n
TYPE I (TOTAL)		24	96	4	25

The results here are surprising in that one would not usually expect a secondary sample's results to be superior to the initial discriminant sample (96 per cent vs. 94 per cent). Two possible reasons are that the upward bias normally present in the initial sample tests is not manifested in this investigation, and/or the model, as stated before, is something less than optimal.

(5) Secondary Sample of Non-Bankrupt Firms

Up to this point the sample companies were chosen either by their bankruptcy status (Group 1) or by their similarity to Group 1 in all aspects except their economic well-being. But what of the many firms which suffer temporary profitability difficulties, but in actuality do not become bankrupt. A bankruptcy classification of a firm from this group is an example of a *Type II error*. An exceptionally rigorous test of the discriminant model's effectiveness would be to search out a large sample of firms that have encountered earnings problems and then to observe the MDA's classification results.

In order to perform the above test, a sample of sixty-six firms is selected on the basis of net income (deficit) reports in the years 1958 and 1961, with thirty-three from each year. Over 65 per cent of these firms had suffered two or three years of negative profits in the previous three years reporting. The firms are selected regardless of their asset size, with the only two criteria being that they were manufacturing firms which suffered losses in the year 1958 or 1961.[32] The two base years are chosen due to their relatively poor economic performances in terms of GNP growth. The companies are then evaluated by the discriminant model to determine their predictive bankruptcy potential.

The results, illustrated below, show that fifteen of the sixty-six firms are classified as bankrupts with the remaining fifty-one correctly classified. The number of misclassifications is actually fourteen, as one of the firms went bankrupt within two years after the data period.

	PREDICTED	
	Bankrupt	Non-Bankrupt
NON-BANKRUPT GROUP ACTUAL	14	52

	Number Correct	Per cent Correct	Per cent Error	n
TYPE II (TOTAL)	52	79	21	66

Therefore, the discriminant model correctly classified 79 per cent of the sample firms. This percentage is all the more impressive when one considers that these firms constitute a *secondary* sample of admittedly *below average* performance. The t-test for the significance of this result is t = 4.8; significant at the .001 level.

Another interesting facet of this test is the relationship of these "temporarily" sick firms' Z scores, and the "zone of ignorance" or gray area described more completely in the next section. Briefly, the "zone of ignorance" is that range of Z scores (see Chart 1) where misclassifications can be observed. Chart 1 illustrates some of the individual firm Z scores (initial sample) and the group centroids. These points are plotted in one dimensional space and, therefore, are easily visualized.

Of the fourteen misclassified firms in this secondary sample, ten have Z scores between 1.81 and 2.67, which indicates that although they are classified as bankrupts, the prediction of bankruptcy is not as definite as the vast majority in the initial sample of bankrupt firms. In fact, just under one-third of the sixty-six firms in this last sample have Z scores within the entire overlap area, which emphasizes that the selection process is successful in choosing firms which showed signs (profitability) of deterioration.

(6) Long-Range Predictive Accuracy

The previous results give important evidence of the reliability of the conclusions derived from the initial sample of firms. An appropriate extension, therefore,

[32] The firms were selected at random from all the firms listed in *Standard and Poor's Stock Guide*, January 1959, 1962, that reported negative earnings.

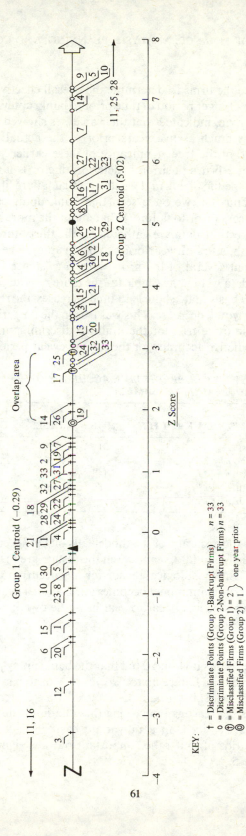

KEY:

† = Discriminate Points (Group 1-Bankrupt Firms) $n = 33$
o = Discriminate Points (Group 2-Non-bankrupt Firms) $n = 33$
⊕ = Misclassified Firms (Group 1) = 2 ⎫ one year prior
⊚ = Misclassified Firms (Group 2) = 1 ⎭

Chart 1.   Individual firm discriminant scores and group centroids—one year prior to bankruptcy ($Z = .012X_1 + .033X_2 + .033X_3 + .006X_4 + .999X_5$).

would be to examine the firms to determine the overall effectiveness of the discriminant model for a longer period of time prior to bankruptcy. Several studies, e.g., Beaver and Merwin, indicated that their analyses showed firms exhibiting failure tendencies as much as five years prior to the actual failure. Little is mentioned, however, of the true significance of these earlier year results. Is it enough to show that a firm's position is deteriorating or is it more important to examine when in the life of a firm does its eventual failure, if any, become an acute possibility? Thus far, we have seen that bankruptcy can be predicted accurately for two years prior to failure. What about the more remote years?

To answer this question, data are gathered for the thirty-three original firms from the third, fourth, and fifth year prior to bankruptcy. The reduced sample is due to the fact that several of the firms were in existence for less than five years. In two cases data were unavailable for the more remote years. One would expect on an *a priori* basis that, as the lead time increases, the relative predictive ability of any model would decrease. This was true in the univariate studies cited earlier, and it is also quite true for the multiple discriminant model. Table 4 summarizes the predictive accuracy for the total five year period.

TABLE 4.   FIVE YEAR PREDICTIVE ACCURACY OF
THE MDA MODEL (INITIAL SAMPLE)

YEAR PRIOR TO BANKRUPTCY	HITS	MISSES	PER CENT CORRECT
1st $n = 33$	31	2	95
2nd $n = 32$	23	9	72
3rd $n = 29$	14	15	48
4th $n = 28$	8	20	29
5th $n = 25$	9	16	36

It is obvious that the accuracy of the model falls off consistently with the one exception of the fourth and fifth years, when the results are reversed from what would be expected. The most logical reason for this occurrence is that after the second year, the discriminant model becomes unreliable in its predictive ability, and, also, that the change from year to year has little or no meaning.

Implications

Based on the above results it is suggested that the bankruptcy prediction model is an accurate forecaster of failure up to two years prior to bankruptcy and that the accuracy diminishes substantially as the lead time increases. In order to investigate the possible reasons underlying these findings the trend in the five predictive variables is traced on a univariate basis for five years preceding bankruptcy. The ratios of four other important but less significant ratios are also listed in Table 5.

TABLE 5. AVERAGE RATIOS OF BANKRUPT GROUP PRIOR TO FAILURE—ORIGINAL SAMPLE

RATIO	FIFTH YEAR		FOURTH YEAR		THIRD YEAR		SECOND YEAR		FIRST YEAR	
	Ratio	Change[a]	Ratio	Change[a]	Ratio	Change[a]	Ratio	Change[a]	Ratio	Change[a]
Working Capital/Total Assets (%) (X_1)	19.5		23.2	+ 3.6	17.6	− 5.6	1.6	−16.0[b]	(6.1)	− 7.7
Retained Earnings/Total Assets (%) (X_2)	4.0		(0.8)	− 4.8	(7.0)	− 6.2	(30.1)	−23.1	(62.6)	−32.5[b]
EBIT/Total Assets (%) (X_3)	7.2		4.0	− 3.2	(5.8)	− 9.8	(20.7)	−14.9[b]	(31.8)	−11.1
Market Value Equity/Total Debt (%) (X_4)	180.0		147.6	−32.4	143.2	− 4.4	74.2	−69.0[b]	40.1	−34.1
Sales/Total Assets (%) (X_5)	200.0		200.0	0.0	166.0	−34.0[b]	150.0	−16.0	150.0	0.0
Current Ratio (%)	180.0		187.0	+ 7.0	162.0	−25.0	131.0	−31.0[b]	133.0	+ 2.0
Years of Negative Profits (yrs.)	0.8		0.9	+ 0.1	1.2	+ 0.3	2.0	+ 0.8[b]	2.5	+ 0.5
Total Debt/Total Assets (%)	54.2		60.9	+ 6.7	61.2	+ 0.3	77.0	+15.8	96.4	+19.4[b]
Net Worth/Total Debt (%)	123.2		75.2	−28.0	112.6	+17.4	70.5	−42.1[b]	49.4	−21.1

[a] Change from previous year.
[b] Largest yearly change in the ratio.

The two most important conclusions of this trend analysis are (1) that all of the observed ratios show a deteriorating trend as bankruptcy approached, and (2) that the most serious change in the majority of these ratios occurred between the third and the second years prior to bankruptcy. The degree of seriousness is measured by the yearly change in the ratio values. The latter observation is extremely significant as it provides evidence consistent with conclusions derived from the discriminant model. Therefore, the important information inherent in the individual ratio measurement trends takes on deserved significance only when integrated with the more analytical discriminant analysis findings.

V.   APPLICATIONS

The use of a multiple discriminant model for predicting bankruptcy has displayed several advantages, but bankers, credit managers, executives, and investors will typically not have access to computer procedures such as the Cooley-Lohnes MDA program. Therefore, it will be necessary to investigate the results presented in Section IV closely and to attempt to extend the model for more general application. The procedure described below may be utilized to select a "cut-off" point, or optimum Z value, which enables predictions without computer support.[33]

By observing those firms which have been misclassified by the discriminant model in the initial sample, it is concluded that all firms having a Z score of greater than 2.99 clearly fall into the "non-bankrupt" sector, while those firms having a Z below 1.81 are all bankrupt. The area between 1.81 and 2.99 will be defined as the "zone of ignorance" or "gray area" because of the susceptibility to error classification (see Chart 1). Since errors are observed in this range of values, we will be uncertain about a *new* firm whose Z value falls within the "zone of ignorance." Hence, it is desirable to establish a guideline for classifying firms in the "gray area."

The process begins by identifying sample observations which fall within the overlapping range. These appear as in Table 6. The first digit of the firm number identifies the group, with the last two digits locating the firm within the group.

Next, the range of values of Z that results in the *minimum number of misclassifications* is found. In the analysis, Z's between (but not including) the indicated values produce the following misclassifications as shown in Table 7.

The best critical value conveniently falls between 2.67–2.68 and therefore 2.675, the midpoint of the interval, is chosen as the Z value that discriminates best between the bankrupt and non-bankrupt firms.

---

[33] A similar method proved to be useful in selecting cut-off points for marketing decisions, see R. E. Frank, A. A. Kuehn, W. F. Massy, *Quantitative Techniques in Marketing Analysis* (Homewood, Ill.: Richard D. Irwin, Inc., 1962), pp. 95–100.

TABLE 6.   FIRM WHOSE Z SCORE FALLS WITHIN GRAY AREA

FIRM NUMBER NON-BANKRUPT	Z SCORE	FIRM NUMBER BANKRUPT
2019*	1.81	
	1.98	1026
	2.10	1014
	2.67	1017*
2033	2.68	
2032	2.78	
	2.99	1025*

* Misclassified by the MDA model; for example, firm "19" in Group 2.

TABLE 7.   NUMBER OF MISCLASSIFICATIONS USING VARIOUS Z SCORE CRITERIONS

RANGE OF Z	NUMBER MISCLASSIFIED	FIRMS
1.81–1.98	5	2019, 1026, 1014, 1017, 1025
1.98–2.10	4	2019, 1014, 1017, 1025
2.10–2.67	3	2019, 1017, 1025
2.67–2.68	2	2019, 1025
2.68–2.78	3	2019, 2033, 1025
2.78–2.99	4	2019, 2033, 2032, 1025

Of course, the real test of this "optimum" Z value is its discriminating power not only with the initial sample, but also with the secondary samples. The results of these tests are even slightly superior to the job done by the computer assignments, with the additional benefit of practical applicability.

Business-Loan Evaluation

Reference was made earlier to several studies which examined the effectiveness of discriminant analysis in evaluating *consumer-loan* applications and, perhaps, these suggest a useful extension of the bankruptcy-prediction model. The evaluation of *business loans* is an important function in our society, especially to commercial banks and other lending institutions. Studies have been devoted to the loan offer function[34] and to the adoption of a heuristic-bank-loan-officer model whereby a computer model was developed to simulate the loan officer function.[35] Admittedly, the analysis of the loan applicant's financial statements is but one section of the entire evaluation process, but it is a very important

[34] D. D. Hester, "An Empirical Examination of a Commercial Loan Offer Function," *Yale Economic Essays*, vol. 2, No. 1 (1962), pp. 3–57.

[35] K. Cohen, T. Gilmore, and F. Singer, "Banks Procedures for Analyzing Business Loan Applications," *Analytical Methods in Banking*, K. Cohen and F. Hammer (eds.) (Homewood, Ill.: Richard D. Irwin, Inc., 1966), pp. 218–251.

link. A fast and efficient device for detecting unfavorable credit risks might enable the loan officer to avoid potentially disastrous decisions. The significant point is that the MDA model contains many of the variables common to business-loan evaluation and discriminant analysis has been used for consumer-loan evaluation. Therefore, the potential presents itself for utilization in the business sector.

Because such important variables as the purpose of the loan, its maturity, the security involved, the deposit status of the applicant, and the particular characteristics of the bank are not explicitly considered in the model, the MDA should probably not be used as the only means of credit evaluation. The discriminant Z score index can be used, however, as a guide in efforts to lower the costs of investigation of loan applicants. Less time and effort would be spent on companies whose Z score is very high, i.e., above 3.0, while those with low Z scores would signal a very thorough investigation. This policy would be advisable to the loan officer who had some degree of faith in the discriminant analysis approach, but who did not want his final decision to depend solely on a numerical score. Also, the method would be particularly efficient in the case of short-term loans or relatively small loans where the normal credit evaluation process is very costly relative to the expected income from the loan. Herein lie important advantages of the MDA model—its simplicity and low cost.

Internal Control Considerations and Investment Criteria

An extremely important, but often very difficult, task of corporate management is to periodically assess honestly the firm's present condition. By doing so, important strengths and weaknesses may be recognized and, in the latter case, changes in policies and actions will usually be in order. The suggestion here is that the discriminant model, if used correctly and periodically, has the ability to predict corporate problems early enough so as to enable management to realize the gravity of the situation in time to avoid failure. If failure is unavoidable, the firm's creditors and stockholders may be better off if a merger with a stronger enterprise is negotiated before bankruptcy.

The potentially useful applications of an accurate bankruptcy predictive model are not limited to internal considerations or to credit evaluation purposes. An efficient predictor of financial difficulties could also be a valuable technique for screening out undesirable investments. On the more optimistic side it appears that there are some very real opportunities for benefits. Since the model is basically predictive the analyst can utilize these predictions to recommend appropriate investment policy. For instance, observations suggest that while investors are somewhat capable of anticipating declines in operating results of selective firms, there is an overwhelming tendency to underestimate the financial plight of the companies which eventually go bankrupt. Firms in the original sample whose Z scores were below the so-called "zone of ignorance" experienced an average decline in the market value of their common stock of 45 per cent from the time the model first predicted bankruptcy until the actual failure date (an average period of about 15 months).

While the above results are derived from an admittedly small sample of very special firms, the potential implications are of interest. If an individual already owns stock in a firm whose future appears dismal, according to the model, he should sell in order to avoid further price declines. The sale would prevent further loss and provide capital for alternative investments. A different policy could be adopted by those aggressive investors looking for short-sale opportunities. An investor utilizing this strategy would have realized a 26 per cent gain on those listed securities eligible for short-sales in the original sample of bankrupt firms. In the case of large companies, where bankruptcy occurs less frequently, an index which has the ability to forecast downside movements appears promising. This could be especially helpful in the area of efficient portfolio selection. That is, firms which appear to be strongly susceptible to downturns, according to the discriminant model, would be rejected regardless of any positive potential. Conversely, firms exhibiting these same downside characteristics could be sold short, thereby enabling the portfolio manager to be more aggressive in his other choices.

VI.   CONCLUDING REMARKS

This paper seeks to assess the analytical quality of ratio analysis. It has been suggested that traditional ratio analysis is no longer an important analytical technique in the academic environment due to the relatively unsophisticated manner in which it has been presented. In order to assess its potential rigorously, a set of financial ratios was combined in a discriminant analysis approach to the problem of corporate bankruptcy prediction. The theory is that ratios, if analyzed within a multivariate framework, will take on greater statistical significance than the common technique of sequential ratio comparisons. The results are very encouraging.

The discriminant-ratio model proved to be extremely accurate in predicting bankruptcy correctly in 94 per cent of the initial sample with 95 per cent of all firms in the bankrupt and non-bankrupt groups assigned to their actual group classification. Furthermore, the discriminant function was accurate in several secondary samples introduced to test the reliability of the model. Investigation of the individual ratio movements prior to bankruptcy corroborated the model's findings that bankruptcy can be accurately predicted up to two years prior to actual failure with the accuracy diminishing rapidly after the second year. A limitation of the study is that the firms examined were all publicly held manufacturing corporations for which comprehensive financial data were obtainable, including market price quotations. An area for future research, therefore, would be to extend the analysis to relatively smaller asset-sized firms and unincorporated entities where the incidence of business failure is greater than with larger corporations.

Several practical and theoretical applications of the model were suggested. The former include business credit evaluation, internal control procedures, and investment guidelines. Inherent in these applications is the assumption that signs of deterioration, detected by a ratio index, can be observed clearly enough to take profitable action. A potential theoretical area of importance lies in the conceptualization of efficient portfolio selection. One of the current limitations in this area is in a realistic presentation of those securities and the types of investment policies which are necessary to balance the portfolio and avoid downside risk. The ideal approach is to include those securities possessing negative co-variance with other securities in the portfolio. However, these securities are not likely to be easy to locate, if at all. The problem becomes somewhat more soluble if a method is introduced which rejects securities with high downside risk or includes them in a short-selling context. The discriminant-ratio model appears to have the potential to ease this problem. Further investigation, however, is required on this subject.

QUESTIONS

1. Examine the five variables (ratios) included in the Altman model and their respective coefficients. Do each variable and the sign of the coefficient make sense to you? Explain.
2. What is multiple discriminant analysis? What are some of its advantages over informal methods?
3. Regression lines are those which produce the smallest sum of the squared deviations from the regression line. Contrast the discriminant analysis objective to that of the regression lines.
4. If your firm were using the Altman model for decision making regarding trade credit, what would your decision be if the score for the credit applicant were:
   a. above 2.99?
   b. below 1.81?
   c. between 1.81 and 2.99?
5. What is meant by the "zone of ignorance"?
6. The data base for this study was industrial firms; is the applicability of the results limited to industrial firms? Discuss.
7. Do you think that the determinants of corporate bankruptcy might change over time? Describe how you could find out.

II | Working Capital Management

4 | Judy Pan, Donald R. Nichols, and O. Maurice Joy

Sales Forecasting Practices of Large U.S. Industrial Firms

Most techniques of financial planning and control rely upon a sales forecast. Students often wonder about the accuracy of such forecasts. This article reports on a survey of large firms and finds correlation between accuracy goals and actual accuracy achieved in forecasting. This implies that where relative accuracy in forecasting is needed, firms are able to develop methods for achieving that accuracy.

Sales forecasting is a crucial part of many financial management activities, including profit planning, capital expenditure analysis, capital structure planning, cash budgeting and merger analysis. In all of these and other financial management areas, accurate sales projections are extremely important. Because of this importance, any prescriptive finance theory should be cognizant of and influenced by the projection and forecasting practices of the firms we prescribe for. Very little is known today about sales forecasting practices in industry, however, and a systematic cataloguing of current sales forecasting practices would assist in documenting and comparing current practices. The purpose of this study is to present some evidence regarding the current state of the art of business sales forecasting practices. Because of the nature of the topic, we necessarily use data from a questionnaire. In the following sections we present this questionnaire, the nature of the data obtained from it, and draw some conclusions about the evidence.

DATA

Data for this study were taken from a questionnaire mailed in mid-1974 to 251 companies selected from *Fortune's* 500 industrial list for 1973. Since we were interested in industry differences in sales forecasting, it was necessary to use

Source. Reprinted by permission from *Financial Management*, Fall 1977, pp. 72–77. Judy Pan is an accountant. O. Maurice Joy and Donald R. Nichols are professor and associate professor, respectively, at the School of Business, University of Kansas.

industry groups that had sufficiently large membership for analysis. We mailed questionnaires to 251 *Fortune* firms in the seven industries that contained 19 or more companies. From this sample, 139 usable responses (55%) were obtained. Exhibit 1 shows some detailed information about the number of questionnaires mailed, usable number returned, and industry subtotals. A sample questionnaire is shown in the appendix.

EXHIBIT 1.   SAMPLE INDUSTRY AND SIZE (SALES) CHARACTERISTICS

Industry	Number of Questionnaires Mailed	Number of Usable Responses	Sales ($ Millions)		
			Under 500	Between 500 and 1,250	Over 1,250
Food and Kindred Products	56	27	8	8	11
Chemicals and Allied Products	52	30	8	12	10
Primary Metals	26	19	6	6	7
Machinery except Electrical	36	27	9	13	5
Electrical and Electronic Machinery Equipment & Supplies	39	17	7	4	6
Petroleum Refining/Oil and Gas Exploration	23	5 ⎫			
Fabricated Metal Products except Machinery Equipment	19	6 ⎬ 19**	8	5	6
Not Classified	—	8* ⎭			
Total	251	139	46	48	45

*Some firms removed their industry code designator from the questionnaire.
**These 19 firms are grouped together as "Other" firms.

Question number two (see the appendix) is worth some special attention, since all questions except for it are more factual in nature. Question two asks for a subjective estimate of the relative sophistication of the firm's forecasting techniques. While the highly subjective nature of the response to this question is philosophically considerably different from the objective responses required in the other questions, the question nevertheless seemed an appropriate way to address the sophistication of techniques issue. An alternative to this approach would have been to ask for a listing of forecasting techniques used; however, such a listing would not necessarily provide an indication of differences in sophistication. All the approaches considered contained some possibility for misinterpretation of the question or the response. Although we recognized the possible shortcomings, we still opted for the subjective format for question two. This variable is more properly described as (and will be referred to as) a *perceived* sophistication score.

DESCRIPTION OF PRACTICES

The survey results are shown in Exhibit 2. Since the findings themselves are straightforward, our discussion in this section will focus on key results and interpretations. In some instances we will introduce data not reflected in Exhibit 2; we will also briefly discuss some of the potential shortcomings of the questionnaire and its results. While problems of questionnaire interpretation of some individual items will be discussed below, one problem that pervades the analysis is the potential "time sensitivity" of the data. Since our survey covers only one year, generalizations of the results across time are clearly hazardous.

1. Most companies perceived the sophistication level of their forecasting techniques as relatively high.

EXHIBIT 2. SURVEY RESULTS

Characteristic	Percentage of Responses in Class				Description of Class*			
	1	2	3	4	1	2	3	4
Perceived sophistication	18	41	30	11			High to low**	
Desired accuracy	20	46	32	3	<5	5–9	Error ± % 10	>10
Achieved accuracy	32	38	28	2	<5	5–9	Error ± % 10	>10
Longest period forecast	4	43	18	35	>5	>3 to 5	Years in future >1 to 3	1
Shortest period forecast	2	66	17	15	<1	1	Months 3	>3 to 12
Revisions per year	2	31	43	23	>12	11 or 12	Number per year 3, 4, or 6	<3
Comparisons per year	4	87	7	2	>12	12	Number per year 3 to <12	<3

*The columns of the "Description of Class" are associated with the respective columns of the "Percentage of Responses in Class." In the "Desired accuracy" row, for example, 20% of the sample reported they had desired accuracy levels less than ± 5% error.

**In the questionnaire shown in the appendix, "Perceived sophistication" has five levels. Since only three firms out of 133 reported their perceived sophistication in level 5 (the lowest), for ease of exposition we have grouped those three firms with the 11 firms in level 4, to give a total of 14 firms, or 11% of the usable sample.

2.   Almost all firms aimed for accuracy of within ± 10%, but only about two-thirds of the companies achieved this goal.
3.   The most frequent "longest length" periods were one year and five years.
4.   The most frequent "shortest length" period was one month.
5.   The most common revision periods were quarterly and monthly.
6.   The vast majority of firms compared forecasts with realizations on a monthly basis.

It bears reemphasizing here that our sample includes only the largest of the U.S. industrial firms. Because of this, it would not be surprising if there were no important "size" effects on forecasting effects. We investigated the possibility of size effects by separating firms into three size categories based on magnitude of sales and performing χ^2 tests to determine if the size of the firms within our sample was associated in any systematic way with any of the seven forecasting variables presented in Exhibit 2. With the exception of perceived sophistication and longest period forecast, there were no important size effects. The larger companies in our sample viewed their forecasting techniques to be more sophisticated and tended to forecast farther into the future than the smaller companies.

There is also the question of industry effects in the responses to the questions. Because of the few number of firms reporting in the petroleum and fabricated metals industries, firms in these two industries were omitted from this part of the analysis. The question of whether industry grouping is independent of any specific forecasting variable was addressed by computing separate χ^2 statistics for the set of cross-classifications involving industry membership and each of the seven specific forecasting variables of Exhibit 2. With the exception of degree of accuracy achieved, industry membership is independent of the forecasting variables at the .05 significance level. This indicates a relatively high degree of interindustry homogeneity with respect to forecasting practices.

RELATIONSHIPS AMONG PERCEIVED SOPHISTICATION, DEGREE OF ACCURACY DESIRED, AND DEGREE OF ACCURACY ACHIEVED

In this section we will explore hypotheses about the relationships among three of the more interesting variables: perceived sophistication, degree of accuracy desired and degree of accuracy achieved. These variables are particularly important because they relate forecasting quality perceptions, aspiration levels and realizations, respectively.

Perceived Sophistication vs. Degree of Accuracy Desired

It might seem reasonable to expect that there would be a close positive relationship between the level of perceived sophistication and the degree of accuracy desired. If this were true, high (low) levels of perceived sophistication would accompany demanding (undemanding) accuracy goals. A positive relationship is plausible because, in a sense, these two variables may be thought of as subjective-objective counterparts. This relationship, if it exists, might be clouded by the data to some extent. The subjective nature of the perceived sophistication variable has been mentioned previously. In addition, the degree of accuracy desired variable may be tempered by past experience and the nature of the industry. Thus it is possible that some respondents may have indicated a relatively poor desired accuracy level because of industry or company specific forecasting difficulties, such as volatility, and yet show usage of relatively sophisticated forecasting practices.

Exhibit 3 shows a cross-classification of the two variables of interest, perceived sophistication and degree of accuracy desired. Applying a χ^2 test to this cross-classification, we found that the probability of observing a χ^2 at least as large as that calculated ($\chi^2 = 12.7$), if the two variables were independent, is less than 5% ($\chi^2_{.05,6} = 12.59$). Consequently, we conclude that perceived sophistication of sales forecasting practices and desired accuracy levels are not independent. Exhibit 3 suggests that observations in the most sophisticated levels (1 and 2) tend to have relatively more ambitious accuracy goals than in the other three levels. In fact, the difference between the mean degree of accuracy desired for perceived sophistication levels 1 and 2 ($\pm 5.9\%$) is significantly greater (*i.e.*, more demanding) at the .05 level than the mean degree of accuracy desired for perceived sophistication levels 3, 4, and 5 ($\pm 7.2\%$). This and following tests of differences between means assume the variances of the populations sampled are finite and equal. The first assumption

EXHIBIT 3.   PERCEIVED SOPHISTICATION VS.
DEGREE OF ACCURACY DESIRED AND ACHIEVED

Perceived Sophistication Level	Degree of Accuracy Desired (D) and Achieved (A)					
	Percent under ± 5%		Percent between ± 5% to ± 9%		Percent over ± 9%	
	D	A	D	A	D	A
1	32	18	12	18	21	15
2	48	55	48	30	28	45
3	8	18	31	42	42	30
4-5	12	8	9	9	9	10
	100	100	100	100	100	100

is fully satisfied, while the second is, based on sample estimates, probably satisfied.

These results support the thesis that higher degrees of perceived sophistication are associated with more ambitious accuracy goals, and the industry or company specific forecasting difficulties mentioned, if they exist, did not produce ambiguous results.

Perceived Sophistication vs. Degree of Accuracy Achieved

Presumably, firms use more sophisticated sales forecasting techniques because the increased level of sophistication can be translated into better forecasts. This plausible presumption implies a positive relationship between the level of perceived sophistication and the degree of forecasting accuracy achieved. In investigating this relationship we have trichotomized the forecasting achievement variable along the same lines as the desired accuracy variable. Results from a cross-classification of the two variables, perceived sophistication and degree of accuracy achieved, are also shown in Exhibit 3. Applying a χ^2 test, we found that the two variables appeared to be independent of one another, as the observed χ^2 (6.31) is less than the critical χ^2 (10.65) at the .10 significance level. This finding of independence is, of course, contrary to the hypothesis that there is a positive relationship between perceived sophistication and achieved forecasting accuracy, at least for the companies and year involved in our sample. It is possible that the industry or firm specific forecasting difficulties alluded to above provide an explanation of the findings, but current knowledge of such difficulties is very limited, and our data were not precise enough to permit investigation of this possibility.

Degree of Accuracy Desired vs. Degree of Accuracy Achieved

We concluded above that there was no systematic relationship between firms' self perception of forecasting sophistication and forecasting accuracy achievements. While that is an important, and somewhat surprising, finding, an even more important question pertains to the relationship between the objectively stated forecasting accuracy goal and the actual forecasting success record. It was not feasible, nor was it our objective, to obtain quantities of historical data for specific time series analyses. Among other things, it would be probable that responses on perceived sophistication, desired accuracy, and achieved accuracy would be related to current conditions. Thus, we directed the respondents to their most recent experience. To the extent that the most recent performance is not representative of normal performance, the responses are biased. Finally, there is also a potential for differing interpretations of the degree of accuracy achieved question. Our objective was to obtain information about accuracy achieved in the original twelve-month forecast, although the response conceivably may relate to accuracy achieved in the latest revision of the annual forecast.

First, a test of independence of the two variables, desired and achieved accuracy, using a cross-classification matrix derived from data in Exhibit 3, indicates that there is some systematic relationship between the two variables as the computed χ^2 is significant at the .01 level. The more pertinent question, however, is whether there is a positive relationship between desired accuracy and achieved accuracy of forecast. The Kendall rank correlation coefficient, a commonly used nonparametric correlation technique, is $+ .363$, which is significantly positive at the .01 level. To corroborate the Kendall test, we also compared mean differences in achieved accuracy results for the three levels of desired accuracy. The mean achieved accuracy groups were as follows:

Desired accuracy classification	Mean achieved accuracy
Under ± 5%	5.0%
± 5% to ± 9%	7.9%
Over ± 9%	12.9%

The mean achieved accuracy of the "over ± 9%" desired accuracy group is significantly poorer than the mean of the "± 5% to ± 9%" group, while the latter group is significantly poorer than the "under ± 5%" mean. Both of these differences are significant at the .05 level. These results, together with the χ^2 and Kendall test, lend support to the hypothesis that desired and achieved accuracy are positively related.

CONCLUSIONS

Our primary purpose in this article has been to describe current sales forecasting practices of major U.S. industrial firms. The results of our survey were consistent with the thesis that large industrial firms recognize the importance of sales forecasting and commit resources to these efforts on a planned, regular basis. The forecasting techniques were perceived by most respondents to be relatively sophisticated, and periodic revisions of the forecasts were common. It also appeared that firms desiring greater accuracy in their forecasts utilized techniques that they felt were more sophisticated than those used by firms desiring less accuracy. Finally, there was evidence of a positive relationship between degree of accuracy desired and achieved accuracy. Keeping in mind the potential shortcomings and problems of the questionnaire results and their interpretation, this last finding has particular importance from the financial management perspective of those involved in designing decision making systems that utilize sales forecasting information. The finding implies that forecasting success is indeed related to forecasting aspirations.

REFERENCES

1. J. C. Chamber, S. K. Mullich, and D. D. Smith, "How to Choose the Right Forecasting Technique," *Harvard Business Review* (July 1971), pp. 45–74.
2. J. G. Gillis, "Legal Aspects of Corporate Forecasts," *Financial Analysts Journal* (January-February 1973), pp. 72–76.
3. Y. Ijiri, J. C. Kinar, and F. B. Putney, "An Integrated Evaluation System for Budget Forecasting and Operation Performance," *Journal of Accounting Research* (Spring 1968), pp. 1–28.
4. R. M. Kirby, "A Comparison of Short and Medium Range Statistical Forecasting Methods," *Management Science* (December 1966), pp. 202–10.
5. Marvin Schiller, Principal Researcher for A. T. Kearney, Inc., in study of *Public Disclosure of Business Forecasts*, Financial Executives Research Foundation (1972).
6. S. S. Stewart, Principal Researcher on *Research Report on Corporate Forecasts* for Financial Analysts Federation (1972).

Appendix QUESTIONNAIRE

Please answer as completely as possible the following questions.

1. The dollar amount of the total sales of your company last year was approximately _____.
2. How would you describe the relative sophistication of your company's forecasting techniques for planning and budgeting on the following scale compared to other companies of your size and industry? (Circle the appropriate number.)

High Sophistication				Low Sophistication
1	2	3	4	5

3. Approximately how much does your company spend on the total forecasting and budgeting function annually?   _____
4. What degree of accuracy does your company realistically desire to achieve in the forecast? (Express in terms of percentage error— you desire the forecast to be within ± what % of actual total sales.)   _____
5. What is the longest time period covered by the budget or forecast? (Express in number of months.)   _____
6. What is the shortest time period included in the budget or forecast?   _____

7. How many times per year does a scheduled revision of the budget
    or forecast occur?   ____

8. How often are actual results compared with budgeted amounts?   ____

9. Approximately what was the percentage error between actual
    results and the budgeted amounts in your annual forecast last
    year?   ____

QUESTIONS

1. Does it make sense that firms would expect to secure high forecasting
    accuracy with more sophisticated methods? Explain.

2. Is it disturbing to you that actual accuracy achieved was independent of
    the perceived sophistication of forecasting methods? Explain.

3. Regardless of the firm's perception of sophistication of methodology, is it
    consistent that those firms with high accuracy goals tended to achieve
    greater accuracy in forecasting than those firms with lower accuracy
    goals? In your explanation, discuss the subjective nature inherent in
    stating the degree of sophistication compared with the objective nature of
    the target accuracy levels.

5 | Lawrence J. Gitman, D. Keith Forrester, and John R. Forrester, Jr.

Maximizing Cash Disbursement Float

As the authors of this article indicate, there are two basic cash management strategies to follow. These are to collect receivables as soon as possible and pay bills as late as possible. This treatise deals with ways to achieve the latter within the constraints of taking discounts and not losing supplier goodwill.

INTRODUCTION

Importance of Cash Management

The management of corporate funds has been a major function of corporate treasurers and bankers for a considerable period of time. Over the past few years increased attention has been devoted to the use of more sophisticated methods of managing corporate cash flows. This increased emphasis can be attributed primarily to the recent high levels of interest rates and also the limited availability of financing alternatives. High interest rates increase the opportunity cost of holding idle cash balances, thereby placing pressure on firms to lower their levels of cash balances. Often, the level of a firm's cash balance is considered indicative of the company's success in managing cash. In general, it appears that businesses have made their money work harder for them in recent years, as cash levels have remained relatively constant while sales have doubled [6].

Cash Management Strategy

Each company is unique in its manner of both receiving and disbursing funds from operations, so that each must utilize cash management strategies based

Source. Reprinted by permission from *Financial Management*, Summer 1976, pp. 15–24. Lawrence J. Gitman is associate professor of finance at the University of Tulsa. D. Keith Forrester is an officer at the Bank of Oklahoma, and John R. Forrester, Jr. is administrator for the Richardson Heights Baptist Church, Richardson, Texas.

upon its own financial condition and objectives. The two basic cash management strategies [4, pp. 169–170] normally applied are: (1) Collect accounts receivables as quickly as possible without losing future sales due to high-pressure collection techniques. (2) Pay accounts payable as late as possible without damaging the firm's credit rating and supplier relationships.

The objective of the *collection system* is to speed up collections by *minimizing* both the amount of mail time for the receipt of payments and the amount of collection float—the latter being the amount of checks in the firm's demand deposit account on which they have not yet received payment from the payor's bank. This enables the company to increase interest income by increasing the amount of investable funds or decrease interest expense by reducing the amount of borrowing. In an effort to minimize collection float, firms have employed several useful tools, one of which is the lock box system. In a lock box system customers send their payments directly to a post office box or drawer located at a major post office [19]. The box or drawer is emptied at least daily by the firm's bank and the contents deposited directly into the firm's account. By strategically locating lock boxes geographically, a firm can reduce mail float—the time it takes for a check mailed by the customer to be deposited in the bank. By reducing both mail float and collection float, such a system should result in savings for the firm if the funds generated are put to more productive uses.

The objective of the *disbursement system* is to slow down payments in order to *maximize* the amount of payment float resulting from all payments (checks) and thereby allow the firm to reduce borrowings or invest excess funds in marketable securities or other productive assets. The goal of the corporate treasurer may be cash conservation, which can be achieved by taking the maximum allowable time to pay bills and by adopting methods of bill paying that result in a need for lower borrowing levels [11]. Methods and procedures for maximizing payment float in order to minimize cash requirements include centralizing payable and disbursement procedures in order to: (1) gain better control over the timing of payments and to streamline banking relationships; (2) insure taking attractive discounts; and (3) employ payment techniques which maximize float by delaying payments until late in the day, by using drafts and by delaying the clearing of checks through the company's bank account [3, 5].

Although the concept of maximizing disbursement float is broadly understood by companies in the United States, it is not a broadly adopted technique since some firms do not wish to endanger their supplier relationships. Some companies find the strategy of maximizing disbursement float inconsistent with their overall business conduct. Other companies are known to go to elaborate means in order to maximize their disbursement float. In some cases, firms use the computer to examine the mailing addresses of check recipients and then draw the check from the most remote bank. Further refinements include taking advantage of snowstorms and airline strikes in order to further slow down payments.

Components of Disbursement Float

Three types of float are generated as a result of the payment process. *Mail float* is the amount of time a check remains in the postal system. *Processing float* is the amount of time it takes for the company to receive the check from the post office until it is deposited in the bank. One aspect of *transit float* deals with how long it takes the check to clear the banking system and be charged against the company's account, which must be funded by the paying company at that time. Such transit float applies to disbursing accounts, and is the float most maximizing disbursing systems seek to maximize. Another aspect of transit float is concerned with the fact that the supplier—the one receiving the check—will receive credit on all checks no more than two days after deposit because of an arbitrary guarantee by the Federal Reserve System [2] that all checks will in effect be cleared within two days. If the Fed cannot clear the checks within two days, then the Fed ends up carrying the float. In this type situation the Fed is providing interest-free money to the collecting company. Because of the Fed's guarantee of availability, the paying company can maximize its transit float for as long as one week, while the supplier (the check depositor) is guaranteed availability of funds within two days after deposit. As a result of the Fed's guarantee of availability in instances where the check takes more than two days to clear, the transit float differs for the supplier and customer. This article is concerned with the transit float of the paying company.

Since the amount of time a check remains in the payment process is very important to the financial manager, he funds the company's bank accounts not when the checks are written or released; rather, he does so when the check is expected to be returned to the bank for payment. Although this strategy would be risky for an individual to use in funding a personal checking account, for large firms writing numerous checks—none of which are unusually large—it is relatively simple, through historical studies, to fund the account on the day the check is expected to clear. The larger the number of checks and the smaller the size of checks, the easier it is to determine with a high degree of accuracy the time at which the checks will clear the account. The longer a payment remains in the system, the greater the amount of earnings that will be generated from investable funds. For example, assume that a company averages $1 million daily in payments to suppliers. Each day these payments remain in the system allows the corporation to increase its investable balances by $1 million. This, in turn, means that a company can annually earn (assuming a 10% opportunity rate, which in this paper is assumed to equal the return the firm could earn by investing the money gained through the increased float in marketable securities) $100 thousand in pre-tax earnings for each additional day that $1 million remains in the disbursement system. With special banking arrangements, a company can earn interest for as long as a week of float, thus considerably increasing its cash reserves.

State of the Art in Cash Management

Over the last few years a great deal of emphasis has been placed on the collection or cash gathering side of the cash flow system, but relatively little attention has been devoted to the disbursement area of cash management. Only in the last few years have companies begun to exploit new, sophisticated, computer-controlled systems [13] with the main purpose of taking advantage of the inefficiencies in both the check collection procedures of the Federal Reserve System and the postal system.

Many large comanies have "played the float" for years. Recently, many corporations have developed effective ways to extend the float a few more days, thereby allowing them, in effect, to use Federal Reserve money interest-free to pay their bills. The company is able to invest its own cash at high interest rates, invest in inventory, or use it to furnish compensating balances to cover the cost of banking services [13]. Levy [11] has developed a heuristic (i.e., a rule of thumb that generates a good—but not necessarily optimal—solution to a problem) applicable to the lock box location problem of managing accounts receivables. Calman [1] has included disbursing activity in his linear programming model that encompasses the entire cash flow system. In this model he includes the cost required by banks to provide services. Pogue, Faucett, and Bussard [14] have expanded Calman's model to more precisely identify costs; they have emphasized minimizing the sum of service fees and the opportunity cost of allocating cash balances to the banks in the system.

The most recent significant development in computerizing disbursement models was underwritten by 8 banks for Phoenix-Hecht Cash Management Services (PHCMS), a computer software designer, to refine the disbursement computer system [13]. By opening accounts in 100 banks nationwide, PHCMS developed a data base of check clearing times between these banks to use for maximizing disbursement float. Their computer model has the ability to specify the most geographically advantageous disbursing point or drawee bank from which to pay suppliers. Although there have been no published models with respect to this particular cash disbursement problem, several banks along with Phoenix-Hecht have developed similar in-house capabilities.

Objective of This Article

In light of the state of the art, in this article a mathematical model is developed and applied to the cash disbursement problem. The disbursement model presented is believed to be an improvement over previous developments, as it incorporates segments of the previously mentioned studies into a workable, efficient model. The model views the disbursement system as the reverse of a check collection system, since check clearing float is maximized instead of collection float being minimized. The model also computes the marginal cost of each additional bank managers would use to help them evaluate the cost of different banks. By applying the techniques used in the warehouse location problem [8] to the quite similar problem of maximizing disbursement float, a heuristic is described that can efficiently and economically provide for the selection of disbursing banks that maximize disbursement float and provide optimal solutions. The cash disbursement model yields optimum disbursement locations given a specific number of possible drawee banks by maximizing transit or check collection float and minimizing account costs for each disbursing bank or group of disbursing banks deemed necessary.

THE CASH DISBURSEMENT PROBLEM

Importance of Cash Disbursement Management

Most large businesses pay their bills—not as received, but rather in batches paid at discrete points in time. Quite often firms pay most of their accounts payable once each month. Of course, when attractive cash discounts are offered, firms pay their bills in order to take advantage of these discounts. Since these firms typically pay their bills with checks, a period of time is likely to elapse between the mailing of the check and the actual withdrawal of funds from its checking account. As a result of this "float" in the check clearing process, a firm is able to reduce borrowings or invest the excess funds in profitable assets. Of course, in order to intelligently do this the firm must arrange for zero-balance accounts with a concentration account at its bank or somehow "scientifically" estimate the amount of checks clearing each day after the checks are issued [19].

Ignoring supplier relations for the moment, in order to efficiently manage its disbursements, the firm should attempt to pay its bills in a fashion that maximizes its disbursement float, thereby delaying the removal of funds from its account and allowing the firm to earn as much on these funds as possible. Of the two aspects of maximizing payables management, one relates to the actual mailing of the check, independent of the day the check is printed or written, or the date that appears on the check. The most important factor is when the company is going to mail the check to the supplier, which could perhaps be 45 days after receipt of invoice, perhaps on the due date, or perhaps one or two days earlier than the due date so that it is received by the supplier on the due date. (This could also include the additional processing time if the payor mails the check to the office of the supplier rather than the lock box.)

The second aspect of maximizing payables is to attempt to maximize transit float. Only two controllable variables exist which allow the firm to manipulate this float—(1) the location, and (2) the number of banks from which the firm makes its disbursements. If one assumes that in order to avoid late fees, payments must be received by the payment date determined by the payor, then the location and number of disbursing banks are the only variables that can be manipulated in order to maximize payables management. This article operates under this assumption. By selecting disbursing locations (assuming the cost of banking services is the same for all banks) in order to maximize total disbursement float, the result should be a positive contribution toward the firm's profits. Of course, at the same time the firm adds additional disbursing banks, it also must provide added balances or fees as compensation for the bank's services. Therefore, the firm must weigh these costs against the added benefits when choosing the optimal system of disbursement banks.

Problem Configuration

The problem with which the firm is faced can be explained using the data presented in Exhibit 1, which depicts in geographic space the three payments to vendors in cities A, B, and C that a firm must make. Exhibit 1 indicates that the firm must make the following monthly payments to firms in the associated cities:

City	Amount
A	$100,000
B	$150,000
C	$125,000

If one assumes that the firm can pay these amounts by a check drawn on a bank in any of the above cities, the question becomes from which city(s) the firm should make its disbursements in order to maximize its disbursement float.

EXHIBIT 1. DIAGRAM OF PAYMENTS TO VENDORS IN CITIES A, B, AND C

A
·

$100,000

B
·

$150,000

C
·

$125,000

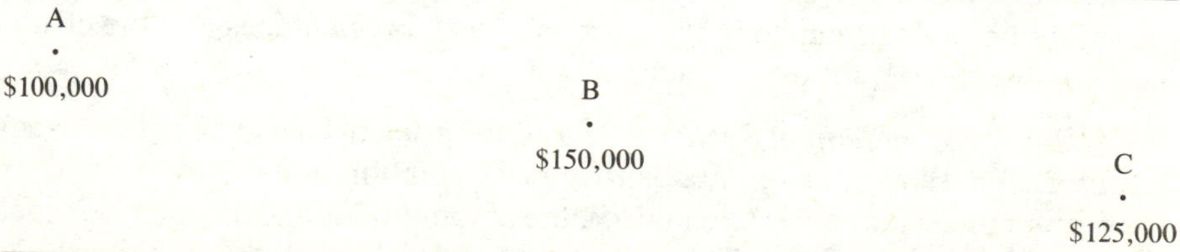

Heuristic Solution

The solution to this disbursement bank selection problem can be obtained heuristically. In order to illustrate the operation of the heuristic procedure, an example is used to show the actual mechanics of the process. To begin with, a table of check clearing times (shown in Exhibit 2) is examined to find the average number of days required for a check to travel from the depository bank (bank where the check is deposited) to the drawee bank (bank on which the check is drawn). Next, the number obtained from the check clearing table is multiplied by the amount of the disbursement to the corresponding city. The resulting product is the total clearing float measured in dollar-days, which are merely the average number of days it takes for a check to clear through the Federal Reserve System or local clearinghouse associations, multiplied by the amount of the payment to a firm in the associated city.

EXHIBIT 2. CHECK CLEARING TIMES (IN DAYS) FOR BANKS A, B, AND C

Drawee Banks	Depository Banks		
	A	B	C
A	0.00	4.71	2.87
B	1.80	0.00	4.00
C	4.08	3.20	0.00

The following steps illustrate the mechanical process involved in arriving at the value of the dollar-day float for each combination of disbursement points. In addition, the optimum number of disbursement or drawee banks will be determined from the available data. In order to keep this sample problem simple, the following analysis is performed on a before-tax basis and only a small dimensional matrix is employed. The firm's opportunity cost of funds is assumed to be 10%, and the monthly cost of each additional bank account is considered to be $150.

The basic operational procedure of the heuristic is simple. Its objective is to maximize the return on float from which the cost of maintaining additional banks can be subtracted to obtain net profit. Using the payment and clearing time data given, the best 1-, 2-, and 3-bank disbursing systems can be determined. Also, the optimum number of drawee banks can be found. The optimum system is that system that maximizes net profit, which is the difference between the savings gained in the form of investable balances and the cost of maintaining the required bank accounts.

Best 1-Bank Disbursement System.   Exhibit 3 presents a matrix of dollar-day float for all possible drawee-depository bank combinations.

By summing each row in the matrix, the amount of dollar-day float for each drawee bank is calculated. The decision criterion for selecting the best dis-

EXHIBIT 3. DOLLAR-DAY FLOAT MATRIX FOR 1-BANK SYSTEM

Drawee Banks	Depository Banks			Total dollar-day float
	A	B	C	
A	0	706,500	358,750	1,065,250
B	180,000	0	500,000	680,000
C	408,000	480,000	0	888,000

bursement system is to choose that drawee bank which maximizes the dollar-day float. In other words, A would be the best 1-bank disbursement system, since it represents the highest total of dollar-day float for the three possible drawee banks.

To determine the value of the dollar-day float, the following equation is applied:

Value of float = (r)[(Dollar-Day Float)/365 days],

where r = firm's opportunity cost of funds. The firm's opportunity cost of funds, which is stated as an annual rate, is divided by 365 days to arrive at a daily earnings rate which is used to determine the value of total dollar-day float. For example, it was found that drawee bank A provided for the greatest amount of dollar-day float. The value of A's dollar-day float is calculated as follows:

Value of float = (.10)[(1,065,250)/365] = $291.85.

Therefore, if we assign a fixed cost of $150 per bank account, the net profit for this system would be $141.85 ($291.85 − $150).

Best 2-Bank Disbursement System. Exhibit 4 presents the dollar-day float matrix for each of the three possible 2-disbursing-bank systems.

To determine the best 2-bank disbursement system, a comparison is made of each paired combination of drawee banks. Again, the combination that

EXHIBIT 4. DOLLAR-DAY FLOAT MATRIX FOR 2-BANK SYSTEM

Drawee Banks		Depository Banks			Total dollar-day float
		A	B	C	
AB	A	0	706,500	0	1,386,500
	B	180,000	0	500,000	
AC	A	0	706,500	358,750	1,473,250
	C	408,000	0	0	
BC	B	0	0	500,000	1,388,000
	C	408,000	480,000	0	

maximizes the total dollar-day float is presumed to be the best disbursing system, which in this case includes banks A and C. Listed below is the total clearing float, value of the float, cost of bank accounts, and the net profit attained from the system:

Clearing float . . . . 1,473,250 (dollar-days)
Value of float $403.63
− Cost of bank accounts (2 × $150) $300.00
Net profit (loss) $103.63

Best 3-Bank Disbursement System.   Exhibit 5 presents the dollar-day float matrix for the 3-disbursement-bank system.

EXHIBIT 5.   *DOLLAR-DAY FLOAT MATRIX FOR 3-BANK SYSTEM*

Drawee Banks		Depository Banks			Total dollar-day float
		A	B	C	
	A	0	706,500	0	
ABC	B	0	0	500,000	1,614,500
	C	408,000	0	0	

The best 3-disbursement-bank system is obviously A, B, and C, since these are the only drawee banks considered. Other drawee banks could have been considered, but for simplicity only the 3 depository banks were considered. The possibility that the optimal configuration may be one that requires the drawee banks to be in cities other than the depository cities is quite likely since this would be consistent with the objective of float maximization. The pertinent information for the 3-bank system follows:

Clearing float . . . . 1,614,500 (dollar-days)
Value of float $442.33
− Cost of bank accounts (3 × $150) $450.00
Net profit (loss) . . . . ($ 7.67)

Optimal Disbursement System

The optimal disbursement system is that combination which provides the maximum net profit attainable from all alternatives considered. Therefore, in the example presented, the one drawee bank system, which is bank A, represents the optimal system since its net profit is greater than any of the other combinations examined.

As this exercise illustrates, the more disbursing points considered, the greater the combinatorial analysis. Therefore, a good heuristic should reduce the amount of time needed to perform the iterative processes and provide for an optimum disbursing system.

DEVELOPMENT AND APPLICATION OF THE WAREHOUSE LOCATION PROBLEM TO THE CASH DISBURSEMENT PROBLEM

The Warehouse Problem

The warehouse problem has been developed in the literature as a special class of mixed integer programming [7]. It deals with the minimization of the costs of maintaining warehouses to support demand and the associated handling and transportation costs of supplying customers. Its solution involves the testing of combinations of warehouses that will economically best (optimally) geographically service the given number of customers. The mathematical model parallels that formulated in equation (1) given in the next section. The mechanics to provide the solution have been improved considerably by Khumawala's [7] branch and bound algorithm and a number of heuristics [16, 18, 20].

The Maximization of Dollar-Day Float

The warehouse location problem provides a "best fit" to the cash disbursement problem by merely converting it into a maximization configuration. The location of disbursing points as they relate to a given customer base remains the same in terms of transportation costs and the fixed costs associated with the points of disbursement. However, instead of m potential warehouses, m potential drawee banks are substituted, and n supplier's deposit banks or payment points are substituted for n customers. The problem then becomes one of maximizing clearing time or dollar-days of float that occur as a result of the payment process of checks to n suppliers drawn on m possible banks. The problem then can be formulated in the following manner:

$$\text{Maximize} \quad \sum_{i=1}^{m} \sum_{j=1}^{n} D_{ij} X_{ij}$$

$$\text{Subject to:} \quad \sum_{i=1}^{m} X_{ij} = 1, \quad \text{for each } j, j=1,2,\ldots,n \tag{1}$$

$$X_{ij} = 0, 1, \quad \text{for all } i, j$$

where C_{ij} = check clearing time in days from its deposit by the supplier at bank j to its presentation at the drawee bank i; V_j = dollars payable to the supplier banking at bank j; $D_{ij} = C_{ij} V_j$ = dollar-day float for payments deposited in bank j and clearing to its presentation at drawee bank i; and X_{ij} = the portion of V_j drawn on bank i.

The reader should recognize that the C_{ij} values in equation (1) would most likely be stochastic. Although the treatment of this variable appears to be deterministic, it would in practice be impossible to know with certainty these clearing times. The specification of the variable could result in problems because the C_{ij} may differ depending upon the drawee bank-depository combination, i, j. Specification of the variances in the model may change the choice of drawee banks and the assignment of payments to these banks. In order not to complicate the model being presented, the C_{ij} variable is, therefore, assumed to be deterministic.

The solution to the maximization of dollar-day float will dictate the number and location of banks that payables will be drawn on. The maximization of float *can* be approached by specifying the number of drawee banks desired. If k represents the number of banks desired, the following constraints (1a) and (1b) must hold:

for k banks,

$$\sum_{i=1}^{m} X_{ij} > 0, \text{ for each } j, j=1,2, \ldots ,n \tag{1a}$$

for m-k banks,

$$\sum_{i=1}^{m} X_{ij} = 0, \text{ for each } j, j=1,2, \ldots ,n. \tag{1b}$$

The optimal solution of the model could be obtained using a branch and bound algorithm [7]. However, several heuristic algorithms are available that can provide solutions within 2% of optimality, but perform with greater efficiency [16, 18, 20]. The solution is normally approached in a logical step-wise manner similar to that described in the previous section.

The Optimum Cash Disbursement Model

To further enhance the model maximizing dollar-day float, the fixed costs for additional bank accounts needed to improve disbursement float can be included in the model. Letting a_i equal the fixed costs of maintaining drawee bank i, equation set (1) is reformulated to maximize net profit from the cash disbursement system in equation set 2, which assumes that the sample payments are for one month. As a result, the daily opportunity cost of funds would be $(r/365)$, where r is the firm's opportunity cost of funds. The cash disbursement model then becomes:

Maximize

$$\frac{r \sum_{i=1}^{m} \sum_{j=1}^{n} D_{ij} X_{ij}}{365} - \sum_{i=1}^{m} a_i Y_i$$

Subject to:

$$\sum_{i=1}^{m} X_{ij} = 1,$$

for each j, j=1,2, . . . ,n   (2)

$$0 \le \sum_{j=1}^{n} X_{ij} \le n_i Y_i,$$

for each i, i=1,2, . . . ,m

$Y_i = 0, 1,$
for each i, i=1,2, . . . ,m

where r/365 = daily opportunity cost of funds assuming monthly dollars disbursed; a_i = fixed costs of having bank account at bank i; n_i = the number of suppliers that can be paid from drawee bank i, which in this case, includes all m of the banks. Therefore, $n_i = m$.

The model then provides the location of the best number of banks, k^*, from which to pay suppliers and also indicates through the X_{ij} values from which of the chosen drawee banks, i, each supplier, j, should be paid in order to maximize the dollar-day float.

COMPUTATIONAL RESULTS

In order to determine the relative effectiveness of the procedure developed in this paper, the monthly disbursements of an actual firm were used to illustrate the practicality of this application. The sample company has monthly payments to be disbursed to 66 different cities from a list of 38 possible drawee banks. The float times represent empirically determined values for the average number of days required for checks placed in each depository bank to clear through each possible drawee bank. Several heuristic rules were applied and each resulted in the same solution; therefore, the resulting solution is believed to be optimal. The data and results of the heuristic solution are summarized in Exhibit 6.

The exhibit indicates what city(s) from which the company should arrange

EXHIBIT 6.   DATA AND SOLUTION OF SAMPLE PROBLEM

Depository bank	Amount of payment	Average days of float to drawee bank chosen	Value of float (@ 6%) associated with drawee banks		
			El Paso	Helena	Miami
Boston	$ 515,000	4.51	$381.81	$	$
New York City	1,937,000	3.96		1,260.91	
Buffalo	11,000	3.88		7.02	
Philadelphia	538,000	4.14		366.13	
Cleveland	881,000	3.32	480.81		
Cincinnati	121,000	3.40	67.63		
Pittsburgh	489,000	3.50		281.34	
Richmond	19,000	4.55	14.21		
Baltimore	6,000	5.10			5.03
Charlotte	34,000	4.08	22.80		
Atlanta	62,000	3.07		31.29	
Birmingham	6,000	6.16		6.08	
Jacksonville	3,000	4.03		1.99	
Nashville	7,000	4.28		4.92	
New Orleans	6,000	5.63		5.55	
Chicago	3,091,000	3.36		1,707.25	
Detroit	295,000	4.05	196.40		
St. Louis	584,000	3.00		288.00	
Little Rock	18,000	4.10		12.13	
Louisville	98,000	3.52	56.71		
Memphis	267,000	3.85		168.98	
Minneapolis	853,000	3.38			473.94
Kansas City	127,000	3.65		76.20	
Denver	18,000	4.16			12.31
Oklahoma City	6,000	3.49			3.44
Omaha	23,000	4.20			15.88
Dallas	229,000	3.64		137.02	
El Paso	2,000	4.97		1.63	
Houston	83,000	3.38		46.12	
San Antonio	1,000	4.21			0.69
San Francisco	149,000	4.18			102.38
Los Angeles	367,000	3.97	239.51		
Portland	22,000	4.29	15.51		
Salt Lake City	9,000	4.98			7.37
Seattle	2,000	4.38	1.44		
Worcester	659,000	5.78		626.14	
Albany	320,000	4.75	249.86		
Rochester	37,000	4.67	28.40		
Allentown	452,000	4.82	358.13		
Akron	610,000	4.31		432.18	
Dayton	37,000	4.31		26.21	
Wheeling	181,000	3.15		93.72	
Columbus	154,000	4.52	114.42		
Raleigh	68,000	4.52		50.52	
Norfolk	12,000	6.03		11.89	

EXHIBIT 6 (*continued*)

Depository bank	Amount of payment	Average days of float to drawee bank chosen	Value of float (@ 6%) associated with drawee banks		
			El Paso	Helena	Miami
Winston-Salem	179,000	3.98	117.11		
Savannah	124,000	4.42		90.10	
Tampa	173,000	5.05		143.61	
Knoxville	60,000	4.75		46.85	
Baton Rouge	272,000	3.47		155.15	
Miami	45,000	3.18	23.52		
Springfield IL	1,174,000	5.13		990.02	
Lansing	85,000	4.94	69.02		
Springfield MO	140,000	3.97		91.36	
Duluth	161,000	4.16			110.10
Helena	1,000	4.47			0.73
Pueblo	35,000	4.37			25.14
Tulsa	24,000	2.84		11.20	
Lincoln	43,000	4.24	29.97		
Lubbock	45,000	3.92			29.00
Beaumont	2,000	4.04		1.33	
Sacramento	154,000	4.40			111.39
San Diego	146,000	4.37		104.88	
Eugene	5,000	4.36	3.58		
Ogden	11,000	4.76		8.61	
Spokane	5,000	4.48			3.68

Total Dollar-Days	= 64,837,440
Value of Float	= $10,658
− Cost of Bank Accounts	= $ 450
Net Profit	= $10,208
CPU Time	≈ 7 seconds

to make its disbursements for each of the depository banks. As is shown in Exhibit 6, the best disbursement system includes 3 banks: El Paso, Helena, and Miami. The total clearing float associated with this sample problem is 64,837,440 dollar-days. By applying the firms' actual opportunity cost of funds of 6% to the total clearing float and dividing by 365 days, the value of the float, which in this case is $10,658 [i.e., (.06)(64,837,440/365 days)], was determined. The net profit of $10,208 was calculated by subtracting from the value of the float the monthly fixed cost of $150 for each of the 3 drawee banks opened [i.e., $10,658 − $150 × 3 banks)].

An important consideration here is that the heuristic procedure usually provides for an optimal solution, which in most cases eliminates the need for more sophisticated techniques such as branch and bound algorithms that normally require more computer CPU time and much more computer core storage.

SUMMARY AND CONCLUSIONS

This presentation has developed a quantitative means by which the accounts payable of a firm can be analyzed to determine the system of disbursement banks that will optimize a firm's check clearing float (ignoring the possibility of manipulating mail times which could be an important factor in maximizing float) and provide benefits through efficient cash management. The maximization of this float increases the amount of time that a firm can invest its available funds and effectively increase its cash reserves or reduce borrowing. The literature does not specifically offer a quantitative solution procedure for the cash disbursement problem. Fortunately, the traditional warehouse location problem can be adapted and applied to select an optimal cash disbursement configuration. The optimum solution can be obtained through the use of a branch and bound algorithm or can be approximated by using one of a number of available heuristics. These solutions can be applied to actual situations to determine if a more profitable disbursement system (drawee bank relationships) is available for minimizing cash requirements and thereby increasing the amount of funds available for investment and/or retirement of debt.

When new disbursement systems are indicated, practical operational considerations exist. In the development of the optimum cash disbursement model, the fixed cost of maintaining a bank account was included for each disbursing bank in the new system. These fixed costs may vary from bank to bank dependent upon the bank's pricing objectives and perhaps its viewpoint of the individual firm's credit standing in the marketplace. However, the following basic consideration is essential to the optimization: the benefits derived by the addition of a new banking relationship for maximizing disbursement float must be offset by the costs associated with the new relationship.

There is a great deal of conjecture that earnings obtained as a result of an optimum cash disbursement system will not be long-lived. Public and private efforts are being made to reduce float as evidenced by the Federal Reserve's attempts to more efficiently perform the check clearing process. They have developed the regional check processing center (RCPC) concept as an effort to reduce float by assisting the check clearing process in high volume areas. Additional efforts to reduce check clearing float have been provided by commercial banks in the form of direct-send programs. These programs depend upon the ability to capture high dollar volume items and physically present them at the drawee bank. They provide a cash management tool that can be used to speed up the collection of checks and pass the benefits on to the bank customer (the supplier) and reduce the disbursement float advantage of the payor (user of the product or service).

Taking advantage of check clearing float may not be a practice that will provide long-term benefits. However, the optimum cash disbursement model will increase earnings for the medium-term. When applied with other disbursing strategies such as paying invoices as late as possible without damaging supplier relationships and credit ratings, the firm's earnings can be further increased. These disbursing strategies should enhance the firm's overall return and allow the firm to better achieve the long-run goal of owner-wealth maximization.

REFERENCES

1. Robert F. Calman, *Linear Programming and Cash Management/Cash ALPHA,* Cambridge, The M.I.T. Press, 1968.
2. *The Federal Reserve System: Purposes and Functions,* Washington, D.C., Board of Governors, September 1974, pp. 20–21.
3. David I. Fisher, *Cash Management,* Ottawa, The Conference Board, Inc., 1973.
4. Lawrence J. Gitman, *Principles of Managerial Finance,* New York, Harper and Row, Inc., 1976.
5. Frederick E. Horn, "Managing Cash," *The Journal of Accountancy* (April 1964), pp. 56–62.
6. "How Business Lives Beyond Its Means," *Business Week* (November 15, 1969), pp. 72, 74, 76.
7. Basheer M. Khumawala, "An Efficient Branch and Bound Algorithm for the Warehouse Location Problem," *Management Science* 18 (August 1972), pp. 718–731.
8. Basheer M. Khumawala, "An Efficient Heuristic Procedure for the Uncapacitated Warehouse Location Problem," *Naval Research Logistics Quarterly* 20 (March 1973), pp. 109–121.
9. Robert L. Kramer, "Analysis of Lock Box Locations," *Bankers Monthly Magazine* (May 15, 1966), pp. 50–53.
10. A. Kuehn and M. Hamburger, "A Heuristic Program for Locating Warehouses," *Management Science* 9 (July 1963), pp. 643–666.
11. Ferdinand K. Levy, "An Application of Heuristic Problem Solving to Accounts Receivable Management," *Management Science* 12 (February 1966), pp. 236–244.
12. James F. Lordan, "Cash Management: The Corporate-Bank Relationship," *The Magazine of Bank Administration* (January 1975), pp. 14–19.
13. "Making Millions by Stretching the Float," *Business Week* (November 23, 1974), pp. 88 and 90.
14. Gerald A. Pogue, Russel B. Faucett, and Ralph N. Bussard, "Cash Management: A Systems Approach," *Industrial Management Review* (Winter 1970), pp. 55–73.
15. Ward L. Reed, Jr., "Cash—The Hidden Asset," *Financial Executive* (November 1970), pp. 54–60.
16. Robert A. Russell, "Heuristic Programming Algorithms for Warehouse Location," in *Scientific and Behavioral Foundations for Decision Sciences,* edited by Laurence J. Moore and Sang M. Lee (1974), pp. 212–213.
17. Frederick W. Searby, "Use Your Hidden Cash Resources," *Harvard Business Review* 46 (March–April 1968), pp. 74–75.

18. R. E. Shannon and J. P. Ignizio, "A Heuristic Programming Algorithm for Warehouse Location," *AIIE Transactions*, Vol. 2, No. 4 (December 1970), pp. 334–339.
19. William J. Tallent, "Cash Management: A Case Study," *Management Accounting* (July 1974), pp. 20–24.
20. M. B. Teitz and P. Bart, "Heuristic Methods for Estimating the Generalized Vertex Median of a Weighted Graph," *Operations Research*, Vol. 16 (1968), pp. 955–961.
21. James C. Van Horne, *Financial Management and Policy*, third edition, Englewood Cliffs, Prentice-Hall, Inc., 1974.
22. Harry L. Winn, Jr., "A Discussion of Issues Related to Disbursing," *Cash Management Forum of the First National Bank of Atlanta* I (Volume 1, Number 2), pp. 2–3, 7.

QUESTIONS

1. Describe how reducing float can be to the firm's advantage if this float has to do with receiving funds as receivables are paid.
2. Explain how increasing cash disbursement float can free funds for the firm.
3. Distinguish among mail float, processing float, and transit float.
4. Explain what will happen if the U.S. system goes to electronic check clearing. How could you tell quickly whether your firm would benefit or be hurt if the Federal Reserve System introduced electronic check clearing system-wide?

PROBLEMS

1. Suppose a large firm normally has $10 million in transit (the money has been mailed by payors but the firm has not yet deposited the funds in its bank). On the average, it takes five days from the time the payors send the checks until the funds are deposited. If this time could be reduced to four days and if short-term funds could be invested at 8 percent, how much per year would this be worth to a firm? The costs associated with reducing transit time from five to four days have been estimated at $40,000 per year.
2. Your company has $500,000 on the average per day in the process of being paid (the checks have been mailed but the funds have not been deducted from your firm's bank account). At the present time, it normally takes four days from the time a check is mailed until it is debited from your account at the bank. How much would it be worth per year if this could be increased to five days (assuming the cost of short-term money is 7 percent)?

6

Bernell K. Stone

The Payments-Pattern Approach to the Forecasting and Control of Accounts Receivable

Professor Stone presents a comprehensive article on the monitoring of accounts receivable. He shows that the methods most commonly used in industry give ambiguous signals, and he presents a thorough analysis of preferred methods.

INTRODUCTION AND OVERVIEW

Under the simplifying assumption that payment behavior is stable from month to month, this paper develops and illustrates forecast and control procedures based on the time distribution of cash flows that arise from credit sales at a point in time. Next, a variety of forecast and control procedures now used in practice are reviewed and evaluated and it is argued that most of the popular procedures are technically deficient. Alternative procedures are then considered for measuring the payment distribution. Here the assumption of stable month-to-month payment behavior is relaxed and seasonals and other factors that can impact payment behavior, such as the level of interest rates and the quality of accounts, are considered. Finally, it is shown how an ability to explain payment behavior makes possible meaningful evaluation of collection performance and how it can assist in making credit policy decisions.

CHARACTERIZING PAYMENT BEHAVIOR: PAYMENT AND BALANCE PATTERNS

A *payment pattern* refers to the time distribution of cash flows that arise from credit sales at a point in time. A *monthly payment pattern* can be characterized by the proportion of credit sales in a given month that become cash flows in that month and a series of subsequent months. Such a pattern can be summarized by a histogram as illustrated in Exhibit 1, where the horizontal axis is time *after* the month in which the sales were made with time measured

Source. Reprinted by permission from *Financial Management*, Autumn 1976, pp. 65–82. The author is Mills B. Lane, professor of banking and finance, George Institute of Technology.

in months. Month zero denotes the month of sale. In this histogram, 10% of the cash flows are received in the month of sale, 40% in the first month after the sale, 30% in the second month, and 10% in the third month.

Once the payment pattern is known, a value of credit sales in a given month can be converted into a schedule of the associated monthly cash flows and the end-of-month receivable balances associated with those credit sales.

Example

January credit sales on a certain product line with credit terms of net 30 were $2,000,000 and were expected to conform to the payment pattern given in Exhibit 1. By applying the payment proportions in the histogram, the following schedules of monthly cash flows and end-of-month receivables associated with January sales are obtained.

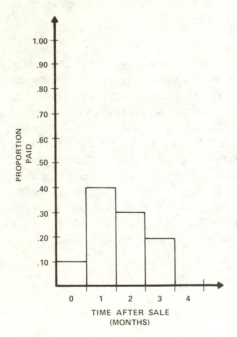

Exhibit 1. A histogram illustrating a monthly payment pattern.

	January	February	March	April
Cash flow	200	800	600	400
Receivables	1800	1000	400	0

This example shows that knowing the schedule of cash flows that arise from a given month's credit sales is equivalent to knowing the schedule of receivables that arise from the same month's credit sales. In effect, there is a receivable balance pattern associated with any payment pattern. The monthly *receivable balance pattern* can be characterized by the fraction of credit sales in a month that remain outstanding at the end of each subsequent month. Exhibit 2 shows the receivable balance pattern associated with the payment pattern of Exhibit 1.

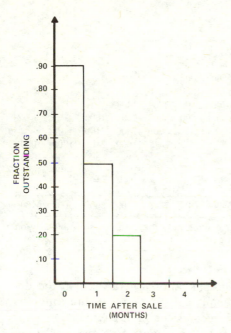

Exhibit 2.   The receivable balance pattern corresponding to the payment pattern of exhibit 1.

These cash flows and receivables are not the monthly totals. Rather, they are only the values associated with credit sales in January. To obtain the total monthly cash flow and end-of-month receivables for March also requires knowledge of the level of credit sales in February and March as well.

Exhibits 3 and 4 present projection matrices that illustrate how knowledge of the payment pattern enables one to convert a schedule of monthly credit sales into the corresponding schedules of total monthly cash flows and total end-of-month receivable balances. The schedule of credit sales is given in the far left-hand column of each exhibit. The procedure for generating the matrix and the monthly totals is straightforward. First, each month's credit sales are converted into a schedule of associated cash flows and receivables. These values are given in the rows of the matrix. Second, monthly totals are obtained by summing down the columns. The values used in Exhibits 3 and 4 are based on the simple payment pattern of Exhibit 1.

EXHIBIT 3.   THE CASH FLOW MATRIX: AN ILLUSTRATION OF THE
CONVERSION OF A CREDIT-SALE FORECAST INTO A
CONDITIONAL FORECAST OF MONTHLY CASH FLOWS

Month	Credit sales	Jan.	Feb.	March	April	May	June	July	Aug.	Sept.	Oct.	Nov.	Dec.
				Monthly cash flows (All figures in thousands)									
Oct.	4000*	800											
Nov.	3000*	900	600										
Dec.	2000*	800	600	400									
Jan.	2000	200	800	600	400								
Feb.	3000		300	1200	900	600							
Mar.	4000			400	1600	1200	800						
Apr.	5000				500	2000	1500	1000					
May	6000					600	2400	1800	1200				
June	7000						700	2800	2100	1400			
July	8000							800	3200	2400	1600		
Aug.	7000								700	2800	2100	1400	
Sept.	6000									600	2400	1800	1000
Oct.	5000										500	2000	1500
Nov.	4000											400	1600
Dec.	3000												300
Total		2700	2300	2600	3400	4400	5400	6400	7200	7200	6600	5600	4400

*Figures for October, November, and December contain only the cash flows for January on projected as if there were perfect conformity to the pro forma pattern.

For expositional purposes, several simplifications were used in the development of Exhibits 3 and 4. First, receipt of all payments within 3 months constitutes a fairly short payment period; second, the same payment behavior has been assumed to occur in every month with no month-to-month variation; and finally, there has been no explicit consideration of bad debts. Extending the method to allow for longer payment periods is easily accomplished by using more nonzero entries in the matrix.

In subsequent sections, payment behavior is allowed to change from month-to-month due to seasonality in payment patterns and dependence of payment behavior on factors such as the state of the economy, the level of interest rates, and the quality of accounts. Further consideration of month-to-month variation in payment behavior is deferred until that point.

A simple way to treat bad debts is to view the credit sales projection as the net value after allowance for bad debts. A more complex but more complete approach is to include a pro forma bad debt recognition pattern. Since it is straightforward to extend the equations given here to reflect bad debts, for the sake of expositional simplicity, the credit sales variable will continue to be viewed as net credit sales. Bad debts will be treated explicitly when measurement issues are considered.

EXHIBIT 4. THE RECEIVABLE MATRIX: AN ILLUSTRATION OF THE
CONVERSION OF A CREDIT-SALE FORECAST INTO A
CONDITIONAL FORECAST OF END-OF-MONTH RECEIVABLES

Month	Credit sales	Jan.	Feb.	March	April	May	June	July	Aug.	Sept.	Oct.	Nov.	Dec.
		End-of-month accounts receivable balances (All figures in thousands)											
Oct.	4000*												
Nov.	3000*	600											
Dec.	2000*	1000	400										
Jan.	2000	1800	1000	400									
Feb.	3000		2700	1500	600								
Mar.	4000			3600	2000	800							
Apr.	5000				4500	2500	1000						
May	6000					5400	3000	1200					
June	7000						6300	3500	1400				
July	8000							7200	4000	1600			
Aug.	7000								6300	3500	1400		
Sept.	6000									5400	3000	1200	
Oct.	5000										4500	2500	1000
Nov.	4000											3600	2000
Dec.	3000												2700
		3400	4100	5500	7100	8700	10300	11900	11700	10500	8900	7300	5700

*Figures for October, November, and December contain only the values for January on projected
as if there were perfect conformity to the pro forma pattern.

Formulas for Monthly Totals

The term *payment horizon* refers to the number of months required for a given
month's credit sales to be completely collected. Thus, receivables associated
with a given month's credit sales are zero at the end of the payment horizon.
The payment horizon is denoted by H, which, for the payment pattern of
Exhibit 1, is 3.

P_i denotes the proportion of credit sales paid i months after the month of
sale. For the payment pattern of Exhibit 1, $P_0 = .10$, $P_1 = .40$, $P_2 = .30$, and
$P_3 = .20$. The P_i's are referred to as *payment proportions;* and the set of such
proportions, $(P_0, \ldots, P_H)$, are a complete numerical summary of the payment
pattern.

If TCF_t denotes total cash flow forecast for month t and if CS_{t-i} denotes the
credit sales received in month t-i, then total cash flow is the sum of the cash
flows from credit sales in month t, month t-1, and so on back to month H, i.e.,

$$TCF_t = P_0 CS_t + P_1 CS_{t-1} + \ldots + P_H CS_{t-H}$$

$$= \sum_{i=0}^{H} P_i CS_{t-i}. \tag{1}$$

The terms in this summation are clearly the nonzero terms in the t-th column of the cash flow matrix. The formula is a symbolic statement of the procedure of adding down the columns to obtain the forecast of the total monthly cash flow.

Letting F_i denote the fraction of the credit sales outstanding i months after the month of sale, the receivable pattern of Exhibit 2 is $F_0 = .90$, $F_1 = .50$, and $F_2 = .20$. (Of course, since the payment horizon is 3 months, $F_3 = 0$.) The F_i's are defined as *balance fractions;* and the set of such fractions, $(F_0, \ldots, F_{H-1})$, is a numerical summary of the receivable balance pattern.

The total values of receivables at the end of month t is the sum of the receivables arising from credit sales in month t, in month t-H, and so on back to those from credit sales H-1 months earlier. If TAR_t denotes total accounts receivable at the end of month t, then

$$TAR_t = F_0CS_t + F_1CS_{t-1} + \ldots + F_{H-1}CS_{t-H+1} \qquad (2)$$

$$= \sum_{i=0}^{H-1} F_iCS_{t-i}.$$

The terms in this summation are clearly the nonzero terms in the t-th column of the receivable matrix. The formula is a symbolic statement of the procedure of adding down the columns of the receivable matrix to obtain the total receivable balance.

Payment Patterns and Control

Control concerns the detection of deviations from expected or intended behavior and the initiation of corrective action where appropriate. For accounts receivable, two levels of control exist. Account-level control concerns the conformity of individual accounts to credit terms. Management control concerns the aggregate behavior of receivables, ideally at the product-line, credit-term level, and thus focuses on the net effect of the company's credit granting and collection effort.

Since payment proportions and balance fractions are measures of payment behavior that are independent of the sales pattern, they are the logical focus of control. Conceptually, using payment patterns for control consists of comparing a pro forma payment distribution with the one that actually occurred and asking if the differences are significant in the sense of exceeding normal month-to-month fluctuations in the payment pattern. For example, assume that a company's historical payment proportions and balance fractions were those summarized in Exhibits 1 and 2. In early March, assume that the report on actual payments for January and February credit sales showed a current balance fraction for January sales of $F_1 = .60$ versus the pro forma value of .50

and a realized value for February sales of $F_0 = .94$ versus the pro forma value of .90. Because the deviations are adverse and larger than usual and because there are two consecutive months of adverse behavior, this report would indicate possible problems and the need for further action.

THE STATE OF CURRENT PRACTICE

The payment-pattern approach to receivable forecasting and control seems simple and straightforward. The reader not familiar with corporate practice might even be asking: "If that is all there is to receivable forecasting and control, why is it perceived to be so hard and why the great concern?"

The fact is that few corporations use payment-pattern measures for forecasting and controlling receivables. The alternatives used in practice and advocated in much of the finance-accounting literature contain serious defects. This section of this article surveys the current state of corporate practice, relates alternative forecasting and control procedures to payment patterns, and indicates why the popular forecast and control procedures typically fail.

Conventional Measures of Receivable Status

The two standard measures used to characterize the status of receivables are average days outstanding and the aging schedule. These measures are presented in most basic finance texts, many accounting texts, and almost any work on financial analysis that deals with receivables, e.g. [1, 3]. They have been the common basis for recommendations on receivable management and control [2, 11]. Of the works known to this author, the only ones using measures of receivable status based on payment-pattern concepts are Lewellen and Edmister [8] and Lewellen and Johnson [9], both of which introduce balance fractions and criticize average days outstanding and the aging schedule.

An Overview of Corporate Practice

There is a dearth of published information on current corporate practice with respect to receivable forecasting and control. This author has surveyed financial officers of nearly 150 companies participating in executive development seminars. The annual sales of these companies ranged from $10 million to $8 billion with 80% having annual sales in the range of $25 million to $250 million. The average sales were just over $100 million. While neither the sample selection nor survey procedure allows meaningful statistical inference to the general population of companies, the results are at least roughly indicative of corporate practice.

Exhibit 5 summarizes the reported use of alternative projection approaches. Over 80% of these companies reported using some systematic procedures to project receivables. Of those using formal methods, the great majority (86%) used either a pro forma projection of average days outstanding or some other ratio of receivables to a measure of sales. Another 10% based projections on the assumption that a certain percentage of receivables are paid in each period. Only 5% (six companies) projected receivables as a linear function of past sales, the projection mode implied by the payment-pattern approach.

In contrast to the diversity of forecasting behavior, Exhibit 5 shows considerably more uniformity in control practice. The great majority of the firms using formal control procedures report that aging schedules are their primary control measure. Almost all these companies also used one or more secondary control measures such as average days outstanding, percent of overdue accounts, percent of doubtful accounts, and bad debt loss rates, but generally regarded them as subordinate information that complements the aging schedule. Of the remaining companies using formal control procedures, approximately 10%, which tended to be smaller companies, used average days outstanding. Only two companies, one of which regarded bad debt loss rates as an equally important control measure, used balance fractions, the measure implied by payment patterns.

Alternative forecast and control procedures used by companies are now elaborated upon and are related to payment patterns. Further comment is also made upon corporate practice.

The Aging Schedule

The aging schedule is the proportion of accounts receivable that are in different age classes. While some companies use weeks, the usual practice seems to be months, which will be used here.

The aging schedule is closely related to the payment pattern. In fact, the projected aging schedule for each month can be obtained directly from the column data of projection matrices such as Exhibit 4. For each column, one simply divides each nonzero value of receivables by the total at the bottom to obtain the proportion in each age class, where the most recent receivables are the bottom of the nonzero column entries.

To illustrate, let A_0, A_1, and A_2 denote the proportion of receivables in each age class. These quantities are labeled *aging fractions*. For the receivables in Exhibit 4, the aging fractions for March and October are:

	A_2	A_1	A_0
March	4/55 = .07	15/55 = .27	36/55 = .66
October	14/89 = .16	30/89 = .34	45/89 = .50

Primary forecast method	% Responses	% Formal model	Primary control measure	% Responses	% Formal model
1. ADO-based projection (see note 2)	26	32	1. Aging schedule (see note 2)	76.0	80.0
2. Ratio projection other than ADO (see note 3)	44	54	2. ADO-based (see note 3)	9.0	9.5
3. Percentage balance (see note 4)	8	10	3. Percentage overdue	4.5	4.8
4. Linear function of past sales (see notes 3 and 5)	4	5	4. Bad debt loss rate	2.5	2.6
5. Pro forma aging schedule (see note 6)	0	0	5. Balance fraction (see note 4)	1.5	1.6
6. No formal systematic procedure (judgement)	15	n.a.	6. Other (see note 1)	1.5	1.6
7. No knowledge	2	n.a.	7. No formal system (see note 5)	6.0	n.a.
8. Incomplete response	2	n.a.	8. Incomplete response	1.0	n.a.
	101	101		102.0	100.1

Notes on Forecasting

1. A number of respondents listed "other" as their primary method. However, their explanation of the method and/or post questionnaire follow-up enabled almost all of these responses to be placed in one of the listed categories.

2. A few respondents listed "average age" as their method. Questtionnaire follow-up indicated that most were using this term synonomously with average days outstanding. A few also listed "pro forma turnover rate" as their primary method. Questionnaire follow-up showed most of these were also variants of the conventional ADO forecast as discussed in the paper; however, a few were closer to the percentage balance method and were grouped under this procedure.

3. Six respondents (4%) reported a "moving ratio" using a weighted average of recent sales. This does involve a linear function of past sales but not a simple linear function. If these responses were reclassified, methods 3 and 5 would change from 44% and 4% to 40% and 8% respectively. However, none of those using a moving ratio assessed weights within a payment-pattern framework.

4. Early versions of the questionnaire did not have "percentage balance" listed as a method; it was added as an explicit choice after being listed under "other" with some frequency. While this omission could bias the early responses against this approach, the questionnaires after its inclusion had a lower selection rate than before.

5. Three of these responses (2%) indicated that the weights were determined via a least-squares regression of accounts receivable on a lagged function of sales.

6. "Pro Forma Aging Schedule" was a possible method. Those few companies indicating this method were reclassified on the basis of questionnaire follow-up, generally as linear function of past sales.

Notes on Control

1. "Other" was listed frequently. Generally, the explanation and/or post questionnaire follow-up enabled most of these to be placed in one of the listed categories. Exceptions are percent over credit limit (.5%), change in quality class composition (.5%), and percent not taking discounts (.5%). Each of these respondents also listed the aging schedule as their primary method.

2. "Aging Schedule" also includes responses, the essence of which was "distribution of overdue accounts" since this is readily derived from the aging schedule by excluding current accounts.

3. ADO includes "turnover measures" and "average age" methods since these are all closely related concepts.

4. Both firms using balance fractions do so implicitly via an adjusted forecast in a lagged regression model rather than directly, i e , they would use realized sales in their receivable forecast equation and then compare differences in theoretical and actual receivables. One of these firms thought that bad debt loss rate was an equally important control measure.

5. Most firms without a formal system and many using ADO measures were either smaller companies or companies for whom receivables were not a significant problem (e.g., because of ability to enforce credit terms by stopping delivery or credit devices such as liberal discounts).

6. Questionnaire follow-up revealed that most firms that were serious about control used seasonalized measures, regardless of their particular control measure. Most larger companies applied their control measures to subunits such as subsidiaries or product lines; most wanted more subunit detail than they were getting.

Comments on Survey Size and Procedures

1. Forecast data is based on a 148 company sample. Control data is based on a 102 company subsample.

2. To assess forecast techniques, respondents were first asked to indicate all methods used to forecast receivables for budgeting, planning, and cash management as opposed to control and then to indicate the primary (most important) method.

3. To assess control techniques, respondents were first asked to indicate all methods used for management control of receivables and then to indicate the primary (most important) method. Because of confusion on early questionnaires (not included in sample), care was taken to differentiate management control (defined as the identification of payment problems and/or detection of changes in overall payment behavior) from account-level control.

4. Fractional weights were assigned when: 1) more than one primary method was indicated; 2) multiple respondents from the same company indicated different primary methods and questionnaire follow-up could not reconcile differences; 3) more than one method was used and no primary method was indicated on either the questionnaire or post questionnaire follow-up.

5. Totals differ from 100% because of rounding.

Despite the fact that the payment proportions used to develop Exhibit 4 were the same in every month, these aging schedules are quite different because the latter depends on both payment behavior and the pattern of sales. When there is no change in payment behavior, rising sales produce a more current aging schedule and falling sales a less current one. As is shown in Appendix A, sufficient conditions for the aging fractions to be independent of sales are extremely restrictive; namely *uniform sales* defined as sales growing at a constant month-to-month rate, a special case being constant month-to-month sales. Uniform sales preclude any kind of annual sales cycle as well as random month-to-month variation.

Throughout this paper, the term *uniform* credit sales means credit sales that grow at a constant month-to-month rate. Uniform credit sales are a slightly more general restriction for the acceptability of aging and average days outstanding than the restriction of constant month-to-month sales stated by Lewellen and Edmister [8], which is a special case of constant growth in which the growth rate is zero.

The dependency of the aging schedule on sales is recognized by most practitioners. For this reason, many of the companies using the aging schedule for control reported that they used a seasonal schedule for comparison purposes. For instance, October's aging schedule would be compared with the one for last October or even an average over several past Octobers. Several companies also reported attempts to correct judgmentally for variations in sales. Most companies described themselves as "extremely dissatisfied" or "dissatisfied" with the aging schedule as a control measure with only a few characterizing themselves as "satisfied" and none as "very satisfied" or "extremely satisfied." Interestingly, larger companies characterized themselves as extremely dissatisfied much more frequently than small companies. Post-questionnaire discussion indicated a consensus view that sales variation was much larger than shifts in payment behavior, so that aging schedules tended to reflect sales changes more than the payment shifts that receivable control is intended to detect.

Most of the larger multiproduct companies reported in questionnaire follow-up that they applied their control measures at subunits such as subsidiaries or product lines. Many expressed frustration at trying to implement exception reports using aging schedules. One problem with implementation was defining a summary measure. Some tried using a sum of either current or overdue aging fractions, e.g., a company might sum the aging fractions in the first two or three age classes. In fact, a few questionnaire responses even listed such summary measures as either the primary control measure or one that is as important as the aging schedule itself.

In questionnaire follow-up, some companies described a very interesting attempt to correct for sales variation. The essence of the procedure was to assume a "pro forma aging schedule" and use realized sales to impute pro forma receivables that would be compared with actual receivables to see if there were deviations from the pro forma behavior. Such companies were very close to discovering balance fractions. In terms of the projection matrices, their problem lay in an attempt to apply aging fractions (which arise from column data) to sales rather than applying the correct procedure of using balance fractions (which apply to row data). The basic problem faced by these companies was that of specifying a pro forma aging schedule when they knew their actual schedules were seasonal.

When use of payment proportions and balance fractions was presented to such companies as sales-independent summaries of payment behavior, the general reaction was favorable in recognizing sales independence as a key criterion for control. The most common questions concerned how to measure payment proportions and/or balance fractions and the extent to which they were stable.

Payment Patterns versus the Aging Schedule

It is claimed in this paper that payment proportions and balance fractions are superior to aging fractions for control. Their obvious advantage over aging fractions is their independence of the level of credit sales. There is no substantive difference in terms of simplicity. The aging schedule is no easier to compute than balance fractions or payment proportions once the receivable data base is properly organized along the lines of the projections matrices illustrated in Exhibits 3 and 4. For stable payment behavior, the number of ratios involved in the aging schedule is the same as the number of balance fractions. In fact, when one uses seasonal aging schedules to reflect seasonal sales, considerably more data is required to use aging fractions. Finally, in the case of time-dependent payment behavior, it is shown subsequently that control is logically organized by the concept of an underlying *basic payment pattern* (defined in the measurement section) that corrects for the effect of seasonals in payment behavior and other factors such as changing interest rates. In contrast, there is no obvious measure of a "basic aging fraction" that corrects for shifts in payment behavior.

Control Based on Average Days Outstanding

There are several closely related one-parameter summary measures of receivable status—average age, average days outstanding, and turnover. Average age is usually defined as the receivable-weighted average of the median number of days in each age class. As a one-parameter summary of the aging schedule, it contains all the defects of the aging schedule plus loss of information due to averaging. In addition, the receivable weighting in computing the average tends to magnify sensitivity to sales.

Average days outstanding (hereafter ADO) is usually measured as the ratio of receivables to a measure of daily sales. With the conventional practice of using annual sales per day as the measure of daily sales, the formula for average days outstanding at the end of month t is

$$ADO_t = 365[TAR_t/(\text{annual credit sales})]. \qquad (3)$$

The usual turnover measure is the ratio of annual sales to receivables, and thus is the reciprocal of the term in brackets. For this reason, average days outstanding and turnover are viewed as essentially equivalent measures.

Computing average sales over a shorter time period than a year can eliminate some of the sales cycle from the ADO measure, but it still leaves the ADO measure quite sensitive to the pattern of sales. To illustrate, the ADO measures for annual, quarterly, and monthly measures of daily sales and average age for the March and October receivables of Exhibit 4 are:

	March	October
ADO (annual)	34	54
ADO (quarterly)	55	45
ADO (monthly)	41	53
Average Age	28	35

Even though the payment proportions used to develop Exhibit 4 were the same in every month, the March and October values of the alternative ADO measures and the average age are quite different. These differences arise solely because of month-to-month sales variation. Except for the unusual special case of uniform sales, both average age and average days outstanding vary with sales even when there is no change in payment behavior.

Almost all companies using ADO-based control measures recognize its dependence on sales and the fact that sales variations can and do mask changes in underlying payment behavior. Most compaies using such measures used a seasonal value as their comparison standard but generally felt ADO-based measures were poor control tools. The usual reason for using ADO-based measures seemed to be simplicity and a perceived lack of any meaningful alternative.

Projection Based on Average Days Outstanding

The essence of forecast procedures based on average days outstanding is to solve the usual defining equation for average days outstanding for total receivables and then to use a pro forma value for average days outstanding to project receivables. For instance, solving equation (3) for total receivables gives

$$TAR_t = ADO_t(\text{annual credit sales})/365. \tag{4}$$

Given a forecast of annual credit sales and a pro forma value of average days outstanding, an associated value is obtained for accounts receivable.

As this formula makes clear, when the relation between receivables and average days outstanding is expressed in terms of average daily credit sales, the value of average days outstanding must generally be a function of time, especially if sales are cyclical. For this reason, most companies use a time dependent value of average days outstanding, usually one based on past history. For instance, the measure of average days outstanding in month t could be based on the average value in the same month in prior years. Then the forecast equation is

$$TAR_t = (\text{average past ADO for month}) \ (\text{annual credit sales})/365.$$

An obvious problem here is that annual credit sales may be unrepresentative of the recent rate of average daily credit sales, especially when sales are highly cyclical. Thus, another way that companies try to improve ADO-based forecast procedures is to use a sales measure for a time period shorter than a year. Quarterly sales seem to be a common substitute, especially for companies doing quarterly financial statement projection. With quarterly sales, the projection equation can be stated as

$$TAR_t = (ADO_t)[(\text{credit sales in previous three months})/Q],$$

where Q is the number of days in the previous 3 months.

Finally, some companies used both a time varying ratio and shorter periods for measuring average receivables. For instance, a synthesis of the two previous equations gives

$$TAR_t = (\text{average past ADO for month})(\text{credit sales in the previous 3 months})/Q.$$

Both the use of more recent measures of average daily sales and of a time dependent ratio are attempts to improve the basic forecast. However, except for such restrictive special cases as uniform sales, these refinements fail to reflect properly the effect of varying sales levels even when payment behavior is stable. Even the use of time varying values for average days outstanding requires joint stability in payment behavior and sales patterns, so that deviations from past sales patterns cannot generally be treated properly.

The underlying problem with ADO-based projections is an attempt to use a single number, and generally a single representative value of sales, to summarize the relationship between receivables and credit sales at a point in time.

Trying to make one number summarize the entire payment pattern is an oversimplification that generally omits important information. Knowledge of payment patterns shows that a complete summary of monthly payment behavior generally requires H numbers, where H is the payment horizon.

The average-days-outstanding method must be viewed as a simple but incomplete forecast framework. Its degree of adequacy depends either on essentially uniform sales or, in the case of cyclical sales, on the joint stability of year-to-year sales and payment patterns.

Follow-up discussions with companies using ADO-based projection indicate that the main reasons for using it are simplicity and the fact that average days outstanding is a universally accepted way of summarizing receivable collections. Almost all companies using ADO-based projection report general dissatisfaction with its accuracy and their ability to reflect what they know about receivable behavior within the ADO framework. The reasons for elaborations on the basic ADO framework such as time varying values are attempts to use more information and cure deficiencies in the basic method.

Ratio-Based Projection

Ratio-based projection refers to any forecast procedure that assumes that receivables at a point in time are proportional to some measure of sales. There appear to be many variations to the ratio projections with varying degrees of sophistication. In fact, the various ADO forecasts can be viewed as a particular type of ratio projection. Thus, ratio-based projection other than ADO-based approaches is now considered.

In its simplest form, ratio projection makes receivables at the end of time period t proportional to sales during that time period. If r denotes the proportionality factor, this relation can be expressed as

$$TAR_t = rCS_t. \tag{5}$$

A simple variant of this equation involves replacing current sales by sales in the previous month (or quarter).

The use of a single constant is incapable of treating the fact that the ratio of sales to accounts receivable typically changes over time. This form of the expression is so simple that it is rarely used. An extension of the simple constant is the use of a "moving ratio" to treat seasonality in the relation of receivables to sales. With monthly projection, this approach assumes that the ratio of receivables to sales in a given month will be the same as the past ratio in that same month. A projection equation for the moving ratio is

$$TAR_t = \left(\frac{TAR_{t-12}}{CS_{t-12}}\right) CS_t. \tag{6}$$

In addition to moving ratio, terms used to describe the projection method included seasonal ratio, sales scaling, and sales shifting. (Another closely related term is "growth scaling". When sales grow at a constant rate g so that $CS_t = CS_{t-12}(1 + g)$, then the moving ratio means receivables show the same growth pattern, i.e., $TAR_t = TAR_{t-12}(1 + g)$.) The central idea of this approach is that shifts in accounts receivable are proportional to shifts in sales. It implicitly assumes that historical relations between sales and receivables persist in the future and that a single value of sales is representative of the entire series of recent sales.

Equation (6) scales sales by the actual ratio of receivables to sales 12 months earlier. A variant of this method is to use the average value on the ratio for a given month over some number of previous years. For instance, if one weighted a given month's values for the past 3 years with weights of .2, .3, and .5 respectively, the formula for the proportionality factor at time t would be

$$r_t = .2\left(\frac{TAR_{t-36}}{CS_{t-36}}\right) + .3\left(\frac{TAR_{t-24}}{CS_{t-24}}\right) + .5\left(\frac{TAR_{t-12}}{CS_{t-12}}\right).$$

Ratio-based projection is another attempt to summarize the relation between receivables and sales by a single number or at least a single number at a point in time. Even with stable payment behavior, the constant ratio requires uniform credit sales to be correct, while the moving ratio requires joint stability of seasonal sales and payment patterns to be an acceptable projection method. When such joint stability exists, then it can be a reasonable way to convert credit sales forecasts into receivable projections.

Ratio projection is often used within the framework of a computer-based financial statement generator. One of the main reasons for using ratios is simply that many of these statement generators require that the user specify relations between financial statement variables in terms of user-specified ratios.

Interestingly, many companies using moving ratios report reasonable to high satisfaction with the accuracy of the receivable forecast for planning purposes but not for control purposes. There are several explanations for this. One is that control generally requires greater accuracy than forecasts for planning (budgeting) and cash management. A second involves the way companies plan. For one-year and two-year cash plans, the most common method of projecting sales is a seasonalized average growth projection, often obtained by scaling some smoothed measure of past sales. Hence, the pro forma sales projections have built into them the required stability, even though the sales ultimately realized may deviate from the historical pattern. This explanation is consistent with the fact that the forecast is adequate for projection purposes but not for control, which requires an ability to deal with what receivables should be for realized sales. Third, for companies making quarterly rather than monthly projections, moving ratios have a built-in smoothing feature that tends to average out month-to-month sales fluctuations. In questionnaire follow up, 3 companies reported being unpleasantly surprised when they shifted from quarterly to monthly projection and found that the quality of their forecasts had deteriorated. This deterioration reflects a major defect of moving ratios, namely, excessive sensitivity to the extent to which a given value of sales is representative of the immediately preceding series of sales.

One attempt to cope with this sensitivity has been to replace the single value of sales at a point in time with a moving average of recent sales. If MAS_t and MAS_{t-12} reflect the moving average of recent sales computed at time t and a year earlier, this refinement of the moving ratio can be expressed as

$$TAR_t = (TAR_{t-12})(MAS_t/MAS_{t-12}). \tag{7}$$

Appendix B relates this projection technique to payment patterns. It shows that, with properly chosen weights, the use of a moving average of past sales in a ratio projection can be viewed as a special case of a payment-pattern projection. However, Appendix B also shows that this technique is generally an inefficient way to use payment-pattern information.

Five of the six companies using a weighted average of past sales within the framework of a moving ratio were among the larger companies surveyed. All used the approach as part of a computer-based projection system, and all but one of the six reported reasonable to high satisfaction with its use for forecasting purposes. The consensus was that it did a good job of reflecting seasonality in receivables and an acceptable job of reflecting the effect of past sales. The most common complaint was an inability to reflect changing business conditions and the fact that the previous year would generally differ from the projected one, so that the ratio interjected a scaling error, a problem noted in Appendix B.

In questionnaire follow-up, all six of these companies indicated that weights were specified judgmentally without any formal statistical measurement designed to find a best set of weights. Several indicated that knowledge of the aging schedule was the primary input to specifying weights and had even described their forecast procedure as aging-schedule-based projection on their questionnaire. None indicated an awareness of balance fractions as the logical basis for specifying weights.

When asked why they did not use a simple lagged function of sales rather than the moving ratio, two basic explanations emerged. Three of these companies had introduced the moving average of sales when they changed from quarterly to monthly projection and found the simple moving ratio no longer satisfactory. Thus, this approach was viewed primarily as a refinement of the simple moving ratio rather than as a representation of receivables as a lagged function of sales. The essence of the other reason was that the use of the ratio tended to correct for misspecification of weights to the extent that past and projected sales patterns were stable.

Percent of Balance

The *percent-of-balance method* of forecasting receivables assumes that payments received in a given month are some constant proportion of the start-of-month receivables. In addition to percent of balance and percentage balance, other practitioners used the terms "percentage payment" and "percent of payment." Still others described it as "monthly turnover." Thus, there seems to be a lack of well-defined terminology for this projection technique. This author is unaware of any reference to it in the finance-accounting literature, although the Cyert-Davidson-Thompson [4] model of bad debt forecasts via a Markov process is conceptually similar.

Accounts receivable at the end of month t is equal to accounts receivable at the end of month $t-1$ less payments made of these receivables in month t plus new credit sales in month t less any bad debts recognized in month t. In the absence of bad debts, this accounting identity can be expressed in the notation of this paper as

$$TAR_t = TAR_{t-1} - TCF_t + CS_t. \tag{8}$$

There seem to be two variants to the percentage balance approach. In one, it is assumed that the total cash flow from receivables in a month is proportional to the starting balance. If q denotes the proportionality factor, then this assumption means that the identity in equation (8) can be rewritten as

$$TAR_t = (1 - q)TAR_{t-1} + CS_t. \tag{9}$$

In the other variant, the proportionality factor between receivables and cash flow is defined in terms of only the cash flow on outstanding receivables. If q^* denotes the fraction of receivables outstanding at the start of a month that are paid off during the month, then $(1 - q^*)TAR_{t-1}$ is the change in receivables initially outstanding and $(1 - P_0)CS_t$ is the net addition from credit sales during the month. In this case, the identity in equation (8) can be written as

$$TAR_t = (1 - q^*)TAR_{t-1} + (1 - P_0)CS_t. \tag{10}$$

Comparison of equations (8) and (9) shows that the two scaling factors must be related by the expression $q = q^* + P_0(CS_t/TAR_{t-1})$. Equation (9) appears to be more commonly used than equation (10), although the latter is more complete and more congruent with the verbal statements of what practitioners say they are doing. However, in the common situation in which there are practically no payments made on credit sales within 30 days, P_0 is essentially zero, q and q* are practically equal, and there is no substantive difference in the two equations.

We have focused attention upon the accounts receivable projection implied by the percent-of-balance method. However, discussions with users of the method indicate that it is employed more often simply to obtain a cash flow projection rather than a receivable projection *per se*. Often the time horizon of the projection is short, e.g., a 3-month rolling cash flow projection.

Whether used to project receivables or cash flow, the use of either q or q* as the basis for projection is a questionable procedure. Like ADO and simple ratio projection, this approach is another attempt to use a single number to summarize payment behavior. Like the other one-number forecasts, these ratios are complete summaries only in the special case of uniform sales.

Like ratio projection, the percent of balance technique can be extended to treat seasonality, although few companies reported trying such extensions. Most users reported general dissatisfaction with the approach.

Linear Functions of Past Sales and Lagged Regression

The payment-pattern approach to forecasting cash flows and receivables expresses the quantities as a linear function of past credit sales. In the survey summarized in Exhibit 5, a number of companies reported using some linear function of past sales. The approach was generally described as a "moving average," "weighted average," or "lagged average," although the weights were generally not normalized in the usual sense of an average. Except for companies using the lagged regression described in the subsequent measurement section, these companies indicated in questionnaire follow-up that the relative importance of each month's credit sales was determined judgmentally rather than by any formal empirical procedure. Some indicated that the basis of judgment was knowledge of the company's aging schedule. Some even described their approach as an aging-schedule-based forecast on the questionnaire.

Most companies applied their model to aggregate sales rather than at the product-line, credit-term level. Nevertheless, a majority of these companies generally described themselves as being "satisfied" to "highly satisfied" with the approach, especially those using a lagged regression to measure the balance fractions.

A Summary of Current Practice

The popular control measures depend on the sales pattern. Thus, the greater the variation in sales, the more likely they are to prove unsatisfactory. Using seasonal measures can help cope with seasonal sales patterns but only to the extent that past patterns repeat exactly. The high general level of dissatisfaction with these measures reflects an inability to separate the effect of sales variation from payment shifts and the fact that normal sales variation is generally much greater than shifts in payment behavior.

The one-parameter forecast techniques (ADO, ratio, and percent of balance) attempt to summarize payment behavior by a single number. Even the attempts to improve these techniques by using seasonal parameters still use a single number at a point in time rather than a set of numbers. Except for companies with an unusual amount of stability in their sales, such one-parameter forecast measures generally produce poor accuracy. Much of the current dissatisfaction with forecasting accounts receivable and the associated cash flows must be imputed to the forecast procedures in widespread use and the fact that they are conceptually incomplete approaches.

In most forecasting situations, there is a trade-off between simplicity and completeness. Except for the unusually stable company, basing forecasts on any of the one-number summaries of the payment behavior must be viewed as erring on the side of oversimplification, especially given the ease with which a set of given payment proportions enables one to fill in forecast matrices such as those illustrated in Exhibits 3 and 4. For computer-based projection with preprogrammed measurement of payment patterns, there is no substantive difference in actual difficulty.

THE MEASUREMENT OF PAYMENT PATTERNS

Alternative ways to use past data to measure payment proportions and balance fractions are now considered. Stable payment behavior is first treated and then measurement when payment behavior shifts over time is considered.

Simple Average

The most straightforward way to estimate payment proportions is to compute the average value realized from past data, i.e.,

$$\hat{P}_i = AVE(CF_{ti}/CS_t)$$

$$= \frac{1}{N} \sum_{t=1}^{N} \frac{CF_{ti}}{CS_t} \qquad 1 = 0, \ldots, H \tag{11}$$

where CF_{ti} is cash flow in month $t+i$ from credit sales in month t and N is the number of months of past history used to compute the average. The caret denotes the fact that the value is an empirical estimate.

The analogous expression for balance fractions is

$$\hat{F}_i = AVE(AR_{ti}/CS_t)$$

$$= \frac{1}{N} \sum_{t=1}^{N} \frac{AR_{ti}}{CS_t} \qquad i = 0, \ldots, H-1 \tag{12}$$

where AR_{ti} is the receivable balance at the end of month $t+i$ due to credit sales in month t.

Lagged Regression

As was indicated in the review of forecasting practice, several companies using a payment-pattern approach to forecasting did so within the framework of a lagged regression in which past receivable balances were regressed on a lagged function of past sales. The regression equation can be expressed as

$$TAR_t = f_0 CS_t + f_1 CS_{t-1} + \ldots = f_{H-1} CS_{t-H+1} + u_t, \tag{13}$$

where $f_0, f_1, \ldots, f_{H-1}$ are the regression coefficients and u_t is the usual error term. Their values represent historical estimates of the relative importance of sales in the previous months in determining the values of outstanding receivables.

Comparison of this regression equation and expression (2) for total receivables shows the two equations have the same structure. Estimating the regression coefficients is a method for imputing balance fractions from past data. The main issue is whether such a regression of receivables on lagged sales is the best way to measure balance fractions. It is argued shortly that it generally is not.

An alternative lagged regression approach can be based on explaining total cash flows rather than receivable balances. The analogous equation for directly estimating the payment proportions is

$$TCF_t = p_0 CS_t + p_1 CS_{t-1} + \ldots + p_H CS_{t-H} + u_t. \tag{14}$$

Again, $p_0, \ldots, p_H$ are regression coefficients and u_t is the usual error term. The regression coefficients are estimates of the payment proportions with the property that they minimize the variance of month-to-month "errors" in their prediction of total cash flow from receivables over the sample of past data. These regression coefficients do not necessarily sum to one; they can be made to do so by simply scaling the estimates. With scaling, the actual estimate of the payment proportion is obtained from the regression coefficients in accord with the expression

$$\hat{P}_i = p_i / (\sum_{j=0}^{H} p_j) \qquad i = 0, \ldots, H.$$

A more complex but more technically correct approach is to use constrained regression in which the least squares estimate is developed subject to the constraint that

$$\sum_{i=0}^{H} p_i = 1.$$

Measurement is one area where explicit note of bad debt considerations is pertinent. When estimation is based on gross credit sales, then the normalization condition should be revised to say that the sum of payment proportions should equal one less the fraction of credit sales written off as bad debts. In fact, payment proportions and bad debt loss rates should be estimated simultaneously as shown below.

Measurement Focus: Payment Proportions versus Balance Fractions

Payment proportions and balance fractions are logically equivalent ways to characterize payment behavior in the sense that knowledge of one implies knowledge of the other. From this equivalence, it would seem that empirical measurement could focus on either payment proportions or balance fractions. The fact that most of the forecast equations for receivables in this article are expressed in terms of balance fractions even suggests that they are the logical focus for measurement. They were in fact the implicit focus of all companies using a lagged regression of receivables on sales. Lewellen and Edmister [8] and Lewellen and Johnson [9] concentrated solely on balance fractions and did not even consider payment proportions.

Contrary to the apparently natural tendency to focus on balance fractions, this author believes that payment proportions are the proper focus for empirical measurement. The primary reason for this preference is that there is no obvious way to impose a normalization restriction of balance fractions, especially in the context of constrained regression.

Note that the normalized balance fractions imply a tautological identity when expressed in terms of the balance fractions, i.e.,

$$1 = \sum_{i=0}^{H} P_i = (1 - F_0) + (F_0 - F_1) + \ldots + (F_{H-2} - F_{H-1}) + F_{H-1}.$$

It is possible to estimate balance fractions, solve for the implied payment proportions, and then recursively adjust the balance fractions until consistent estimates are obtained. However, such a circuitous procedure is unnecessarily complex when the payment proportions can be estimated directly.

A second reason involves treatment of bad debts. By focusing measurement on payment patterns, one obtains a comparatively simple problem structuring for simultaneous estimation of bad debt and payment behavior. For instance, if GCS_t denotes gross credit sales at time t, BD_t denotes total bad debts realized in month t and primes denote values expressed in terms of gross credit sales, then the joint estimation of payment patterns and bad debt loss rates can be expressed in the lagged regression framework as

$$BD_t = \sum_{t=0}^{H} B_i' \, GCS_{t-1}$$

$$TCF_t = \sum_{t=0}^{H} P_i' \, GCS_{t-1}$$

subject to the joint constraint that

$$\sum_{i=0}^{H} P_i' + \sum_{i=0}^{H} B_i' = 1.$$

The associated balance fraction is given by

$$F_t' = 1 - \sum_{i=0}^{t} P_i' - \sum_{i=0}^{t} B_i'.$$

The reason for the "nice" structuring is that payment proportions and bad debt loss rates characterize flows that occur in a single month, while balance fractions represent the net effect of flows over the preceding months.

Constant versus Time-Varying Payment Behavior

The estimation of payment patterns via either the simple average method or the lagged regression implicitly assumes that the payment proportions are the same from month-to-month aside from random disturbances. In most companies, payment behavior shifts in response to a variety of factors. Some product lines may have a seasonal variation in their payment pattern. Also, payment behavior typically shifts in response to economic variables such as the level of interest rates and the state of the economy. Moreover, changes in the quality of receivables and shifts in the company collection effort can also alter payment behavior.

The way to allow for variation in payment behavior over time is to have a different set of payment proportions and balance fractions in each month. As before, total cash flows and receivables are projected by first developing the row of the projection matrix and then summing down columns. Control is still based on comparing pro forma and realized values. The only increase in complexity is the nominal requirement for more data.

Measurement in the Presence of Shifting Payment Behavior

Allowing for time varying payment proportions and balance fractions provides the conceptual generality necessary to develop forecasts in the presence of shifting payment behavior. However, without additional structuring, it provides neither for meaningful empirical measurement of payment behavior nor for a coherent framework for either control or performance evaluation. Variation in payment behavior can be meaningfully structured by assuming that there is a stable underlying payment pattern characterized by a constant set of payment proportions and associated balance fractions. Actual payment behavior can be shifted from these underlying values by other factors such as seasonality, interest-rate levels, and company collection effort.

Some illustrative estimation equations are now developed to show how the postulate of a basic underlying payment pattern leads to a meaningful conceptual framework for empirical measurement.

Seasonality

Seasonality of payment behavior refers to systematic changes in payment proportions over the course of a quarter or year. It is important to distinguish it from the seasonal receivables and cash flows that arise from seasonal sales.

To illustrate the measurement of a yearly seasonal, let S_{mi} denote the seasonal shift in the payment proportion P_i for month m of the year (where the months are indexed from 1 to 12 with January being 1). The regression equation for jointly estimating the basic payment proportions and the seasonal shift is

$$\frac{CF_{ti}}{CS_t} = P_i + \sum_{m=1}^{12} S_{mi}D_{mt} + u_{ti}, \tag{15}$$

where D_{mt} is a dummy variable that is one if time t occurs in month m of the year, and zero otherwise; and u_{ti} is the usual residual error.

Credit managers, who are accustomed to correcting the standard receivable measures for seasonality, tend to worry about seasonal payment behavior. In this author's experience, payment proportions for highly seasonal sales are often not significantly seasonal, especially when estimated at the product-line, credit-term level.

Readers are warned to beware of measurement induced seasonals. These can be caused by measuring a payment pattern for overall sales when sales subunits each have a different but stable (non-seasonal) payment pattern and the mix of sales subunits has a stable relative seasonal. Of course, instability in the sales mix itself means a degradation in the ability to impute an overall payment pattern to characterize total sales.

Accounting practice can be another source of spurious seasonals. For instance, in a company that recognized bad debts on a quarterly basis, this every-third-month adjustment to receivables gave the appearance of a small quarterly cycle in payment behavior. It vanished when bad debts were recognized monthly.

Interest-Rate Effects

To illustrate the inclusion of interest-rate effects along with seasonal effects, let I_t be a measure of the level of interest rates in month t and $\bar{I}$ be a measure of "normal" interest rates. A regression equation for jointly estimating the basic payment pattern, any yearly seasonal, and interest rate shifts is

$$\frac{CF_{ti}}{CS_t} = P_i + \sum_{m=1}^{12} S_{mi}D_{tm} + a_i(I_t - \bar{I}) + u_{ti}, \tag{16}$$

where the coefficient a_i measures the sensitivity of payments i months after the sale to deviations in interest rates from the so-called normal level.

Synthesis of Measurement

Equations (15) and (16) illustrate how past data can be used to estimate both basic payment proportions and the way that payment behavior shifts in response to a yearly seasonal and interest rates. Other appropriate factors can be added to the estimation equation in an analogous fashion and their explanatory importance assessed.

It is noted that equations (15) and (16) are extensions of the simple average approach to estimation and not lagged regression. Analogous relationships can be put in the lagged regression framework by, for example, extending the lagged regression to reflect a seasonal variation in payment behavior by adding a seasonal constant to equation (14), i.e.,

$$TCF_t = \sum_{m=1}^{12} C_m \Delta_{mt} + \sum_{i=0}^{H} p_i CS_{t-1} + u_t, \tag{17}$$

where Δ_{mt} is the seasonal dummy that is one when time period t is month m and zero otherwise. However, including shifts in the payment pattern from effects such as interest rates requires modification of the sales coefficients and usually leads to nonlinear estimation problems requiring recursive techniques.

Dealing with time dependent payment behavior complicates considerably the estimation problem compared to the estimation of simple averages in a stable environment. Dealing with these econometric issues is beyond the scope of this paper. The reader is referred to econometric texts such as Johnston [7] and Theil [14] and related literature such as references [5, 6, 10, 12, 13]. The objective here is not to specify completely all pertinent factors that can influence payment behavior or to deal extensively with the many statistical issues that arise in this type of measurement problem. Rather, the intent is to structure the problem sufficiently to make clear the basic conceptual approach implied by the postulate of the existence of an underlying stable payment pattern.

Measurement Focus and the Need for Disaggregation

In the course of this article, it has been mentioned several times that the logical focus for receivable forecasting and control is the product-line, credit-term level. A more precise criterion for the logical measurement focus is that payment proportions should be assessed for sales units that can logically be expected to have the same payment behavior. Credit terms are often more important than product lines.

When payment proportions are measured for sales mixtures with different underlying payment patterns, then the imputed payment pattern is an average of those for the particular sales mix in the sample. The use of such averages for forecasting and control involves an implicit assumption that the same sales mix will prevail in the future. Hence, the basic benefit of payment-pattern measures, independence of sales, is lost. Moreover, to the extent that the sales mix shifts over the sample period, measurement precision is unnecessarily sacrificed and the company foregoes control quality and forecast confidence.

The criterion of focusing measurement on sales units expected to have stable payment behavior can even go beyond the product-line, credit-term level. For instance, in a company that classified accounts into 5 credit quality classes, this author has found that measurement of payment patterns for different quality classes is an easy but particularly beneficial refinement. Deciding how far to go in refining measurement involves two basic issues. One is theoretically attainable accuracy. The other is trading off the greater measurement cost and accuracy with the benefits of tighter control and possibly improved decision making and performance measurement.

PERFORMANCE EVALUATION AND DECISION MAKING

Meaningful measures of the performance of a company's collection effort must be based on measures of behavior that do not depend on factors beyond the control of those responsible for collections, e.g. the sales pattern, the level of interest rates, and the quality of the accounts, the latter being determined by the company's credit granting decisions. Underlying basic payment proportions and balance fractions represent such measures.

An Example

A Fortune 100 company instituted a major program to speed up collections in 1973 because of apparently deteriorating collections. As sales declined and interest rates rose throughout the first 9 months of 1974, both the aging schedule and unadjusted balance fractions indicated further deterioration in receivables despite even greater collection effort. There was talk of replacing the credit manager and reorganizing the collection function. Then, as interest rates declined in late 1974 and 1975 and sales stopped falling and then increased, there was apparently dramatic improvement in collection behavior as measured by both the aging schedule and an indication of some improvement even on the basis of unadjusted balance fractions. However, when basic payment patterns were measured with correction for seasonals, interest-rate effects, and receivable quality, the picture was dramatically different. It indicated a large favorable shift in the basic payment patterns for almost every product line within a month of the initiation of the new collection program in 1973 that was followed by further month-to-month improvements that continued into mid-1974 when the impact of the new collection effort fell to near zero. Interestingly, when both the aging schedule and the unadjusted balance fraction indicated significant improvement, the basic balance fraction had stabilized in that it showed no statistically significant change. The explanation for the difference in the unadjusted balance fraction and the basic balance fraction was primarily the effect of interest rates, especially in product lines with discounts that were foregone by almost all customers when interest rates were high. This interest-rate effect was reinforced by a normal seasonal in some product lines and lower quality of accounts arising from the extension of credit to poorer risks as sales declined.

Credit Policy Decisions

Making intelligent credit policy decisions (such as relaxing or tightening credit granting, changing discount terms, introducing or eliminating discounts) requires knowledge of how the decisions will impact payment behavior. The "explanation" of payment behavior inherent in the measurement of basic payment patterns is useful input to such decisions. In the company of the example above, measuring payment patterns at the product-line, credit-term level for different credit quality classes led to the relaxation of credit granting in some product lines and the tightening in others and the revision of discount terms in several product lines.

SUMMARY AND CONCLUSIONS

Payment proportions and balance fractions are two closely related sets of ratios that completely summarize the conversion of credit sales into cash flows and receivable balances. These ratios are independent of the pattern of credit sales, a key property for a meaningful summary of company payment experience first recognized in the pioneering works of Lewellen and Edmister [8] and Lewellen and Johnson [9].

Implications for Forecasting

Popular forecast techniques (average days outstanding, ratios, and percentage balance) are based on one-number summaries of the relation of credit sales to receivables. Except for the special case of uniform sales (or of jointly stable seasonal sales and payment behavior for seasonal forecast parameters), these one-number summaries do not properly reflect the dependence of receivables on sales. Hence, their use introduces structural forecast error into both receivable and cash flow projections.

For the typical company, the payment-pattern approach to receivable forecasting promises greater forecast accuracy within a logically consistent framework that places no restrictions on sales patterns. For the company that cannot measure payment patterns with any meaningful statistical accuracy, the approach indicates the inherent uncertainty in receivable levels and cash flows.

Given the apparently widespread dissatisfaction with current forecast procedures, there seems to be a clear need for the use of improved methods.

Implications for Control

Rather than the usual aging schedule, control should focus on monitoring payment proportions, bad debt loss rates, and balance fractions. Meaningful control should focus on the patterns at the product-line, credit-term level. Realized values should be compared to pro forma values implied by past data with adjustment made for factors that shift payment behavior such as seasonals and interest rates. In effect, the control focus should be the basic payment pattern. By eliminating measurement noise arising from sales variation, seasonal payment behavior and other factors, more precise control is attainable at any given level of administrative effort.

Implications for Performance Evaluation

The proper focus for the evaluation of company collection effort is impact on basic payment patterns. Either realized payment patterns or sales dependent measures such as the aging schedule can give spurious indications of company performance.

Implications for Information System Design

A basic principle of modern information systems theory is the idea of working backward from the decision to be made to the required data to the implied data gathering and data organization. The two projection matrices illustrated in Exhibits 3 and 4 are the basic data-structure units for a receivable information system. The various forecast equations define key data manipulation. The measurement section specifies the types of data that must be captured. Thus, the decision foundations and much of the data identification and organization necessary to develop a decision-centered receivable information system are provided.

REFERENCES

1. W. H. Beaver, "Financial Statement Analysis," Chapter 5 in *Handbook of Modern Accounting,* Sidney Davidson, editor, New York, McGraw-Hill Book Co., 1970.
2. H. Benishay, "Managerial Control of Accounts Receivable: A Deterministic Approach," *Journal of Accounting Research* (Spring 1965), pp. 114–132.
3. L. A. Bernstein, *Financial Statement Analysis,* Homewood, Illinois, Richard D. Irwin, Inc., 1974.
4. R. M. Cyert, H. J. Davidson, and G. L. Thompson, "Estimation of the Allowance for Doubtful Accounts by Markov Chains," *Management Science* (April 1962), pp. 287–301.
5. Z. Griliches, "A Note on the Serial Correlation Bias in Estimates of Distributed Lags," *Econometrica* (January 1961), pp. 65–73.
6. A. W. Jastram, "A Treatment of Distributed Lags in the Theory of Advertising Expenditures," *Journal of Marketing* (July 1955), pp. 36–46.
7. J. Johnston, *Econometric Models,* second edition, New York, McGraw-Hill Book Co., 1972.
8. W. G. Lewellen and R. O. Edmister, "A General Model for Accounts Receivable Analysis and Control," *Journal of Financial and Quantitative Analysis* (March 1973), pp. 195–206.

9. W. G. Lewellen and R. W. Johnson, "Better Way to Monitor Accounts Receivable," *Harvard Business Review* (May–June 1972), pp. 101–109.
10. N. Liviatan, "Consistent Estimation of Distributed Lags," *International Economic Review* (January 1963), pp. 44–52.
11. G. L. Marrah, "Managing Receivables," *Financial Executive* (July 1970), pp. 40–44.
12. T. W. McGuire, J. U. Farley, R. E. Lucas, Jr. and W. L. Ring, "Estimation and Inference for Linear Models in which Subsets of the Dependent Variables are Constrained," *Journal of the American Statistical Association* (June 1972), pp. 348–368.
13. T. W. McGuire and D. L. Weiss, "Logically Consistent Market Share Models II," *Journal of Marketing Research* (August 1976), pp. 296–302.
14. H. Theil, *Principles of Economics*, New York, John Wiley, 1971.

Appendix A. THE FUNCTIONAL DEPENDENCY OF THE PARAMETERS OF VARIOUS FORECAST AND CONTROL PROCEDURES ON BALANCE FRACTIONS AND THE SCHEDULE OF CREDIT SALES

This appendix develops formulas expressing the parameters of popular techniques as functions of balance fractions and the schedule of credit sales. It considers sufficient conditions for these parameters to be complete summaries when payment behavior is stable.

AGING FRACTIONS

Let A_{jt} denote the fraction of receivables in age class j at time t. The convention is adopted that the most current receivables are indexed by $j = 0$. The formula that relates the aging fraction to the balance fractions and the schedule of credit sales is

$$A_{jt} = F_j CS_{t-j} \Big/ \sum_{i=0}^{H-1} F_i CS_{t-i} \qquad j = 0,1, \ldots ,H-1.$$

A time subscript is used here because the aging schedule generally changes from month to month even when the balance fractions are constant.

In the special case of uniform sales that grow at a constant month-to-month rate of g, the expression for the balance fraction simplifies to

$$A_{jt} = F_j(1 + g)^{-j} / \sum_{i=0}^{H-1} F_i(1 + g)^{-i} \qquad j = 0,1, \ldots ,H-1.$$

Here, the aging schedule is the same in every month.

For constant month-to-month credit sales, the growth rate g is zero and the expression above simplifies to

$$A_{jt} = F_j / (\sum_{i=0}^{H-1} F_i) \qquad j = 0,1, \ldots ,H-1.$$

In the special case of constant sales, the aging schedule is simply a normalized schedule of balance fractions.

AVERAGE DAYS OUTSTANDING AND AVERAGE AGE

If the conventional ADO measure is used based on the ratio of total receivables to a measure of average daily sales, then with a Q-day quarter as the time period, it is found that

$$ADO_t = \frac{TAR_t}{\text{average daily sales}} = \frac{Q \sum_{i=0}^{H=1} F_i CS_{t-i}}{\sum_{i=0}^{2} CS_{t-i}}.$$

With the conventional approximation that the average age of the receivables arising from sales i months prior to time t is 30i + 15, the overall average age of receivables is

$$\text{average age} = \sum_{i=0}^{H-1} F_i CS_{t-i}(30i + 15) / \sum_{i=0}^{H-1} F_i CS_{t-i}.$$

When payment behavior is stable, both average days outstanding and average age depend on sales. They will be constant only for restrictive assumptions about sales such as uniform sales.

RATIO FORECASTS

The following expression relates the receivable-to-sales ratio to balance fractions and sales levels:

$$r_t = TAR_t/CS_t = \sum_{i=0}^{H-1} F_i CS_{t-i}/CS_t$$

$$= F_0 + F_i \left(\frac{CS_{t-1}}{CS_t}\right) + F_2 \left(\frac{CS_{t-2}}{CS_t}\right) + \ldots + F_{H-1} \left(\frac{CS_{t-H+1}}{CS_t}\right).$$

The moving ratio approach of equation (6) requires the consistency of the following expression in each month:

$$\frac{\sum_{i=0}^{H-1} F_i CS_{t-i}}{CS_t} = \frac{\sum_{i=0}^{H-1} F_i CS_{t-i-12}}{CS_{t-12}}.$$

For the constant ratio to be independent of the sales pattern requires restrictive conditions such as uniform sales. In contrast, the moving ratio allows for seasonal sales variation but requires year-to-year stability of seasonal patterns to within a scale factor.

PERCENT OF BALANCE PARAMETERS

The two variations of the percent of balance method were characterized by the parameters q and q*. By definition, q is the ratio of total cash flow to total receivables in the previous periods, i.e.,

$$q \equiv \frac{TCF_t}{TAR_{t-1}} = \frac{\sum_{i=0}^{H} P_i CS_{t-i}}{TAR_{t-1}} = \frac{(1 - F_0)CS_t + \sum_{i=1}^{H} (F_i - F_{i+1})CS_{t-i}}{\sum_{i=0}^{H} F_i CS_{t-i-1}}.$$

By definition, q* is the ratio of cash flow from receivables outstanding at the end of the previous period to those receivables, i.e.,

$$q^* \equiv \frac{TCF_t - P_0 CS_t}{TAR_{t-1}} = \frac{\sum_{i=1}^{H} (F_i - F_{i+1})CS_{t-i}}{\sum_{i=0}^{H} F_i CS_{t-i-1}}.$$

Appendix B. THE RELATION BETWEEN FORECASTS BASED ON A MOVING RATIO USING WEIGHTED AVERAGES OF PAST SALES AND PAYMENT-PATTERN PARAMETERS

The ratio between total receivables at time t and 12 months earlier can be expressed as

$$\frac{TAR_t}{TAR_{t-12}} = \frac{\sum_{i=0}^{H-1} F_i CS_{t-i}}{\sum_{i=0}^{H-1} F_i CS_{t-12-i}}.$$

Let $W_i = F_i/(\sum_{i=1}^{H-1} F_i)$ denote a normalized balance fraction. By multiplying both the numerator and denominator of the right-hand side of this expression by $1/(\sum_{i=1}^{H-1} F_i)$,

$$\frac{TAR_t}{TAR_{t-12}} = \frac{\sum_{i=0}^{H-1} W_i CS_{t-i}}{\sum_{i=0}^{H-1} W_i CS_{t-12-i}}$$

is obtained. This last expression is clearly a moving ratio involving a weighted average of credit sales. It has the structure of equation (7). This result shows that the moving-ratio forecast based on a weighted average of past sales is equivalent to a payment-pattern projection when the weights are based on normalized balance fractions. It also shows that any other choice of weights in equation (7) must be an incomplete characterization of the dependency of receivables on the sales pattern. The aging schedule is appropriate only when sales are constant and payment behavior is stable.

This expression shows that the standard moving-ratio projection with a single value of sales is an extreme case of assigning the entire weight to the current value of sales. This overweighting of the current value is the reason for the unnecessary sensitivity of the receivable forecast to the value of sales used and the reason that companies have moved to the intuitively more acceptable approach of weighting several values.

While a moving ratio in the form of equation (7) is a logically correct way to project receivables when weights are based on normalized balance fractions, it is unnecessarily redundant. Once the balance fractions are known, equation (2) is all that is necessary. Moreover, once it is recognized that payment behavior can shift over time, using a ratio based on balance-fraction weighted sales rather than the simple use of balance fractions introduces an element of statistical noise that can improperly scale the correct forecast.

QUESTIONS

1. Distinguish between the monthly payment pattern and the receivable balance pattern. Draw diagrams of each which are consistent with one another.
2. For companies showing variations in days' sales outstanding, variations in sales patterns were reported as being a more important cause than changing payments patterns. Use this information to explain why a receivables monitoring vehicle such as days' sales outstanding would produce ambiguous signals at times.
3. Assume that your firm is using the monthly payment pattern method to monitor accounts receivable. The control limits could be pierced because of internal problems associated with easing of credit standards, or departure from norms could result from fundamental changes in the economic environment. Explain how departures from norms might be caused by (a) an economic recession, (b) tight money, (c) excess capacity in your industry. Should your credit policy and enforcement *always* be adjusted to keep within the control limits?

PROBLEM

1. The Burned Corporation is uncertain whether its growing A/R balance is a warning flash or not. Its business has been profitable, but A/R increased almost six times, while sales increased only about four times over the

period January 31–April 30, 1976. Records of their collection experience show the following information:

MONTH OF SALE	SALES FOR MONTH	COLLECTED IN JANUARY	COLLECTED IN FEBRUARY	COLLECTED IN MARCH	COLLECTED IN APRIL
January	25	5	7.5	10	2.5
February	45	—	9	13.5	18
March	80	—	—	16	24
April	100	—	—	—	20
A/R balance		22.2	48.9	89.0	124.5

a. Analyze the firm's collection experience using at least two different methods. If an average period is used, use ninety days. Sales for November and December were 2 and 4, respectively.

b. What is the status of the "collection experience"?

c. Sales for the next four months are forecast to be $90, $75, $60, and $50, respectively. What will receivables be on August 31, 1976?

7 | James L. Pappas and George P. Huber

Probabilistic Short-Term Financial Planning

This article presents a framework for determining a firm's optimal line of credit. In addition to providing valuable descriptive material regarding lines of credit, the authors develop a model to show how imperfect forecast information may be translated into confidence statements about cash strategies assuming that specified lines of credit are used. In so doing, the authors demonstrate another area in which probabilistic material is useful in managerial finance.

Companies typically arrange lines of credit or more formal credit agreements with banks primarily to assure availability of funds on short notice. The need for such funds may stem from seasonal fluctuations in working capital requirements, from a continuing need for additional permanent capital coupled with the desire to seek funds in the capital market at less frequent intervals than would be necessary without bank credit, from a relatively unstable relationship between cash inflows and disbursements, or from a number of other such factors.

The financial manager is responsible for minimizing the cost of the funds obtained subject to the requirement that a credit agreement provides the amount of liquidity needed. Thus, he must examine all factors that can influence cost associated with all the credit sources available. This evaluation is not aimed solely at selecting the least-cost credit arrangement. For example, funds obtained by means of an informal line of credit may well cost less than a similar amount acquired through a contractual agreement. However, with an informal line of credit the firm risks the loss of funds in times of a credit crunch, since such agreements typically do not contractually obligate the bank. Moreover, under line of credit agreements the interest rate is typically not final until the time of borrowing. With the formal credit agreement, on the other hand, the bank is legally obligated to supply the funds, and the interest rate charged is frequently specified. Thus, the two forms of credit arrangement are dissimilar in significant

Source. Reprinted by permission from *Financial Management*, Autumn 1973, pp. 36–44 The authors are professors of business in the Graduate School of Business, University of Wisconsin.

ways. Hence, they cannot be evaluated as alternatives only on the basis of expected cost. Rather, their comparison is a form of cost-benefit analysis.

THE COST OF CREDIT

Ex post analysis of the cost of a credit agreement is simple; one merely divides the annual dollar cost incurred by the average annual usable funds obtained. Costs are typically composed of the commitment fee plus interest cost on average borrowing. Usable funds are the amount borrowed less any positive difference between the compensating balance requirement and the normal account balance. If the normal account balance should exceed the compensating balance requirement, then usable funds would equal the amount borrowed. Estimating the expected cost of a credit agreement is equally as simple. One merely uses estimates of the projected borrowing levels and the resulting costs.

An illustration is provided in Exhibit 1. In this example, ABC Company is assumed to have negotiated a $50 million credit arrangement calling for a .5% commitment fee charged on the unused portion of the credit limit, a 9% interest charge on outstanding borrowings, a 20% compensating balance against borrowed funds, and a 10% compensating balance on the unused portion of the credit limit. With an average borrowing of $20 million and a normal account balance of $1 million, the interest cost to ABC is 13.9%, calculated by dividing the $1.95 million costs by the $14 million average usable funds obtained. The 13.9% is an annual interest rate provided the credit agreement extends over a twelve month period. If the life of the arrangement is shorter, an appropriate adjustment must be made to determine the effective annual yield [cf. 9, pp. 229–232].

The importance to the cost of funds of the relationship between the amount specified by the credit agreement and average usable funds required can be demonstrated by modifying this example slightly. Assume that instead of a $50 million credit agreement, ABC had negotiated a $75 million agreement but still had required average usable funds of $14 million. In that case, ABC's average borrowing would have been $22.8 million and the interest cost would have increased to 16.5%. The increased borrowing stems from the need to cover the larger compensating balance for the unused portion of the commitment, and the higher cost results from the interest on the increased borrowing plus the larger commitment fee.

Similarly, a change in borrowing time pattern also has a significant impact on cost. For example, if ABC had needed an average of only $10 million in usable funds, average borrowing would have been $15.5 million with the $50 million agreement, and the actual interest cost of funds obtained would have been 15.7%.

Exhibit 2 provides an expanded picture of the impact of alternative credit terms and usage patterns on borrowing costs. The data in this exhibit demonstrate the importance to a financial manager of obtaining a good estimate of credit requirements.

EXHIBIT 1.   INTEREST COST CALCULATION FOR ABC CORPORATION'S $50 MILLION CREDIT ARRANGEMENT

[In thousands]

Dollar Costs		
Interest on average borrowing = 9.0% × $20,000 =		$ 1,800
Commitment fee on unused portion of credit limit = 0.5% × $30,000 =		150
Total Costs		$ 1,950

Usable Funds†		
Average Borrowing		$20,000
Less: 20% compensating balance on borrowing	($4,000)	
10% compensating balance on unused portion of credit limit	($3,000)	($ 7,000)
		$13,000)
Plus: Normal bank balance		1,000
Average Usable Funds		$14,000

$$\text{Interest Cost} = \frac{\text{Dollar costs}}{\text{Avg. usable funds}} = \frac{\$1,950}{\$14,000} = 13.93\%$$

† So long as the compensating balance requirement exceeds the firm's normal bank balance, the relationship between usable funds (UF) and average borrowing (AB) is given by the following expressions where normal balances are represented as (NB) and the credit limit as (CL):

$$(UF) = (AB) - \alpha(AB) - \beta((CL) - (AB)) + (NB)$$
$$= (1 - \alpha + \beta)AB - \beta(CL) + NB,$$

and

$$AB = \frac{UF + \beta(CL) - (NB)}{(1 - \alpha + \beta)}$$

Here
α = the compensating balance requirement on outstanding borrowing,
and
β = the compensating balance requirement on the unused portion of the credit limit.

ESTIMATING CREDIT REQUIREMENTS

Since both the maximum credit that the firm will require and the time pattern of borrowing are stochastic, or uncertain, they cannot be specified precisely at the time a credit agreement is negotiated. This means that they must be estimated. Unfortunately, the typical approach to forecasting the borrowing needs for a firm does not provide the information necessary to properly evaluate alternatives.

EXHIBIT 2. COST IMPACT OF ALTERNATIVE CREDIT ARRANGEMENTS

CREDIT LIMIT	AVERAGE USABLE FUNDS	COMPENSATING ON BORROWING	BALANCE ON UNUSED PORTION OF CREDIT LIMIT	COMMITMENT FEE ON UNUSED PORTION OF CREDIT LIMIT	INTEREST RATE ON BORROWING	AVERAGE BORROWING	COST OF USABLE FUNDS
(000,000)	(000,000)	(%)	(%)	(%)	(%)	(000,000)	(%)
$50	$14	20	10	0.5	9.0	$20.00	13.93
50	10	20	10	0.5	9.0	15.55	15.72
50	20	20	10	0.5	9.0	26.67	12.58
50	14	30	0	0.5	9.0	18.57	13.05
50	14	20	10	0.0	9.5	20.00	14.64
75	14	20	10	0.5	9.0	22.78	16.51
75	14	30	10	0.5	9.0	25.63	18.23
75	15	20	10	0.0	9.5	23.89	16.84

For most firms, estimating both the size and time pattern of credit needs is accomplished by developing a pro forma cash budget. At first glance, this method seems to provide the information necessary to develop a least-cost credit agreement. The cumulative pro forma cash balance shows the maximum financing requirement, and the cash budget indicates monthly borrowing needs so that an average borrowing figure can be calculated. Given these data, the firm appears to be in a position to negotiate a favorable credit agreement.

Unfortunately, the orthodox cash budget not only fails to provide the data needed for a thorough credit analysis, but it is also likely to be misleading with respect to projected funds requirements. The problem stems from the inability of the simple cash budget to depict those characteristics of future cash flows of primary importance in decision making. The traditional cash budget is typically based solely on forecasted single valued estimates for cash inflows and outflows. Use of single valued estimates leads to several difficulties. First, there is the problem of uncertainty. Actual cash flows are stochastic and, hence, can be expected to vary from their expected levels. The problem of uncertainty about cash flows is frequently handled by establishing a desired minimum cash balance position, which, in effect, is a safety stock against uncertainty and the lack of synchronization of cash inflows and outflows. Even though the size of the safety stock is related to variability of cash flows, this approach still fails to provide the data necessary to evaluate the choice of any particular minimum level of cash.

In addition, there is evidence that the inability to accurately estimate borrowing needs leads to the establishment of excessively large safety stocks, which result in a high cost of borrowing. A recent survey found that a group of 39 major U.S. corporations had an average of about 37% excess cash on hand compared to compensating balance requirements of their loan agreements. In all likelihood, this means that not only were average borrowing levels substantially above the optimum, but also excessively large loan agreements had been negotiated. Another recently reported example [1] showed a large Midwestern firm paying 28% for its bank credit for precisely these reasons.

A second problem arising from the cash budget approach to financial planning lies in the estimation of cumulative borrowing needs. This approach does not reveal intra- and inter-period cash flow relationships, and these influence the pattern of cumulative net cash flows. For example, activities associated with greater than expected cash inflows may also require greater than expected expenses or outflows. Similarly, if sales and revenues fall below expectations, it is likely that cash outflows will also be lower than their expected value. Such a situation is reflected by a significant intra-period correlation of cash flows.

In addition, it is reasonable to expect important inter-period cash flow correlations. If, for example, sales exceed expectations in one period, it is frequently the case that they will also be higher than initially expected in the following period. Similarly, if a firm experiences higher than expected costs in its production system, the factors that led to the added costs may well cause a similar pattern in succeeding periods. Given either intra- or inter-period correlations of cash flows, the simple cash budget procedure for projecting financial requirements will provide misleading data.

A SIMULATION APPROACH TO ESTIMATING CASH NEEDS

Fortunately, a rather simple extension of cash budgeting methodology provides the information necessary to correctly analyze alternative credit possibilities. The extension involves the use of a simulation model. Such a model provides more accurate answers than can a simple cash budget to such questions as: What is the maximum amount of credit that the firm is likely to require? What is the expected average borrowing figure? Additionally, the simulation approach provides other much needed information by answering questions like: What is the probability that the maximum borrowing requirement will exceed any given dollar amount? What are the probabilities associated with positive loan balances in any given month? What is the probability that the firm will be able to repay all borrowing by the end of the planning period?

Overall, simulating cash flows should provide a positive economic benefit, but it does require more extensive data than the usual cash budget approach. Instead of identifying simply the expected value for each monthly inflow and outflow, simulation requires that we estimate the probabilities of other possible flows, as well as intra- and inter-period cash flow correlation coefficients. While this may appear formidable, we will demonstrate that whatever source of information is used for developing point forecasts of expenditures and receipts is usually sufficient for developing distribution forecasts.

Developing Distribution Forecasts from Historical Data

It may be that we have accurate data of our historical expenditures and receipts and believe that their future values will be a straight-forward extrapolation of their past values. If this is the case, then we should compute the probability distributions for future time periods as follows.

1. Using either trend analysis or a seasonal model, construct a forecasting model that would have accurately predicted the recent history of the firm's cash flows (expenditures and receipts). (The reader is referred to the Nelson text [4] for an excellent exposition on this process.)
2. Use the model to develop an estimate of the expected cash flow, $\hat{Y}_t$, in each period covered by the data, and subtract the actual cash flow, Y_t, from the

expected cash flow to compute the forecast error, $e_t = \hat{Y}_t - Y_t$, for each time period, t. Draw a histogram or probability distribution of these errors. It has a mean of zero.

3. Modify this parent distribution for use at each point t, to account for the fact that the forecast, $\hat{Y}_t$, of any point that is far removed from the center of the historical data will be less accurate than the forecast of a point closer to the mean, $\bar{t}$, of the time periods examined. Since the points we are forecasting are outside the range of the historical data, their probability distributions will have greater variance than the average variance calculated in the forecasting model. We can adjust for this by multiplying each of the errors shown in the histogram developed in step 2 by an adjustment factor, δ_t, for each future period we plan to incorporate into our analysis, while retaining the original probability for each. The term δ_t, which is to unity as the standard deviation for any Y_t^* is to the standard deviation of Y_t^* at $\bar{t}$, is algebraically correct for least squares forecasts and is offered here as a heuristic for other forecasts [cf. 5]. The equation for δ_t is:

$$\delta_t = \sqrt{1 + \frac{1}{N} + \frac{(t - \bar{t})^2}{\sum\limits_{t=1}^{N} (t - \bar{t})^2}}, \tag{1}$$

where N is the number of data points used to obtain the least squares trend line or the parameters of a seasonal model. This adjustment procedure has the effect of appropriately increasing the variance of the estimate, $\hat{Y}_t$, for each forecast period, t. As can be seen from inspection of the formula for δ_t or from the forthcoming example calculation, only if N is quite small or t is much larger than $\bar{t}$, is δ_t significantly different from unity.

4. Use the model to forecast the expected cash flow for each of future time periods important to the bank credit arrangement.

5. Estimate the probability distribution for each of the future time periods by adding the mean of the distribution (computed in step 4) to the values of the probability distribution of historical errors, computed in step 3, i.e., shift the probability distribution from a mean of zero to a mean estimated by the forecasting model.

Working through a simple example should clarify this methodology. In Exhibit 3 we have graphed a least squares trend model of a hypothetical cash receipts pattern assumed to exhibit no seasonality. A histogram of the error terms is also provided. In the example, 19 periods of data have been used, so the first period of our forecast would be designated as $t = 20$.

To develop the estimate of the cash receipts distribution for $t = 20$, we begin by estimating the adjusted probability distribution for the residual or error

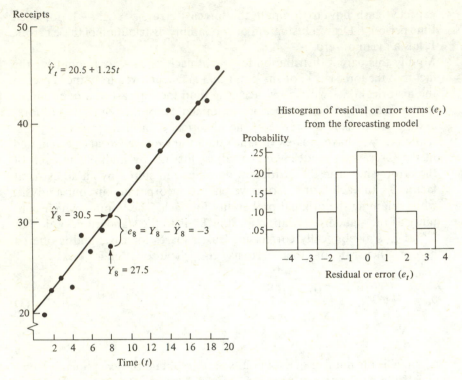

Exhibit 3.   Graph of the least squares forecasting model.

terms as outlined in step 3 above. In this case, δ_{20}, the adjustment factor, is 1.026, found in the following manner:

$$\delta_{20} = \sqrt{1 + \frac{1}{19} + \frac{(20 - 9.5)^2}{\sum\limits_{t=1}^{19} (t - 9.95)^2}} = 1.026. \tag{2}$$

Multiplying each value on the horizontal axis of the distribution in Exhibit 3 by the adjustment factor provides the histogram shown in Exhibit 4.

Finally, the relevant probability distribution for cash receipts in period 20 is developed by using the forecasting model to estimate the expected cash receipt, $\hat{Y}_{20}$, and adding that expected receipt to each of the residual or error terms in Exhibit 5. The value of $\hat{Y}_{20}$ is found as follows:

$$\hat{Y}_{20} = 20.5 + 1.25(20) = 45.5. \tag{3}$$

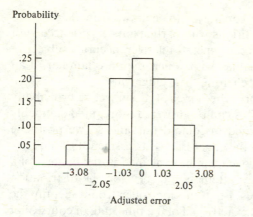

Exhibit 4.   Adjusted histogram for the residual or error term for period 20.

Adding 45.5 to each possible outcome in Exhibit 4 leads to the probability distribution shown in Exhibit 5. A similar distribution would be constructed for receipts and disbursements in each period within the planning horizon.

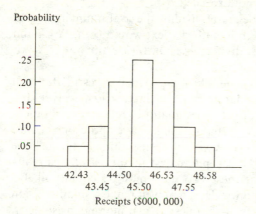

Exhibit 5.   Probability distribution of receipts for period 20.

Judgmental Estimation of Probability Distributions

The above approach provides both point and distribution forecasts for cash flows when we can count on historical flows to be predictive of future flows in an algebraically straightforward manner. However, when historical cash flows will not be representative of future flows, either point forecasts or distributed forecasts used in simulation must be obtained judgmentally. They may be obtained after much discussion and use of reference data, but they are nonetheless professional judgments.

The topic of subjective probability estimation has been actively studied in recent years and has been reviewed by Peterson and Beach [6], Slovic and

Lichtenstein [8], and Huber [2]. The conclusion to be drawn from field studies or studies made under field-like conditions with participants experienced with the judgments required is that experts can generate relatively accurate subjective probability distributions about variables with which they are familiar, if an appropriate procedure is used when eliciting their judgments.

Which of the several available approaches for eliciting subjective probability distributions is most appropriate? This can be answered more understandably after one approach has been examined in some detail, and so we postpone discussing it until we have presented the equal-fractile assessment technique.

The *equal-fractile assessment* approach can be explained in the context of a controller or other financial manager attempting to develop the distribution for a particular month's expenditures. First, the controller would identify the expenditure expected to be exceeded exactly half of the time and, of course, not exceeded the other half of the time. That is, the equal-fractile assessment approach involves, first, estimating the median, the $\hat{Y}_{.50}$ point on the probability distribution of possible expenditures. His second step is to consider just those expenditure levels falling below $\hat{Y}_{.50}$ and identify the expenditure level that would be as likely to be exceeded as not exceeded.

What the controller has done is to begin subdividing the continuum into equal parts. So far, $X_{.50}$ and $X_{.25}$ have been identified. Next would come $X_{.75}$, and in most cases by having the controller divide these quartiles, estimates of $X_{.125}$, $X_{.375}$, $X_{.625}$, and $X_{.875}$ would be obtained.

During the assessment process, it is generally useful to help the estimator with his consistency and to have him consider again the estimates he has given. If a second analyst is involved, he might direct the estimator to reflect for a moment about the expenditure levels below $X_{.25}$ that he thinks have about one chance in four of occurring, and the levels above $X_{.75}$ that he also thinks have just one chance in four of occurring. Then the second analyst might ask if it is really true, in the estimator's opinion, that these two outcomes are equally likely? After considering this question, the controller might well make a small revision to one or more of his estimates. Aside from the question of minor inconsistencies, we must recognize that most estimators involved in a dialogue such as this are thinking more analytically than they are accustomed to do. In addition to helping the estimator clarify his thinking, this "on-line checking" helps avoid the problem of cumulating errors, which is possible, of course, when successive judgments are made using earlier judgments as reference points.

Approaches to eliciting probability distributions can be categorized according to whether they involve equal-fractile assessment, betting, direct probability estimation, or scale estimation. The *betting* approach would require the controller to pretend that he was in a gambling situation and to state how much he would be willing to bet on the relevant events (outcomes), such as cash outflows falling in a certain range. The subjective probability estimates would be derived from the bets, using the assumptions that the controller is attempting to maximize his imaginary expected payoff and that his is cognitively capable of doing this. Since these assumptions about human behavior and ability have been found to be unjustified in many situations, the betting approach is receiving less attention now than it did in the past and is not recommended here.

The *direct probability estimation* approach would require the controller to state the probabilities of relevant events (outcomes), i.e., estimate the relative proportion of times that an event (outcome) would occur. This is cognitively more difficult than making the indifference judgments, the judgments about whether two events are equally or not equally likely to occur, required by the fractile assessment approach. Combined with the fact that this would require the controller to have some understanding of probability, while the fractile assessment approach does not, this cognitive difficulty causes us not to suggest direct probability estimation.

Scale estimation would require the controller to estimate cash flows that would or would not be exceeded a certain proportion of the time, e.g., to tell someone the expenditure level that he expects to see exceeded only 10% of the time. Again, making such an estimate is cognitively a very difficult task [cf. 7,3].

As a consequence of these considerations, we recommend the equal-fractile assessment approach for subjectively estimating cash flows.

Estimating Intra- and Inter-Period Correlation Coefficients

There are two types of intercorrelations of interest in credit analysis. The first is the correlation between cash inflows and outflows. If historical data are used to develop the distribution forecasts for these two variables, then these same data can also be used to compute the correlation between them simply by following the usual algebraic procedures.

If expert judgments are used to develop the distribution forecasts, those of the cash inflows should be developed first and used as "givens" when the controller or other expert provides the distribution forecasts of the cash outflows. In effect, then, these latter forecasts are made from conditional probability distributions. Research suggests that such judgments can be quite accurate. In computing the correlation coefficient we would require only the means of the two distributions. These would be used in the same fashion as historical data to compute an estimate of the correlation coefficient.

The other type of intercorrelation of interest is the correlation between cash receipts of adjacent time periods. Here again, irrespective of whether historical data or subjective estimates are used to develop the distribution forecasts, these same data can also be used to compute the inter-period correlation. If expert judgments are used, we insure that estimates for successive months are conditional estimates by reminding the individual providing the data of his estimate for the mean of the distribution of receipts for the preceding period and asking him to reconcile it with the current month.

Simulating a Company's Cash Flow Pattern

Once the distributions of periodic cash inflows and outflows and the correlations have been estimated, the financial manager is in a position to simulate the net cash flow pattern for his firm. This will provide a much clearer picture of the costs and benefits of alternative credit possibilities.

Simulation in this case consists of running repeated trials in which a projected cash budget is generated. Data for each trial are drawn randomly from the distributions developed above (with the proper inter- and intra-period correlations), and the resulting cash flow patterns themselves are formed into frequency distributions.

Assume that, through the technique described above, the cash flow distributions have been estimated for ABC's receipts and disbursements over the next twelve months. It was found that the distributions could be accurately described by the beta function with the upper and lower limits given in Exhibit 6 lying ± 3 standard deviations from the means. The intra- and inter-period correlations were estimated from historical data.

Using these estimates, we proceeded to simulate the firm's net cash flows over the twelve month planning horizon. Each simulation resulted in a pro forma cash budget. Successive iterations produced frequency distributions for each cash flow characteristic relevant for credit cost analysis.

A 100 trial simulation resulted in the following output for ABC Company's cash flow analysis: (1) During the planning period the expected average borrowing was $15.1 million; (2) the distribution of average borrowing was such that there is less than a 5% chance that average borrowing will fall outside the range $11.2–$19.0 million dollars; (3) the expected maximum borrowing requirement was $49.5 million; (4) there is a 95% probability that the maximum borrowing will not exceed $56.9 million, and a 99% probability that it will be below $60.6 million; and (5) the probability that the loan balance will be zero in any given month was found to be

Month	1	2	3	4	5	6	7	8	9	10	11	12
Probability	.95	.87	.65	.27	0.0	0.0	0.0	0.0	0.0	0.0	.51	1.00

With this information ABC Company's financial manager is in a position to evaluate alternative forms of bank credit agreements. In this case ABC must arrange a $60.6 million credit agreement to be 99% sure that it would provide all the funds necessary. This is considerably above the maximum borrowing requirement of $45,000 one would obtain using only the expected values of receipts and disbursements from Exhibit 6 in a standard pro forma cash budget analysis. This clearly indicates the danger of possibly establishing too low a credit limit. The opposite result is also possible. That is, without adequate information about the distribution of cash flows, a financial manager is likely to "play safe" by establishing an excessively large credit agreement.

EXHIBIT 6.   PARAMETERS FOR THE CASH FLOW DISTRIBUTIONS FOR ABC COMPANY

[In thousands]

		MONTH											
		1	2	3	4	5	6	7	8	9	10	11	12
Receipts	Upper Estimate	24	23	20	15	9	9	8	7	13	46	60	45
	Expected	19	17	15	11	6	6	5	4	10	38	50	38
	Lower Estimate	13	12	11	8	4	4	4	2	5	28	47	30
Disbursements	Upper Estimate	20	19	19	18	18	19	21	23	25	28	26	23
	Expected	17	16	16	14	13	14	15	16	18	20	20	18
	Lower Estimate	15	15	14	11	10	10	10	12	13	14	15	14

Intraperiod correlation = .75
Interperiod correlation = .50

The form of the credit arrangement that ABC's financial manager chooses is not important for our purposes here. It will depend not only on ABC's needs, but also on alternatives available. The important point is that, armed with the output from the simulation, the financial manager is able to fully evaluate alternative courses of action. He can, for example, examine the expected costs of obtaining credit from different sources with varying terms. He is also able to determine the cost associated with reducing the risk of a funds shortage through establishment of a larger credit agreement.

REFERENCES

1. C. Todd Conover, "The Case of the Costly Credit Agreement," *Financial Executive* (September 1971), pp. 41–48.
2. G. Huber, "Methods for Quantifying Subjective Probabilities and Multi-Attribute Utilities," *Decision Sciences* (July 1974).
3. A. H. Murphy and R. L. Winkler, "Subjective Probability Forecasting of Temperature: Some Experimental Results," in preprint, *Proceedings of the Third Conference on Probability and Statistics in Atmospheric Science*, Boulder, Colorado, American Meteorological Society, June 1973.
4. C. R. Nelson, *Applied Time Series Analysis for Managerial Forecasting*, San Francisco, Holden-Day, Inc., 1973.
5. B. Ostle, *Statistics in Research*, Ames, Iowa, Iowa State University Press, 1963.
6. C. R. Peterson and L. R. Beach, "Man as an Intuitive Statistician," *Psychological Bulletin* (1967), pp. 29–46.

7. C. R. Peterson, K. J. Snapper, and A. H. Murphy, "Credible Interval Temperature Forecasts," *Bulletin of the American Meteorological Society* (October 1972).
8. P. Slovic and S. Lichtenstein, "Comparison of Bayesian and Regression Approaches to the Study of Information Processing in Judgment," *Organizational Behavior and Human Performance* (November 1971).
9. J. F. Weston and E. F. Brigham, *Essentials of Managerial Finance*, 3rd edition, Hinsdale, Illinois, The Dryden Press, 1974.

QUESTIONS

1. Explain why it is costly to arrange for a line of credit greater than what will be needed.
2. Why is it impossible at the beginning of the year to know the effective interest rate on the funds you will borrow from the bank for seasonal needs?
3. Explain how to perform the *simulations which could be used to establish the distribution of likely borrowing needs* for each month in the period ahead. It may be helpful to make a diagram to chart the process.
4. Describe how the analyst might extract the relevant probabilistic information which serves as the input for the simulation.
5. Once the probabilistic information is obtained from the simulation, how might it be used for strategic decision making regarding the needed line of credit?

PROBLEM

1. The Pappas Corporation is negotiating a $100 million credit arrangement. The commitment fee to be charged on the unused portion of the credit limit will be 0.65 per cent. Outstanding loans will have an interest charge of 12.5 per cent. Borrowed funds require a 25 per cent compensating balance, while a 15 per cent compensating balance on the unused portion of the credit limit will be needed. Normal account balances for the Pappas Corporation total $9 million.
    a. If the outstanding average borrowing is expected to be $45 million, what will the average usable funds and the interest cost be?
    b. If the firm had negotiated a $125 million agreement, but still required the same average usable funds (as in part a), what would its average borrowings have been, and what interest would it now be paying? Briefly discuss what caused the change in borrowing.

III | Decisions Involving Long-Term Assets

8 | *Lawrence J. Gitman and John R. Forrester, Jr.*

A Survey of Capital Budgeting Techniques Used by Major U.S. Firms

Students often ask if the analytical methods they are learning are really used in industry. This article shows, among other things, that most large firms use the so-called sophisticated capital budgeting techniques. In context with earlier studies, this article shows that such usage is increasing.

The capital budgeting decision process remains one of the key decision areas confronting the contemporary financial manager, since its results help mold the firm's future opportunities. Academicians have preached the use of the more sophisticated approaches to capital budgeting analysis and have suggested that certain adjustments for risk be made. Support for the use of quantitative risk-adjustment was provided by the findings of Petty and Bowlin in their Winter 1976 *Financial Management* article [7] concerned with the use of quantitative methods by financial managers. This article surveys the level of sophistication used in capital budgeting by the nation's leading firms. Where possible, the findings of this study are related to comparable previous studies.

SAMPLE SELECTION, RESPONSE, AND CHARACTERISTICS

The large business firms utilized in this study were selected on the basis of two factors: 1) stock price growth, and 2) total dollars of capital expenditures. All of the sample firms came from a list of 600 companies which experienced the greatest stock price growth over the 1971–1976 period as reported in *Forbes* [12, pp. 186–206]. The sample was in effect limited to those firms having exhibited the type of growth which would be expected to accompany increased levels of capital expenditure. The firms also appeared in a list of the

Source. Reprinted by permission from *Financial Management,* Fall 1977, pp. 66–71. Lawrence Gitman is associate professor of finance at the University of Tulsa, and John R. Forrester, Jr. is administrator of the Richardson Heights Baptist Church in Richardson, Texas.

500 companies having made the greatest dollar capital expenditures during 1969 as reported in *Forbes* [11, pp. 111–118]. These 1969 data were used since they reflected the behavior of firms during an inflationary or expansionary period. Questionnaires personally addressed to the chief financial officer of the firm were mailed in June, 1976, to 268 firms appearing on both lists [10].

One hundred and ten responses were received, with 103 completed questionnaires (38.4% of the 268 firms). To become more familiar with the characteristics of the respondents, a few questions were asked pertaining to the firm and its chief financial officer. Job titles of those primarily responsible for capital budgeting analysis as well as the completion of the questionnaire were: Vice President of Finance, Treasurer, Director of Planning, Director of Capital Programs, or Director of Facilities Management. As can be seen in Exhibits 1 and 2, the firms responding primarily were manufacturing firms with total assets in excess of $100 million.

EXHIBIT 1.   *INDUSTRY CLASSIFICATION OF RESPONDENTS*

	Responses	
Classification	Number	Percent
Distributor	4	3.9
Manufacturer of Durables	35	34.0
Manufacturer of Non-durables	41	40.0
Service Company	23	22.1
Total Responses	103	100.0

EXHIBIT 2.   *ASSET SIZE OF RESPONDENT FIRMS*

	Responses	
Asset Size	Number	Percent
Less than $100 million	0	0.0
$100 to $500 million	10	9.7
$500 to $1 billion	22	21.4
More than $1 billion	71	68.9
Total Responses	103	100.0

CAPITAL BUDGETING STATISTICS

A portion of the questionnaire was devoted to determining various statistics describing the respondent firms' capital budgeting activities: Exhibits 3, 4, and 5 provide these data. Capital budgets of over $100 million were in the majority, and the number of projects formally analyzed averaged 238 per respondent per year. These data indicate that the responding firms were actively engaged in capital budgeting evaluation and analysis. An open-ended question relating to project size elicited a wide range of responses with an average size of $3,375,000. All of the respondents indicated that a minimum outlay of $10,000 or more was required in order to justify formal analysis of a proposed project: because of the response choices given (See Exhibit 4), this result may be a bit misleading since the questionnaire's minimum was $10,000. Of projects formally analyzed, two-thirds of the respondents have an acceptance rate of over 75%. This suggests that projects are not formally analyzed unless they are expected to meet the firm's acceptance criteria.

EXHIBIT 3. SIZE OF ANNUAL CAPITAL BUDGET

Size of Annual Capital Budget	Responses	
	Number	Percent
Less than $10 million	0	0.0
$10 to $50 million	11	11.2
$50 to $100 million	23	23.5
More than $100 million	64	65.3
Total Responses	98	100.0

EXHIBIT 4. PROJECT SIZE FOR FORMAL ANALYSIS

Project Size	Responses	
	Number	Percent
Greater than $10,000	31	31.3
Greater than $50,000	27	27.3
Greater than $100,000	23	23.2
Greater than $500,000	12	12.1
Greater than $1,000,000	6	6.1
Total Responses	99	100.0

EXHIBIT 5. PERCENT OF PROJECTS ACCEPTED

Percent Accepted	Responses	
	Number	Percent
Less than 10%	4	4.1
10 to 25%	1	1.0
25 to 50%	5	5.1
50 to 75%	20	20.6
75 to 90%	34	35.1
More than 90%	33	34.1
Total Responses	97	100.0

CAPITAL BUDGETING PROCEDURES

Respondents were asked to indicate whether their firms utilize a central review committee. The responses to this "yes-no" question indicated that a great majority of the firms do: 76 of 101 respondents indicated that their firms utilize the committee, while the other 25 indicated they did not.

The respondents were asked to choose one of a number of possible areas to identify which division or department has the responsibility for analyzing capital expenditure proposals—Finance, Operations, Planning, or Production. The responses to this question are shown in Exhibit 6. Total responses (123) exceed the number of respondents, because a number of respondents picked more than one choice, since the responsibility for capital budgeting analysis in their firm was shared between two or more departments. Exhibit 6 clearly indicates that in the majority of firms the responsibility for analyzing capital budgeting projects is that of the Finance or Planning Departments.

EXHIBIT 6.   DIVISION OF DEPARTMENT RESPONSIBILITY

Division or Department	Responses	
	Number	Percent
Finance	74	60.2
Operations	16	13.0
Planning	30	24.4
Production	3	2.4
Total Responses	123	100.0

The capital budgeting process can be viewed as consisting of four stages: 1) project definition and estimation of cash flows; 2) project analysis and selection; 3) project implementation; and 4) project review. Exhibit 7 indicates that the *most difficult* aspect of the capital budgeting process involves defining projects and estimating their cash flows. This result is not surprising since specification of cash flows involves numerous forecasts and tax-related decisions. Since what is viewed as "most difficult" might not be considered "most important," the respondents were asked which stage of the capital budgeting process is most critical. The responses, also shown in Exhibit 7, indicate that project definition and estimation of cash flows is the *most critical* stage. These results confirm those of Fremgen [2, pp. 24–25] who in his 1973 study found

EXHIBIT 7.   MOST DIFFICULT AND MOST IMPORTANT STAGES OF CAPITAL BUDGETING PROCESS

Stage	Responses			
	Most Difficult		Most Critical	
	Number	Percent	Number	Percent
Project Definition and Cash Flow Estimation	65	64.3	53	52.0
Financial Analysis and Project Selection	15	14.9	34	33.3
Project Implementation	7	6.9	9	8.8
Project Review	14	13.9	6	5.9
Total Responses	101	100.0	102	100.0

that most firms believed that the definition and estimation of project cash flows were both the most difficult and most critical parts of the capital budgeting process.

CAPITAL BUDGETING TECHNIQUES

One of the goals of this study was to determine the capital budgeting techniques most commonly used by the nation's leading business firms: by comparing the findings with the results of previous studies, the progress of business firms toward the use of more sophisticated techniques was assessed. Another area of interest was the cost of capital or cutoff rate utilized by these firms.

Several capital budgeting techniques are available for use in evaluating projects. Net Present Value, Benefit/Cost Ratios (or Profitability Index), and the Internal Rate of Return (or Discounted Rate of Return) are quite "sophisticated," since they explicitly consider the value of money. Although there are numerous "unsophisticated" capital budgeting techniques, the best known are the Rate of Return (or Average Rate of Return) and the Payback Period. The respondents were asked to indicate the primary and secondary technique used, given a choice of the three sophisticated and two unsophisticated techniques mentioned. Their responses are summarized in Exhibit 8. From the total number of responses to the question on primary technique in use (112), it can be seen that some respondents consider more than one technique to be a primary tool.

EXHIBIT 8.   CAPITAL BUDGETING TECHNIQUES IN USE

Technique	Primary		Secondary	
	Number	Percent	Number	Percent
Internal (or Discounted) Rate of Return	60	53.6	13	14.0
Rate of Return (Average Rate of Return)	28	25.0	13	14.0
Net Present Value	11	9.8	24	25.8
Payback Period	10	8.9	41	44.0
Benefit/Cost Ratio (Profitability Index)	3	2.7	2	2.2
Total Responses	112	100.0	93	100.0

The results indicate a strong preference for sophisticated capital budgeting techniques as the primary tool of analysis, and the use of internal rate of return as the dominant technique, confirming the findings of Fremgen [2] and Petty, Scott, and Bird [8, pp. 162–165]. A 1972 study by Klammer [4, pp. 387–395] showed that the use of sophisticated techniques increased from 19 percent of the firms in 1959 to 38 percent in 1964, and to 57 percent in 1970. The 1973 study by Fremgen [2, pp. 20–22] also confirmed this trend. This study supports these earlier findings and suggests that the use of sophisticated techniques is continuing to increase (57 percent of firms in 1970, 66 percent of responses in 1976). Petty, Scott, and Bird [8, p. 170] also show that "almost one-half of the respondents expressed that the firm has moved to more quantitative and formal analysis."

Exhibit 8 indicates that the most popular secondary (or supplementary) technique used is the payback period. The popularity of this technique has prevailed for years. In Fremgen's 1973 study, the payback period was found to be the most popular technique. Although Fremgen did not specifically ask for secondary techniques, it is apparent from his study that the use of payback was secondary to the use of the internal rate of return as has been suggested by numerous authors such as Gitman [3, pp. 290–291]. The use of net present value as a supplementary technique was reported by nearly 26 percent of the respondents, but only 9.8% used it as a primary technique, which suggests that it is not utilized by most firms in a primary role but does find favor as a secondary tool of analysis.

Respondents were asked to indicate which of a number of possible cost of capital values best described that of their firm. The responses to this question are summarized in Exhibit 9. At the time they responded, most of the firms had a cost of capital of 10 to 15 percent or more. 83.1 percent of the firms had costs of capital between 10 and 20 percent. Although this finding does not enhance our knowledge of the techniques being used, it does provide a general idea about the requirements for project acceptance even though these findings may only apply to a particular point in time.

EXHIBIT 9.   COST OF CAPITAL OR CUTOFF RATE

| | Responses | |
Rate	Number	Percent
Less than 5%	0	0.0
5 to 10%	9	9.5
10 to 15%	57	60.0
15 to 20%	22	23.1
More than 20%	7	7.4
Total Responses	95	100.0

CAPITAL RATIONING

Respondents were asked to indicate "yes or no" on whether their firm made a competitive allocation of a *fixed* budget to competing projects. Of the 100 responses to this question, 52 indicated "yes" while the remaining 48 responded "no." Hence, about half of all large firms operate in a capital rationing environment in which they attempt to allocate a fixed budget on a competitive basis. The principal causes of capital rationing are presented in Exhibit 10. Nearly 70 percent of the respondents indicated that the major cause of capital rationing was a limit placed on borrowing by the internal management. This confirms the finding of Fremgen [2, pp. 23–24] who disclosed that "the most prevalent cause of capital rationing is a limitation on borrowing." When the other causes of borrowing limitations imposed by outside agreements (10.7 percent) or external management (3.2 percent) are added, the total of 83 percent suggests that capital rationing results from some type of debt limitation.

EXHIBIT 10.   MAJOR CAUSE OF CAPITAL RATIONING

Cause	Responses	
	Number	Percent
Debt Limit Imposed by Outside Agreement	10	10.7
Debt Limit Placed by Management External to the Organization	3	3.2
Limit Placed by Borrowing by Internal Management	65	69.1
Restrictive Policy Imposed upon Retained Earnings for Dividend Payout	2	2.1
Maintenance of a Target Earnings Per Share or Price-Earnings Ratio	14	14.9
Total Responses	94	100.0

RISK AND UNCERTAINTY

The final aspect of the capital budgeting process investigated was the treatment of risk and uncertainty. The literature of capital budgeting emphasizes the importance of giving some consideration to the differing risks associated with different projects. Two questions were included in the questionnaire on whether the firms explicitly consider risk and uncertainty, and, if so, what methods they use. Of 100 respondents, 71 percent indicated they gave explicit consideration to risk and uncertainty, while 29 percent said "no." This suggests that a great majority of large firms give explicit consideration to risk and uncertainty, and it confirms Fremgen's 1973 study [2, p. 22], which found 67 percent of the firms responding affirmatively.

The respondents were asked to indicate which of four possible techniques they used to adjust for risk and uncertainty and to indicate any other techniques used. Responses to the four choices are shown in Exhibit 11. Other responses included: sensitivity analysis, simulation, and risk models. A few respondents use more than one technique (103 responses from 100 respondents). The most popular technique (43 percent of responses) involves adjusting the minimum rate of return upward.

EXHIBIT 11. METHODS USED TO ADJUST FOR RISK AND UNCERTAINTY

Method	Responses	
	Number	Percent
Increase the Minimum Rate of Return or Cost of Capital	44	42.7
Use Expected Values of Cash Flows (Certainty-Equivalents)	27	26.2
Subjective Adjustment of Cash Flows	19	18.5
Decrease Minimum Payback Period	13	12.6
Total Responses	103	100.0

The popularity of the risk-adjusted rate of return is not surprising since it is one of the easiest approaches available for risk adjustment. Petty, Scott, and Bird [8, p. 170] recognized the use of this technique in their 1975 survey and contended that more sophisticated risk-adjustment techniques would not be employed until risk can be measured more precisely and one can show its effect on the firm's cost of capital. The second favored approach was expected values, and the third most popular technique was the subjective adjustment of cash flows. As one might expect from a reading of capital budgeting texts [1, 6, 9], the use of either risk-adjusted discount rates or certainty equivalents is quite common (approximately 69 percent of the responses) among the nation's leading business firms. These results again seem to confirm those of Fremgen [2, pp. 22–23], who found both of these techniques to be quite popular.

SUMMARY AND CONCLUSIONS

This article has presented the findings of a survey of capital budgeting techniques sent to a sample of 268 major companies experiencing high stock price growth and known to make large capital expenditures. Based upon the 103 usable responses received, the findings were analyzed on the basis of five major areas.

The first section presented basic statistics describing respondent firms. The second section on capital budgeting procedures disclosed that most firms have a central review committee which chooses proposals and that the responsibility for analysis normally is within the Finance or Planning Departments. The respondents also indicated that the most difficult and most important stage of the process involves the definition and estimation of cash flows. The third section showed that sophisticated techniques for primary analysis were most popular, particularly the internal rate of return. For secondary analysis, the use of the payback period was indicated by a large number of respondents. It was found that most firms at the time of the survey used costs of capital or cutoff rates of 10 to 20 percent; the majority of responses were in the 10 to 15 percent range. The fourth section showed that most firms make capital expenditures on a competitive basis to allocate a fixed budget. It was found that the major cause of capital rationing was a debt limit which was imposed internally by management. The final section found that most firms give explicit consideration to risk and uncertainty, and that the use of risk-adjusted discount rates and/or certainty equivalents to adjust for risk is quite popular.

In summary, it is evident that the major firms in the U.S. are utilizing many of the tools of analysis presented in the financial theory for analyzing capital budgeting projects. And, as indicated in previous studies (Fremgen [2] and Petty, Scott, and Bird [8]), firms are continuing to move forward in the adoption of more sophisticated tools of analysis.

REFERENCES

1. Harold Bierman, Jr., and Seymour Smidt, *The Capital Budgeting Decision,* 3rd ed., New York, Macmillan, 1971.
2. James M. Fremgen, "Capital Budgeting Practices: A Survey," *Management Accounting* (May 1973), pp. 19–25.
3. Lawrence J. Gitman, *Principles of Managerial Finance,* New York, Harper and Row, 1976, Ch. 13, 14.
4. Thomas Klammer, "Empirical Evidence of the Adoption of Sophisticated Capital Budgeting Techniques," *Journal of Business* (July 1972), pp. 387–397.
5. James C. T. Mao, "Survey of Capital Budgeting: Theory and Practice," *Journal of Finance* (May 1970), pp. 349–360.
6. Jerome Osteryoung, *Capital Budgeting: Long Term Asset Selection,* Columbus, Ohio, Grid, 1974.
7. J. William Petty and Oswald D. Bowlin, "The Financial Manager and Quantitative Decision Models," *Financial Management* (Winter 1976), pp. 32–41.
8. J. William Petty, David F. Scott, Jr., and Monroe M. Bird, "The Capital Expenditure Decision-Making Process of Large Corporations," *The Engineering Economist* (Spring 1975), pp. 159–172.
9. David G. Quirin, *The Capital Expenditure Decision,* Homewood, Illinois, Irwin, 1974.
10. Standard and Poor's, Inc., *Register of Corporations, Directors, and Executives,* Vol. 1, New York, Standard and Poor's, Inc., 1976.
11. "The 500 Biggest Corporations by Capital Expenditures," *Forbes* (May 15, 1970), pp. 111–118.
12. "Who's Where in the Stock Market," *Forbes* (January 1, 1976), pp. 186–206.

13. Ronald B. Williams, "Industry Practice in Allocating Capital Resources," *Managerial Planning* (May/June 1970), pp. 15–22.

QUESTIONS

1. Explain what is meant by capital rationing. Would you say that it is significant that 52 percent of the responding firms indicated that they do indeed ration capital? Why?
2. Explain what methods are used to consider risk or uncertainty by the firms in the sample.
3. What part of capital budgeting would be the most difficult for you if you were the financial manager of a firm? Is your answer consistent with those indicated by managers of the sample firms?

9 Peter W. Bacon

The Evaluation of Mutually Exclusive Investments

This article presents the differences in analytical treatment necessary in capital budgeting for mutually exclusive investments depending upon whether or not the firm rations capital. Recall from the previous article that 52 percent of the responding firms ration capital.

It is widely recognized that the two most commonly recommended measures of investment desirability—net present value (NPV) and internal rate of return (IRR)—can occasionally give conflicting signals regarding the relative ranking of mutually exclusive projects. Moreover, most textbook writers seem to agree that the source of the problem lies in differing assumptions regarding the rate at which cash flows will be reinvested.

Despite this general agreement, ambiguity persists regarding an appropriate solution to the problem. Although most authors imply that the NPV method is theoretically superior to the IRR method in dealing with the mutually exclusive problem, the most commonly recommended solution involves the specification of a reinvestment rate and the calculation of comparative terminal values rather than NPV's. The question of how to select an appropriate reinvestment rate has often been left to the reader's imagination.

It appears to be desirable, therefore, to demonstrate to students and practitioners alike that 1) computation of comparative terminal values is unnecessary because the NPV method, properly implemented, always ranks projects correctly, and 2) the choice of an appropriate discount (reinvestment) rate depends importantly upon assumptions of capital availability. If funds are not rationed, use of cost of capital as the discount (reinvestment) rate leads to theoretically correct decisions. In capital rationing situations, however, the decision maker must develop a discount (reinvestment) rate based upon internal investment opportunities.

MUTUALLY EXCLUSIVE PROBLEM

The nature of the problem can be demonstrated by means of a simple example. A firm whose cost of capital is 10% is considering two mutually exclusive

Source. Reprinted by permission from *Financial Management*, Summer 1977, pp. 55–58. Peter W. Bacon is professor of finance at Wright State University.

projects, A and B. Both projects cost $40,000, but project A provides cash flows of $20,000 each year for the next three years while project B generates no benefits until year 3 when $70,000 is received. Because of these timing differences, the IRR and NPV give conflicting rankings: $IRR_A \cong 23.4\% >$ $IRR_B \cong 20.5\%$. However, using a 10% discount rate, $NPV_A = \$9,737 <$ $NPV_B = \$12,592$.

TERMINAL VALUES

A widely recommended solution to the problem involves the calculation of comparative terminal values. Terminal values for each project under several reinvestment assumptions are presented in Exhibit 1, column 2. At reinvestment rates less than approximately 16%, project B has the higher terminal value. Higher reinvestment rates reverse the ranking.

EXHIBIT 1.   COMPARISON OF MUTUALLY EXCLUSIVE PROJECTS UNDER ALTERNATIVE REINVESTMENT ASSUMPTIONS

	(1) NPV at Assumed Discount (Reinvestment) Rate		(2) Terminal Value at Assumed Reinvestment Rate		(3) Net Terminal Value at Assumed Reinvestment Rate		(4) Present Value of Net Terminal Value at Assumed Reinvestment Rate	
Rate	A	B	A	B	A	B	A	B
10%	$9,737	$12,592	$66,200	$70,000	$12,560	$16,760	$9,737	$12,592
16%	$4,918	$ 4,846	$70,112	$70,000	$ 7,676	$ 7,564	$4,918	$ 4,846
18%	$3,486	$ 2,604	$71,448	$70,000	$ 5,726	$ 4,278	$3,486	$ 2,604

Exhibit 1 also extends the concept of terminal value to one of net terminal value (NTV). The NTV approach explicitly accounts for any differences in initial cash outlays by subtracting the terminal value of the outlays (computed by compounding at the reinvestment rate) from the terminal value of the inflows.

Comparison of columns 1 and 3 implies that the NPV and NTV approaches consistently lead to identical conclusions; *i.e.*, the project with the highest NTV always has the highest NPV. Moreover, when the present value of the NTV (PVNTV) is computed (Exhibit 1, column 4) the numerical answer is identical to that produced by the NPV method, assuming that the same rate is used in either calculation. Thus, it would appear that calculation of NTV or PVNTV is unnecessary. Instead, the analyst need only calculate NPV using the assumed reinvestment rate as the discount rate.

TERMINAL VALUE VERSUS PRESENT VALUE

The equivalence of the NPV, NTV, and PVNTV approaches can be demonstrated symbolically as follows:

$$NTV = \sum_{t=0}^{n} B_t(1 + r)^{n-t} - \sum_{t=0}^{n} 0_t(1 + r)^{n-t}$$

where B_t = net cash benefits at end of year t,
      n = life of the longest lived project,
      r = reinvestment rate,
      0_t = net cash outflows in year t.
  Dividing each side of the equation by $(1 + r)^n$ yields

$$\frac{NTV}{(1 + r)^n} = \sum_{t=0}^{n} \frac{B_t}{(1 + r)^t} - \sum_{t=0}^{n} \frac{0_t}{(1 + r)^t}.$$

The right hand side of the equation is, of course, the familiar NPV calculation. The left hand side represents the PVNTV. Thus, the project with the highest NPV will always have the highest NTV and PVNTV provided the same rate used to compute terminal values is also used to compute present values. The appendix demonstrates that these conclusions hold even when the reinvestment rate changes over time.

CHOICE OF DISCOUNT RATE

The previous section indicated that the choice of reinvestment rate is critical to the proper implementation of the NPV method since the reinvestment rate must be used as the discount rate when calculating NPV. The selection of an appropriate reinvestment rate, in turn, depends importantly on assumptions regarding the availability of capital. If sufficient capital is available to undertake all projects for which return exceeds the cost of capital, the appropriate reinvestment rate is in fact the future cost of capital. This is true despite the fact that the firm may be earning a return greater than the cost of capital.

To better understand this key point, return to the earlier example. Further assume that if project A is selected, its benefits will be reinvested at 18%, generating a NTV of $5,726, and a NPV and PVNTV of $3,486. Since these values exceed those of project B using an 18% reinvestment or discount rate, it appears, at first blush, that project A is preferred.

Notice, however, that if funds are *not* rationed, project A's interim cash flows merely reduce the amount of new external financing requirements in future years; the firm could undertake identical future incremental investments by investing in project B today (rather than A), and raising $20,000 externally at the end of years 1-3. Thus, reinvestment of project A's cash flows saves the firm the cost of a comparable amount of externally raised capital. Therefore, the relevant reinvestment rate is the cost of capital.

A comparison of these two alternative courses of action is presented in Exhibit 2, which assumes an external cost of capital of 10% and a marginal rate of return on internal investments of 18%. Clearly, alternative B would generate greater terminal wealth for shareholders than alternative A, and is, therefore, the preferred approach. Notice also that the difference in the two terminal values is $3,800—the same difference that resulted when a 10% reinvestment rate was assumed in Exhibit 1, column 2. Finally, observe that the difference in the present values of the two terminal values is $2,855—a result that is identical to the one obtained when the NPV method was employed using 10% as the discount rate (see Exhibit 1, column 1).

The important conclusion is that when capital is not rationed, cost of capital is in fact the reinvestment rate, even though the firm's cut-off rate exceeds the cost of capital. The fact that one project generates more cash flows in any given year simply means that less capital will have to be raised. Thus the reinvestment rate is equivalent to capital costs saved, *i.e.,* the cost of capital, and a comparison of the NPV's using cost of capital as the discount rate yields the correct answer.

EXHIBIT 2. COMPARISON OF MUTUALLY EXCLUSIVE COURSES OF ACTION

Alternative A	
Terminal value of investment in Project A and reinvesting cash flow at 18% internally	$71,448
Alternative B	
Terminal value of investment in Project B (no reinvestment)	$70,000
Plus—Terminal value of investing $20,000 per year internally at 18% (funds obtained from external financing)	71,448
Minus—Terminal value of external financing of $20,000 per year at 10%	(66,200)
Terminal value of Project B	$75,248
Terminal value advantage of Project B ($75,248 − 71,448) =	$3,800
Present value of terminal value advantage of Project B (at 10%)	$2,855

CAPITAL RATIONING

If capital is severely rationed, however, the acceptance of project A may permit the acceptance of future projects that would not or could not be undertaken if project B were selected. In this case, the analyst must determine the rate of return on these future marginal projects and use this rate as the discount rate. If, in the previous example, acceptance of project A permits investments of $20,000 to be undertaken in each of the next three years that would otherwise be foregone, the return on those investments should serve as the discount rate. If that rate exceeds 16%, project A is preferred. Lower rates favor project B.

Unfortunately, this simple example belies the complexity of determining the future reinvestment rate in capital rationing situations. Technically, the correct discount (reinvestment) rate cannot be determined until an optimal selection of current and future projects has been made. The optimal solution, in turn, depends upon the discount (reinvestment) rate employed. Thus, mathematical programming is usually required to arrive at optimal solutions.

As a practical matter, however, satisfactory results are likely to be obtained by using the expected mean return on the firm's total capital budget as the discount rate when ranking mutually exclusive projects under capital rationing [2]. In fact, it should be recognized that correct decisions can be made without *precise* knowledge of the future reinvestment rate. Graphing the NPV's for each project under a variety of reinvestment rate assumptions will reveal the *range* of rates at which one project is superior to the other. The decision maker can then estimate whether or not the future reinvestment rate will fall within that range.

CONCLUSIONS

The purpose of this paper is to clear up some of the ambiguities that surround the problem of choosing between mutually exclusive projects. Theoretically correct decisions will always arise by proper implementation of the NPV method. In the case of capital rationing, the discount rate must reflect the internal investment opportunities of the firm. If capital is not rationed, however, cost of capital is the relevant reinvestment rate and should be used as the discount factor in NPV calculations.

REFERENCES

1. R. Conrad Doenges, "The Reinvestment Problem in a Practical Perspective," *Financial Management* (Spring 1972), pp. 85–90.
2. Carlton L. Dudley, Jr., "A Note on Reinvestment Assumptions in Choosing

Between Net Present Value and Internal Rate of Return," *Journal of Finance* (September 1972), pp. 907–915.
3.   James C. Van Horne, *Financial Management and Policy*, 4th edition, Englewood Cliffs, Prentice-Hall, Inc., 1977.
4.   J. Fred Weston and Eugene F. Brigham, *Managerial Finance*, 5th edition, Hinsdale, Dryden Press, 1975.

Appendix

If the reinvestment rate is expected to change over time, NTV would be computed as follows:

$$NTV = \sum_{t=1}^{n} C_t \prod_{j=t+1}^{n} (1 + r_j)$$

where C_t = cash flow at end of period t, and
$\quad\quad r_j$ = reinvestment rate during period j.
Dividing each side of the equation by

$$\prod_{j=1}^{n} (1 + r_j)$$

produces

$$\frac{NTV}{\prod\limits_{j=1}^{n} (1 + r_j)} = \sum_{t=0}^{n} C_t \prod_{j=1}^{t} \frac{1}{(1 + r_j)}.$$

For example, let $C_0 = -\$20,000$, $C_1 = \$10,000$, $C_2 = \$10,000$, $C_3 = \$10,000$, $r_1 = .10$, $r_2 = .15$, and $r_3 = .2$.

$$NTV = (-\$20,000)\,(1.1)\,(1.15)\,(1.2) + (\$10,000)\,(1.15)\,(1.12)$$

$$+ (\$10,000)\,(1.2) + \$10,000 = \$5,440$$

and

$$\frac{NTV}{\prod\limits_{j=1}^{n} (1 + r_j)} = \frac{\$5,440}{(1.1)\,(1.15)\,(1.12)} = \$3,583.66 = PVNPV.$$

More conventionally:

$$\text{NPV} = \frac{-\$20,000}{(1)} + \frac{\$10,000}{(1)\,(1.1)} + \frac{\$10,000}{(1)\,(1.1)\,(1.15)}$$

$$+ \frac{\$10,000}{(1)\,(1.1)\,(1.15)\,(1.2)} = \$3,583.66.$$

QUESTIONS

1. Explain what is meant if Projects A and B are independent versus being mutually exclusive.
2. If the firm does not ration capital, what, conceptually, is the best estimate of the firm's reinvestment rate? Explain.
3. If the firm does ration capital, what do you propose as a good way to estimate the firm's rate of return on reinvestment?
4. The author of this article showed that reinvestment rates would differ if the firm did or did not ration capital. Refer to the previous article, and indicate what percentage of large firms ration capital. Generate a hypothesis as to the seriousness of capital rationing as the firm size decreases. Explain the reasons for your hypothesis.

10 | James C. Van Horne
A Note on Biases in Capital Budgeting Introduced by Inflation

Professor Van Horne shows that if inflation is properly estimated and used in projecting future cash flows then no biases exist due to inflation. The reason for this is that expected inflation will impact both the future cash flows and the cost of capital. However, if inflation is not properly recognized in both the forecasts and the cost of capital, biases will appear in capital budgeting analyses.

In the allocation of capital to investment projects, it is unlikely that optimal decisions will be reached unless anticipated inflation is embodied in the cash-flow estimates. Often, there is a tendency to assume that price levels remain unchanged throughout the life of the project. Frequently this assumption is imposed unknowingly; future cash flows are estimated simply on the basis of existing prices. However, a bias arises in that the cost-of-capital rate used as the acceptance criterion embodies an element attributable to anticipated inflation, while the cash-flow estimates do not. Although this bias may not be serious when there is modest inflation, it may become quite important in periods of high anticipated inflation. The purpose of this note is to investigate the nature of the bias and how it arises.

I. COST-OF-CAPITAL RATE

Consider a situation in which the cost-of-capital rate is used as the hurdle rate for project selection and there is no capital rationing. If a project meets the acceptance criterion, capital is available to finance it at the cost-of-capital rate. Suppose, also, that the acceptance of any investment project or group of projects will not alter the risk complexion of the firm as a whole. Finally, assume for simplicity that the firm has a capital structure consisting entirely of equity. Actually, the implications for the problem at hand are the same if debt is artially employed.

There is general agreement that security prices depend not on past changes

Source. Reprinted by permission from *Journal of Financial and Quantitative Analysis*, January 1971, pp. 653–658. James C. Van Horne is A. P. Giannini Professor of Finance at Stanford University.

in prices, but on future anticipated ones.[1] Inflation is defined as a rise in the general level of prices for goods and services, which in turn results in a decline in the purchasing power of a unit of money. While there is disagreement as to what index is most representative of purchasing power,[2] we bypass this problem and assume that a single index exists that portrays effectively the general price level at various moments in time. The anticipated rate of inflation is defined as the expected annual rate of change in this index. For simplicity, we assume that this rate is the same for all future periods.

Generally, the market value of a share of common stock is considered to be the present value of all expected future dividends, discounted at a required rate of return, k, determined by the market. Thus,

$$P_0 = \sum_{t=1}^{\infty} \frac{D_t}{(1 + k)^t} \tag{1}$$

where: P_0 = market price per share at time 0, and
D_t = the dividend expected by investors at the margin to be paid at the end of the period t.
For the continuous case, equation (1) becomes:

$$P_0 = \int_0^{\infty} D_t e^{-kt} dt. \tag{2}$$

In the case of an all-equity capital structure, the required rate of return, k, becomes the cost of capital. This rate can be thought of as being comprised of two parts:

$$k = i + \theta, \tag{3}$$

where: i = the risk-free rate, and
θ = a risk premium to compensate investors for the uncertainty associated with their receiving the expected stream of dividends.
If the corporation were expected to exist in perpetuity, i might be represented by the current yield on a perpetual default-free bond.[3] As the rate is expressed

---

[1] See Irving Fisher, *The Theory of Interest* (New York: The MacMillan Company, 1930), Chapter 2, from which most of the work on yields and inflation stems.
[2] See Martin Bronfenbrenner and Franklyn D. Holzman, "Survey of Inflation Theory," *American Economic Review*, LIII (September 1963), pp. 597–99.
[3] We assume that no call feature exists on the instrument and that investors pay no taxes on dividends and capital gains.

in nominal terms, embodied in it is an element attributable to anticipated inflation from time 0 into perpetuity. Whether this element corresponds exactly to the rate of anticipated inflation, as denoted by changes in the price index, depends upon the preference functions of investors relative to the price index employed.[4]

II. ESTIMATING CASH FLOWS

Having affirmed that anticipated inflation is embraced in the acceptance criterion—namely, the cost of capital, k—it is important to consider its impact on the project itself. The expected cash flows of a project are affected by anticipated inflation in several ways.[5] If cash inflows arise ultimately from the sale of a product, these inflows are affected by expected future prices. As for cash outflows, inflation affects both expected future wages and material costs. Note that future inflation does not affect depreciation charges on the asset. Once the asset is acquired, these charges are known with certainty.[6] The effect of anticipated inflation on cash inflows and cash outflows will vary with the nature of the project. In some cases, cash inflows, through price increases, will rise faster than cash outflows; while in other cases the opposite will hold. This phenomenon has given rise to the famous controversy of whether or not wages lag behind prices in times of inflation so that real wages decline and real profits increase.[7]

With the recognition of inflation, estimates of expected future cash flows must be modified to take account of the anticipated rate of inflation. One way is to adjust estimates made under an assumption of no future inflation by an

[4] In one study, Robert Mundell, "Inflation and Real Interest," *Journal of Political Economy*, LXXI (June 1963), pp. 280–83, contends that nominal rates of interest may contain less than the full rate of anticipated inflation. The reason is that inflation may influence wealth variables in such a manner as to lower the real rate of interest.

[5] Again, it is important to stress that we have assumed that the acceptance of the project does not alter the risk complexion of the firm as a whole.

[6] For further analysis of this point, see Brian Motley, "Inflation and Common Stock Values: Comment," *Journal of Finance*, XXIV (June 1969), pp. 530–35.

[7] Bronfenbrenner and Holzman, "Inflation Theory," pp. 647–49; R. A. Kessel and A. A. Alchian, "The Meaning and Validity of the Inflation-Induced Lag of Wages Behind Prices," *American Economic Review*, L (March 1960), pp. 43–66; G. L. Bach and Albert Ando, "The Redistributional Effects of Inflation," *Review of Economics and Statistics*, XXXIX (February 1957), pp. 1–13; and Thomas F. Cargill, "An Empirical Investigation of the Wage-Lag Hypothesis," *American Economic Review*, LIX (December 1969), pp. 806–16.

inflation adjustment factor. The net-present value of a project then could be determined by:

$$NPV_0 = \sum_{t=1}^{n} \frac{[I_t(1 + \alpha\Gamma)^t - O_t(1 + \beta\Gamma)^t][1 - T] + F_tT}{(1 + k)^t} - C_0 \qquad (4)$$

where: NPV_0 = the expected value of net-present value of the project at time 0,

n = final period in which cash flows are expected,

I_t = expected value of cash inflow in period t in the absence of future inflation,

Γ = anticipated rate of inflation as denoted by expected annual rate of change in the price index,

α = portion of Γ applicable to cash inflows,

O_t = expected value of cash outflows in period t in the absence of future inflation,

β = portion of Γ applicable to cash outflows,

T = corporate tax rate,

F_t = depreciation charges on the asset in period t, which are known with certainty, and

C_0 = cost of project at time 0, which is assumed to be known with certainty.

The values α and β represent the expected sensitivity of cash inflows and outflows to inflation, assuming this sensitivity is invariant with respect to t. If the latter assumption does not hold, α and β can be made to vary with t. Added sophistication (in equation (4)) can be achieved by breaking down the cash inflows and cash outflows into individual components. For example, we might subdivide cash outflows into wages and material costs and calculate the sensitivity of each to Γ. If the project is expected to have a salvage value, the effect of inflation on this value must be recognized explicitly.

If a project has a net-present value greater than zero, as depicted by equation (4), it provides an inflation-adjusted return greater than that required by investors at the margin. As a result, its acceptance should result in a higher market price per share.[8]

The real problem, of course, is not in specifying an equation to deal with the impact of inflation, but in estimating the inputs that go into it. In some measure, price expectations appear to be related to past changes in price. Moreover, these expectations seem to be based more heavily on recent past price behavior than upon more distant past price behavior. Several empirical

---

[8] For the logic behind this statement, see James C. Van Horne, *Financial Management and Policy* (Englewood Cliffs, N.J.: Prentice-Hall, Inc., 1968), p. 130.

studies have documented these relationships.[9] If some weighted average of past changes in prices can be used to predict future changes, Γ in equation (4) can be estimated. Estimates of the expected sensitivity of cash inflows and outflows to Γ are best based upon past relationships between cash flows and actual inflation for similar types of projects. While we do not wish to belittle the difficulties associated with these estimates, our principal purpose is to point out the bias that arises if expected inflation is not incorporated in the cash-flow estimates for an investment project.

To illustrate this bias, assume that a project which cost $100,000 at time 0 was under consideration and was expected to provide cash-flow benefits over the next 5 years. Assume further straight-line depreciation and a corporate tax rate of 50 per cent. Suppose that cash flows were estimated on the basis of price levels at time 0, with no consideration to the effect of future inflation upon them, and that these estimates were:[10]

	Period				
	1	2	3	4	5
Expected cash inflow	$30,000	$40,000	$50,000	$50,000	$30,000
Expected cash outflow	10,000	10,000	10,000	10,000	10,000
	20,000	30,000	40,000	40,000	20,000
Times 1—tax rate	.50	.50	.50	.50	.50
	10,000	15,000	20,000	20,000	10,000
Depreciation · tax rate	10,000	10,000	10,000	10,000	10,000
Net cash flow	$20,000	$25,000	$30,000	$30,000	$20,000

If the firm's measured cost of capital were 12 per cent, the net-present value of the project would be −$3,192. As this figure is negative, the project would be rejected.

However, the results are biased in the sense that the discount rate embodies an element attributable to anticipated future inflation, whereas the cash flow estimates do not. Suppose that the existing rate of inflation, as measured by changes in the price-level index, were 5 per cent, and that this rate was expected to prevail over the next 5 years. If both cash inflows and cash outflows were expected to increase at this rate, the net-present value of the project would be:

---

[9] See Phillip Cagan, "The Monetary Dynamics of Hyperinflation," in Milton Friedman, ed., *Studies in the Quantity Theory of Money* (Chicago: University of Chicago Press, 1956), pp. 23–117; and William E. Gibson, "Price-Expectations Effects on Interest Rates," *Journal of Finance*, XXV (March 1970), pp. 19–34.

[10] Again, we have assumed that selection of the project will not affect the risk complexion of the firm as a whole.

$$NPV_0 = \sum_{t=1}^{5} \frac{[I_t (1.05)^t - O_t (1.05)^t] [.5] + 20,000_t [.5]}{(1.12)^t} - 100,000 \qquad (5)$$

$$= \$5,450.$$

Because the net-present value is positive, the project would be acceptable now, whereas before it was not. To reject it under the previous method of estimating cash flows would result in an opportunity loss to stockholders, for the project provides a return in excess of that required by investors at the margin.

The example serves to illustrate the importance of taking anticipated inflation into account explicitly when estimating future cash flows. Too often, there is a tendency not to consider its effect in these estimates. Because anticipated inflation is embodied in the required rate of return, not to take account of it in the cash-flow estimates will result in a biased appraisal of the project and, in turn, the possibility of a less than optimal allocation of capital. While our example has been framed in terms of a project whose acceptance does not alter the risk complexion of the firm, anticipated inflation can and should be recognized when this assumption is relaxed.[11]

QUESTIONS

1. Explain why, if the rate of inflation were expected to increase future cash flows, the cost of both debt and equity (and hence the cost of capital) would be expected to be high to account for this inflation.
2. Would your analysis be unbiased if you correctly anticipated inflation and built it into your future cash flow estimation, but the market had not yet anticipated inflation so your cost of capital was low? Explain.
3. Explain why in periods of inflation your analyses would tend to be biased downward against projects if you did not incorporate price increases into cash flow estimations.

---

[11] If expected cash flows are expressed as a probability tree reflecting series of conditional probabilities over time, each possible future cash flow should embody an assumption with respect to the rate of future inflation. This rate should be treated as stochastic. The project then could be evaluated according to the expected value of net-present value and the standard deviation of the probability distribution of possible net-present values, where the risk-free rate is used as the discount factor. This risk-return approach can be extended to handle the marginal impact of a project on the expected value and standard deviation of the probability distribution of net-present values for the firm as a whole. See James C. Van Horne, "The Analysis of Uncertainty Resolution in Capital Budgeting for New Products," *Management Science,* 15 (April 1969), pp. 376–82.

11

O. Maurice Joy and Jerry O. Bradley*

A Note on Sensitivity Analysis of Rates of Return

One method for dealing with uncertainty in capital budgeting analysis is to compute rates of return (IRR) or net present values (NPV) under various possible outcomes of the uncertain variable(s). Thus, for given forecasting errors of such variables as sales, one can generate information on the magnitude of error in the decision variable IRR or NPV. The authors perform sensitivity analyses on several variables, then show how sensitive the IRR is to changes in these variables.

In a specific analysis, a sensitivity study may show that a highly uncertain variable such as asset life is not important because, within the range of possible outcomes, it does not seriously influence the rate of return. On the other hand, uncertainty in other variables— for example, sales—may produce a very large variation in rate of return. Where the NPV or IRR are highly sensitive to variations in the uncertain variable, the analyst may wish to spend time and money to secure better information on this critical variable.

I. INTRODUCTION

Capital budgeting theory is founded on discounted cash flow techniques. The most pervasive capital budgeting problem is the single project accept-reject decision. Under *certainty*, the firm would accept the project if its net present value, using the riskless interest rate, were positive, or equivalently, if the project's internal rate of return exceeded the riskless interest rate.[1] Under

Source. Reprinted by permission from *Journal of Finance*, December 1973, pp. 1255–1261. The authors are in the Finance Department at the University of Kansas.

* The authors acknowledge the comments of Frank Reilly and John Tollefson on an earlier draft of this paper.

[1] It is well known that the internal rate of return will lead to erroneous or ambiguous decisions under certain conditions. However, for a very commonplace class of cash flow patterns such that the internal rate of return is finite and unique, and *initial* cash flows are outflows, followed by cash

uncertainty (where uncertainty and risk have coincidental meanings) the single project accept-reject investment decision is analogously evaluated: the firm would accept the project if the net present value of the expected cash flows, using a discount rate that reflects the degree of risk inherent in the project, were positive. Alternatively, the project would be accepted if its expected internal rate of return exceeded its risk adjusted cost of capital.[2]

It has often been suggested that capital budgeting theory has overemphasized the development of such techniques with little regard for the typically poor data used in project evaluation and the effect that errors in capital budgeting inputs have on project profitability. Some recent studies have investigated this question. Solomon [7] and House [3] investigated sensitivity analysis on an *ad hoc* basis and Huefner ([1] and [2]) recently investigated the sensitivity of present value to input data errors in a more general and systematic fashion.[3]

The purpose of this paper is to further study the sensitivity question, adding generality where possible. Like the Solomon study we investigate the sensitivity of the after-tax internal rate of return to input errors; however, our analyses and consequently our inferences are more general. He reported the effect of errors in pre-tax cash flows, assuming straight line depreciation and a constant tax rate, while we evaluate the effect of errors in *post* tax cash flows.[4] Our study is more closely related to the Huefner studies, the primary differences being that we investigate the sensitivity of internal rates of return rather than present value and we concentrate more on the *relative* importance of alternative input errors and the effect that the *levels* of the capital budgeting variables have on project profitability sensitivity.

II. ERRORS IN CAPITAL BUDGETING INPUTS

The internal rate of return is that discount rate that equates the net present value of all cash flows to zero. Assuming discrete cash flows with only one net cash outflow, the initial investment,[5] this may be mathematically stated as:

---

inflows, the internal rate of return will correctly resolve the accept-reject decision. In addition, the internal rate of return apparently is more widely understood by corporate practitioners (see Mao [4]).

[2] For a detailed exposition see Tuttle and Litzenberger [8]. For a contrary position see Robichek and Meyers [5], who advocate discounting certainty equivalent cash flows at the riskless interest rate rather than using risk adjusted discount rates.

[3] In a different content, Sarnat and Levy [6] have investigated the relationship between the internal rate of return and some investment rules of thumb.

[4] This change is not made without cost. Errors in pre-tax cash flows are conceptually easier to posit since they are the cash flow stream that is directly estimated. Our cash flows may alternatively be thought of as a pre-tax cash flows if the internal rate of return is also designated as a pre-tax internal rate of return.

[5] That is, a *point* outflow, *stream* of inflows pattern.

$$-c_0 + \sum_{t=1}^{n} \frac{c_t}{(1 + r)^t} = 0,$$ (1)

where

c_0 = expected initial investment,

c_t = expected cash inflow in period t,

n = expected project life,

r = expected internal rate of return.

The definitions of the variables in equation (1) reflect that they are *expected* or *estimated* quantities, not generally known with certainty.

Now the *actual* or realized (but *ex ante* unknown) rate of return on the project will be found from the following equation:

$$-c_0^* + \sum_{t=1}^{n^*} \frac{c_t^*}{(1 + r^*)^t} = 0,$$ (2)

where

c_0^* = actual initial investment,

c_t^* = actual cash flow in period t,

n^* = actual project life,

r^* = actual internal rate of return.

These quantities are distinguished from their counterparts in (1) in that they are the realized results that are generally unknown until the project is completed. We are interested in analyzing the effect of discrepancies between expected and realized input data on the difference between expected and realized rates of return. We will analyze a fairly broad class of projects characterized by constant percentage declining cash flows.

III. CONSTANT PERCENTAGE DECLINING CASH FLOWS

For a cash inflow pattern that declines at a constant per cent per period,[6] the expected (actual) cash inflow in any period, c_t (c_t^*), may be expressed as a

---

[6] A special member of the constant percentage declining cash flow family is the constant cash flow case, where the decline rate equals zero.

function of the expected (actual) cash inflow in period one and the expected (actual) per period decline rate. That is:

$$c_t = c_1(1 - d)^{t-1} \qquad t = 1, \ldots, n$$

and,

$$c_t^* = c_1^*(1 - d^*)^{t-1} \qquad t = 1, \ldots, n$$

where

c_1 = expected cash inflow in period one,

d = expected percentage decline rate of cash flow per period, a constant $(0 \leq d \leq 1.00)$,

c_1^* = actual cash inflow in period one,

d^* = actual percentage decline rate of cash flow per period, a constant $(0 \leq d^* \leq 1.00)$.

Inserting these definitions of c_t and c_t^* into equations (1) and (2), and dividing through each question by its initial investment (to put cash inflows on a per dollar of initial investment basis) yields:

$$-1 + \frac{c_1}{c_0} \sum_{t=1}^{n} \frac{(1 - d)^{t-1}}{(1 + r)^t} = 0 \qquad (3)$$

$$-1 + \frac{c_1^*}{c_0^*} \sum_{t=1}^{n^*} \frac{(1 - d^*)^{t-1}}{(1 + r^*)^t} = 0. \qquad (4)$$

Equations (3) and (4) are reformulations of (1) and (2) where cash flows decline at a constant per cent per year and are independent of the absolute size of the initial investment, as the cash flow coefficients c_1/c_0 and c_1^*/c_0^* respectively represent the size of the expected and actual cash flow in period one relative to the original investment.

Now define:[7]

$$k_c = \% \text{ error in cash flow coefficient} = \frac{c_1^*/c_0^* - c_1/c_0}{c_1/c_0}$$

---

[7] A *positive* error in an input variable is defined to be one that causes $r^* > r$, that is $k_r > 0$. A *negative* error is an input variable causes $r^* < r$ and $k_r < 0$. Positive (negative) errors in life and cash flow coefficient are thus the result of underestimating (overestimating) n and c_1/c_0, but positive (negative) errors in decline rates are caused by overestimating (underestimating) d.

$$k_n = \% \text{ error in project life} = \frac{n^* - n}{n}$$

$$k_d = \% \text{ error in decline rate} = \frac{d - d^*}{d}$$

$$k_r = \% \text{ error in internal rate of return} = \frac{r^* - r}{r}$$

and (4) may be restated as:

$$-1 + \frac{c_1(1 + k_c)}{c_0} \sum_{t=1}^{n(1 + k_n)} \frac{[1 - d(1 - k_d)]^{t-1}}{[1 + r(1 + k_r)]^t} = 0. \tag{5}$$

Equations (3) and (5) may be used to perform a sensitivity analysis on the internal rate of return. Equation (3) may be used to establish the levels of c_1/c_0, n, d and r. Then the sensitivity of r to errors in these input variables may be measured by choosing a representative range of percentage error terms (k_d, k_n and k_d) and determining k_r from equation (5). There are an infinite number of combinations of c_1/c_0, n, d and r that could be analyzed, but we have chosen to restrict the analysis to sample points that are representative of a broad class of capital investment projects.

The majority of capital budgeting projects are probably in the 10–20% rate of return range and the choice of 5, 10 and 20 year lives in very representative of the range of most project lives. Decline rates of 10% and 50% were chosen as representative decline rates.[8] The descriptive dimensions of our analysis are portrayed by the following (arbitrary) terms:[9]

Rate of return: low (10%)—high (20%)

Live: short (5 years)—moderate (10 years)—long (20 years)

Decline rate: small (10%)—large (50%).

Taking all possible combinations of these three parameters establishes twelve points around which we will investigate the sensitivity of r to errors in c_1/c_0, n and d.[10] There is no theoretical limit to the range of possible error values, but we have chosen to restrict the analysis to errors of $\pm 50\%$. Figure 1 is a graphical representation of the sensitivity of r errors in the three input variables, depicting

[8] We also investigated but do not report, the 0% and 30% decline rate cases.

[9] These terms are qualitatively descriptive of the parameter ranges in the study but, obviously, may not be as descriptive for certain companies or industries.

[10] Fixing (choosing) r, n and d establishes the level of c_1/c_0.

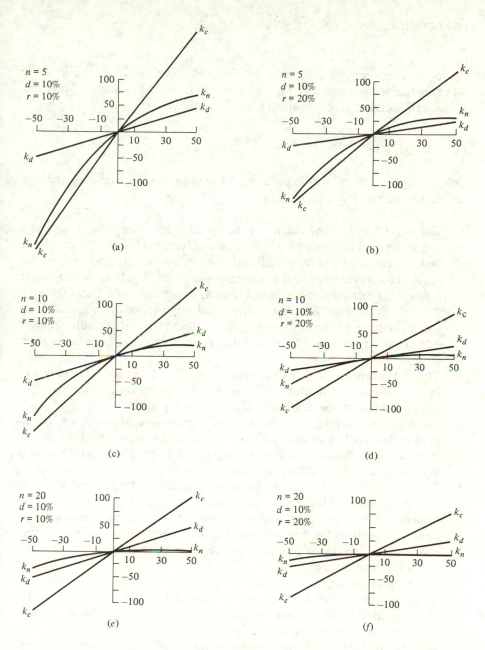

Figure 1. $k_r - vs - k_c$, k_d, and k_n. k_r is measured on the vertical axis; k_c, k_d, and k_n are measured on the horizontal axis. All k's are in percent units.

the results of a computer analysis of the values of k_r induced by k_c, k_n and k_d for six of the twelve sample points. Figure 1 contains all the 10% decline results and is illustrative of the results obtained from the analysis.

IV.   RESULTS

Other things equal and within the range of parameter values investigated, the sensitivity analysis indicates that:

1.   The larger (smaller) the magnitude of the error in either c_1/c_0, n or d, the larger (smaller) the resultant error in rate of return. This result is intuitive, underscoring that the functional relationship between k_r and each of the three causal percentage errors is monotonic increasing. But, for long lived projects the relationship between k_r and k_n flattens out (see F in Figure 1).

2.   It's difficult to generalize about the *relative* importance of k_c, k_d and k_n as the magnitude of the error increases or decreases. The result appears dependent on the *level* of the variables c_1/c_0, d and n and the *sign* of the error.

3.   The higher (lower) the rate of return the less (more) sensitive it is to errors in c_1/c_0, n or d.[11] (This and #4 below may be seen by comparing right and left hand sides of the sensitivity diagrams in Figure 1).

4.   The higher (lower) the rate of return, the more (less) sensitive it is to errors in cash flow coefficient and decline rate *relative* to life errors. That is, as r increases, cash flow errors (k_c and k_d are two different kinds of such errors) become more important relative to errors in life.

5.   The longer (shorter) the life, the less (more) sensitive rate of return is to cash flow coefficient and life errors, but the more (less) sensitive rate of return is to decline rate errors. (This and #6 below may be seen by scanning down either the right or left hand side of Figure 1.) Note also the severe magnification or leveraging of errors induced in r by negative errors in c_1/c_0 and n for short lived projects.

6.   The longer (shorter) the life, the more (less) sensitive rate of return is to cash flow coefficient and decline rate errors *relative* to life errors. For all moderate and long-lived project results, the effect of *positive* errors in either dimension of cash flow is more potent than comparable positive errors in life. The same is true for the effect of *negative* errors for all long-lived project types.

7.   The higher (lower) the decline rate, the more (less) sensitive rate of return is to cash flow coefficient and decline rate errors, but the less (more) sensitive rate of return is to life errors. (This and #8 below are not shown on Figure 1 which has only 10% decline rate points).

---

[11] This and other generalizations that relate to rate of return are further substantiated by unreported observations with $r = 40\%$.

8. The higher (lower) the decline rate, the more (less) sensitive rate of return is to cash flow coefficient and decline rate errors *relative* to life errors. For decline rates of 30% or more, either kind of cash flow error is always more crucial than life errors.

V.   CONCLUSIONS

For *most* instances where errors are within $\pm 50\%$, errors in estimating cash flows (k_c and k_d) induce larger resultant errors in rate of return than do equal size errors in life. There are exceptions: when project life is ten years or less, life errors can become the predominant factor, but over the range of rates of return, lives, cash flow coefficients and decline rates covered by this study, rate of return is generally more sensitive to cash flow errors. This implies that cash flow predictions are the more crucial aspect of the capital budgeting estimation problem and that downside errors in cash flow estimation will not generally be compensated by equal upside life errors.[12]

Errors in rates of return are linearly related to cash flow errors, but are not linearly related to life errors. Consequently, while equal absolute valued positive and negative cash flow errors induce proportionate positive and negative rate of return errors, this is not so for life errors: the errors are more pronounced on the negative side. Alternatively stated, rate of return is more sensitive to downside life errors than upside ones.

Holding the magnitude of the input errors constant, as expected rate of return increases, the magnitude of the induced percentage errors in rate of return *decreases*. Thus, projects that offer relatively large expected rates of return are *less* sensitive to errors in cash flow and life than are projects with relatively small expected returns. This is counter-intuitive and implies that the uncertainty surrounding the capital budgeting parameters for marginal projects may be greater than for projects with higher expected rates of return.[13]

Other things equal, rate of return errors are largest when projects are short lived. This, together with the asymmetric $k_r - k_n$ function, indicates that short projects are potentially very risky.[14] This contradicts the concept of using payback as a risk screening device since payback criteria tend to favor short lived projects.

[12] For long lived projects with high rates of return, errors in life of up to $\pm 50\%$ are usually of little consequence. In particular, for such projects there is little serendipity from underestimating project lives.

[13] This presumes, of course, that the accuracy of estimation of input parameters is independent of the expected level of return.

[14] This conclusion assumes that the magnitudes of the errors of estimation are independent of project life, which implies that cash flows in the *far* future may be estimated with the same precision as cash flows in the *near* future. This assumption is certainly questionable.

Some of these conclusions are intuitive, some are not. But in any event, the analysis provides some basis for estimating the effect that errors in capital budgeting parameters have on the resultant rates of return. It also indicates where the emphasis should be placed in estimating parameters of proposed capital budgeting projects.

REFERENCES

1. R. J. Huefner, "Analyzing and Reporting Sensitivity Data," *Accounting Review* (October 1971), pp. 717–732.
2. ———, "Sensitivity Analysis and Risk Evaluation," *Decision Sciences* (July 1972), pp. 126–135.
3. W. C. House, Jr., "The Usefulness of Sensitivity Analysis in Capital Investment Decision Making," *Management Accounting* (February 1966), pp. 22–29.
4. J. C. T. Mao. "Survey of Capital Budgeting: Theory and Practice," *Journal of Finance* (May 1970), pp. 349–360.
5. A. A. Robichek and S. C. Myers, "Conceptual Problems in the Use of Risk-Adjusted Discount Rates," *Journal of Finance* (December 1966), pp. 727–730.
6. M. Sarnat and H. Levy, "The Relationship of Rules of Thumb to the Internal Rate of Return: A Restatement and Generalization," *Journal of Finance* (June 1969), pp. 479–490.
7. M. B. Solomon, Jr., "Uncertainty and Its Effect on Capital Investment Analysis," *Management Science* (April 1966), pp. B-334–B-339.
8. D. L. Tuttle and R. H. Litzenberger, "Leverage, Diversification and Capital Market Effects on a Risk-Adjusted Capital Budgeting Framework," *Journal of Finance* (June 1968), pp. 427–443.

QUESTIONS

1. Describe how sensitivity analysis could be used for dealing with uncertainty on an individual project with uncertain future returns.
2. What happens to the importance of life (of project) errors if expected life is short? Explain.
3. Under which circumstances are errors in estimated cash flow more important, long life or short life? Explain.
4. What happens to the sensitivity of errors in cash flow, life, or decline rate if the expected rate of return is low?

12 David B. Hertz

Risk Analysis in Capital Investment

This article by David Hertz was the first to describe the Monte Carlo simulation method for capital investment analysis under risk or uncertainty. Although articles have since appeared on various details of the method, none has provided the comprehensive and definitive treatment given here.

The simulation method has several advantages. First, simulation enables the analyst to handle very complicated problems. Second, compared with the single-valued estimate approach, simulation allows the experts providing input data to indicate the probable accuracy of their estimates as well as expected values. Third, the method enables the analyst to make a sensitivity analysis of any stochastic variable merely by holding all other variables constant (presumably at their expected values). Finally, since the output is a probability distribution of NPV or IRR, decision makers have substantial information about the reward-risk profile of the project. For example, output data could include the worst, best, most likely, and expected outcomes, and the probabilities would be estimated for IRR > cost of capital, IRR > 0, IRR > riskless rate, IRR > "sensational," NPV > "ruinous" outcome, or NPV > 0.

The most problematic aspects of the method are securing appropriate input data, incorporating interdependence among the variables, correct modeling of the project variables, and correct specification of independence or correlation of cash flows over time.

Of all the decisions that business executives must make, none is more challenging—and none has received more attention—than choosing among alternative capital investment opportunities. What makes this kind of decision so demanding, of course, is not the problem of projecting return on investment under any given set of assumptions. The difficulty is in the assumptions and in their impact. Each assumption involves its own degree—often a high degree—of uncertainty; and, taken together, these combined uncertainties can multiply

Source. Reprinted by permission from *Harvard Business Review*, January–February 1964, pp. 95–106, Copyright © 1963 by the President and Fellows of Harvard College; all rights reserved. The author is a director of McKinsey & Company, Inc.

into a total uncertainty of critical proportions. This is where the element of risk enters, and it is in the evaluation of risk that the executive has been able to get little help from currently available tools and techniques.

There is a way to help the executive sharpen his key capital investment decisions by providing him with a realistic measurement of the risks involved. Armed with this measurement, which evaluates for him the risk at each possible level of return, he is then in a position to measure more knowledgeably alternative courses of action against corporate objectives.

NEED FOR NEW CONCEPT

The evaluation of a capital investment project starts with the principle that the productivity of capital is measured by the rate of return we expect to receive over some future period. A dollar received next year is worth less to us than a dollar in hand today. Expenditures three years hence are less costly than expenditures of equal magnitude two years from now. For this reason we cannot calculate the rate of return realistically unless we take into account (a) when the sums involved in an investment are spent and (b) when the returns are received.

Comparing alternative investments is thus complicated by the fact that they usually differ not only in size but also in the length of time over which expenditures will have to be made and benefits returned.

It is these facts of investment life that long ago made apparent the shortcomings of approaches that simply averaged expenditures and benefits, or lumped them, as in the number-of-years-to-pay-out method. These shortcomings stimulated students of decision making to explore more precise methods for determining whether one investment would leave a company better off in the long run than would another course of action.

It is not surprising, then, that much effort has been applied to the development of ways to improve our ability to discriminate among investment alternatives. The focus of all of these investigations has been to sharpen the definition of the value of capital investments to the company. The controversy and furor that once came out in the business press over the most appropriate way of calculating these values has largely been resolved in favor of the discounted cash flow method as a reasonable means of measuring the rate of return that can be expected in the future from an investment made today.

Thus we have methods which, in general, are more or less elaborate mathematical formulas for comparing the outcomes of various investments and the combinations of the variables that will affect the investments.[1] As these techniques have progressed, the mathematics involved has become more and more

---

[1] See for example, Joel Dean, *Capital Budgeting* (New York, Columbia University Press, 1951); "Return on Capital as a Guide to Managerial Decisions," *National Association of Accounts Research Report No. 35*, December 1, 1959; and Bruce F. Young, "Overcoming Obstacles to Use of Discounted Cash Flow for Investment Shares," *NAA Bulletin*, March 1963, p. 15.

precise, so that we can now calculate discounted returns to a fraction of a per cent.

But the sophisticated businessman knows that behind these precise calculations are data which are not that precise. At best, the rate-of-return information he is provided with is based on an average of different opinions with varying reliabilities and different ranges of probability. When the expected returns on two investments are close, he is likely to be influenced by "intangibles"—a precarious pursuit at best. Even when the figures for two investments are quite far apart, and the choice seems clear, there lurks in the back of the businessman's mind memories of the Edsel and other ill-fated ventures.

In short, the decision-maker realizes that there is something more he ought to know, something in addition to the expected rate of return. He suspects that what is missing has to do with the nature of the data on which the expected rate of return is calculated, and with the way those data are processed. It has something to do with uncertainty, with possibilities and probabilities extending across a wide range of rewards and risks.

The Achilles Heel

The fatal weakness of past approaches thus has nothing to do with the mathematics of rate-of-return calculation. We have pushed along this path so far that the precision of our calculation is, if anything, somewhat illusory. The fact is that, no matter what mathematics is used, each of the variables entering into the calculation of rate of return is subject to a high level of uncertainty. For example:

The useful life of a new piece of capital equipment is rarely known in advance with any degree of certainty. It may be affected by variations in obsolescence or deterioration, and relatively small changes in use life can lead to large changes in return. Yet an expected value for the life of the equipment—based on a great deal of data from which a single best possible forecast has been developed—is entered into the rate-of-return calculation. The same is done for the other factors that have a significant bearing on the decision at hand.

Let us look at how this works out in a simple case—one in which the odds appear to be all in favor of a particular decision:

The executives of a food company must decide whether to launch a new packaged cereal. They have come to the conclusion that five factors are the determining variables: *advertising and promotion expense, total cereal market, share of market for this product, operating costs,* and *new capital investment.* On the basis of the "most likely" estimate for each of these variables the picture looks very bright—a healthy 30% return. This future, however, depends on each of the "most likely" estimates coming true in the actual case. If each of these "educated guesses" has, for example, a 60% chance of being correct, there is only an 8% chance that *all five* will be correct (.60 × .60 × .60 × .60 × .60). So the "expected" return is actually dependent on a rather unlikely coincidence. The decision-maker needs to know a great deal more about the *other* values used to make each of the five estimates and about what he stands to gain or lose from various combinations of these values.

This simple example illustrates that the rate of return actually depends on a specific combination of values of a great many different variables. But only the expected levels of ranges (e.g., worst, average, best; or pessimistic, most likely, optimistic) of these variables are used in formal mathematical ways to provide the figures given to management. Thus, predicting a single most likely rate of return gives precise numbers that do not tell the whole story.

The "expected" rate of return represents only a few points on a continuous curve of possible combinations of future happenings. It is a bit like trying to predict the outcome in a dice game by saying that the most likely outcome is a "7." The description is incomplete because it does not tell us about all the other things that could happen. In Exhibit 1, for instance, we see the odds on throws of only two dice having six sides. Now suppose that each die has 100 sides and there are eight of them! This is a situation more comparable to business investment, where the company's market share might become any one of 100 different sizes and where there are eight different factors (pricing, promotion, and so on) that can affect the outcome.

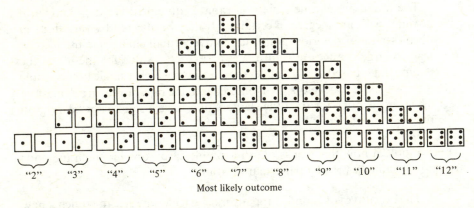

Most likely outcome

Exhibit I.   Describing uncertainty—a throw of the dice.

Nor is this the only trouble. Our willingness to bet on a roll of the dice depends not only on the odds but also on the stakes. Since the probability of rolling a

"7" is 1 in 6, we might be quite willing to risk a few dollars on that outcome at suitable odds. But would we be equally willing to wager $10,000 or $100,000 at those same odds, or even at better odds? In short, risk is influenced both by the odds on various events occurring and by the magnitude of the rewards or penalties which are involved when they do occur. To illustrate again:

> Suppose that a company is considering an investment of $1 million. The "best estimate" of the probable return is $200,000 a year. It could well be that this estimate is the average of three possible returns—a 1-in-3 chance of getting no return at all, a 1-in-3 chance of getting $200,000 per year, a 1-in-3 chance of getting $400,000 per year. Suppose that getting no return at all would put the company out of business. Then, by accepting this proposal, management is taking a 1-in-3 chance of going bankrupt.
>
> If only the "best estimate" analysis is used, management might go ahead, however, unaware that it is taking a big chance. If all of the available information were examined, management might prefer an alternative proposal with a smaller, but more certain (i.e., less variable), expectation.

Such considerations have led almost all advocates of the use of modern capital-investment-index calculations to plead for a recognition of the elements of uncertainty. Perhaps Ross G. Walker sums up current thinking when he speaks of "the almost impenetrable mists of any forecast."[2]

How can the executive penetrate the mists of uncertainty that surround the choices among alternatives?

Limited Improvements

A number of efforts to cope with uncertainty have been successful up to a point, but all seem to fall short of the mark in one way or another:

1. *More accurate forecasts*. Reducing the error in estimates is a worthy objective. But no matter how many estimates of the future go into a capital investment decision, when all is said and done, the future is still the future. Therefore, however well we forecast, we are still left with the certain knowledge that we cannot eliminate all uncertainty.

2. *Empirical adjustments*. Adjusting the factors influencing the outcome of a decision is subject to serious difficulties. We would like to adjust them so as to cut down the likelihood that we will make a "bad" investment, but how can we do that without at the same time spoiling our chances to make a "good" one?

[2] "The Judgment Factor in Investment Decisions," *HBR*, March–April 1961, p. 99.

And in any case, what is the basis for adjustment? We adjust, not for uncertainty, but for bias.

For example, construction estimates are often exceeded. If a company's history of construction costs is that 90% of its estimates have been exceeded by 15%, then in a capital estimate there is every justification for increasing the value of this factor by 15%. This is a matter of improving the accuracy of the estimate.

But suppose that new-product sales estimates have been exceeded by more than 75% in one-fourth of all historical cases, and have not reached 50% of the estimate in one-sixth of all such cases? Penalties for overestimating are very tangible, and so management is apt to reduce the sales estimate to "cover" the one case in six—thereby reducing the calculated rate of return. In doing so, it is possibly missing some of its best opportunities.

3. *Revising cutoff rates.* Selecting higher cutoff rates for protecting against uncertainty is attempting much the same thing. Management would like to have a possibility of return in proportion to the risk it takes. Where there is much uncertainty involved in the various estimates of sales, costs, prices, and so on, a high calculated return from the investment provides some incentive for taking the risk. This is, in fact, a perfectly sound position. The trouble is that the decision-maker still needs to know explicitly what risks he is taking—and what the odds are on achieving the expected return.

4. *Three-level estimates.* A start at spelling out risks is sometimes made by taking the high, medium, and low values of the estimated factors and calculating rates of return based on various combinations of the pessimistic, average, and optimistic estimates. These calculations give a picture of the range of possible results, but do not tell the executive whether the pessimistic result is more likely than the optimistic one—or, in fact, whether the average result is much more likely to occur than either of the extremes. So, although this is a step in the right direction, it still does not give a clear enough picture for comparing alternatives.

5. *Selected probabilities.* Various methods have been used to include the probabilities of specific factors in the return calculation. L. C. Grant discusses a program for forecasting discounted cash flow rates of return where the service life is subject to obsolescence and deterioration. He calculates the odds that the investment will terminate at any time after it is made depending on the probability distribution of the service-life factor. After calculating these factors for each year through maximum service life, he then determines an overall expected rate of return.[3]

Edward G. Bennion suggests the use of game theory to take into account

---

[3] "Monitoring Capital Investments," *Financial Executive*, April 1963, p. 19.

alternative market growth rates as they would determine rate of return for various alternatives. He uses the estimated probabilities that specific growth rates will occur to develop optimum strategies. Bennion points out:

> "Forecasting can result in a negative contribution to capital budget decisions unless it goes further than merely providing a single most probable prediction. . . . [With] an estimated probability coefficient for the forecast, plus knowledge of the payoffs for the company's alternative investments and calculation of indifference probabilities . . . the margin of error may be substantially reduced, and the businessman can tell just how far off his forecast may be before it leads him to a wrong decision."[4]

Note that both of these methods yield an expected return, each based on only one uncertain input factor—service life in the first case, market growth in the second. Both are helpful, and both tend to improve the clarity with which the executive can view investment alternatives. But neither sharpens up the range of "risk taken" or "return hoped for" sufficiently to help very much in the complex decisions of capital planning.

SHARPENING THE PICTURE

Since every one of the many factors that enter into the evaluation of a specific decision is subject to some uncertainty, the executive needs a helpful portrayal of the effects that the uncertainty surrounding each of the significant factors has on the returns he is likely to achieve. Therefore, the method we have developed at McKinsey & Company, Inc., combines the variabilities inherent in all the relevant factors. Our objective is to give a clear picture of the relative risk and the probable odds of coming out ahead or behind in the light of uncertain foreknowledge.

A simulation of the way these factors may combine as the future unfolds is the key to extracting the maximum information from the available forecasts. In fact, the approach is very simple, using a computer to do the necessary arithmetic. (Recently, a computer program to do this was suggested by S. W. Hess and H. A. Quigley for chemical process investments.[5])

To carry out the analysis, a company must follow three steps:

[4] "Capital Budgeting and Game Theory," *HBR*, November–December 1956, p. 123.

[5] "Analysis of Risk in Investments Using Monte Carlo Techniques," *Chemical Engineering Symposium Series 42: Statistics and Numerical Methods in Chemical Engineering* (New York, American Institute of Chemical Engineering, 1963), p. 55.

1.   Estimate the range of values for each of the factors (e.g., range of selling price, sales growth rate, and so on) and within that range the likelihood of occurrence of each value.

2.   Select at random from the distribution of values for each factor one particular value. Then combine the values for all of the factors and compute the rate of return (or present value) from that combination. For instance, the lowest in the range of prices might be combined with the highest in the range of growth rate and other factors. (The fact that the factors are dependent should be taken into account, as we shall see later.)

3.   Do this over and over again to define and evaluate the odds of the occurrence of each possible rate of return. Since there are literally millions of possible combinations of values, we need to test the likelihood that various specific returns on the investment will occur. This is like finding out by recording the results of a great many throws what per cent of "7"s or other combinations we may expect in tossing dice. The result will be a listing of the rates of return we might achieve, ranging from a loss (if the factors go against us) to whatever maximum gain is possible with the estimates that have been made.

For each of these rates the chances that it may occur are determined. (Note that a specific return can usually be achieved through more than one combination of events. The more combinations for a given rate, the higher the chances of achieving it—as with "7"s in tossing dice.) The average expectation is the average of the values of all outcomes weighted by the chances of each occurring.

The variability of outcome values from the average is also determined. This is important since, all other factors being equal, management would presumably prefer lower variability for the same return if given the choice. This concept has already been applied to investment portfolios.[6]

When the expected return and variability of each of a series of investments have been determined, the same techniques may be used to examine the effectiveness of various combinations of them in meeting management objectives.

PRACTICAL TEST

To see how this new approach works in practice, let us take the experience of a management that has already analyzed a specific investment proposal by con-

[6] See Harry Markowitz, *Portfolio Selection, Efficient Diversification of Investments* (New York, John Wiley and Sons, 1959); Donald E. Fararr, *The Investment Decision Under Uncertainty* (Englewood Cliffs, New Jersey, Prentice-Hall, Inc., 1962); William F. Sharpe, "A Simplified Model for Portfolio Analysis," *Management Science*, January 1963, p. 277.

ventional techniques. Taking the same investment schedule and the same expected values actually used, we can find what results the new method would produce and compare them with the results obtained when conventional methods were applied. As we shall see, the new picture of risks and returns is different from the old one. Yet the differences are attributable in no way to changes in the basic data—*only to the increased sensitivity of the method to management's uncertainties about the key factors.*

Investment Proposal

In this case a medium-size industrial chemical producer is considering a $10 million extension to its processing plant. The estimated service life of the facility is 10 years; the engineers expect to be able to utilize 250,000 tons of processed material worth $510 per ton at an average processing cost of $435 per ton. Is this investment a good bet? In fact, what is the return that the company may expect? What are the risks? We need to make the best and fullest use we can of all the market research and financial analyses that have been developed, so as to give management a clear picture of this project in an uncertain world.

The key input factors management has decided to use are:

1. Market size.
2. Selling prices.
3. Market growth rate.
4. Share of market (which results in physical sales volume).
5. Investment required.
6. Residual value of investment.
7. Operating costs.
8. Fixed costs.
9. Useful life of facilities.

These factors are typical of those in many company projects that must be analyzed and combined to obtain a measure of the attractiveness of a proposed capital facilities investment.

Obtaining Estimates

How do we make the recommended type of analysis of this proposal?

Our aim is to develop for each of the nine factors listed a frequency distribution or probability curve. The information we need includes the possible range of values for each factor, the average, and some ideas as to the likelihood that the various possible values will be reached. It has been our experience that for major capital proposals managements usually make a significant investment in time and funds to pinpoint information about each of the relevant factors. An objective analysis of the values to be assigned to each can, with little additional effort, yield a subjective probability distribution.

Specifically, it is necessary to probe and question each of the experts involved—to find out, for example, whether the estimated cost of production really can be said to be exactly a certain value or whether, as is more likely, it should be estimated to lie within a certain range of values. It is that range which is ignored in the analysis management usually makes. The range is relatively easy to determine; if a guess has to be made—as it often does—it is easier to guess with some accuracy a range rather than a specific single value. We have found from past experience at McKinsey & Company, Inc., that a series of meetings with management personnel to discuss such distributions is most helpful in getting at realistic answers to the a priori questions. (The term "realistic answers" implies all the information management does *not* have as well as all that it does have.)

The ranges are directly related to the degree of confidence that the estimator has in his estimate. Thus, certain estimates may be known to be quite accurate. They would be represented by probability distributions stating, for instance, that there is only 1 chance in 10 that the actual value will be different from the best estimate by more than 10%. Others may have as much as 100% ranges above and below the best estimate.

Thus, we treat the factor of selling price for the finished product by asking executives who are responsible for the original estimates these questions:

1. Given that $510 is the expected sales price, what is the probability that the price will exceed $550?
2. Is there any chance that the price will exceed $650?
3. How likely is it that the price will drop below $475?

Managements must ask similar questions for each of the other factors, until they can construct a curve for each. Experience shows that this is not as difficult as it might sound. Often information on the degree of variation in factors is readily available. For instance, historical information on variations in the price of a commodity is readily available. Similarly, management can estimate the variability of sales from industry sales records. Even for factors that have no history, such as operating costs for a new product, the person who makes the "average" estimate must have some idea of the degree of confidence he has in his prediction, and therefore he is usually only too glad to express his feelings. Likewise, the less confidence he has in his estimate, the greater will be the range of possible values that the variable will assume.

This last point is likely to trouble businessmen. Does it really make sense to seek estimates of variations? It cannot be emphasized too strongly that the less certainty there is in an "average" estimate, *the more important it is to consider the possible variation in that estimate.*

Further, an estimate of the variation possible in a factor, no matter how judgmental it may be, is always better than a simple "average" estimate, since it includes more information about what is known and what is not known. It is, in fact, this very *lack* of knowledge which may distinguish one investment possibility from another, so that for rational decision making it *must* be taken into account.

This lack of knowledge is in itself important information about the proposed investment. To throw any information away simply because it is highly uncertain is a serious error in analysis which the new approach is designed to correct.

Computer Runs

The next step in the proposed approach is to determine the returns that will result from random combinations of the factors involved. This requires realistic restrictions, such as not allowing the total market to vary more than some reasonable amount from year to year. Of course, any method of rating the return which is suitable to the company may be used at this point; in the actual case management preferred discounted cash flow for the reasons cited earlier, so that method is followed here.

A computer can be used to carry out the trials for the simulation method in very little time and at very little expense. Thus, for one trial actually made in this case, 3,600 discounted cash flow calculations, each based on a selection of the nine input factors, were run in two minutes at a cost of $15 for computer time. The resulting rate-of-return probabilities were read out immediately and graphed. The process is shown schematically in Exhibit 2.

Data Comparisons

The nine input factors described earlier fall into three categories:

1. *Market analyses.* Included are market size, market growth rate, the firm's share of the market, and selling prices. For a given combination of these factors sales revenue may be determined.

2. *Investment cost analyses.* Being tied to the kinds of service-life and operating-cost characteristics expected, these are subject to various kinds of error and uncertainty; for instance, automation progress makes service life uncertain.

3. *Operating and fixed costs.* These also are subject to uncertainty, but are perhaps the easiest to estimate.

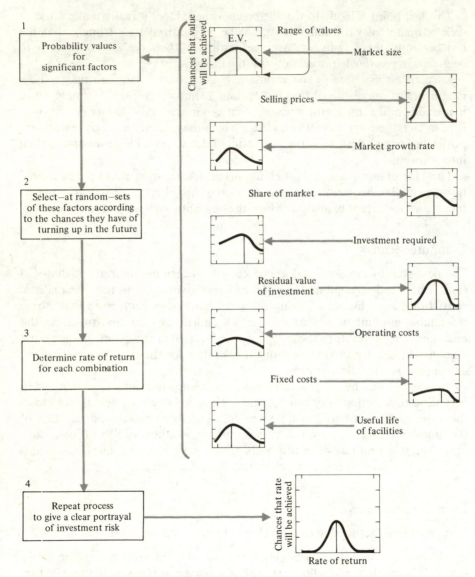

Exhibit 2.   Simulation for investment planning. E. V. = expected value = average or the "one best estimate."

These categories are not independent, and for realistic results our approach allows the various factors to be tied together. Thus, if price determines the total market, we first select from a probability distribution the price for the specific computer run and then use for the total market a probability distribution that is logically related to the price selected.

We are now ready to compare the values obtained under the new approach with the values obtained under the old. This comparison is shown in Exhibit 3.

EXHIBIT 3.   COMPARISON OF EXPECTED VALUES UNDER OLD AND NEW APPROACHES

	CONVENTIONAL "BEST ESTIMATE" APPROACH	NEW APPROACH
Market Analyses		
1. *Market size*		
Expected value (in tons)	250,000	250,000
Range	—	100,000–340,000
2. *Selling prices*		
Expected value (in dollars/ton)	$510	$510
Range	—	$385–$575
3. *Market growth rate*		
Expected value	3%	3%
Range	—	0–6%
4. *Eventual share of market*		
Expected value	12%	12%
Range	—	3%–17%
Investment Cost Analyses		
5. *Total investment required*		
Expected value (in millions)	$9.5	$9.5
Range	—	$7.0–$10.5
6. *Useful life of facilities*		
Expected value (in years)	10	10
Range	—	5–15
7. *Residual value (at 10 years)*		
Expected value (in millions)	$4.5	$4.5
Range	—	$3.5–$5.0
Other Costs		
8. *Operating costs*		
Expected value (in dollars/ton)	$435	$435
Range	—	$370–$545
9. *Fixed costs*		
Expected value (in thousands)	$300	$300
Range	—	$250–$375

Note: Range figures in right-hand column represent approximately 1% to 99% probabilities. That is, there is only a 1 in a 100 chance that the value actually achieved will be respectively greater or less than the range.

Valuable Results

How do the results under the new and old approaches compare?

In this case, management had been informed, on the basis of the "one best estimate" approach, that the expected return was 25.2% before taxes. When we ran the new set of data through the computer program, however, we got an expected return of only 14.6% before taxes. This surprising difference not only is due to the fact that under the new approach we use a range of values; it also reflects the fact that we have weighted each value in the range by the chances of its occurrence.

Our new analysis thus may help management to avoid an unwise investment. In fact, the general result of carefully weighing the information and lack of information in the manner I have suggested is to indicate the true nature of otherwise seemingly satisfactory investment proposals. If this practice were followed by managements, much regretted overcapacity might be avoided.

The computer program developed to carry out the simulation allows for easy insertion of new variables. In fact, some programs have previously been suggested that take variability into account.[7] But most programs do not allow for dependence relationships between the various input factors. Further, the program used here permits the choice of a value for price from one distribution, which value determines a particular probability distribution (from among several) that will be used to determine the value for sales volume. To show how this important technique works:

Suppose we have a wheel, as in roulette, with the numbers from 0 to 15 representing one price for the product or material, the numbers 16 to 30 representing a second price, the numbers 31 to 45 a third price, and so on. For each of these segments we would have a different range of expected market volumes; e.g., $150,000–$200,000 for the first, $100,000–$150,000 for the second, $75,000–$100,000 for the third, and so forth. Now suppose that we spin the wheel and the ball falls in 37. This would mean that we pick a sales volume in the $75,000–$100,000 range. If the ball goes in 11, we have a different price and we turn to the $150,000–$200,000 range for a sales volume.

Most significant, perhaps, is the fact that the program allows management to ascertain the sensitivity of the results to each or all of the input factors. Simply by running the program with changes in the distribution of an input factor, it is possible to determine the effect of added or changed information (or of the lack of information). It may turn out that fairly large changes in some factors do not significantly affect the outcomes. In this case, as a matter of fact, management was particularly concerned about the difficulty in estimating market growth. Running the program with variations in this factor quickly

[7] See Frederick S. Hillier, "The Derivation of Probabilistic Information for the Evaluation of Risky Investments," *Management Science*, April 1963, p. 443.

demonstrated to us that for average annual growths from 3% and 5% there was no significant difference in the expected outcome.

In addition, let us see what the implications are of the detailed knowledge the simulation method gives us. Under the method using single expected values, management arrives only at a hoped-for expectation of 25.2% after taxes (which, as we have seen, is wrong unless there is no variability in the various input factors—a highly unlikely event). On the other hand, with the method we propose, the uncertainties are clearly portrayed:

PERCENT RETURN	PROBABILITY OF ACHIEVING AT LEAST THE RETURN SHOWN
0%	96.5%
5	80.6
10	75.2
15	53.8
20	43.0
25	12.6
30	0

This profile is shown in Exhibit 4. Note the contrast with the profile obtained under the conventional approach. This concept has been used also for evaluation of new product introductions, acquisitions of new businesses, and plant modernization.

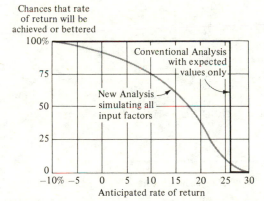

Exhibit 4.   Anticipated rates of return under old and new approaches.

COMPARING OPPORTUNITIES

From a decision-making point of view one of the most significant advantages of the new method of determining rate of return is that it allows management

SELECTED STATISTICS

	Investment A	Investment B
Amount of investment	$10,000,000	$10,000,000
Life of investment (in years)	10	10
Expected annual net cash inflow	$ 1,300,000	$ 1,400,000
Variability of cash inflow		
1 chance in 50 of		
being *greater* than	$ 1,700,000	$ 3,400,000
1 chance in 50 of		
being *less** than	$ 900,000	($600,000)
Expected return on investment	5.0%	6.8%
Variability of return		
on investment		
1 chance in 50 of		
being *greater* than	7.0%	15.5%
1 chance in 50 of		
being *less** than	3.0%	(4.0%)
Risk of investment		
Chances of a loss	Negligible	1 in 10
Expected size of loss		$ 200,000

Chances that rate
of return will be
achieved or bettered

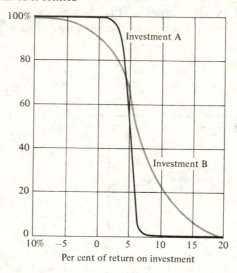

Per cent of return on investment

Exhibit 5.   Comparison of two investment
opportunities. *In the case of negative figures
(indicated by parentheses), "less than" means "worse
than."

194

to discriminate between measures of (1) expected return based on weighted probabilities of all possible returns, (2) variability of return, and (3) risks.

To visualize this advantage, let us take an example which is based on another actual case but simplified for purposes of explanation. The example involves two investments under consideration, A and B.

When the investments are analyzed, the data tabulated and plotted in Exhibit 5 are obtained. We see that:

Investment B has a higher expected return than Investment A.

Investment B also has substantially more variability than Investment A. There is a good chance that Investment B will earn a return which is quite different from the expected return of 6.8%, possibly as high as 15% or as low as a loss of 5%. Investment A is not likely to vary greatly from the expected 5% return.

Investment B involves far more risk than does Investment A. There is virtually no chance of incurring a loss on Investment A. However, there is 1 chance in 10 of losing money on Investment B. If such a loss occurs, its expected size is approximately $200,000.

Clearly, the new method of evaluating investments provides management with far more information on which to base a decision. Investment decisions made only on the basis of maximum expected return are not unequivocally the best decisions.

CONCLUSION

The question management faces in selecting capital investments is first and foremost: What information is needed to clarify the key differences among various alternatives? There is agreement as to the basic factors that should be considered—markets, prices, costs, and so on. And the way the future return on the investment should be calculated, if not agreed on, is at least limited to a few methods, any of which can be consistently used in a given company. If the input variables turn out as estimated, any of the methods customarily used to rate investments should provide satisfactory (if not necessarily maximum) returns.

In actual practice, however, the conventional methods do *not* work out satisfactorily. Why? The reason, as we have seen earlier in this article, and as every executive and economist knows, is that the estimates used in making the advance calculations are just that—estimates. More accurate estimates would be helpful, but at best the residual uncertainty can easily make a mockery of corporate hopes. Nevertheless, there is a solution. To collect realistic estimates for the key factors means to find out a great deal about them. Hence the kind of uncertainty that is involved in each estimate can be evaluated ahead of time. Using this knowledge of uncertainty, executives can maximize the value of the information for decision making.

The value of computer programs in developing clear portrayals of the uncertainty and risk surrounding alternative investments has been proved. Such programs can produce valuable information about the sensitivity of the possible outcomes to the variability of input factors and to the likelihood of achieving various possible rates of return. This information can be extremely important as a backup to management judgment. To have calculations of the odds on all possible outcomes lends some assurance to the decision-makers that the available information has been used with maximum efficiency.

This simulation approach has the inherent advantage of simplicity. It requires only an extension of the input estimates (to the best of our ability) in terms of probabilities. No projection should be pinpointed unless we are *certain* of it.

The discipline of thinking through the uncertainties of the problem will in itself help to ensure improvement in making investment choices. For to understand uncertainty and risk is to understand the key business problem—and the key business opportunity. Since the new approach can be applied on a continuing basis to each capital alternative as it comes up for consideration and progresses toward fruition, gradual progress may be expected in improving the estimation of the probabilities of variation.

Lastly, the courage to act boldly in the face of apparent uncertainty can be greatly bolstered by the clarity of portrayal of the risks and possible rewards. To achieve these lasting results requires only a slight effort beyond what most companies already exert in studying capital investments.

QUESTIONS

1. What is a "stochastic" variable?
2. Draw a picture of a probability distribution for NPV. Label on it the type of information obtainable from this probability distribution, if it were known.
3. Draw NPV probability distributions for projects A and B, each with the same mean and variance but such that you would obviously prefer A to B.
4. Describe the Monte Carlo simulation method of capital budgeting as proposed by Hertz. In your description, explain how the input information is secured, how the simulation is accomplished, and how the results might be interpreted. Highlight the strengths and weaknesses of this simulation technique.
5. List the five efforts to cope with uncertainty indicated by Hertz; point out what improvement they offered and where they fell short.

PROBLEMS

1. You are given the following probability distribution for the outlay (O) on a project.

    P (O = $100,000) = 0.2
    P (O = $110,000) = 0.3
    P (O = $120,000) = 0.4
    P (O = $130,000) = 0.1

    As an exercise for what it means to take random samples, take one hundred random samples from the above probability distribution and record the results on a histogram. Summarize the results.
    Hint:
    a. To accomplish the random sampling, let the digits

        0, 1   represent $100,000
        2, 3, 4   represent   110,000
        5, 6, 7, 8 represent   120,000 and
        9   represent   130,000

    b. If you do not have a random digit table, use arbitrarily selected columns of digits from present value tables. Use the digits which are the furthest to the right of the decimal point.
2. You have the following information for a project:

    Outlay = $100,000
    Cost of capital = 10 percent
    Salvage value = $0.0
    Cash flow: P (CF = 10,000) = 0.3
                   P (CF = 15,000) = 0.5
                   P (CF = 20,000) = 0.2

    Life of project: P (L =   8 years) = 0.2
                      P (L = 10 years) = 0.4
                      P (L = 12 years) = 0.3
                      P (L = 14 years) = 0.1

    Ignore tax and depreciation; make ten trials for NPV and plot a histogram of the results. (Assume that cash flows are perfectly correlated through time; i.e. whatever the outcome of a random sample of the CF distribution, that is the CF for each year over the life of the project.)

IV | Sources and Forms of Long-Term Financing

13

Ronald C. Lease, Wilbur G. Lewellen, and Gary G. Schlarbaum*

The Individual Investor: Attributes and Attitudes

The ultimate purchasers of corporate securities are individual investors, and their desires, expectations, fears, and greed all bear on how readily securities may be issued by corporations and on the costs these issuers must pay for the funds obtained. Accordingly, it is valuable to learn as much as possible about individual investors. This paper provides a unique body of data on the age, income, wealth, investment objectives, and rate of return expectations of the active individual participant in the American securities market. The authors attempt to find out who the individual investors are, how they make their decisions, how they deal with their brokers, what their portfolios consist of, and how well in fact they have done as portfolio managers.

Source. Reprinted by permission from *Journal of Finance*, May 1974, pp. 413–433. The authors are, respectively, associate professor of finance at the University of Utah, professor of management at Purdue University, and associate professor of management at Purdue University.

* The paper presents a preliminary report on a National Bureau of Economic Research study. Grateful acknowledgment is made of the financial support provided for the study by the Investment Company Institute, the Krannert Graduate School of Purdue University, the Purdue Research Foundation, the College of Business Administration of the University of Utah, and—especially—the brokerage house discussed in the text, whose cooperation in providing data made the study possible. The latter firm's understandable desire for anonymity precludes the accolade it so richly deserves, but does not diminish the authors' sincere appreciation for its contribution. A special debt is also owed to Mr. William Elbring of Purdue University for his crucial assistance with the construction of the computer infrastructure for the larger investigation of which the current analysis represents only a part. Professors Frank Bass, Donald King, and Edgar Pessemier of Purdue, Professors Ramon Johnson and James Jenkins of Utah, Professor Donald Farrar of UCLA, and Messrs. Frank Conran and Harvey Katz of the Research Department of the New York Stock Exchange provided equally indispensable inputs to the design and execution of the research methodology. Responsibility for the findings and their interpretation, of course, remains with the authors. In particular, those findings have not yet undergone the full critical review accorded the NBER's studies, and should not be regarded as an official NBER publication.

In its role as the final arbiter for the allocation for our scarce capital resources, the American securities market has been the object of continuing close scrutiny by both the scholarly community and the architects of public policy. The predominant concern has been to ensure and maintain conditions under which the flow of investment funds will in fact be channeled to those enterprises whose products are most in demand by the consuming public. As has occurred in many areas of economic activity, however, there has been a steadily increasing tendency toward an institutionalization of the relevant processes—i.e., toward a withdrawal of the individual capital supplier to a position of derivative rather than direct participation in the market.

Commercial and mutual savings banks, and savings and loan associations, of course, have for many years performed the intermediation function of collecting small amounts of *debt* capital from widely-dispersed individual savers, and repackaging those amounts in larger units for the ultimate borrower. The emergence on a grand scale of a similar mechanism in the *equities* market, on the other hand, is a much more recent phenomenon. The significant growth in the common stock portfolios of mutual funds, pension trusts, and insurance companies has occurred primarily since 1950—but over that interval this growth has brought about a clear reversal of the relative roles of the individual and the institution in allocating ownership funds among competing enterprises. Between 1961 and 1971 alone, for example, the fraction of NYSE public trading volume by total dollar value which was accounted for by institutions rose from 39 per cent to 68 per cent; even as judged simply by the number of shares traded, the gain was from 33 per cent to 60 per cent.[1] Indeed, since 1959, individual investors in the aggregate have consistently been net sellers of corporate common stocks.[2]

It is, of course, not so much the case that the individual has been *displaced* by the institution as it is that he has chosen to divert his funds *to* the institution, for administration on his behalf. Such a decision may reflect a feeling that he lacks the requisite portfolio management expertise, that necessary information on companies he might invest in is not available to him on the same basis as it is to the professional, that the commitment of time and energy needed to become both informed and skillful is too great, or that transactions costs for the modest investor are excessive.

Whatever the reasons for increasing institutionalization, the trend has been viewed with alarm by commentators ranging from William McChesney Martin ("I'm very concerned about the liquidity of the stock market, and I've talked to corporate heads who are worried to death about it."[3]), to the Chairman of

---

[1] New York Stock Exchange, *1973 Fact Book* (New York, NYSE, June 1973), p. 54.

[2] R. C. Klemkosky and D. F. Scott, Jr., "Withdrawal of the Individual Investor from the Equity Markets," *Michigan State University Business Topics*, Spring 1973.

[3] "Small Investors Forced Out," *Commercial and Financial Chronicle*, June 1, 1972.

the SEC (". . . we are already starting to witness a decline in the unique ability of this country's capital market system to raise capital for many thousands of corporations throughout the country."[4]), to *Fortune* magazine ("How the Terrible Two-Tier Market Came to Wall Street."[5]). The pernicious effects attributed to the individual investor's relegation to a secondary form of participation are (1) that, in the short run, market price volatility is accentuated by the large-bloc trades of institutions, and (2) that, over the long term, the capital allocation process will be less efficient and less appropriate since institutions have typically tended to concentrate their holdings in a relatively small number of companies.

In the face of these concerns, we should expect to be confronted with a rich body of evidence about the characteristics, attitudes, portfolio selection rules, and realized investment returns of the small investor. As it happens, however, we appear to know surprisingly little about him. There have, of course, been some broadbased survey efforts, but these have dealt almost exclusively with aggregate demographic patterns,[6] rather than with investment strategies and decision processes. Similarly, the portfolio performance of the individual over time has, for all practical purposes, been *represented*—by simulation,[7] or by inferences from general market price index movements and randomly selected portfolios—rather than *observed*, from actual individual transactions data. Therefore, while we have come to know a great deal about the investment propensities and performance characteristics of institutions,[8] counterpart evidence for the individual remains submerged. As Professor Friend has remarked, "Our lack of knowledge about the market experience of different [individual] investor groups is even more impressive than the gaps in the available data on the performance of the stock market as a whole."[9] Or, in Adam Smith's terminology, "We have the most elaborate machinery possible for tracking prices, but that is like bending over buffalo tracks and saying 'Yes, many buffalo pass this way.' Very good if there are a lot of buffalo all going in the

---

[4] "Departing the Market—the Small Investor," *Wall Street Journal*, May 7, 1973.

[5] *Fortune*, July 1973.

[6] For example, the NYSE *1973 Fact Book* (*op. cit.*) and the *1973 Mutual Fund Fact Book* (Washington, D.C., Investment Company Institute, 1973).

[7] L. Fisher and J. H. Lorie, "Rates of Return on Investments in Common Stocks," *Journal of Business*, July 1968.

[8] Among the key investigations are I. Friend, M. Blume, and J. Crockett, *Mutual Funds and Other Institutional Investors: A New Perspective*, New York, McGraw-Hill, 1970; M. C. Jensen, "The Performance of Mutual Funds in the Period 1945–64," *Journal of Finance*, May 1968; M. C. Jensen. "Risk, the Pricing of Capital Assets, and the Evaluation of Investment Portfolios," *Journal of Business*, April 1969; W. F. Sharpe, "Mutual Fund Performance," *Journal of Business*, January 1966. See also: J. H. Lorie and M. T. Hamilton, *The Stock Market: Theories and Evidence*, Homewood, Illinois, Irwin, 1973.

[9] I. Friend and J. deCani, "Stock Market Experience of Different Investment Groups," *American Statistical Association: Business and Economic Proceedings, 1966*.

same direction."[10] It is the intent of the study reported on here to begin more usefully to address the question of the composition and direction of the herd.

THE STUDY AND ITS CONTEXT

That effort was made possible through the cooperation of a large national retail brokerage house, headquartered in New York City. The firm agreed to make available to the authors both a mailing list of its present customers and historical data on the complete transactions activity of a large sample of those customers. Organized around this data base, the thrust of the investigation was twofold: first, to determine, from a broad-scale mail questionnaire survey, the demographic characteristics, investment strategy patterns, information sources, asset holdings, market attitudes and perceptions, and framework of broker relationships displayed by the customer population; second, to create from the account transactions file an historical record of portfolio positions and realized investment returns for the group, spanning a range of market conditions over a substantial portion of the last decade. In effect, the objective was to find out who the individual investor is, how he makes his decisions, how he deals with his broker, what his portfolio consists of, and how well in fact he has done as a portfolio manager. While several of these elements of the project are still in process—and would be precluded from our discussion here because of space constraints in any event—the analysis of the questionnaire responses is virtually completed, and is the focus of the present paper. Even as it stands, it provides a unique body of data on the motives, style, and makeup of the active individual participant in the American securities market.

THE SAMPLE

The survey subjects were chosen at random by the investigators from the brokerage firm's list of all the accounts which had been open with it over the full interval January 1, 1964, through December 31, 1970. This period was chosen partly for reasons of data availability (the corresponding transactions file existed in machine-readable tape form at the firm only back to 1964), partly for reasons of eventual comparability with previous studies (investment performance measures for institutions covering a substantial portion of the period have been published), partly because it encompassed a decent spectrum of external market conditions (three major uptrends and two sizeable declines), and partly in order to deal with individuals who had been "in the market" long enough to have developed both a behavior pattern and a rich store of experiences from which to respond.

[10] Adam Smith, *Super Money*, New York, Random House, 1972, p. 13.

A sample of 3000 such accounts was selected, stratified according to the geographical distribution of all American shareholders, as reported by the NYSE surveys[11]—residence location being the only dimension of an individual customer's circumstances which was discernible *ex ante*. Based on questionnaire pretest results, a sample of 3000 was deemed sufficient to generate a volume of responses which would give rise to sub-category cell sizes adequate for the effective application of certain statistical techniques (e.g., cluster analysis and A.I.D.) considered useful to the study.[12] From the list of 3000, some 500 accounts were eliminated on the basis of the addresses supplied, because they were clearly corporate, institutional, foreign, or investment club accounts. A questionnaire was sent to each of the remaining 2500, during the summer of 1972. Responses were received from just over 1000 of these, for a return rate of roughly 40 per cent.[13]

THE QUESTIONNAIRE

The survey instrument contained some 130 separate questions, spanning 12 pages. It was designed in conjunction with the advice and counsel of the cooperating brokerage firm, behavioral scientists at Purdue having extensive experience with questionnaire surveys, and the research staff of the NYSE. Three pretests were conducted before settling on a final format. Required responses included the checking of multiple-choice categories, frequency and importance ratings and rankings, and the insertion of dollar values for various classes of asset holdings and items of income and expenditure. The respondent's name was not solicited, and he was assured of anonymity in the survey. The completed forms have not—and will not—be turned over to the brokerage house involved; only the project investigators have access to the raw data. Subsequent to the survey, the underlying address file was also destroyed, rendering it impossible for us to associate even the survey group as a whole with the response records. While this action precludes specific follow-up mailings, except from a new random draw of accounts, the exigencies of preserving anonymity were deemed to be of overriding importance. Presumably, the relatively high response rate reflected this guarantee.[14] By and large, the participants filled in the forms completely and—to all appearances—carefully.

[11] NYSE, *1971 Fact Book*, and *1973 Fact Book*, *op. cit.*

[12] The 3000 selected represent approximately 10 per cent of *all* the firm's accounts which were open from January 1964 to December 1970.

[13] Distributed very much in line with the underlying geographical pattern of the mailing. No region was significantly under- or over-represented in the response matrix.

[14] In that connection, a "reminder" postcard went to the sample 10 days after the initial mailing, as a device to prompt responses. Finally, a somewhat shortened version of the original questionnaire was sent out a month later to pick up any potential stragglers. 726 of the "long form," and 264 of these "short form," returns comprise the total response file.

Of the 1300 replies received, only 40 had to be discarded as unusable. We are, therefore, well satisfied with the quality of the data.[15]

DEMOGRAPHY OF THE SAMPLE

Those data portray the survey group to be heavily male, relatively old, and reasonably affluent. Its characteristics are summarized in Table 1. We find that four out of five of the respondents are men, that four out of five are married, that nearly a third are age 65 or older, that just under half enjoy an annual (family) income exceeding $25,000, that the great majority of those employed work in professional and managerial occupations, and that more than half have attained at least the bachelor's degree level in their educational backgrounds. Not listed in the table, but reported on the questionnaire, was a mean household size of 2.8 persons; just 38 per cent of the respondents indicated that their households contained dependent children. Finally, of the 68 per cent of the group which was actively employed, more than four-fifths worked for profit-seeking enterprises, as opposed to governmental or non-profit organizations.

TABLE 1. DEMOGRAPHIC CHARACTERISTICS OF THE SAMPLE

Age:		Education:	
Under 21	<1%	Less than H.S.	11%
21–34	3%	H.S. Graduate	12%
35–44	12%	Some College	23%
45–54	29%	BA/BS or better	54%
55–64	26%		
65 and over	30%	Occupation:	
		Professional and Technical	27%
Sex:	80%	Managerial and Proprietor	29%
Male	20%	Clerical, Sales, and Service	7%
Female		Craftsman, Operative, and Labor	3%
		Farmer and Farm Laborer	2%
Marital Status:		Nonemployed	
Married	80%	(Retired, Housewives, Students, Unemployed)	32%
Unmarried	20%		
		Residence Location:	
Family Income:		Large City	40%
Under $5,000	2%	Small City	23%
$5,000–$9,999	8%	Suburban	30%
$10,000–$14,999	15%	Rural	7%
$15,000–$24,999	30%		
$25,000 and over	45%		

[Sample Size = 990]

[15] See, also, the discussion below.

REPRESENTATIVENESS OF THE SAMPLE

Distinctive as these attributes may be, in comparison with the circumstances of the general U.S. population, most of them are not especially surprising, given the underlying basis for sample assembly. There is, for example, evidence that securities ownership is heavily concentrated within the upper age and income segments of the community;[16] consequently, we would expect to find a disproportionate number of such individuals among any list of brokerage house customers. Similarly, the fact that the sample was constrained to encompass only individuals whose accounts had been open over an *entire* seven-year test period would virtually ensure that the group would turn out to be somewhat older than even a random draw of brokers' customers, let alone the population as a whole. The real issue, therefore, is not whether the sample resembles the community, but whether it resembles the share-*holding-and-trading* community well enough to permit a generalization of any findings which emerge from it to the broader circumstances of the latter group.

In that connection, it *is* possible to draw some reasonably firm conclusions, because quite specific standards of comparison are available. The NYSE in particular not only publishes an ongoing demographic survey of U.S. share-owners,[17] but also has separated out those data for "heads of households" as a distinct sub-group.[18] By the nature of the sampling procedure for our questionnaire (many of the accounts were joint accounts), we clearly would expect the household head to be the individual who *would* normally complete and return the form; indeed, 90 per cent of the respondents so identified themselves on the questionnaire.

Apart from the NYSE evidence—which does, of course, deal with share-holders in the aggregate, rather than exclusively with brokerage house customers—we made it a point to draw a random "control group" sample of somewhat over 2000, from the roster of *all* the cooperating firm's accounts which were open as of mid-summer 1972, without regard either to their geographic location or the length of time they had been customers. After eliminating the non-individual and foreign accounts, a questionnaire was mailed (followed by the standard reminder) to the approximately 1850 which remained. Completed, usable forms were returned by a total of 760 from this group—providing

[16] J. Bossons, "The Distribution of Assets Among Individuals of Different Age and Wealth," pp. 394–428 in: R. W. Goldsmith (Ed.), *Institutional Investors and Corporate Stock*, New York, National Bureau of Economic Research, 1973. The discussion contains a review of past studies as well.

[17] NYSE *Fact Book, op. cit.* All shareholders, not merely those who own NYSE stocks, are covered by the survey.

[18] *A Detailed Look at the Individual Investor: Marketing Highlights from the 1970 NYSE Share-ownership Study*, New York, NYSE Research Department, 1971.

us with an additional test of the peculiarities, if any, of the attributes of our basic study sample.

The relevant comparisons are shown in Table 2, and both the similarities and the differences among the four groups are apparent.[19] Unquestionably, both samples chosen from the broker customer list have higher incomes, more education, and are more heavily in the professional and managerial employment ranks than is true of the great mass of shareholders. The latter, of course, include individuals who have received the shares they own by gift, inheritance,[20] purchase through a bank, or under some compensation program of their employers, rather than explicitly through dealings with a brokerage firm. They are not, therefore, necessarily people having money under conscious, active management—as would be a fair description of our two samples[21]—and the differences in the observed demographic characteristics fit reasonable *a priori* notions.

The wide disparity in the male/female percentage composition of the "All Shareholder" group vis-à-vis the other three samples has an equally logical explanation. Shares may be *registered* in the name of a wife, or minor children, for a variety of estate and tax reasons, even though both the investment decision and the investment funds *originate* with the husband/father. We would thus expect to find not only that our questionnaire was typically filled out by the head of the relevant household—whatever the formal designation on the account involved—but that this individual would most often be a male. The very clear consistency across the study, control, and NYSE household-head samples with regard to sex proportions confirms that hypothesis, and lends credibility to the appropriateness of our study group precisely for inquiring about individuals' investment strategies and decision processes. This argument is buttressed by the answers to the direct question on the form: 75 per cent of the respondents reported that they formulated portfolio decisions for the entire household, another 15 per cent said they shared that responsibility, and a final 8 per cent indicated they at least made all the selections for their *own* accounts. Our conclusion therefore is that, while half of all nominal share *owners* may be women, something like 80 to 90 per cent of all investment *decision-makers* are men[22]—and that we do have data from the right sort of people.

---

[19] The NYSE data are from the 1970 shareowner survey (which is the latest available), as reported in the 1971 and 1973 *Fact Books*. Except for dollar income levels—an adjustment to which is indicated in Table 2—the demographics of the "All Shareholder" group have been sufficiently stable over the last decade or so that comparison with our samples drawn in 1972 is legitimate.

[20] We are tempted by, but will refrain from, the classification "widows and orphans."

[21] Although no activity test was imposed as a criterion for customer inclusion in the sample. Accordingly, we are not dealing solely with large, active traders or speculators.

[22] We hasten to add, however, that this is not a value judgment about the logical ordering of the universe; merely a description of extant circumstances. The NYSE suggests a similar decision formulation scenario (*A Detailed Look at the Individual Investor, op. cit.*, p. 4).

TABLE 2. COMPARISONS OF SAMPLE DEMOGRAPHICS

	STUDY GROUP	CONTROL GROUP	ALL U.S. SHAREHOLDERS*	SHAREHOLDER HEADS OF HOUSEHOLDS**
Age:				
Under 21	<1%	<1%	7%	2%
21–34	3%	16%	15%	11%
35–44	12%	20%	19%	19%
45–54	29%	25%	25%	28%
55–64	26%	20%	20%	23%
65 and over	30%	19%	14%	17%
Average Age (yrs.)[1]	57	50	47	50
Sex:				
Male	80%	84%	50%	85%
Female	20%	16%	50%	15%
Family Income:				
Under $5,000	2%	2%	—	8%
$5,000–$9,999	8%	7%	—	20%
$10,000–$14,999	15%	15%	N.A.	30%
$15,000–$24,999	30%	34%	—	27%
$25,000 and over	45%	42%	—	15%
Average Income[2]	$26,500	$24,400[3]		$18,500[4]
Education:				
Less than H.S.	11%	7%	13%	12%
H.S. Graduate	12%	10%	30%	28%
Some College	23%	24%	21%	18%
BA/BS or better	54%	59%	36%	42%
Occupation:				
Prof. & Technical	27%	31%	23%	—
Mgr. & Prop.	29%	29%	14%	—
Clerical, Sales, Svc.	7%	10%	18%	N.A.
Craft & Labor	3%	5%	8%	—
Farm	2%	1%	1%	—
Nonemployed	32%	24%	36%	—

* NYSE 1970 Survey (1971 *Fact Book*).

** NYSE 1970 Survey (*A Detailed Look at the Individual Investor*).

[1] Calculated from interval mid-points. Assumes "Under 21" category has an average age of 18, and the "Over 65" group an average of 72.5, based on age-65 life expectancy of 15 years.

[2] Calculated from interval mid-points, assuming the average for the "$25,000 and over" category to be $40,000.

[3] The actual average implied by the distribution shown is $26,100 as of the questionnaire survey date for the Control Group, which was mid-1973. The reported figure of $24,400 reflects a downward adjustment equal to the rate of increase in per capita U.S. personal income between July 1972 and July 1973 (Economic Statistics Bureau, *Handbook of Basic Economic Statistics*, Vol. 27, Washington, D.C., 1973) in order to put the Control Group income figures on a basis consistent with those of the Study Group—the latter, as indicated, having been surveyed in mid-1972.

[4] Again, this figure is adjusted upward for increases in U.S. per capita personal income between mid-1970 (the NYSE survey date) and mid-1972. The raw average from the distribution portrayed is $16,900.

The "Control Group" depicted provides perhaps the key interpretive link in support of this contention. It appears from those responses that the general run of the cooperating brokerage firm's customers are quite representative of the broader shareholder head-of-household population. The two age distributions are virtually identical, as are the male/female proportions in the respective totals. The one real difference is the higher level of education within the control group, which clearly accounts for its heavier relative contingent of professional and managerial personnel[23] and, accordingly, its higher average income. None of the latter differences are dramatic, however, nor—as suggested above—particularly surprising. Consequently, it seems fair to infer that the clientele of the firm in question is apt to be not unlike that of the typical brokerage house[24] nor even, in most dimensions, the typical shareowning household.

The remaining issue, therefore, is whether there is anything aberrant about the basic "Study Group" sample on which our analysis will be focused, and which was drawn from a list specifically of longer-term customers of the firm—pursuant to the ultimate objective of matching its reported attributes and attitudes to a record of actual account transactions and portfolios, over that same long period. Quite obviously, the tabulation reveals that the one distinguishing feature of the study group is its high average age; the distributions of each of its other characteristics correspond very closely to those of the control group in every respect.[25] This phenomenon, of course, is the inevitable result of restricting the list to accounts which were open for at least seven years[26]—and it is instructive, in that regard, to consider whether the resulting sample looks any different than might be anticipated by reason of longevity alone.

In particular, if we hypothesize that the sample would have been a "typical" one as of the *start* of the period under consideration (i.e., was equivalent to a

---

[23] As compared with the "All Shareholder" group, since a similar breakdown explicitly for heads of households was unavailable. Nonetheless, we can state with some confidence that the occupational differences between the control and household-head groups would be more modest. Thus, a shift from a 50/50 male/female composition to an 85/15 one would undoubtedly diminish both the "unemployed" and "clerical, sales, and service" job category percentages, thereby moving the revised distribution closer to that of the broker customer sample.

[24] An expectation which would be supported by an examination of the nature of the firm itself. It has been around for a while, is in fact predominantly a retail house, offers a full range of all forms of securities and commodity trading activity, is one of the larger firms in the country, and has offices with nationwide coverage. Indeed, its customer population is almost inescapably "typical," which is one of the major reasons we sought its cooperation to begin with. On the other hand, our hope at some point is to be able to test that belief directly through questionnaire mailings to a sampling of customers of other houses as well.

[25] The higher proportion of unemployed in the study group than in the control group is purely an age-related outcome; the increase is in the "retired" category.

[26] Really some eight-and-one-half years, since the sample was chosen in mid-1972 from the customer list, even though 1964 through 1970 was the investigation interval for the supplementary transactions data.

true random draw from the community of all U.S. shareholders, by age distribution, as of 1964) and that effectively the only condition which was imposed on the group was that of following it longitudinally through time, rather than allowing for entry and exit by taking a fresh cross-section each year, it turns out that the 57.1-year average age we observe for the study group as of its mid-1972 sampling date is almost exactly that which would have emerged from having "frozen" on a representative early-1964 shareowner list; the latter figure is 56.9 years.[27] Given the complementary evidence that, in all other demographic dimensions, the study and control groups are virtually identical—and that the brokerage firm's underlying clientele appears decently representative—we would argue that our 990-man basic sample is indeed an appropriate one from which to generalize about the behavior, attitudes, and circumstances of that segment of the individual investor population which can be thought of as having "money under management." It is, we believe, precisely this contituency which is of primary interest for purposes of addressing the matter of patterns of market participation by the individual investor. The only peculiarity of our study group is simply a direct reflection of the mechanics of imposing a requirement of historical account continuity for sample eligibility. Moreover, a sufficient spectrum of demographic circumstances exists *within* the group to allow us to go beyond inferences merely about *aggregate* behavior and style. In all, then, we deem it legitimate both to focus on that sample for analysis, and to extrapolate from it as a microcosm.

QUALITY OF THE RESPONSES

A concern which is always present in a survey context, however, is that of the quality of the responses received, even if the survey group itself is properly constituted. That problem can be approached from several different standpoints, the most subjective of which relates to the apparent conscientiousness of the respondents. As indicated earlier, only 4 per cent of the returned forms were so poorly executed (few items completed, illegible answers, multiple or contradictory responses, and/or clear instances of deliberate misrepresentations) that they could not be processed for inclusion. Further, the average completion rate of the questions on the *usable* replies was some 95 per cent—i.e., the typical participant left blank only 5 per cent of the total interrogatories on the form.[28]

[27] The 1965 NYSE shareowner survey is the one nearest the beginning date of our study interval, and the age distribution reported in it was used in the calculations. Since average shareholder age has been almost constant during the last 15 years (NYSE *1971 Fact Book*, p. 47), this adaptation should create no distortions. The calculations were made in the manner indicated in the note to Table 2.

[28] Rather than either discarding an entire questionnaire, or leaving it out of any analysis requiring the particular response which was omitted, a procedure was developed for filling in these few "missing values." It involved clustering all 990 questionnaires according to common demographic

Such a performance bodes well for the level of care and attention lavished by the respondents.

A second, and somewhat more rigorous, criterion would be the extent of the internal logic of certain of the cross-sectional response patterns: are they generally congruent with reasonable expectations? In that connection, we examined the responses for their consistency with some twenty of the most obvious conceivable hypotheses about individual investment behavior and circumstances—by calculating the coefficients of correlation between the values of the relevant pairs of questionnaire replies. In each instance, the observed relationship was directly in line with the only plausible *a priori* scenario, and was evidenced by a correlation coefficient significant at the .001 level or better. Among the discernible patterns, to which specific questionnaire items (discussed in detail below) gave concrete expression, are those catalogued in Table 3. All have an undeniably high degree of intuitive appeal and, while we clearly cannot thereby verify that *every* underlying individual response was both sincere and accurate, there are at least no blatant outrages in the broad profile.

TABLE 3. QUESTIONNAIRE RESPONSE PATTERNS

A. Significant *positive* correlations between:
   (1) Annual income and (2) total wealth;
   (1) Age and (2) percentage of portfolio invested in "income" securities;
   (1) Age and (2) rating of dividend income as a portfolio objective;
   (1) Expressed interest in dividend income and (2) percentage of portfolio invested in "income" securities;
   (1) Extent of use of margin transactions and (2) expressed interest in short-term capital gains as a portfolio objective;
   (1) Frequency of short sales and (2) expressed interest in short-term capital gains as a portfolio objective.

B. Significant *negative* correlations between:
   (1) Annual income and (2) percentage of portfolio invested in "income" securities;
   (1) Age and (2) size of immediate-family household;
   (1) Extent of use of margin transactions and (2) expressed interest in dividend income as a portfolio objective;
   (1) Frequency of short sales and (2) expressed interest in dividend income as a portfolio objective.

Finally, we do have an interesting direct test, which is seldom attainable in survey investigations, of what is commonly referred to as the possible "non-

attributes, using the Howard-Harris Clustering Algorithm. Five groups emerged. For any missing item on a given form, then, there was inserted the mean or modal response (as applicable, depending on the nature of the question at issue) obtained from the *other* questionnaires belonging to the specific cluster into which the form fell. Lansing and Morgan (J. B. Lansing and J. N. Morgan, *Economic Survey Methods*, Ann Arbor, University of Michigan, 1971, p. 170) provide the rationale.

response bias." As we outlined previously, the cooperating brokerage firm supplied a full portfolio transactions record for each of the 2500 accounts in our sample, covering the period 1964 through 1970. Accordingly, the question-naires were coded when they were sent out and, before the underlying address list was destroyed to prevent any later reconstruction of the group, each questionnaire returned was mated to the transactions file for the specific account in question, using an arbitrary numbering scheme. We thereby have, for all 990 questionnaire responses, a mapping—albeit now completely anonymous—of the reply form into the corresponding *individual* record of portfolio activity. It is this link which we plan subsequently to draw upon in order to identify which classes of investors (by demographic features, investment strategies, and other attributes) have done well, and which have done poorly, as personal portfolio managers. More importantly for present purposes, this data matrix allows us to test very conveniently whether there is any significant difference between the character of the questionnaire respondents and non-respondents, in a variety of account activity dimensions.

We chose to examine 18 distinct such measures—including the total dollar volume of trading in the account between 1964 and 1970, the total number of transactions executed within that period, the number of different corporations whose securities were traded, the percentage of the account's transactions which were on margin, the percentage which were short sales, the percentage break-down of the traded securities by NYSE, AMEX, and OTC classification, and so on—which seemed of likely usefulness as indices of "trading style" differences among individuals. We then attempted a linear discriminant analysis, based on these independent variables, aimed at determining whether it was possible to distinguish the respondents from the non-respondents. That effort failed. The discriminant function performed well below the 5 per cent confidence level in predicting the respective memberships of the two groups.[29] Indeed, it was able to classify correctly only 61 per cent of the relevant individual accounts—essentially, no better than a purely random achievement within a population constituted in 60/40 non-respondent/respondent proportions to begin with. It would appear, therefore, that the 990 questionnaire returnees *are* very much like their absent brethren in terms of the profile of their portfolio activities over the study period.[30] There is, on that basis, no particular reason to suspect that either the demographic or the investment strategy information on the returned forms would contain biases due to any peculiarities of the specific individuals who chose to respond.

---

[29] The critical "F" value at the 5 per cent level was 1.60, and the calculated "F" was 1.11.

[30] Eventually, of course, when the data are in place, we shall be able to address this issue in another crucial dimension—whether the questionnaire respondents have realized *returns* from their portfolios which differ from those realized by the non-respondents.

INVESTMENT STRATEGIES

Those responses portray the individual investor to be primarily a "funda-mental" analyst who perceives himself to hold a balanced, and well-diversified, portfolio of income and capital appreciation securities. He asserts that he invests predominantly for the long run, and is prone to use one of the broad-based market indexes as the benchmark by which to judge his personal invest-ment performance results. He also supplements his direct securities purchase activities quite frequently with ownership of mutual fund shares. The pertinent data, cast in the form of the replies to the questionnaire interrogatories, are presented in Table 4.

We see that almost two out of every three respondents describe themselves as using either an entirely or heavily fundamental personal approach to the evaluation of individual securities. Approximately one-fourth typically rely instead on their brokers or some other professional source of advice for recom-mendations, and only 4 per cent are technical traders. The result, as they see it, is a portfolio consisting of income and capital appreciation securities in roughly 40/60 proportions. Given that, on average, this package contains shares of stock in between 10 and 15 different corporations, it would seem that the benefits of diversification are regarded as compelling by the sample; indeed, we may infer that the respondents have (at least potentially) eliminated 90 per cent or more of the "non-systematic" risk from their respective portfolios.[31] Approximately half use mutual fund shares as an additional such vehicle.[32]

According to the group, long-term capital appreciation is the paramount investment concern, with dividend income and intermediate-term gains running distant seconds, and short-term gains clearly at the bottom of the list.[33] In appraising their success in achieving these ends, the respondents frequently use one of the standard stock price indexes as a criterion, but as many have developed an alternative "internal" benchmark instead—presumably, some amalgam of historical equity market movements and accumulated subliminal notions of a "fair" return. In any case, the sample claims that it rejects both risk-free investment yields, and mutual fund performance records, as explicit external criteria. This would suggest that, in their minds, the portion of invest-ment funds which they commit to equities under personal management is in fact regarded as a distinctive sub-category with distinctive attributes and aspirations associated with it.

[31] See J. L. Evans and S. H. Archer, "Diversification and the Reduction of Dispersion: An Empirical Analysis," *Journal of Finance*. December 1968.

[32] In each of these areas, the control group's responses were quite similar. For example, 62 per cent were fundamental analysts in whole or in part; only 4 per cent used a technical approach; the mean portfolio consisted of about 9 common stocks; and 57 per cent of the group had, at some point, owned mutual fund shares.

[33] Again, the control group replies also placed long-term capital appreciation comfortably at the top of the hierarchy.

TABLE 4. INDIVIDUALS' INVESTMENT OBJECTIVES AND STRATEGIES (QUESTIONNAIRE RESPONSES)

Which of the following approaches do you most frequently take in evaluating securities and/or reaching investment decisions?

42%   Fundamental Approach, i.e., analysis of such fundamental factors as general business conditions, industry outlook, earnings, dividends, quality of management, etc.

4%   Technical Approach, i.e., analysis of market factors such as stock price movements, supply vs. demand, amount of odd-lot trading, resistance levels, short interest, charts, etc.

23%   Combination of fundamental and technical approaches.

20%   Rely primarily on brokerage firm or account executive for recommendations.

7%   Rely primarily on paid investment newsletters or investment counselors' advice.

4%   Other.

If you divided your present securities portfolio into just two categories, (1) primarily income securities and (2) primarily capital appreciation securities, what percentages would be:

41%   Primarily income securities.*

59%   Primarily capital appreciation securities.*

The following list contains some frequent objectives that investors have in owing shares of common stock. Please rate each of these objectives in terms of their importance to you where: 4 = Very Important; 3 = Important; 2 = Slightly Important; 1 = Irrelevant.

1.84   Short-term capital gains.*

2.45   Intermediate-term capital appreciation.*

3.56   Long-term capital appreciation.*

2.65   Dividend income.*

In how many different corporations do you currently own stock?

1%	None	24%	6 to 9
7%	1 or 2	26%	10 to 15
15%	3 to 5	27%	More than 15

[*Mean value, calculated from interval mid-points and assuming average in "More than 15" category is 20, comes to 11 different companies*]

Which of the following do you use as the primary standard against which to compare your portfolio performance?

42%   Dow Jones Industrial Average, NYSE Index, Standard & Poor 500, or similar index.

2%   Average performance of mutual funds.

1%   Portfolio performance of friends or family.

45%   Your personal standard or pre-determined rate.

6%   Interest rate on savings accounts.

4%   Other.

Have you ever owned shares in a mutual fund?

57%   Yes   43%   No

In how many mutual funds do you currently own shares?

56%	None	7%	3 or 4
34%	1 or 2	3%	More than 4

* Figures represent mean values over all responses, with equal weight given to each.

We inquired specifically about those aspirations, and are tempted to conclude from the responses that most brokerage house customers must have subscriptions to the *Journal of Business*. To the question, "What annual percentage rate of return, before taxes, do you think is attainable on a regular basis from investments in common stocks, with moderate skill and understanding on the investor's part?" the answers were:

20%   0–5% Average Annual Return

49%   6–10% Average Annual Return

20%   11–15% Average Annual Return

7%   16–20% Average Annual Return

2%   21–25% Average Annual Return

2%   Above 25% Average Annual Return.

The median response, obviously, lies in the "6–10%" category and would be nearer the upper end of that range if we hypothesized a uniform distribution within it. Alternatively, the mean value, assuming such a distribution within *each* category,[34] comes out to 9.3 per cent.

In either form, the consensus reply is eminently consistent with the empirical evidence we have available from the University of Chicago studies[35] about historical rates of return on portfolios of NYSE stocks over the very long term (the appropriate horizon, according to our sample). For that matter, the sample's expectations are not only realistic, but may even be somewhat pessimistic, if viewed against the empirical data for more recent market intervals.[36] Part of this apparent pessimism might simply be a reflection of transactions costs (which were not considered in the Chicago studies, but were likely to have been implicitly netted out to some degree in our questionnaire responses), but much of it must result from the still-fresh memories of the sobering equity market experiences of the late 1960's and early 1970's.

Some interesting comparative figures, which bear on this last point, emerged from a subsequent inquiry as to the participants' impressions of their *actual* average annual before-tax portfolio returns over the last five years. Whereas both the mean and the median values of the reported "realized" distribution

[34] And assuming the "Above 25%" segment to consist of a flat spread from 26 to 30 per cent.

[35] L. Fisher and J. H. Lorie, "Rates of Returns on Investments in Common Stocks," *op. cit.* They report a compound pre-tax annual rate of return of 9.3 per cent, for an investment divided equally among all NYSE stocks as of January, 1926, and held to December, 1965.

[36] Fisher and Lorie, *ibid.*, portray returns generally in the 10-to-15 per cent per annum range, before taxes, since World War II, for NYSE investments held five years or longer.

were almost identical to those of the "attainable" array depicted above, the dispersion was noticeably greater—largely because approximately one-in-ten of the respondents admitted to a net *negative* portfolio yield between 1967 and 1972. In effect, then, the survey sample has a conception of expected long-run equity returns which is not only empirically plausible but which (logically) is rather more focused than the distribution of actual performance results over a particular shorter period.[37]

THE DECISION PROCESS

The questionnaire also provides some insights into the decision framework which underlies the indicated goals and attitudes, as well as into certain dimensions of the mechanics of the process. Table 5 summarizes the relevant responses, and suggests that roughly half the sample spends less than five hours a month, and less than $15 a year, on collecting the information for and making the decisions about the securities in its portfolios. Both of these figures are more modest than the authors' forecasts, and they convey an image of the individual's investment activities which falls well short of heavy involvement and close monitoring.[38] Of the money which *is* spent, the great bulk goes for subscriptions to the standard financial periodicals.

With regard to the perceived *quality* of information obtained, the group appears to consider the private messages it gets from its account executives, and the public ones from its journals and newspapers, of generally equal credibility and usefulness. The lower opinions of the more customized services of professional counselors and research organizations would seem to be consistent with the low level of expenditures thereon. Banks clearly are thought of as unhelpful in rendering advice.[39]

The vast majority of the respondents now do, and always have, transacted their securities business through a brokerage firm. Four out of five have tried more than one such house over the years—three being the mean and median

---

[37] Perhaps equally interesting, and highly supportive, is the counterpart evidence from the control group—which, as noted, was surveyed in 1973 rather than 1972. Its replies to the "attainable return" question produced a distribution which was indistinguishable from that of the study group. On the "realized return" query, however, the distribution was shifted markedly downward; the mean/median values were in the vicinity of only 4 per cent per annum; and nearly 30 per cent of the respondents reported they had been losing money in recent years. Hence, this younger (by seven years) group, which was sampled a year later, held precisely the same view of "normal" common stock portfolio yields, even though it felt itself to have done much less well in actuality in the period just prior to the survey.

[38] Apparently that's why account executives make all those telephone calls. 52 per cent of the control group also reported devoting under five hours per month to analysis and decision-making.

[39] The ranking of these sources was identical, and the ratings differed by an average of just 0.07, in the control group's responses.

TABLE 5. THE INVESTMENT DECISION FRAMEWORK (QUESTIONNAIRE RESPONSES)

Approximately how many hours do you spend per month in investment analysis and decision-making for your securities portfolio?

34%	Less than 3 hours.
21%	3 to 5 hours
18%	5 to 10 hours
12%	10 to 20 hours
6%	20 to 30 hours
9%	More than 30 hours

During the last year, approximately how much money did you spend for: (1) Subscriptions to investment and business periodicals; (2) Subscription advisory services; (3) Professional investment counselling?

	Periodical Subscriptions	Subscription Advisory Services	Professional Counselling
Nothing	31%	71%	92%
Less than $15	16%	6%	1%
$15 to $50	34%	8%	2%
$50 to $100	15%	7%	1%
$100 to $250	3%	6%	1%
Over $250	1%	2%	3%

The following list contains some common sources of information that investors use in making portfolio decisions. Please rate each of them in terms of their *usefulness* to you, where: 4 = Almost Always Useful; 3 = Generally Useful; 2 = Occasionally Useful; 1 = Never Useful or Never Used.

1.28	Banks*
2.14	Investment Research Subscriptions*
2.78	Brokerage Houses*
1.85	Professional Investment Counsellors*
2.69	Financial Periodicals*

How did you make (a) your *first* acquisition of common stock, and (b) your *most recent* acquisition?

	First	Most Recent
Bought through a bank.	5%	1%
Bought through a stock broker.	82%	93%
Obtained from my employer.	5%	3%
Obtained as a gift or inheritance.	7%	1%
Obtained in some other way.	1%	2%

How many different brokerage houses have you had an account with?

22%	1	27%	3
25%	2	14%	4
12%	5 or more		

(*continued*)

218

TABLE 5 (*Continued*)

Do you *presently* have an account with more than one brokerage house?

37%   Yes   63%   No

Have you ever engaged in any of the following market operations? If so, please check and then rate your degree of success with that activity, where: 5 = Very Successful; 4 = Somewhat Successful; 3 = Neutral; 2 = Somewhat Unsuccessful; 1 = Very Unsuccessful:

	Have Done	Success Rating*
Used a margin account	46%	3.67
Purchased a put or call option.	15%	2.90
Sold a stock short.	23%	2.99
Purchased a convertible security.	35%	3.71
Purchased a warrant.	42%	3.38

* Figures represent mean values over all responses, with equal weight given to each.

number—although most are dealing with but one firm at the moment.[40] A substantial percentage of the group, in their activities, have engaged in one or more of the "sophisticated" forms of market participation: short sales, margin purchases, and the like. Of these, margin dealings, convertible securities, and warrants have been the most popular, and are thought of as having generated the best results. Over all, therefore, the picture is one of an individual who is far from preoccupied with managing his portfolio and who gets most of his information from public sources—but who has shopped around reasonably carefully for a brokerage firm to work with,[41] and who is willing at least to try some of the more exotic investment vehicles in search of an edge.

THE PORTFOLIO CONTEXT

The search has been conducted in a very distinctive milieu. Because our underlying interest was not merely in the common stock transactions of the investor sample, but also with the dimensions of the *total* asset portfolios of the group, we asked on the questionnaire that the participant identify the dollar value (to the nearest $100) of his present holdings in some 15 separate asset categories. In each instance, current market values rather than original cost figures were

[40] Approximately 80 per cent of the total commission business of the sample was attributed on the questionnaire to the firm from which the account list was drawn, implying that the corresponding transactions file will in fact pick up all but a few of the relevant trades.

[41] Interestingly, the reasons given for moving from one firm to another were primarily "negative" ones—i.e., dissatisfaction with the original house rather than a positive appeal from the new one.

requested. The level of response was gratifying,[42] and the results are condensed in Table 6.

TABLE 6. THE INDIVIDUAL INVESTOR ASSET PORTFOLIO
(QUESTIONNAIRE RESPONSES)

ASSET CATEGORY	SAMPLE MEAN	SAMPLE MEDIAN	% HAVING ZERO HOLDINGS
Common Stock	$105,500	$ 40,800	2%
Preferred Stock	5,100	0	69%
Mutual Fund Shares	9,100	0	56%
Government Bonds	31,900	0	73%
Corporate Bonds	13,500	0	70%
Warrants/Puts/Calls	1,000	0	87%
Savings Account	22,900	6,100	16%
Checking Account	4,200	1,400	5%
Commodity Futures	1,100	0	96%
Personal Residence	43,900	36,000	18%
Other Real Estate	59,800	0	51%
Equity in Own Firm	49,600	0	79%
Personal Property	15,600	10,000	3%
Insurance Cash Value	16,200	7,400	15%
Other Assets	6,800	0	84%
Total Assets	$386,200	$101,700	

The reported mean asset holdings of the group aggregate to the impressive sum of $386 thousand,[43] of which $156 thousand, or approximately 40 per cent, is in direct equity investments—among them a small quantity of warrants, puts, and calls. 27 per cent of this represents ownership of the common shares of "external" firms, whereas the other 13 per cent is comprised of holdings in the company which *employs* the investor/respondent (obviously, 'employment' as a sole proprietor, partner, or majority stockholder-manager in many cases). These amounts easily swamp the $9 thousand of indirect ownership participation embedded in mutual fund shareholdings, and suggest a predominance of equity capital under personal administration as the group style. A fair-sized helping of fixed-income claims shows up in the portfolios as well: an average of $73 thousand in bonds, savings accounts, and preferred stock, constituting somewhat under one-fifth of total assets.

[42] This request was by far the most onerous on the questionnaire, and exhibited the lowest fraction of usable responses. Nonetheless, 83 per cent of the returned "long" forms did contain the relevant data (the question appeared only on the long-form version; see footnote above). No attempt was made to fill in any missing values, via clustering, for this question.

[43] The "other assets" classification does *not* include any allowance for vested rights to pension or other prospective compensation program benefits.

In many respects, however, these mean values are markedly less interesting than the medians, simply because the former are affected for our group quite drastically by a relatively few large observations—by several multimillionaires, in particular. In fact, as the last column in the tabulation documents, the great majority of the sample have no holdings at all in many of the indicated categories. Accordingly, we consider the median figures listed to provide a much more meaningful picture of the set of "typical" circumstances involved.

Those circumstances portray an individual whose total asset portfolio is in the (more familiar) vicinity of $100 thousand,[44] but of which direct equity investments still represent 40 per cent. Such commitments are barely surpassed in the aggregate by the combined worth of the man's house, furniture, automobiles, and other personal possessions. Life insurance and a modest savings account fill out the rest of the package. It would seem, therefore, if our sample *is* as useful a guide to the individual market participant population as we alleged it above to be, that most people with "money under management" *really* have money under management: They invest in common stocks to the virtual exclusion of everything else, with any funds they have left after satisfying their family's core living needs.[45]

INVESTOR OPINIONS

Such a behavior pattern—along with the observed portfolio strategies which give it expression—is, of course, the outgrowth of a host of individual perceptions and attitudes. While many of those are destined to remain permanently obscure, we did attempt in the investigation to elicit at least some indication both of the investor's subjective evaluation of his market environment, and of his self-defined personal role therein. Table 7 presents the responses to certain of the key inquiries in this area, each of which requested the subject to rate, on a five-point scale, the degree of his agreement with a specific proffered statement of opinion.[46]

---

[44] A multiple of perhaps four to five times annual earnings, based on the probable median implied by the income distribution recorded in Table 1. We had originally contemplated requesting figures for personal liabilities as well as assets, on the questionnaire, but concluded that the extra burden would very likely cost us too much in lowered response rates. For subsequent, more detailed analyses, however, some reasonable estimates of liabilities for individuals in the relevant age and income brackets *can* be made, since we have a breakdown of the various asset categories against which any borrowings would formally take place.

[45] There appear no *a priori* grounds for thinking that the survey year 1972 would be a peculiar one, in terms of the over-all composition of the group's portfolios. Regrettably, we do not have an additional verification from the "control group" in this instance, because they were sent the short-form questionnaire which did not include the asset-value request.

[46] The statement sequence in this tabulation is not that which was on the questionnaire, and other statements not shown were interspersed.

TABLE 7. ATTITUDES OF THE INDIVIDUAL INVESTOR
(MEAN VALUES OF QUESTIONNAIRE RESPONSES)

Please indicate your reaction to each of the following statements by using a rating scale of one to five, where: 5 = Strongly Agree; 4 = Moderately Agree; 3 = Neither Agree nor Disagree; 2 = Moderately Disagree; 1 = Strongly Disagree.

4.09 I enjoy investing and look forward to more such activity in the future.

3.94 Relying exclusively upon mutual fund investments reduces the personal satisfaction I obtain from making my own investments.

2.50 Over the next five years, my common stock holdings as a percentage of my entire investment portfolio will decrease substantially.

3.58 The individual investor who manages his own portfolio of stocks is likely to fare better financially than the investor who puts his money into mutual funds.

3.31 I am substantially better informed than the average investor.

2.82 Compared with mutual fund management fees, the brokerage commissions on individuals' common stock transactions are excessive.

2.12 The individual investor tends to be a more important force in the financial markets than the institutional investor.

3.60 A relatively small group of investors are making money consistently on the basis of "insider information."

2.70 The SEC regulations afford ample protection for the small investor.

3.61 To make money, an investor must be prepared to take substantial risks.

3.88 Security prices are not predictable in the short run.

2.56 The individual investor who regularly trades securities is likely to fare better financially than the individual who holds out for the long run.

The ratings suggest that the survey group's passion for direct market participation has its origins in considerations of fun as well as profit. The respondents claim to enjoy investing, to feel they would sacrifice a fair portion of that pleasure if they let institutions administer their funds, and to plan on a still larger relative commitment to equity securities under personal management in the future.[47] Presumably, such attitudes are heavily influenced by the fact that the group basically feels its portfolio selections can outperform those of institutions over time, that it is also more knowledgable than its individual investor contemporaries, and that the brokerage commissions it incurs are highly competitive with institutional management fees. While all three beliefs are strongly optimistic, they are perhaps essential prerequisites to a serious involvement in direct investment activity.

[47] If a sample of the size at issue here were drawn from a population whose actual constituent individual opinions were, say, *uniformly* distributed across the rating scale of one through five (which seems the most pessimistic possibility), the likelihood that the sample mean would differ from the true "neutral" value of 3.00 by as much as 0.15 would be less than one in 100; the chance that it would differ by as much as 0.50 would be less than one in 10,000. Since all the averages shown in the table depart from 3.00 by at least 0.18, all should comfortably pass the standard tests of significance.

Moreover, whatever their objective merits, they should not be construed as evidence of a naive view of life on the part of the respondents; reactions to the other statements indicated would belie that characterization. For example, the respondents were under no illusions (1) that the individual continues to be the dominant market force, (2) that there aren't some people around who are beating them at the investment game by getting to information first, (3) that the SEC is insulating them fully from concerns about being exploited, or (4) that they do not have to expose themselves to substantial risks in order to achieve the worthwhile portfolio returns they think are attainable.

Indeed, further evidence of sobriety emerges in the responses to the last two items listed. The consensus clearly is that short-term stock price movements *cannot* be predicted with any confidence and, accordingly, that the frequent trader is very apt to do poorly. We interpret these combined attitudes as equivalent to concurrence with the "random walk" hypothesis.[48]

In their entirety, therefore, the sentiments expressed are consistent with the "hard" data answers reported above for other portions of the questionnaire, and they contain definite elements not only of realism but even of cynicism. Nonetheless, the group does assert a claim to differential investment skill— which may not be surprising but which must (and subsequently will) be appraised empirically from the actual transactions record.

SUMMARY

The widespread concern about the potential—some would say imminent— disappearance of the individual investor from direct participation in the equity securities marketplace demands a careful examination of the latter's circumstances and decision processes. Certainly, until there becomes available a decent body of evidence on the small investor's personal situation, his self-perceptions, the portfolio returns he has experienced, and the nature of his investment strategy deliberations, neither the financial community nor the regulatory authorities are in much of a position to contemplate actions with which to counteract his withdrawal or otherwise beneficially influence his behavior. The investigation outlined here comprises the beginnings of a concerted attempt to provide information relevant to such appraisals. While the space constraints of the present forum inevitably preclude any more than an introductory treatment, we have sought to portray both the objectives of the analysis and the character of the sample on which it will be based—and have presented in some detail the initial findings which have emerged. These offer what we believe is a revealing preliminary look at the attributes and attitudes of a representative

---

[48] The form in which initially we planned to phrase the question, but from which we were sensibly dissuaded.

group of individuals who have had equity investment funds under conscious personal management during the decade of the 1960's. The underlying data are unarguably unique; we find them uncommonly fascinating; and it is our hope that others may find them at least moderately useful.

QUESTIONS

1. Relate how knowledge of investor attitudes and attributes could provide some information on each of the following.
    a. cost of capital for the firm
    b. dividend policy or investment policy for the firm
    c. capital structure for the firm
2. Do the correlations listed in Table 3 make sense to you? Explain.
3. Summarize the approaches most frequently used by individuals to evaluate securities and to reach investment decisions.
4. What is the average number of stocks held by investors in the sample? Would you call this a diversified portfolio?
5. What percentage of investors own one or more mutual funds? What does your answer to this question add to your answer to Question 4 above?
6. Comment on the annual percentage rate of return, before taxes, that investors considered to be attainable.
7. Comment on the differences between the mean and median asset portfolios of Table 6. Why do the authors place more reliance on the median figures as being representative?

14

J. B. Silvers

Liquidity, Risk, and Duration Patterns in Corporate Financing

In this article, Professor Silvers discusses the use of debt financing from 1961 to 1975 by U.S. corporations. Among other things, he shows that, although debt to asset ratios have increased, debt maturity and duration have increased, thereby decreasing financial risk during the period.

RECENT FINANCIAL HISTORY

The financial behavior of corporations has changed markedly in the 1961–75 period covered by this study. More debt has been utilized and less of a liquid asset cushion has been maintained. Exhibit 1, which is based on the total manufacturing industry data provided by the *FTC Quarterly Financial Report for Manufacturing*, reveals an increase in debt (total liabilities) from 34% of total capital in 1961 to almost 50% in 1973. Liquidity, over the same period measured by the ratio of liquid assets to current liabilities, fell from 48% to 24%. Cash and marketable securities as a percent of total assets also dropped to about half their initial 10% level before recovering slightly in the early 1970's.

Not only did corporations increase their debt load, they made more extensive use of bank debt. The proportion of total capital furnished by banks doubled over the 1961–75 period, while the non-bank proportion rose relatively modestly and then fell in the 1970's. Presumably, this bank debt was of shorter maturity than financing from non-bank sources. On the other hand, Exhibit 2, which details these trends, also reveals that long term bank debt (more than one year) rose in tandem with short term bank debt. These apparent trends towards more debt, less liquidity, and more extensive use of bank debt appear to be only incidentally affected by recessions (indicated by the shaded areas in the graphs including the "growth recession" of 1967).

These secular trends raise the question of whether the financial risk of insolvency has increased. To provide an answer, it is necessary to consider

Source. Reprinted by permission from *Financial Management*, Autumn 1976, pp. 54–64. J. B. Silvers is professor of finance, Case Western Reserve University.

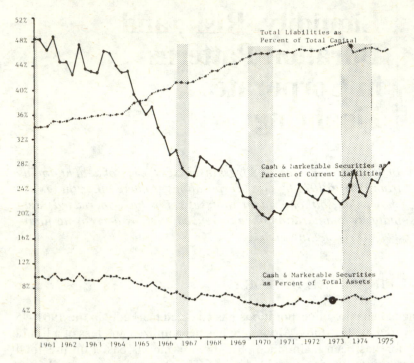

Exhibit 1.   Measures of financial risk and liquidity manufacturing sector 1961–1975 quarterly.

Source.   Constructed by the author from *FTC Quarterly Financial Report for Manufacturing,* Federal Trade Commission, Washington, D.C., 1961–1975.

the components of financial risk and how this risk should be measured. In terms of the conventional measure of debt-to-equity ratios, the answer is clearly positive. However, this simple measure misses much of the complexity of the financing decision. In addition to the common textbook focus on various gross debt ratios, the distribution of maturities of the debt used in the capital structure is of great importance to managers [1, 2]. They do not always fully hedge their position by matching asset and liability maturities. For example, the ratio of fixed assets to total assets has remained at approximately 50% over the 1961–75 period, while other liability relationships have fluctuated greatly (see Exhibits 1 and 2). Certainly, one must look beyond the debt-to-equity ratio or other simple relationships to measures of the full maturity structure of corporate liabilities and assets.

This paper addresses two basic questions. First, what has been the actual behavior of the maturity structure over recent years? That is, were debt structures as "bad" as was conveyed by the press, and have these financial

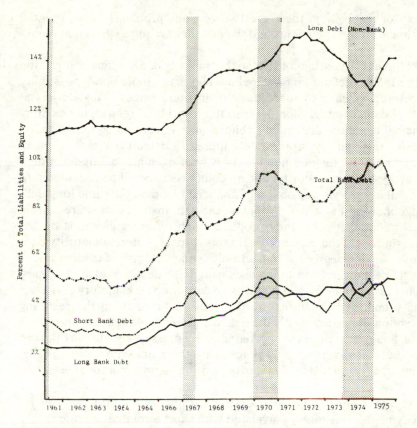

Exhibit 2.   Debt as a percent of total capital manufacturing sector 1961–1975 quarterly.

Source.   Constructed by the author from *FTC Quarterly Financial Report for Manufacturing,*
Federal Trade Commission, Washington, D.C., 1961–1975.

structures improved during the current recovery? Second, how can the debt
maturity decisions of corporate managers be explained?

FINANCIAL RISK AND MATURITY STRUCTURE

The concept of financial risk has several dimensions. One facet of financial
risk as perceived by the markets is that the additional leverage added to
corporate capital structures has had an effect on the stability of earnings and
prices [6]. However, the ultimate risk is that of bankruptcy. Certainly decreased liquidity and increased reliance on bank debt would constitute *prima
facie* evidence to most observers of increased risk of this sort. With regard to

bankruptcy or insolvency, there are two obvious problems—the potential failure to make interest payments and the default of required principal repayments.

Earlier studies [7] have demonstrated that in times of economic contraction such as the 1930's, default on principal payments is a more likely possibility and, therefore, is reflected more directly in bond prices. This "crisis at maturity" phenomenon rests on the idea that retiring or refinancing existing debt principal is a more demanding obligation than continuing interest payments. Using this logic, short term debt increases default risk more than an equivalent amount of long term debt. By way of example, a long-term debt obligation (say 40 years maturity) and an equity issue could be considered to be more similar vis-à-vis this notion of financial risk than the same long debt issue and a one year bank loan. Although the debt instruments share certain similar debt characteristics, they produce much different demands on the financial resources of the corporation. In this respect, different maturity debt should have varying degrees of impact on the financial risk of insolvency.

To determine if financial risk increases with rising debt, it is also necessary to examine the matching of debt maturity to corporate asset maturity. If asset and liability maturity structures are perfectly matched, then the resulting hedged position should leave only the risk of unpredictable aberrations in cash flows. This line of thinking is supported in a recent paper by Morris [9], who concludes that a risk averter would hedge in just this manner. According to his study, deviation from a matched maturity position might occur for at least two reasons.

The first reason would be if the operating earnings of the firm available for interest payments were highly correlated with short term interest rate levels. In that case, interest payments for servicing short term debt financing would rise and fall with operating earnings and, thus, would be effectively a variable cost. Such a situation would no doubt influence the financial leverage employed by the firm as well as its financial risk.

The second reason for such behavior would be the superior ability of a manager to forecast interest rate levels (also explored by Grove [4, 5]). If the manager could accurately forecast a fall in interest rates, then he would be justified in temporarily increasing the financial risk of the firm by adding short term debt at the margin while expecting to refinance it later with longer term debt at a lower interest rate. Of course, by taking no action, a limited form of this behavior results, since the maturity of existing debt drops by one year for each year of inaction.

In addition to the preceding two reasons, maturity structure levels might be expected to change for a variety of environmental reasons ranging from the availability of various types of capital in the financial markets to the particular experiences of the company and manager in question. The important point, however, is that little reason exists to expect stable debt maturity structures—in the corporate sector.

BEHAVIOR OF THE MATURITY STRUCTURE, 1961–1975

The evidence presented in Exhibits 1 and 2 provides only limited insight into the maturity structure. The fixed categories of debt (bank and non-bank) and other liabilities (accounts payable, etc.) imply that the composition and maturity of each group is invariant across time. But as Exhibit 2 illustrates, bank debt, for example, can change in composition over time and the maturity of the non-bank long term debt category can vary substantially. Thus, it is important to determine the average maturity of each category of corporate liability and the resulting overall average for all liabilities rather than relying on percentage distributions as in Exhibits 1 and 2.

The data from the FTC on the aggregate manufacturing sample used in this study allows a rough approximation of this sort. For long debt categories (bank and non-bank), a final maturity and weighted average maturity can be determined by assuming equal amortization at a level annual rate equal to the portion of each due within one year. Thus a $1 million face value bond with $100,000 due within one year would have an estimated final maturity of 10 years and an average maturity (weighted by the payment due in each year) of 5.5 years. For other major categories such as accounts payable, a maturity equal to the average payment period is reasonable. Unfortunately, the maturity estimate for a few relatively smaller categories must be somewhat subjective due to lack of more precise data. Specifically, constant maturity estimates were as follows: short term bank loans (six months), accrued taxes (one year), and other current liabilities (one year). Although these are not based on actual observations, the magnitude of these categories relative to all liabilities is small and their maturities are probably not subject to large changes. Thus, any errors will have a minimal effect on the overall weighted average maturity index. The overall average can be calculated using equation (1), where P_t is the payment due in period t, T is the number of years remaining to maturity, $\overline{M}$ is the weighted average maturity, and F_T is the face value of the debt.

$$\overline{M} = \sum_{t=1}^{T} (t) (P_t) \Big/ \sum_{t=1}^{T} (P_t) = \sum_{t=1}^{T} (t) (P_t)/F_T \qquad (1)$$

Although the procedure is cumbersome, it is fairly straightforward and reveals some interesting insights as shown by the upper (dotted) line in Exhibit 3. The weighted average maturity for total liabilities ($\overline{M}$) reveals no secular trend but does exhibit a great deal of cyclical variation. Maturities tend to reach a minimum during a recessionary period (shaded area of the graph) and

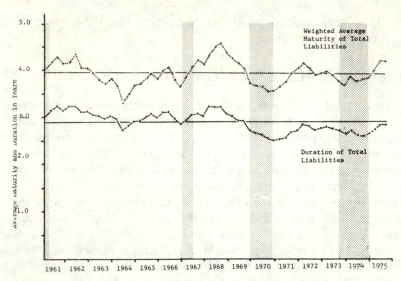

Exhibit 3.   Weighted average maturity and duration of total liabilities manufacturing sector 1961–1975 quarterly.

Source.   Constructed by the author from *FTC Quarterly Financial Report for Manufacturing,* Federal Trade Commission, Washington, D.C., 1961–1975.

peak long before the recessionary downturn begins. The maturity peaked five quarters before the 1970 recession and six before the 1973–74 downturn. Although this is an interesting observation, the data over the total period reveal many other fluctuations around the fairly stable mean, which should be investigated.

An alternative way of approaching the maturity structure data is to apply the concept of duration as formulated by Macaulay [8] and used later by a number of authors in analyzing bond portfolios (Fisher and Weil [3]), financial institutions' balance sheets (Samuelson [10]), and the general maturity structure question (Grove [4, 5]). The principle behind duration is that maturity is misleading due to the time value of money. For instance, the difference in present value terms between one dollar received from a one-year bond and one dollar received from a five-year bond at maturity is much greater than between a 21-year and a 25-year bond, yet the difference in maturity in both cases is four years. By weighting the year of payment by the present value of the payment (rather than just the dollar amount), equation (1) can be modified to produce the parallel measure of duration. Specifically, where P_t is the payment due in period t, T is the final maturity date, R is the appropriate discount rate of interest, and $\overline{D}$ is the resulting duration, then

$$\overline{D} = \sum_{t=1}^{T} (t) \left[P_t/(1 + R)^t\right] \Big/ \sum_{t=1}^{T} \left[P_t/(1 + R)^t\right]. \qquad (2)$$

Obviously since the present value of distant payments is less than their nominal value, the duration of a cash stream will always be less than its maturity for a non-zero value of R. For shorter term obligations, maturity and duration will be very close; but for longer term bonds the difference is large. For instance, the duration of a 6% semiannual coupon bond with a one year maturity is 0.985 years. But with a 20 year maturity, the duration using a 6% discount rate is only 11.904 years (see Fisher and Weil [3]).

Duration calculations are also somewhat sensitive to the choice of the discount rate. Hopefully, this rate incorporates the opportunity costs of cash flows over the interim period. For this paper, the monthly AAA utility rate for newly issued bonds averaged over the quarter was utilized in discounting. Certainly a great deal of conceptual argument is possible over this rate. However, an error of even two percentage points (i.e., 6% rate rather than 4%), ssuming a true average liability maturity in the neighborhood of four years, would produce a negligible difference in average durations.

The results of the duration calculations are presented in both Exhibits 3 and 4. In Exhibit 3 it can be seen that the results for maturity data are only slightly modified in the alterntive duration format. The peaks and valleys are flattened by the application of present values. However, the general shape of the duration curve is the same with the exception of a very slight secular downtrend. This occurs as the result of the upward drift of interest rates (used to discount future cash flows) over the 1961–75 period.

In Exhibit 4, the duration of the components of total liability duration ($\overline{D}$) are presented. All these except short term bank loans and accounts payable demonstrate pronounced cyclical and secular movement. The relatively stable total liability duration was achieved by offsetting movements of the component sources. Specifically, the decreasing duration levels of non-bank debt (Exhibit 4) appear to have been largely offset by the increasing use of long term bank loans (Exhibit 2). The average duration of total bank loans to the manufacturing sector (Exhibit 4) has risen from 1.5 years to around 2.0 years over the 15 year period.

CHANGES IN FINANCIAL RISK, 1961–1975

Although the average maturity and duration of total liabilities has fluctuated around a relatively constant mean value, the dispersion of maturities of the various sources of financing has decreased over this period. The duration of total liabilities remained around 3.0 years while the non-bank debt duration dropped from 8 to 6 years and the total bank debt duration climbed from 1.5 to 2.0 years. In other words, debt from all sources has become more homogeneous with respect to maturity. Therefore, even though there has been a pronounced shift to more bank debt, which historically has carried shorter

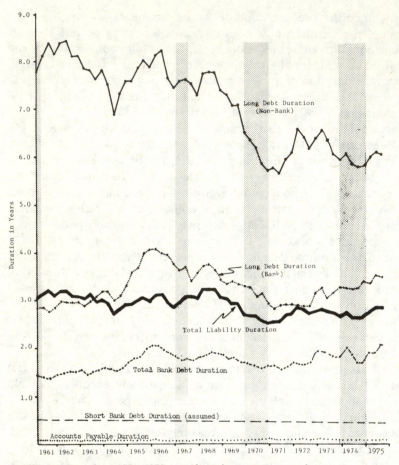

Exhibit 4.   Durations 1961–1975 manufacturing sector quarterly.

Source.   Constructed by the author from *FTC Quarterly Financial Report for Manufacturing,* Federal Trade Commission, Washingtion, D.C., 1961–1975.

maturities than non-bank debt, the maturity (duration) of bank debt has increased sufficiently to leave total liability maturity (duration) unchanged.

The increased maturity (duration) of bank debt implies a smaller proportional amount of debt would be approaching maturity at any given time. Therefore, following the crisis-at-maturity logic, the actual financial risk of insolvency from debt financing might have decreased over this period, even though the average maturity of all liabilities remained the same. As a result, it is possible that the increased financial risk coming from the larger proportion of debt used relative to equity was offset by the decreased financial risk of debt financing. Total financial risk of combined debt and equity sources could have remained relatively stable contrary to the indications of common simple ratios.

This conclusion cannot be reached without reservation. Even the more precise debt groupings used in this paper, for instance, mask variations within each group. Also, the duration of equity financing might have increased or decreased over this period. Both of these factors could shift overall financial risk either up or down. Nevertheless, it is important to observe that overall financial risk, as measured by the liability maturity structure, might have decreased rather than increased as is commonly assumed.

No conclusion concerning financial risk is possible, however, without some assessment of the degree of hedging used by firms. Hedging refers to the level of asset maturity and duration relative to that of the liability accounts. Unfortunately, asset maturity is much more difficult to determine both conceptually and empirically due to the uncertain life of long term corporate assets. Any such estimate must be regarded with suspicion particularly with respect to its absolute value. Nevertheless, even an asset maturity *index* rather than a true value should be useful in determining the degree of matching behavior.

As a first step, the final maturity of plant and equipment (representing roughly half of manufacturing assets) was approximated by the years of straight line depreciation remaining in the net book value account (book value/current depreciation change). To the extent that the sample includes corporations which report depreciation and book values using accelerated depreciation, the resulting estimate will seriously underestimate the true book life remaining. However, assuming that the proportion of firms so reporting was stable over the sample period, then the asset maturity index would be consistent if not accurate on an absolute scale. The resulting average life span from the FTC sample was 8.5 years—a plausible estimate at least. Assuming the yearly cash flow recovery equals the straight line depreciation (another gross assumption which ignores all actual operating or salvage cash flows), a weighted average maturity and duration for the plant and equipment accounts was calculated. Equations (1) and (2), the standard maturity and duration relationships, were utilized in making these estimates.

The maturity and duration estimate for other assets was more defensible with the maturity of cash at zero years, marketable securities at 0.10 years (arbitrary), accounts receivable at the collection period (average of 0.132 years), inventories at the turnover period and other assets at one year (arbitrary). In reality the overall asset maturity and duration were dominated by movements in the plant and equipment variable, thus rendering precise estimates of other categories less critical.

The results of this asset maturity and duration index are presented in Exhibit 5. It is striking to note the relative stability of asset maturity and duration figures. These strongly imply that (1) the asset maturity structure is far less a subject of manipulation by management than the liability structure,

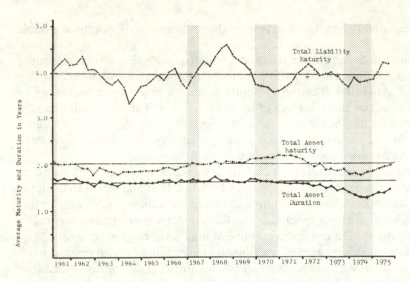

Exhibit 5.   Total asset maturity and duration and total liability weighted average maturity manufacturing sector 1961–1975 quarterly.

Source.   Constructed by the author from *FTC Quarterly Financial Report for Manufacturing*, Federal Trade Commission, Washington, D.C., 1961–1975.

(2) asset maturity matching alone is not sufficient to explain liability maturity behavior, and (3) on a secular basis the difference between asset maturity and liability maturity (a measure of financial risk) has not deteriorated significantly but has fluctuated considerably. The ratio of asset maturity to liability maturity at peak and trough periods, where the differences might be greatest, provides evidence on the final point as follows:

TOTAL ASSET MATURITY/TOTAL LIABILITY MATURITY

Date	Peak ratio	Trough ratio
1962		.49
1964	.60	
1966		.52
1967	.59	
1968		.51
1970	.64	
1972		.53
1973	.56	
1975		.49

While this table represents some shift in relative risk, the movement is not as dramatic as might be expected from the other conventional measures utilized in the introductory section of this paper. The peak and trough ratios, which

reflect the relative degree of hedging, are fairly stable, but the cyclical variation in relative asset and liability maturities is clear. Since asset maturity
matching does not explain liability maturity behavior, a more detailed study of
the maturity structure decision is obviously required.

DETERMINANTS OF THE MATURITY STRUCTURE

In an earlier section of this paper several basic reasons were hypothesized as
to why the maturity structure might vary over the sample period. In expanded
form these are explained as follows.

According to the *matching hypothesis,* managers adjust liability maturities
(and thus durations) to match the corresponding level of asset maturities,
which in turn are dictated by product-market and production and organization
decisions.

The *interest rate forecast hypothesis* states that managers forecast interest
rates and shorten the maturity structure when long rates are expected to fall
and lengthen maturities when rates are expected to rise, thus minimizing
expected total interest expense over the long run.

Under the *availability hypothesis,* the availability of corporate capital in the
financial markets dictates the type of debt used (and thus the average maturity) with managers preferring longer maturities (lower financial risk). However, market sources offer shorter and shorter maturities as conditions tighten
and risks increase.

With the *substitution hypothesis* internal funds flow (e.g., new equity
resulting from retained earnings) is used to substitute or reduce shorter term
debt. Larger returns on equity are applied to the repayment of short term debt
as a way to reduce financial risk. A variation of the ''availability hypothesis''
also supports this behavior with shortfalls in internal funds reducing the firm's
ability to support longer term debt, thus forcing it to the shorter term markets.

If reasonable surrogates can be found, then statistical tests of each of the 4
hypotheses are possible in a multiple regression format. However, notably
missing from these hypotheses are industry or company specific variables
such as the correlation between operating earnings and short term interest
rates (see Morris [9]). Of course in an aggregate sample such as the FTC data,
such interesting variables cannot be tested, although they may be important.

Matching was tested by including the asset duration as an independent
variable. The current return on equity (PAT/Book Equity) was included in the
regression to represent the level of internal funds generated and available for
substitution of higher risk debt. Availability was represented by the debt
ratio—the idea being that higher debt ratios would ultimately result in reduced
availability. Finally, the yield spread (long AAA newly issued utility rates less
the commercial paper rate) was used as the interest rate expectation variable.

Following the expectations hypothesis of the term structure literature, the anticipation was that management would interpret a positive spread as a signal that higher general rates would follow.

The base equation tested was of the following form:

$$\underset{\text{Duration}}{\text{Total Liability}} = a_0 + a_1 \left(\overset{\text{SUBSTITUTION}}{\underset{\text{Equity}}{\text{Return on}}} \right)$$

$$+ a_2 \left(\overset{\text{MATCHING}}{\underset{\text{Duration}}{\text{Asset}}} \right)$$

$$+ a_3 \left(\overset{\text{AVAILABILITY}}{\frac{\text{Total Liabilities}}{\text{Total Assets}}} \right)$$

$$+ a_4 \left(\overset{\text{INTEREST FORECAST}}{\text{Long-Short Spread}} \right) + \hat{e}$$

EMPIRICAL RESULTS

The hypotheses as proposed were all generally supported by the regression results presented in Exhibit 6. In addition to testing the base relationship for total liabilities as in the preceding equation, similar regressions were also run for the bank and non-bank subcategories with equally encouraging results.

The regressions were run (a) for the total 59 quarter period extending through the third quarter of 1975 and (b) for a 52 quarter period running through the fourth quarter of 1973 when the FTC sample underwent a substantial reclassification and redefinition of accounting categories. Although some of the coefficients were slightly altered between the two sample periods, the significance and signs of the equation parameters remained stable.

All of the coefficients for the relationship in line (1a) of Exhibit 6, which describes total liability duration behavior, are significantly different from zero at the 97.5% level, and the signs are as hypothesized.

Although these results are interesting, the total liability duration, as indicated in prior discussion, gives an incomplete picture of the maturity structure. Both the proportion of financing among the various sources and the mean maturity of each source have changed substantially. However, similar regressions on the two main sub-categories also support these results. Lines (2a) and (2b) in Exhibit 6 present the results for the non-bank duration. They are as expected except that the interest forecast variable is less significant.

EXHIBIT 6. REGRESSION RESULTS, MANUFACTURING SECTOR 1961–75 [t-RATIOS IN PARENTHESES]

Dependent variable	Constant	Substitution Return on equity	Matching Asset duration	$\frac{\text{Debt}}{\text{assets}}$	Availability Long debt duration	Short interest rate	Interest rate forecast Yield spread	R^2
1961–75 (n=59)								
1a. Total liability duration	+2.345	+.1280 (2.326)	+.8496 (3.541)	-2.959 (5.761)			+.0609 (3.185)	.69
2a. Long debt duration (non-bank)	+8.140	+.4288 (2.967)	+2.387 (3.787)	-14.69 (10.89)			+.0569 (1.132)	.85
3a. Total bank duration	-1.161	+.2260 (4.228)	-.1803 (0.741)	+3.682 (4.450)	+.1422 (3.046)		+.0287 (1.645)	.64
4a. Total bank duration	-0.989	+.2178 (3.914)	-.2537 (0.917)	+4.059 (3.812)	+.1309 (2.567)	-.0177 (0.568)	+.0116 (0.334)	.64
1961–73 (n=52)								
1b. Total liability duration	+2.297	+.1359 (2.211)	+.8581 (2.087)	-2.903 (4.903)			-.0473 (1.913)	.61
2b. Long debt duration (non-bank)	+8.151	+.4973 (3.111)	+2.278 (2.130)	-14.71 (9.554)			+.0363 (0.564)	.82
3b. Total bank duration	-1.674	+.2822 (6.610)	+.3594 (1.320)	+3.404 (5.302)	+.0920 (2.594)		-.0214 (1.360)	.78
4b. Total bank duration	-1.838	+.2343 (5.154)	+.4706 (1.783)	+5.535 (5.082)	+.0520 (1.375)	+.0771 (2.365)	-.1110 (2.724)	.81

This is perhaps due to the possibility that such forecasts have their impact through switches *between* bank and non-bank debt (thus showing up in the overall liabilities results) and less through changes in the duration of sub-categories of financing. On the other hand, substitution, asset maturity matching, and availability all have a stronger influence in terms of the absolute value of the coefficients and their statistical significance. The overall explanatory power of this sub-equation in terms of R^2 also surpasses that for the total liability regression.

For the bank debt variable the availability proxy was broadened to include the long term debt duration in equations (3a) and (3b) and the short term interest rate in equations (4a) and (4b). The logic for the first was that the availability of bank debt would be positively influenced by the presence of longer term durations for the long term debt sources. This would imply less immediate refinancing demands and thus greater ability to support shorter term (bank) debt. In the final equation the short term interest rate was included to further reflect the tightness of the market.

The behavior of total bank loan durations in lines (3a-b) and (4a-b) in Exhibit 6 is much as expected with some interesting exceptions. Interest forecast proxies are again less significant for this sub-sample. However, the signs of the interest forecast variables are reversed and significant for equation (4b), indicating a lengthening of durations when rates are expected to fall and a shortening when they are thought to be rising. This reverse behavior may be a reflection of the fact that desired overall duration changes, in reaction to altered interest expectations, are achieved by shifting between the bank and non-bank sources rather than by changing the durations of all forms of debt. This reverse sign also may reflect the parallel and opposite desire of banks to lock up high long term rates in the face of falling interest levels. Unfortunately, without a full supply and demand model of the financial system, it is impossible to determine the full underlying factors. In addition, asset duration, not too surprisingly, has negligible impact on bank loan duration. On the other hand, the substitution (Return on Equity) variable is more highly significant, again supporting the idea that higher volumes of internal funds are used to retire shorter term bank debt and/or support additional longer term bank borrowing.

For the full sample period the debt ratio and the long debt duration were significant. In the truncated period (1961–73) the short term interest rate variable was also significant.

Of course the large unanswered question concerns the increased use of debt sources in the aggregate, which is an issue parallel to the maturity structure focus of this study. It might be that the perceived duration of equity sources (which can be defined, as in [3]) has changed in such a manner as to leave the duration of all capital sources relatively stable on average over the period in spite of the rising proportion of debt capital. This speculation was explored in the preceding section. However, without more evidence regarding equity durations, this possibility must remain only a speculation.

CONCLUSIONS

This paper has provided some insight into the complex choice of debt maturities by corporate management. The patterns of debt maturity and duration over time provide evidence that these choices have not resulted in large increases in financial risk. Furthermore, attempts were made to explain observed maturity structures for the manufacturing sector by reasonable behavioral variables.

One might conclude from these results that corporate maturity structures are subject to substantial variations as economic conditions change. A large portion of these changes can be attributed to risk aversion, expected interest cost minimization, and availability factors. Thus, it is clear that the maturity structure is an important policy variable for corporate management in addition to the traditional choice between debt and equity.

REFERENCES

1.   G. Donaldson, *Corporate Debt Capacity,* Boston, Division of Research, Harvard Business School, 1961.
2.   G. Donaldson, *Strategy for Financial Mobility,* Boston, Division of Research, Harvard Business School, 1969.
3.   L. Fisher and R. L. Weil, "Coping With the Risk of Interest Rate Fluctuations: Returns to Bond Holders from Naive and Optimal Strategies," *Journal of Business* (October 1971).
4.   M. A. Grove, "A Model of the Maturity Profile of the Balance Sheet," *Metroeconomica* (Jan.–April 1966).
5.   M. A. Grove, "On 'Duration' and the Optimal Maturity Structure of the Balance Sheet," *The Bell Journal of Economics and Management Science* (Autumn 1974).
6.   R. A. Haugen and D. W. Wichern, "The Intricate Relationship Between Financial Leverage and the Stability of Stock Prices," *Journal of Finance* (December 1975).
7.   R. Johnson, "Term Structure of Corporate Bond Yields as a Function of Risk of Default," *Journal of Finance* (May 1967).
8.   F. R. Macaulay, *The Movements of Interest Rates, Bond Yields, and Stock Prices in the United States Since 1856,* New York, National Bureau of Economic Research, 1938.
9.   J. R. Morris, "On Corporate Debt Maturity Strategies," *Journal of Finance* (March 1976).
10.   P. Samuelson, "The Effects of Interest Rate Increases on the Banking System," *American Economic Review* (March 1945).

QUESTIONS

1. Explain why firms have increased their use of debt during the period 1961–1975.
2. Banks have been traditional suppliers of short-term funds and still are. However, this study shows that bankers are providing more long term funds than previously. What reasons can you provide for banks' willingness to provide longer-term funds?
3. Explain why a given amount of long-term debt could entail less financial risk for a firm than the same amount of short-term debt.
4. Contrast term-to-maturity of a debt obligation with its duration (that is, define each and explain how they are related and how they are different).

15 | Brian M. Neuberger and Carl T. Hammond

A Study of Underwriters' Experience with Unseasoned New Issues

Corporations issuing securities to obtain financing should know something about investment bankers. This study shows that the cost of flotation (due to underpricing) varies systematically among underwriters. It would, therefore, seem important for the firm to be aware of this and select an underwriter with some knowledge of what to expect.

I. INTRODUCTION

One of the phenomena on Wall Street during the sixties was the new issues market. During the decade new issues became a popular investment alternative, particularly in the bull markets of 1962, 1966, and 1968. The height of enthusiasm occurred in the hot new issues market of the fiscal year 1968–1969 when 2,171 issues were offered to the public. This interest in new issues was followed by studies such as Reilly and Hatfield [12], McDonald and Fisher [9], the SEC [13], and others, all of which show that there is a downward bias in the issue price of new issues. Why this downward bias is present was treated later by Logue [5]. Although these studies also suggest that there is a difference in the pricing behavior by individual underwriters, none of the previous studies has addressed itself specifically to this point.

Therefore, the purpose of this study is (1) to evaluate the performance of the underwriters of unseasoned new issues from 1965 to 1969 and (2) to test the hypothesis that there is a significant difference in the short-run price appreciation of underwriters' portfolios of unseasoned new issues.

The new issues market involves three parties: the investor, the issuer, and the underwriter. This study will approach the situation from the perspective of the investor.[1] The primary objective of the investor is the appreciation of his

Source. Reprinted by permission from *The Journal of Financial and Quantitative Analysis,* March 1974, pp. 165–177. Brian Neuberger is professor of finance at San Diego State University. Carl T. Hammond is with Price Waterhouse and Co.

[1] For an in-depth discussion of all three parties, see Logue [7].

capital. If some underwriters experience appreciation that is significantly higher than others, then the investor should consider the underwriter as a variable in his evaluation of prospective new issues.

McDonald and Fisher [9] were the first to suggest that there was a difference in the pricing behavior of underwriters, and this idea was studied more closely by Logue [6]. Logue's study, based on his above-mentioned dissertation [5], discusses the difference in performance of prestigious and nonprestigious underwriters. The underwriters were segregated using Hayes' system [2] which identified prestigious underwriters based on tombstone advertising. Logue found that in one month from the date of issue, prestigious underwriters' issues appreciated 20.8 percent, versus 52.1 percent for nonprestigious underwriters. The difference is significant, and he concludes, "this difference can be explained in part by differences in the issues themselves and by the way in which each segment responds to various stimuli."

For example, using regression analysis and testing ten independent variables, Logue found the only variable significant to prestigious underwriters was that of the "secondary issue" variable. Statistical variance in this variable means that as a greater percentage of the shares offered is secondary (proceeds accrue to shareholders instead of the corporation), the lower the appreciation of the issue. The explanation Logue offers in part is, "Because the secondary sellers' demands for liquidity may be more postponable than those of the firm . . . they may be in a bargaining position such that they can force the investment banker to seek a higher price. . . ." Logue goes on to interpret other significant differences between prestigious and nonprestigious underwriters. Unfortunately, since he considers the sample of 250 issues only in terms of prestigious and nonprestigious underwriters, the question of individual underwriter performance is left unanswered.

Although the investor is interested in both the short-run and long-run appreciation of new issues, this study will only consider the short run. The primary reason is based on the findings of the McDonald-Fisher study [9], which stated, "The implications are that short-term holdings were highly profitable to initial subscribers, but that initial price behavior did not have significant predictive value to investors making purchase decisions at the market rice a short time after the offering."

In other words, once the initial price bias is adjusted, the investor should expect subsequent price movement to follow efficient market rules where the primary attribute is risk.[2] In a related SEC study, out of 49 issues rising 100 percent or more one month following the date of issue, only 14 were still above the offering price two years later [10].

---

[2] For an opposing view, see Reilly-Hatfield [12] and Reilly [11].

II. THE SAMPLE

The sample contains 48 underwriters chosen with three concerns in mind. The first concern was to choose underwriters large enough to be able to critically select new companies seeking public financing. Therefore, all underwriters managing over 50 common equity issues totaling at least $100 million in value from 1960 to 1969 were considered. This produced 23 underwriters. The second concern was to choose underwriters that participated heavily in the common equity market during the sixties. We decided to consider all under-writers that managed at least 20 common equity issues and participated in 700 or more issues from 1960 to 1969. This produced an additional 14 under-writers. Third, we wanted to select underwriters with experience in new common issues.[3] We defined this criterion of experience as the management of 20 common equity issues from 1960 to 1969 of which at least four were new issues during 1969. This produced an additional 11 underwriters. Table 1 summarizes the total underwriter population for this study.

The three concerns can be broken down into five different characteristics as shown in Table 1. The total underwriter population is 750, of which 130 exhibit at least one of the five characteristics. Out of the 130 underwriters, 48 met one of the three concerns. It is important to note that all underwriters selected managed at least 20 common equity issues from 1960 to 1969, and that 39, or 81 percent, of these underwriters had four new common issues during 1969.

The portfolios for these underwriters are composed of all unseasoned new issues (companies offering stock publicly for the first time) from 1965 through 1969. Regulation "A" offerings (under $300,000) and mutual funds were excluded. Market conditions for this period varied. The Dow Jones Industrial Average indicated two major bull markets and two major bear markets from 1965 through 1969.

III. TEST METHODOLOGY

Simply stated, the hypothesis for this study is tested by determining the average excess appreciation for each underwriter's portfolio and comparing them with each other using an analysis of variance. If the individual under-writers used similar pricing behavior, the average excess appreciation among underwriters would be equivalent and our hypothesis would not be confirmed.

---

[3] New common issues were taken from the *New Issue Performance Directory* [4]. A close examination of issues listed in this source shows that they are not all unseasoned new issues. The number of seasoned issues is minor, and the list is sufficiently different to distinguish it from a list of common equity offerings.

TABLE 1. *UNDERWRITERS EXHIBITING SAMPLE SELECTION CRITERIA*

	Number of Underwriters	
Characteristic	Population	Sample
1. Underwriters involved in investment banking from 1960 to 1969 750		48
2. Selection criteria for the sample		
a. Concern 1: Large underwriters meeting (1) and (2) below 23		23
(1) Managed over $100 million in common equity issues from 1960 to 1969 50		35
(2) Managed at least 50 common equity offerings from 1960 to 1969.............................. 24		24
b. Concern 2: Active underwriters meeting (1) and (2) below 32		32
(1) Participated in over 700 common equity offerings from 1960 to 1969 33		32
(2) Managed at least 20 common equity offerings from 1960 to 1969.............................. 74		48
c. Concern 3: Experienced underwriters in new issues meeting (1) and (2) below 38		38
(1) Managed at least 4 new common equity offerings during 1969 95		39
(2) Managed at least 20 common equity offerings from 1960 to 1969.............................. 74		48
3. Underwriters exhibiting at least one of the criteria mentioned in 2 above 130		48

The source of issues comprising each underwriter's portfolio, the date of issue, and the issue price were taken from *1960-1969: A Decade of Corporate and International Finance* [3]. Subsequent prices were taken primarily from the *Commercial and Financial Chronicle* which reports on most new issues.[4]

The method employed in this study is similar to that used by McDonald-Fisher. There are three time periods under consideration: (1) date of issue to one week following date of issue, (2) date of issue to one month following date of issue, and (3) one week to one month following date of issue.[5]

---

[4] If subsequent price information was not available in the *Commercial and Financial Chronicle* [1], then the issue was omitted from the study. Out of 1,110 issues, 816 (or 73.5 percent) qualified.

[5] Bid prices as reported by the *Commercial and Financial Chronicle* [1] were used for the one-week and one-month price. The one-week price was the first reported price which was at least three days and not more than ten days after the date of issue. The only exceptions to this were stocks which remained in syndication after the issue date; for these stocks, the first reported price was used. The one-month price was the price reported three weeks after the date used for the one-week price.

Excess appreciation was calculated for each issue as:

$$X_{it} = R_{it} - R_{mt}$$

where R_{it} is the return on issue i in period t and R_{mt} is the return on the over-the-counter average in the same period.

The excess appreciation was accumulated by underwriter u and mean excess appreciation $\bar{x}$ was determined by:

$$\bar{x} = \frac{\Sigma \, x_{ut}}{n_u}$$

where n is the number of issues for each underwriter.

The hypothesis is tested by using the F statistic in the analysis of variance formula:

$$F = \frac{\sum\limits_{}^{k} n_u \, (\bar{x}_u - \bar{x}.)^1 \left(\dfrac{1}{k-1}\right)}{\sum\limits_{}^{k} \, (\sum\limits_{}^{n} x_u^2 - [(\sum\limits_{}^{n} x_u)^2 \, / \, n_u]) \, / \, \dfrac{1}{(N-k)}}$$

where

x_u is the underwriter's excess appreciation for each issue,
$\bar{x}_u$ is the average excess appreciation for each underwriter,
$\bar{x}.$ is the excess average appreciation for all issues,
 k is the total number of underwriters,
 n is the number of issues for each underwriter, and
N is the total number of issues for all underwriters.

IV. THE RESULTS

F Statistic

The F statistic results are summarized in Table 2. The one-week period is significant at the 1 percent level and the one-month period is significant at the 5

TABLE 2.   F STATISTIC

Period 1	Period 2	Period 3
1.641*	1.474**	0.851

*Significant at .01 level
**Significant at .05 level

percent level. This means that there is a significant difference in the appreciation of underwriters' portfolios of unseasoned new issues from the date of issue to one week or one month later. In other words, the investor should consider the underwriter of a new issue because the price appreciation is significantly different among underwriters.

The appreciation from the one-week price to the one-month price is not significant. This would indicate that any short-run adjustment of price occurs during the first week, and is consistent with findings of previous studies. For the investor, this would mean that he should consider a short holding period and rapid turnover as a more effective trading technique than holding for eventual predetermined appreciation.[6]

Total Issues

The excess appreciation for all issues tested is comparable to that of other studies (see Table 3). Most of the differences can be attributed to the different sampling techniques and time frames. For example, the lower appreciation found in this study during the one-month holding period can be explained in part by the predominance of large underwriters which appear to experience lower returns. (See also discussion on appreciation by underwriters.)

TABLE 3.   RESULTS OF STUDIES OF UNSEASONED NEW ISSUES

Study	Time Frame	Number of Issues	Appreciation	
			Immediately after Offering	One Month after Offering
Reilly-Hatfield	1963-1965	53	9.9	8.7
McDonald-Fisher	1969	142	28.5	34.6
Logue	1965-1969	250	—	41.7
Neuberger-Hammond	1965-1969	816	17.0	19.1

Table 4 shows total issues segregated as "secondary" and "nonsecondary."[7] Logue [11] found a significant difference in his "secondary issue" variable as discussed earlier in this paper, and these results support his contention that stockholders can demand a higher offering price.

[6] Logue [8], using a different analysis technique which considers risk, recommends holding issues three months after the date of issue.

[7] The proceeds of a secondary issue accrue solely to the stockholders. A primary issue's proceeds, in contrast, accrue to the corporation. A combination issue is primary and secondary. In this study, nonsecondary issues will be defined as primary and combination issues.

TABLE 4. *SUMMARY OF EXCESS APPRECIATION BY CATEGORY*

Category	Number of Issues	Period 1	Period 2	Period 3
Total issues	816	17.0% (33.9)	19.1% (45.7)	0.8% (19.0)
Secondary issues	313	10.9% (24.5)	10.9% (35.7)	−1.1% (14.2)
Nonsecondary issues	503	20.9% (38.6)	24.3% (50.3)	2.0% (21.4)

Note: Standard deviation is in parentheses.

Underwriters

The average excess appreciation by underwriter is summarized in Table 5.[8] The immediate and maybe the most important point to come from Table 5 is the fact that no underwriter had negative average excess appreciation during the first week after offering. This is the result of underpricing, as suggested by this and other studies. Also, underwriters are able to support the price of an issue by making a market in that issue if it falls below the offering price.

TABLE 5. *SUMMARY OF AVERAGE EXCESS APPRECIATION FOR 48 UNDERWRITERS*

		Period 1	Period 2	Period 3
First Quartile	High	37.6%	45.5%	8.2%
	Low	22.2	27.7	4.0
Second Quartile	High	21.3%	26.9%	4.0%
	Low	15.5	18.3	0.6
Third Quartile	High	15.3%	17.3%	0.3%
	Low	7.8	6.6	−1.7
Fourth Quartile	High	7.7%	6.4%	−2.2%
	Low	1.0	−9.2	−18.6

The one-month range of 45.5 percent to −9.2 percent is considerably wider than that of the one-week period. It is interesting to note this in light of the fact that the F statistic was smaller for the one-month period. We would expect the opposite; that is, the wider range in appreciation values would give a larger F statistic. The results show that the appreciation averages for individual underwriters are bunched more in the one-month period. This would suggest that after the market adjusts for any downward bias in pricing and begins influencing price based on risk, we find underwriters with similar risk-oriented

---

[8] See Appendix for individual underwriter performance.

portfolios, and therefore their price performance consolidates around related percentages.

The difference between the one-week and one-month results (period 3) shows half the sample with positive excess appreciation and half with negative excess appreciation. This could be the result of investors capturing their short-run gains and the excessive selling pressure lowering the market price, just as excessive buying pressure raised the market price the week after the offering. Although the difference among underwriters is not significant for this time period, it is important to note that only half of the underwriters were able to protect their short-run gains for one month.

Out of 48 underwriters selected, 25 are prestigious underwriters as defined by Hayes [2]. Table 6 shows that prestigious underwriters experience lower appreciation than less prestigious underwriters. The number of prestigious underwriters is definitely skewed toward the lower quartiles.

TABLE 6.   NUMBER OF PRESTIGIOUS AND NONPRESTIGIOUS
UNDERWRITERS IN EACH QUARTER

	Period 1		Period 2		Period 3	
	P*	NP**	P*	NP**	P*	NP**
First	2	10	2	11	5	7
Quartile	(8%)	(43%)	(8%)	(48%)	(20%)	(30%)
Second	6	6	7	4	6	6
Quartile	(24%)	(26%)	(28%)	(18%)	(24%)	(26%)
Third	8	4	6	6	7	5
Quartile	(32%)	(18%)	(24%)	(26%)	(28%)	(22%)
Fourth	9	3	10	2	7	5
Quartile	(36%)	(13%)	(40%)	(8%)	(28%)	(22%)
Total	25	23	25	23	25	23
	(100%)	(100%)	(100%)	(100%)	(100%)	(100%)

*P = prestigious underwriters
**NP = nonprestigious underwriters

These findings are consistent with Logue [6] as discussed earlier in this paper. He believes the reasons for this are attributable mainly to the fact that prestigious underwriters are involved with large issues, and that there is an inverse relationship between the issue size and appreciation. Also, many fringe underwriters enter the new issues market only in times of great activity when new issues tend to appreciate rapidly.

V. CONCLUSION

The investor who is interested in participating in the new issues market is supported by the fact that research has shown there is an apparent downward bias in the pricing of new issues. This study expands the previous research by evaluating the performance of specific underwriters. Average short-run portfolio appreciation for each underwriter was compared using an analysis of variance, and the difference was significant from the issue date to one week and to one month later. This leads us to conclude that the investor should consider the underwriter as a significant variable in the appreciation of new issues.

Once market activity had eliminated the initial pricing bias established by the underwriters, the issues studied performed so that no significant distinction was apparent among underwriters. In addition, the difference for all issues in the one-week-to-one-month time period was minor. Therefore, concerning trading technique, it appears that a short holding period and rapid turnover strategy would be more effective than holding for eventual predetermined appreciation.

Finally, the analysis of two other partitions of the sample resulted in differences from which inferences can be drawn. This study found, first, that secondary issues appreciated less than nonsecondary issues, and, second, that prestigious underwriters' portfolios appreciated less than those of nonprestigious underwriters.

Appendix
AVERAGE SHORT-RUN EXCESS APPRECIATION BY UNDERWRITER

Name	Number of Issues	Excess Appreciation		
		Period 1	Period 2	Period 3
Allen & Co., Inc.	19	29.6%	32.5%	2.0%
		(25.7)	(32.0)	(14.0)
Auchincloss, Parker & Redpath	16	20.2	20.7	− 1.5
		(35.2)	(54.3)	(16.0)
Bache & Co., Inc.	18	14.5	10.1	− 4.3
		(51.1)	(56.1)	(12.4)
Barthe & Co., J.	11	18.0	26.4	7.0
		(22.1)	(26.3)	(8.5)
Bear Stearns & Co.	14	2.8	6.1	2.7
		(9.1)	(20.8)	(16.2)
Becker & Co., A. G.	10	32.1	35.7	4.2
		(56.3)	(53.1)	(15.0)
Blair Securities Corp.	29	37.6	42.5	2.5
		(46.7)	(71.8)	(33.4)
Blyth & Co., Inc.	15	7.8	6.6	− 1.1
		(14.3)	(18.1)	(10.3)
Courts & Co.	15	35.2	36.8	− 0.8
		(44.6)	(51.9)	(11.6)

Name	Number of Issues	Excess Appreciation		
		Period 1	Period 2	Period 3
Dain, Kalman & Quail, Inc.	13	26.9% (54.2)	25.8% (52.6)	− 0.4% (14.1)
Dempsey-Tegeler & Co.	26	31.1 (41.0)	31.8 (45.7)	0.2 (13.2)
Dominick & Dominick, Inc.	14	15.5 (25.9)	5.2 (26.7)	− 8.3 (17.1)
duPont & Co., F. I. Allyn, Inc. A. C.	29	1.0 (9.3)	− 5.3 (20.0)	− 6.7 (13.4)
Eastman, Dillon, Union Securities & Co.	22	10.1 (23.6)	12.7 (34.8)	1.6 (16.8)
Eppler, Guerin & Turner, Inc.	11	13.5 (21.1)	17.3 (34.6)	3.9 (27.6)
First Boston Corp.	5	5.9 (17.3)	1.7 (28.1)	−5.1 (12.0)
Glore, Florgan & Co., Wm. R. Staats, Inc.	19	5.3 (16.3)	1.7 (23.9)	− 3.9 (11.8)
Goldman, Sachs & Co.	27	6.3 (14.2)	10.1 (22.9)	2.8 (10.9)
Goodbody & Co.	23	18.1 (31.0)	25.5 (52.8)	3.7 (23.3)
Gregory & Sons	19	28.9 (48.5)	39.4 (63.0)	6.3 (18.8)
Hayden, Stone, Inc.	16	11.8 (20.1)	17.7 (39.2)	4.0 (25.1)
Hornblower & Weeks, Hemphill, Noyes	19	5.2 (10.7)	4.8 (17.0)	− 0.8 (9.3)
Hutton & Co., E. F.	9	13.8 (23.8)	15.7 (43.0)	− 0.3 (15.1)
Hutton & Co., W. E.	13	3.9 (10.4)	3.1 (21.7)	− 1.1 (16.1)
Kidder, Peabody & Co.	23	7.7 (27.3)	6.4 (39.7)	− 2.2 (12.8)
Kleiner Bell & Co.	11	30.2 (43.2)	29.7 (61.0)	− 3.8 (18.4)
Lehman Brothers	25	19.4 (32.1)	26.5 (41.2)	5.4 (14.1)
Loeb, Rhoades & Co.	7	10.2 (26.4)	− 9.2 (34.8)	−18.6 (18.9)
Lomansey & Co., Myron A.	20	21.3 (56.4)	26.3 (47.4)	7.4 (28.8)
McDonald & Co.	10	14.1 (18.7)	11.0 (20.8)	− 2.9 (7.3)
Merrill Lynch, Pierce Fenner & Smith, Inc.	28	5.7 (14.3)	4.1 (18.7)	− 1.7 (8.7)
Mitchem, Jones & Templeton, Inc.	14	36.1 (48.2)	45.5 (58.9)	6.0 (16.6)
Paine, Webber, Jackson & Curtis	23	16.4 (28.0)	18.3 (39.8)	0.3 (12.8)

Name	Number of Issues	Excess Appreciation		
		Period 1	Period 2	Period 3
Plohn & Co., Charles	31	17.1%	23.8%	4.8%
		(38.8)	(57.3)	(28.9)
Rauscher Pierce & Co.	15	16.7	16.5	− 2.3
		(27.2)	(46.0)	(14.6)
Reynolds & Co.	7	15.7	23.4	6.7
		(21.5)	(31.5)	(23.2)
Shearson, Hammill & Co., Inc.	15	2.2	6.9	4.0
		(12.3)	(23.8)	(14.5)
Shields & Co., Inc.	17	15.6	22.1	3.4
		(33.0)	(56.4)	(27.1)
Smith, Barney & Co., Inc.	7	15.3	19.5	2.6
		(16.9)	(25.8)	(8.7)
Suplee, Mosley, Close & Kerner Inc.	17	21.9	35.7	8.2
		(45.1)	(78.4)	(39.4)
Unterberg, Towbin & Co., C. E.	28	27.5	29.4	1.1
		(24.5)	(37.8)	(18.8)
Van Alstyne, Noel & Co.	18	9.1	6.6	− 3.0
		(23.3)	(34.1)	(18.2)
Walker & Co., G. H.	18	8.7	5.9	− 2.7
		(17.6)	(20.1)	(11.7)
Walston & Co., Inc.	28	20.3	24.1	1.2
		(41.8)	(56.4)	(17.4)
Weis, Voisin, Cannon Inc.	12	12.1	12.3	0.1
		(17.0)	(46.5)	(35.2)
Wheat & Co., Inc.	9	2.2	0.1	− 1.0
		(26.4)	(28.1)	(14.5)
White Weld & Co.	33	23.0	24.0	− 0.9
		(50.2)	(62.8)	(15.0)
Witter (Dean) & Co. Inc.	20	12.8	20.1	4.7
		(21.7)	(36.9)	(15.4)

Note: Standard deviation is in parentheses.

REFERENCES

1. *Commercial and Financial Chronicle.* 1965–1970.
2. Hayes, S. L., III. "Investment Banking: Power Structure in Flux." *Harvard Business Review,* March–April 1971, pp. 136–152.
3. Hillstrom, Roger, and Robert Kind, eds. *1960–1969: A Decade of Corporate and International Finance.* New York: IDD, Inc., 1970.
4. Lack, Arthur, ed. *New Issue Performance Directory.* New York: New Issue Outlook, Inc., 1970.
5. Logue, D. E. "An Empirical Appraisal of the Efficiency of the Market for First Public Offerings of Common Stock." Unpublished Ph.D. dissertation, Cornell University, 1971.

6. _____. "On the Pricing of Unseasoned Equity Issues: 1965–1969." *Journal of Financial and Quantitative Analysis,* January 1973, pp. 91–103.
7. _____. "Premia on Unseasoned Equity Issues." *Journal of Economics and Business,* Spring/Summer 1973, pp. 133–141.
8. _____. "Risk-Adjusted Performance of Unseasoned Common Stock Offerings." *The Quarterly Review of Economics and Business,* vol. 12 (1972).
9. McDonald, J. G., and A. K. Fisher. "New Issue Stock Price Behavior." *The Journal of Finance,* March 1972, pp. 97–102.
10. Murphy, James P. "List of Registrants and Related Information." Working papers for testimony in SEC Hot Issue Investigation, February 28, 1972.
11. Reilly, Frank K. "Further Evidence on Short-Run Results for New Issue Investors." *Journal of Financial and Quantitative Analysis,* January 1973.
12. Reilly, Frank K., and Kenneth Hatfield. "Investor Experience with New Stock Issues." *Financial Analysts Journal,* September–October 1969, pp. 73–80.
13. U.S. Securities and Exchange Commission. *Institutional Investors Study.* Washington, D.C.: U.S. Government Printing Office, 1971.
14. _____. *Special Study of the Securities Markets.* Washington, D.C.: U.S. Government Printing Office, 1963.

QUESTIONS

1. If a particular underwriter systematically prices securities so that his or her investors receive high returns in comparison with another underwriter's, what is the implication for the financial manager?
2. What logical reason is there for an underwriter to "underprice" an issue? How does underpricing affect investor returns? If you were an investor, which would you desire, more or less underpricing (if you were to buy stock from the underwriter)? If you were the issuing firm, which would you prefer?
3. Explain how it could be possible for the more prestigious underwriters to underprice issues more than less prestigious underwriters.
4. If underwriters believed that the securities markets were efficient, would they feel the need to underprice issues?

16

Richard S. Bower

Issues in Lease Financing

Leasing as a source of capital is increasing in importance. The lessee has the use of the asset, while the lessor buys the asset and receives lease payments, the depreciation privilege, and the residual value. Unlike the owner of the asset, the lessee has foregone the salvage value and tax savings due to depreciation. The entire lease payment is tax deductible, while only the interest component of a loan is deductible.

The literature in finance includes some controversy as to how the asset user should analyze the lease or buy decision. Professor Bower presents the major opposing views, then reconciles the methods of analysis for the decision maker. He synthesizes earlier methods in a way which shows that the only real differences are those dealing with the discount rates to be applied to the lease payments, the tax shelters, and the salvage value.

The advantages of becoming the lessee in a long-term, irrevocable financial lease arrangement are not so obvious that corporation executives can ignore their critical evaluation. A number of academic analysts who will be considered individually here have offered such counsel. Unhappily, the advice does not agree in all respects, and the proponents of variant approaches tend to emphasize their points of disagreement rather than their points of agreement, i.e., Johnson & Lewellen [7, pp. 816–818] and Mitchell [8, pp. 308–309]. It is more profitable to summarize points of agreement, reconcile or resolve disagreements and seek an easily used decision format.

AGREEMENT AND DISAGREEMENT

All of the academic approaches require inputs that include purchase price of the asset to be leased, A_0; lease payment at the end of a period, R_j; depreciation charge relevant for tax payment at the end of a period, D_j; cash operating cost expected to occur in a period if the asset is purchased but not if it is leased, O_j; expected after-tax salvage value of the asset at the end of the last period covered by the lease agreement, V_n; pre-tax interest rate on term loans "comparable" to the lease, r; after-tax cost of capital for the corporation, k; the corporate income tax rate, t; and number of periods covered by the lease agreement, n. Additionally, the several approaches concentrate on how the asset is to be

Source. Reprinted by permission from *Financial Management*, Winter 1973, pp. 25–34. The author is Commissioner, New York State Public Service Commission.

acquired, leaving to more conventional capital budgeting the prior decision on whether it is to be acquired at all. The advocates of each of the academic approaches also pretend to no more than an approximation of the right decision because they take leasing as a decision to be made given predetermined financing and investment policies, rather than as a decision to be made jointly as part of the determination of these policies.

Johnson and Lewellen [7, pp. 815–817] discuss the problem of improperly mixing financing and investment decisions in lease evaluation. Associating investment projects with particular financing that happens to be projected for the same period is certainly a source of error when there is no relationship linking the investment and financing. Failing to recognize a true link is just as likely to lead to error, and neglecting the risk differences among investment projects that call for different financing assures that capital budgeting-financing decisions will be less than optimal. In leasing there is a choice involving both operating flows and financing flows. In this case anything less than a joint analysis of assets, claims and the optimal mix of the two must limit the decision to an approximation of the ideal.

The approaches differ regarding relevant alternatives and the choice of a best summary measure of comparison. The relevant alternatives are expressed in terms of outstanding principal of the loan equivalent, P_j; loan payment at the end of period, L_j; interest component of the loan payment, I_j; principal component, Q_j; present value of the lease claim, B_0; and in discount rates to be applied to cash flows in each category, X_m, that are intended to reflect opportunity costs. The summary measure is either the increment in net present value of owner's wealth, NAL, or the pre-tax interest rate on the lease, i. Exhibit 1 reports each approach and shows how it differs from others. (Some license is used in presenting the various approaches, but there is no known distortion in representation.)

Exhibit 1 depends on an equation that can be used to express any of the approaches. It is

$$\text{NAL} = A_o - \sum_{j=o}^{n} \frac{R_j}{(1 + X_2)^j} + \sum_{j=o}^{n} \frac{tR_j}{(1 + X_3)^j} - \sum_{j=o}^{n} \frac{tD_j}{(1 + X_4)^j}$$
$$- \sum_{j=o}^{n} \frac{tI_j}{(1 + X_5)^j} + \sum_{j=o}^{n} \frac{O_j(1 - t)}{(1 + X_6)^j} - \frac{V_n}{(1 + X_7)^n}.$$
$$(1)$$

The interpretation of the equation depends on the approach, but it may aid intuition to view it in one of the possible ways and to assume "correct" discount rates. If the first two terms on the right hand side combine to have a positive value, then the lease payments have a smaller present value than the asset being leased. If the next three terms have a positive value, then the present value of tax savings from the lease exceeds that of the tax savings associated with a buy

EXHIBIT 1. APPROACHES TO LEASE EVALUATION

APPROACH	SUMMARY MEASURE	EXCLUDED FLOWS OF OTHER COMMENTS	EQUIVALENT LOAN CALCULATION*	DISCOUNT RATE USED FOR:					
				X_2	X_3	X_4	X_5	X_6	X_7
Beechy [1, 3]	i	tL_j is used instead of tR_j in the 3rd term of the equation.	$P_o = A_o$ $B_o = \sum_{j=o}^{n} (R_j/(1+r)^j)$ $L_j = R_j(P_o/B_o)$	i	i	i	i	i	i
Bower, Herringer, Williamson [4]	NAL		$P_o = A_o$ $B_o = \sum_{j=o}^{n} (R_j/(1+r)^j)$ $L_j = R_j(P_o/B_o)$	r	k	k	k	k	k
Doenges [5] Mitchell [8] Wyman [12]	$i(1-t)$	I_j is excluded. Wyman provides a probability distribution of rates.	None	$i(1-t)$	$i(1-t)$	$i(1-t)$	—	$i(1-t)$	$i(1-t)$
Findlay [6]	NAL	Certainty equivalents of O_j and V_n are used in the 6th and 7th terms.	$P_o = \sum_{j=o}^{n} (R_j/(1+r)^j)$ $L_j = R_j$	r	$r(1-t)$	$r(1-t)$	$r(1-t)$	$r(1-t)$	$r(1-t)$
Johnson and Lewellen [7]	NAL	I_j is excluded.	None	$r(1-t)$	$r(1-t)$	k	—	k	k
Roenfeldt and Osteryoung [10]	$i(1-t)$	I_j is excluded. Certainty equivalents of O_j and V_n are used in the 6th and 7th terms.	None	$i(1-t)$	$i(1-t)$	$i(1-t)$	$i(1-t)$	$i(1-t)$	$i(1-t)$
Vancil [11]	NAL		$P_o = A_o$ $L_j = R_j$	r	k	k	k	k	k

* Only the first two or three equations required to produce the equivalent loan flows are shown in each box. The remaining equations are the same for each approach. The full set of equations for Beechey's approach is:

$$P_o = A_o \qquad B_o = \sum_{j=o}^{n} (R_j/(1+r)^j) \qquad L_j = R_j(P_o/B_o) \qquad I_j = rP_j - 1 \qquad Q_j = L_j - I_j \qquad P_j = P_j - 1 - Q_j.$$

and borrow alternative. If the last two terms have a positive value, then after-tax operating savings with the lease have a present value that exceeds that of the after-tax salvage sacrificed by leasing instead of buying. Summing all terms provides the net present value advantage of leasing to the corporations' shareholders. Setting NAL equal to 0 and solving for i provides the pre-tax interest rate on the lease.

The differences among the seven approaches should not obscure rather general agreement on the handling of the first and the last two terms in the basic equation. The first term, the purchase price of the asset to be leased, represents the initial outlay that will be avoided if the asset is acquired through the lease. The last two terms include conventional project flows with risk characteristics and financing mix implications that fail to distinguish them from the flows usually considered in capital budgeting. In two of the approaches this is reflected by adjusting the flows to their certainty equivalents, and in three others by discounting at k, the company's cost of capital. Only in the two methods of lease evaluation that find a single solving rate is there a suggestion of a different kind of treatment, and for the authors of these methods this seems to be an acknowledged oversight [2], an area outside their concern [5, 8], or a matter to be handled by Hertz-type simulation [11]. On the first and last two terms of the basic equation academicians may disagree in the style of handling they recommend, but not in the substance of their advice.

Disagreement is more significant in treatment of terms 2, 3, 4, and 5 of the basic equation, the terms that include lease payments, and the tax shelter acquired or given up if the lease is accepted. The disagreement is most obvious and most easily reconciled in the decision to include or exclude the tax deduction associated with interest on the equivalent loan. Findlay includes the tax deduction on interest and proceeds by discounting the lease payments at the pre-tax loan rate. He then discounts the lease tax shelter acquired and the depreciation and interest tax shelter sacrificed at the after-tax loan rate. Because he assumes an equivalent loan equal to the lease payments' present value, his procedure has a result identical to excluding the interest shelter and discounting the other three flows involved at the after-tax loan rate (see the appendix). More formally:

If $P_o = \sum_{j=o}^{n} \dfrac{R_j}{(1 + r)^j}$,

Then $- \sum_{j=o}^{n} \dfrac{R_j}{(1 + r)^j} + \sum_{j=o}^{n} \dfrac{tR_j}{(1 + r(1 - t))^j} - \sum_{j=o}^{n} \dfrac{tD_j}{(1 + r(1 - t))^j}$

$$- \sum_{j=o}^{n} \frac{tI_j}{(1 + r(1 - t))^j}$$

$$\text{Equals} - \sum_{j=0}^{n} \frac{R_j}{(1 + r(1 - t))^j} + \sum_{j=0}^{n} \frac{tR_j}{(1 + r(1 - t))^j} - \sum_{j=0}^{n} \frac{tD_j}{(1 + r(1 - t))^j}.$$

(2)

Thus, the approaches used by Roenfeldt and Osteryoung [9], by Doenges [5], Mitchell [8], and Wyman [11] and by Beechy [1, 3] have all implicitly assumed Findlay's equivalent loan [6]. If purchase price, operating saving, and salvage are handled in the same way in each case, which seems in keeping with the general agreement described above, then all of these approaches will indicate the same decision on any lease proposal.

Setting aside for the moment the disagreements that are still unreconciled in Bower, Herringer and Williamson [4], Johnson and Lewellen [7] and Vancil [10], we now have the first of two decision formats that executives might use to approximate a correct decision on a lease alternative. The format can be demonstrated with the illustration that appears in Johnson and Lewellen [7, p. 820–822]. Exhibit 2 presents that illustration, provides present values at the cost of capital, k, for purchase price, after-tax operating savings and after-tax salvage, and offers present values at rates from 0 to .14 for the lease payment, the lease payment tax shelter and the depreciation tax shelter. The purchase price net of salvage and the operating expenses that will now be covered by the lessor are the benefits associated with leasing. The lease payments, less any net additional tax shelter they provide, are the costs of leasing. The benefits, which everyone seems to agree should be discounted at the cost of capital, are $16,206. (It should be clarified that while there may be agreement that k is the right rate to use, there is unlikely to be agreement on a single estimate of k.) The benefits in question appear in Exhibit 2 and are graphed in Exhibit 3. These two exhibits also show the costs of the lease discounted at various rates; therefore they satisfy preferences for both present value and internal rate summary measures.

This lease has a net disadvantage at after-tax interest rates below .0399 and a net advantage at rates above this figure. At .04, the after-tax interest rate provided in the illustration, the net advantage is $5. This decision format indicates a borderline choice in favor of the lease or, more pragmatically, a choice that should make very little difference to the owners of the lessee corporation even if executives are using 8% as the appropriate pre-tax borrowing rate when that rate is correctly 6% or 10%. This may be a quite common outcome, i.e., one in which the decision will depend not on the type of quantitative analysis presented here but on the wide variety of other considerations that influence executives' actions. Exhibit 3, decision format #1, with its tabular and graphic presentation, indicates not only when the choice to accept or reject a lease is obvious, but also when the choice is inconsequential.

EXHIBIT 2. *AN ILLUSTRATION FROM JOHNSON AND LEWELLEN*

YEAR, j	PURCHASE PRICE, A_o	LEASE PAYMENT, R_j	TAX SHELTER Lease payment, tR_j	Depreciation, tD_j	AFTER-TAX OPERATING SAVING, $O_j(1-t)$	AFTER-TAX SALVAGE, V_n
0	15000					
1		4200	2100	2500	500	
2		4200	2100	2000	500	
3		4200	2100	1500	500	
4		4200	2100	1000	500	
5		4200	2100	500	500	1050

$t = .5$
$k = .12$
$r = .08$

PRESENT VALUE AT $k = .12$	A_o	R_j	tR_j	tD_j	$O_j(1-t)$	V_n
	+15000		+10500	−7500	+1802	−596

r	R_j	tR_j
.0	−21000	+10500
.02	−19797	+9898
.04	−18698	+9349
.06	−17692	+8846
.08	−16769	+8385
.10	−15921	+7961
.12	−15140	+7570
.14	−14119	+7209

LEASE	
Benefit	Cost
16206	18000
	17063
	16201
	15410
	14680
	14006
	13383
	12806

258

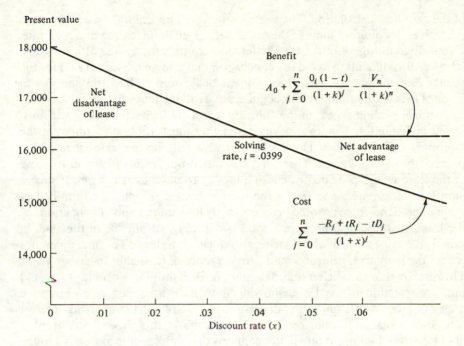

Exhibit 3.   Decision format # 1

FURTHER DISAGREEMENT

Exhibit 3, which is a simple way of presenting the approaches taken by Beechy [1, 2, 3], Doenges [5], Mitchell [8], Wyman [11], Findlay [6], and Roenfeldt and Osteryoung [9] indicates that the choice on the illustration's lease is a matter of indifference. In contrast, Johnson and Lewellen find the choice in favor of the lease to be important and obvious. They calculate the net advantage of the lease as $1043, not $5. The source of this difference is disagreement with a single element of the other approaches: the discount rate applied to the depreciation tax shelter.

The approaches reconciled earlier all suggest the after-tax interest rate, $r(1 - t)$, as the discount rate for the depreciation shelter. Johnson and Lewellen use the cost of capital, k. The present value figures in the depreciation column of Exhibit 2 indicate that this causes other approaches to estimate the present cost of the depreciation shelter as $6852, while Johnson and Lewellen estimate it as $5813, the difference of $1039 mentioned above.

Johnson and Lewellen's selection of k as the discount rate is understandable but unappealing. It is understandable because k is the rate used in discounting depreciation shelters in conventional capital budgeting, where the shelter is part of the cash flow calculation. The selection of k is unappealing, though, because it involves discounting some of the tax shelter given up in leasing at a high rate, k, and discounting all of the tax shelter that comes with leasing at a low rate, $r(1 - t)$. It is difficult to avoid the conclusion that a higher discount rate for the shelter element of lease cost does a great deal more to bias the analysis in favor of leasing than it does to recognize any real difference in risk.

The unappealing aspect of the Johnson and Lewellen rate selection is illustrated in Exhibit 4. The lease payments in that illustration, discounted at the interest rate of an equivalent loan, have a present value just equal to the purchase price of the asset involved. Therefore, a loan with payments identical to those of the lease would provide just enough money to purchase the asset. If such a loan were negotiated, and this is the loan explicit in Findlay and implicit in other approaches, then it would involve exactly the same stream of obligations as the lease. It would also produce a total tax shelter over the life of the asset in exactly the same amount as the shelter provided by the lease. The only difference is that the loan arrangement would provide more of its shelter in earlier years. This is shown in the shelter and net columns of Exhibit 4. Format #1 would indicate rejection of the lease, showing it to have a solving rate above the after-tax interest rate and a net disadvantage of $183 at the after-tax interest rate. But format #1 is not really required to make this choice, because it is apparent from looking at the shelter columns that unless depreciation is a much more risky source of shelter than a lease payment, the buy and borrow alternative with its earlier tax savings is superior to the lease. Although the choice seems apparent, it is not the one that Johnson and Lewellen would advise. Their approach would show a net advantage for the lease in this illustration of $701. This finding is due entirely to the use of a higher rate, k, with the depreciation shelter.

A FINAL DISAGREEMENT

The present value approaches offered by Bower, Herringer and Williamson and by Vancil differ from the approaches reflected in Exhibit 3 in two respects. First, they use different equivalent loans to calculate the interest tax shelter sacrificed in leasing, and secondly they discount all tax shelter terms at the rate k rather than at $r(1 - t)$. The first difference is easily reconciled; the second is the cause of the introduction of Exhibit 6 at the close of this section.

Earlier, it was shown that discounting lease payments at the after-tax interest rate, $r(1 - t)$, is identical to discounting the same lease payments at the pre-tax interest rate, r, and then generating the implied interest in each year, multiplying that interest by the tax rate and discounting the resulting interest tax shelter at the after-tax rate, $r(1 - t)$. As a result it is understood that all the approaches considered so far, including Johnson and Lewellen, assume that a lease has a

EXHIBIT 4. AN ILLUSTRATION OF JOHNSON AND LEWELLEN

	LEASE FLOWS			BUY AND BORROW FLOWS				
YEAR, j	Payment, R_j	Shelter, tR_j	Net, $R_j(1 - t)$	Payment, L_j	Interest, I_j	Depreciation (SOYD), D_j	Shelter, $t(I_j + D_j)$	Net, $L_j - t(I_j + D_j)$
1	3200	1600	1600	3200	1022	4259	2640	560
2	3200	1600	1600	3200	848	3407	2128	1072
3	3200	1600	1600	3200	660	2555	1607	1593
4	3200	1600	1600	3200	456	1703	1080	2120
5	3200	1600	1600	3200	238	852	545	2655
Sum	16000	8000	8000	16000	3224	12776	8000	8000

$$A_o = 12776 \quad r = .08$$
$$V_n = 0 \quad k = .12$$
$$O_j = 0 \quad t = .5$$

loan equivalent. This analytic use of an equivalent loan comes very close to removing questions of financial structure from the lease decision. It determines the borrowing that could take place within the debt limit if there were no commitments to make lease payments, and it presumes that this borrowing *would* take place if the lease was not signed. The borrowing sacrificed is clearly one cost of the lease, and the lost interest tax shelter associated with that borrowing is just as clearly a second cost.

Although Bower, Herringer and Williamson and Vancil calculate the cost of borrowing sacrificed or the value of the lessor's claim against the company in the same way Findlay and the others do, they presume that the borrowing that would take place if leasing were rejected would be equal to the purchase price of the asset. As a result, they calculate their interest tax shelter from an equivalent loan equal to the purchase price of the asset rather than equal to the present value of the lease payments. Their presumption and calculation seem much less satisfactory than the more common alternative. In particular, difficulty may arise where the purchase price is above the present value of lease payments, so additional borrowing, if it occurs, could threaten debt limits and affect discount rates. The disagreement on the equivalent loan to be used in generating the interest tax shelter is properly resolved by rejecting the Bower, Herringer and Williamson and Vancil alternatives in favor of the alternative explicit in Findlay and implicit elsewhere.

There is now no remaining disagreement among approaches on how to calculate tax shelter gained or lost by leasing. The only disagreement is on the rate to be used in discounting. Johnson and Lewellen's use of k with the depreciation shelter was rejected because it involved discounting one type of tax shelter at a rate higher than another type. However, that rejection does not imply that k is the wrong rate if consistently applied to all tax shelters.

Discounting tax shelters by the after-tax equivalent of the interest rate assumes not only that the shelter flow is certain enough to be discounted at the rate r in calculating the firm's market value, but also that the flow will be borrowed against using a loan supported only by the initial tax shelter and by the further shelter of the loan's own interest. The after-tax interest rate, $r(1 - t)$, therefore, is too low a rate to apply to tax shelter terms. The rate r is the proper rate if the flows are as certain as the loan obligations, but even this rate is likely to be too low. Tax rates can and do change, income is not available to be offset in every year, and there are costs and institutional difficulties in transferring shelters to others. In addition, the years in which a tax shelter will be of least use are the years when business is bad for everyone, income is low and tax relief is public policy. There is risk in tax shelter flows, and most of it may be systematic. In view of all these factors, perhaps k is a closer estimate of the rate that applies than r.

This final disagreement has no obvious resolution. To recognize the disagreement and still permit executives to take advantage of the broad agreement on other matters, decision format #2 is offered. In format #1 the executive was presented a table and graph which took k as given in calculating the benefits of leasing, assumed that tax shelters should be discounted at $r(1 - t)$, and let the executive look at the decision implications associated with different interest rates. In decision format #2, which is applied to the earlier illustration in Exhibit 5 and Exhibit 6, the executive looks at the decision implications associated with different tax shelter discount rates. Agreement among academicians is exploited by using the cost of capital, k, in calculating benefits that involve purchase price, operating saving and salvage and by using the appropriate interest rate, r, in calculating the present cost of the lease payments. The tax shelter effect is then calculated for rates of discount from 0 to 14%.

The summary columns to the right in Exhibit 5 and the graphic presentation in Exhibit 6 take on a different form than those in the table and graph of format #1. Here, the seven terms of the basic equation are rearranged so that cost of purchasing (COP) depends on purchase price, depreciation tax shelter, cash operating cost avoided by leasing, and salvage value:

$$COP = A_o - \sum_{j=o}^{n} \frac{tD_j}{(1 + X)^j} + \sum_{j=o}^{n} \frac{O_j(1 - t)}{(1 + k)^j} - \frac{V_n}{(1 + k)^j}. \tag{3}$$

The cost of leasing (COL) depends on lease payment, lease tax shelter and the interest tax shelter lost by leasing:

$$COL = \sum_{j=o}^{n} \frac{R_j}{(1 + r)^j} - \sum_{j=o}^{n} \frac{tR_j}{(1 + X)^j} + \sum_{j=o}^{n} \frac{tI_j}{(1 + X)^j}. \tag{4}$$

Format #2 tells a somewhat different story from format #1 and a very different story from Johnson and Lewellen. When the tax shelter is discounted at $r(1 - t)$, 4%, the net advantage of leasing is $5, just as it was in decision format #1 in Exhibit 3. At all discount rates above 4.07% the lease has a net disadvantage. If the estimates k and r are felt to be tightly bound, and if the executive making the decision holds the view that the proper tax shelter discount rate is well above $r(1 - t)$, then he will conclude from decision format #2 in Exhibit 6 that a decision to sign this lease agreement could be of very little financial benefit to the company's owners and could do them damage.

CONCLUSION

This article has reviewed various *ad hoc* approaches to the lessee's decision that have been proposed. It is made clear that these approaches disagree substantively on very few points and that they lead to a composite approach referred to here as decision format #2 (Exhibit 6), which puts the executive in a position to

EXHIBIT 5. AN ILLUSTRATION FROM JOHNSON AND LEWELLEN

YEAR, j	PURCHASE PRICE, A_o	LEASE PAYMENT, R_j	TAX SHELTER Lease payment, tR_j	TAX SHELTER Depreciation, tD_j	TAX SHELTER Loan interest,* tI_j	AFTER-TAX OPERATING SAVING, $O_j(1-t)$	AFTER-TAX SALVAGE, V_n
0	15000						
1		4200	2100	2500	671	500	
2		4200	2100	2000	556	500	
3		4200	2100	1500	433	500	
4		4200	2100	1000	300	500	
5		4200	2100	500	156	500	1050

$t = .5$
$k = .12$
$r = .08$

PRESENT VALUE AT $k = .12$, $r = .08$

	PURCHASE PRICE, A_o	LEASE PAYMENT, R_j	tR_j	tD_j	tI_j	$O_j(1-t)$	V_n
	15000	16769	10500	7500	2116	1802	596

COST OF:

	tR_j	tD_j	tI_j	Purchasing	Leasing
0	10500	7500	2116	8706	8385
.02	9898	7164	2019	9042	8890
.04	9349	6852	1929	9354	9349
.06	8846	6564	1846	9642	9769
.08	8385	6296	1768	9910	10152
.10	7961	6046	1697	10160	10505
.12	7570	5813	1630	10393	10829
.14	7209	5596	1567	10610	11127

* The loan is calculated as Findlay's equivalent loan in Exhibit 1. The loan schedule is:

Year	Loan balance year start	Interest at .08	Principal repayment	Loan balance year end
1	16769	1342	2858	13911
2	13911	1113	3087	10823
3	10823	866	3334	7489
4	7489	599	3889	3888
5	3888	311	3889	—

264

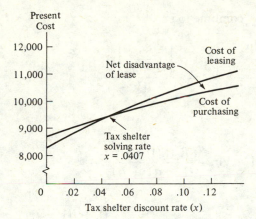

Exhibit 6.   Decision format # 2

make his own judgment on the principal disagreement. Using decision format #2 or some more artistic derivative of it, executives may be better able to take advantage of the advice academicians have made available.

Appendix

For a two period lease Findlay [6] calculates

$$P_o = \frac{R_1}{(1 + r)} \frac{R_2}{(1 + r)^2}$$

$$P_1 = \frac{R_2}{(1 + r)}$$

and includes P_o plus the lost interest tax deduction, discounted at $r(1 - t)$,

$$\frac{P_o rt}{(1 + r(1 - t))} + \frac{P_1 rt}{(1 + r(1 - t))^2}$$

among the disadvantages of the lease. This is equivalent to simply discounting R_1 and R_2 at $r(1 - t)$,

$$\frac{R_1}{(1 + r(1 - t))} + \frac{R_2}{(1 + r(1 - t))^2}.$$

The two sets of flows used by Findlay combine to be

$$\frac{R_1}{(1 + r)} + \frac{R_2}{(1 + r)^2} + \frac{\left[\dfrac{R_1}{(1 + r)} + \dfrac{R_2}{(1 + r)^2}\right] rt}{(1 + r(1 - t))} + \frac{\left[\dfrac{R_2}{(1 + r)}\right] rt}{(1 + r(1 - t))^2}.$$

Rearranging, this is

$$R_1/(1 + r) + \frac{R_1 rt/(1 + r)}{(1 + r(1 - t))} + R_2/(1 + r)^2 + \frac{R_2 rt/(1 + r)^2}{(1 + r(1 - t))}$$

$$+ \frac{R_2 rt/(1 + r)}{(1 + r(1 - t))^2}.$$

Multiplying the first term by $(1 + r(1 - t))/(1 + r(1 - t))$ the first two terms are

$$\frac{R_1(1 + r(1 - t)) + R_1 rt}{(1 + r)(1 + r(1 - t))} = \frac{R_1 + R_1 r - R_1 rt + R_1 rt}{(1 + r)(1 + r(1 - t))},$$

or

$$\frac{R_1(1 + r)}{(1 + r)(1 + r(1 - t))} = \frac{R_1}{(1 + r(1 - t))}.$$

Multiply the third and fourth term to set all three R_2 terms over $(1 + r(1 - t))^2$ and going through the appropriate manipulations for all terms in the numerator reduces the R_2 terms to

$$\frac{R_2}{(1 + r(1 - t))^2}.$$

REFERENCES

1. Thomas H. Beechy, "The Cost of Leasing: Comment and Correction," *Accounting Review* (October 1970), pp. 769–773.
2. Thomas H. Beechy, *A Note on the Analysis of Leasing* (Mimeo).
3. Thomas H. Beechy, "Quasi-Debt Analysis of Financial Leases," *Accounting Review* (April 1969), pp. 375–381.
4. Richard S. Bower, Frank C. Herringer, and J. Peter Williamson, "Lease Evaluation," *Accounting Review* (April 1966), pp. 257–265.
5. E. Conrad Doenges, "The Cost of Leasing," *Engineering Economist* (Winter 1971), pp. 31–44.

6. M. Chapman Findlay III, *Financial Lease Evaluation Survey and Synthesis* (Mimeo), Abstracted in Donald E. Fisher, editor, *Proceedings of the 1973 Annual Meeting of the Eastern Finance Association*, April 12–14, 1973, Storrs, Connecticut, p. 136.
7. R. W. Johnson, and W. G. Lewellen, "Analysis of the Lease or Buy Decision, *Journal of Finance* (September 1972), pp. 815–823.
8. G. B. Mitchell, "After-Tax Cost of Leasing," *Accounting Review* (April 1970), pp. 308–314.
9. Rodney L. Roenfeldt and Jerome S. Osteryoung, "Analysis of Financial Leases," *Financial Management* (Spring 1973), pp. 74–87.
10. Richard F. Vancil, "Lease or Borrow—New Method of Analysis," *Harvard Business Review* (September 1961), pp. 122–136.
11. Harold E. Wyman, "Financial Lease Evaluation Under Conditions of Uncertainty," *Accounting Review* (July 1973), pp. 489–493.

QUESTIONS

1. Explain each portion of the NAL equation offered in the Bower article.
2. On what rationale would *all* flows related to the lease versus borrow-buy decision be discounted at $r(1 - t)$?
3. Explain why some flows, such as those involving tax shelters or salvage value, might be discounted at k, the cost of capital.
4. What difference does it make in the solution whether tax shelter benefits are discounted at $r(1 - t)$ or k?
5. Given that a difference of opinion does exist among theorists as to the correct discount rates to use, what do you think of the proposal by Professor Bower to let the executive determine the most appropriate interpretation?
6. Refer to Exhibit 3. If the firm has an opportunity cost of funds which is greater than the indifference point, in this case 0.0399, which is preferable, the lease or purchase?

17

Ivar W. Sorensen and Ramon E. Johnson

Equipment Financial Leasing Practices and Costs: An Empirical Study

This study is a systematic exploration of practices and costs derived from a sample of lease contracts. The main results are that lease costs appear high and that terms vary widely among lessors. This means, in general, that financial managers should invest time to understand lease options and how to analyze them, and then managers should shop for the best deal.

INTRODUCTION

The literature on leasing provides an abundance of information from two perspectives. On the trade press side are publications claiming advantages or disadvantages of leasing [1, 2, 7, 10, 13]. These tend to approach the subject on descriptive, intuitive, or authoritative bases and do not provide theoretical or analytical guidelines. On the other side, there have been numerous theoretical treatises on how to compare the cost of leasing with purchase alternatives [3, 5, 12] or what to expect under efficient capital markets [6, 9, 11]. The theoretical literature has refined our ability to understand and analyze leases, and it has clarified what we should expect to observe in practice.

If financial lease contracts can be considered debt instruments, and if the relevant capital market is efficient, we should expect the cost of leasing to approach the cost of debt [6] (or at least the cost of debt plus a risk premium for salvage value uncertainty). While there is not an abundance of empirical work on leasing, two such studies have inferred high returns for leasing firms or high costs of leasing for asset users. McGugan and Caves [8] reported evidence of profit rates for leasing firms in excess of competitive norms. In general this could only be true if rates of return on individual contracts were high. In another study, Gudikunst and Roberts [4] evaluated specific lease contracts

Source. Reprinted by permission from *Financial Management*, Spring 1977, pp. 33–40. Ivar Sorensen is financial vice president of Polar Manufacturing Co., Holdingford, Minnesota. Ramon Johnson is professor of finance at the University of Utah.

using analytical methods proposed in the academic literature. They found that virtually every lease contract studied was more costly than the alternative, regardless of the analytical method used. One objective of this research is to secure information on costs of leasing, but the general goal of the paper is to perform a systematic descriptive study on a sample of lease contracts. The study was made possible because four leasing firms allowed contracts in their files to be examined.

Data were gathered on 520 retail financial lease contracts for several categories of equipment. These contracts were studied and descriptive material relating to asset costs, asset types, maturities, prepayments, collateral, default remedies, and treatment of investment tax credit was generated. Estimates of leasing cost rates were computed; univariate and multivariate relationships of these variables with cost rates were obtained.

DATA SOURCE

Data were obtained from the records of four non-bank leasing firms in Salt Lake City, Utah. These four lessors had offices in Arizona, California, Colorado, Idaho, Oregon, Texas, Utah, Washington, and Western Canada. Because access to information was limited to contracts still on the lessor's books no *ex post* data on contracts that had terminated was available. Further, the identity of any lessee had to be confidential, and contact with individual lessees with reference to specific lease contracts was prohibited.

THE SAMPLE AND SAMPLE STATISTICS

The 520 financial lease contracts in the sample were written in Salt Lake City, Utah, during the period 1970 through March of 1975. Every lease contract studied was a financial lease; the lessee was responsible for asset selection and physical acquisition, maintenance, taxes, insurance, and liability. The leases were all non-cancellable. Default remedies were repossession, declaration of all remaining payments due and payable, and deficiency claims.

Outlay Cost of Assets

The distribution of outlay cost for the sample is shown in Exhibit 1. Contracts included in the sample ranged from $134 to $200,000 in outlay cost to the lessor. The sample mean was $9863. Exhibit 1 shows that the asset cost distribution was highly skewed upward. Thirty-nine percent of the contracts were less than $2500, and only 3.7 percent were larger than $40,000.

EXHIBIT 1. OUTLAY COST OF ASSETS

	Number of Contracts	Percent
Less than $2,500	206	39.6
$2,501–$5,000	90	17.3
$5,001–$10,000	85	16.3
$10,001–$20,000	67	12.9
$20,001–$40,000	53	10.2
$40,001–$200,000	19	3.7
Mean $9863	520	100.0

Prepayment Requirements

Almost every contract required some prepayment, the equivalent of the down payment on a loan. Prepayments for this sample ranged from zero to 19.5 percent of original cost, with a mean of 9.5 percent. Sixty-five percent of the contracts required prepayments in the 10.01 to 15.00 percent range. Exhibit 2 shows the distribution of required prepayments for the sample.

EXHIBIT 2. PREPAYMENT REQUIREMENTS

Prepayment (Percent)	Number of Contracts	Percent
Zero	2	.4
0.01–5.00	78	15.0
5.01–10.00	98	18.9
10.01–15.00	339	65.1
15.01–20.00	3	.6
Mean 9.3	520	100.0

Length of Lease Period

With few exceptions, the sample leases required monthly payments. For the leases included in this study, contract maturities ranged from 12 to 84 months, as summarized in Exhibit 3. Most of the terms were 3 or 5 years. For example,

EXHIBIT 3. LENGTH OF LEASE PERIOD

Months	Number of Contracts	Percent
6–12	7	1.3
13–14	60	11.5
25–36	208	40.0
37–48	44	8.5
49–84	201	38.7
Mean 44	520	100.0

forty percent carried 36-month maturities, and slightly less than 38 percent carried 60-month maturities.

Collateral

In this sample, 121 contracts, or 23 percent, were secured by personal guarantees, by third party guarantees, or by claims on assets of the lessee. While not called for in the master contracts, such collateral was obtained through separate documentation of specific guarantees, co-signatures, and filing of security interest notices with appropriate authorities.

Treatment of Investment Tax Credit (ITC)

Investment tax credit may be retained by lessors or passed on to lessees. Seventy percent of the 520 contracts in the sample were written such that lessors retained the investment tax credit.

Lessor

Information categorized by the lessor firm (Exhibit 4) indicated some differences in mean outlay cost of contracts and in prepayment percentages among firms. Average maturities appeared to be about the same among firms, except for Firm 3 which wrote smaller asset cost leases and shorter maturities than the others. Contracts showed substantial differences by lessors regarding percent of contracts requiring collateral and percent of contracts where the lessor retained the ITC.

Asset Category

Contracts were grouped by asset category in Exhibit 5 showing that the largest outlay cost was for construction and the smallest was for office equipment. Prepayments were also highest for construction equipment, while the lowest were for autos and trucks. Average maturities ranged from 42 months for autos and trucks to 48 months for hospital and medical equipment. Collateral was required most frequently on autos and trucks, and the ITC was retained by lessors most frequently on construction equipment. Comparison of Exhibits 4 and 5 suggests that contracts written by different lessors were more divergent in characteristics than contracts written for different asset categories.

ANALYTICAL INVESTIGATION

It was possible to compute *ex ante* rates of return on investment for the lessors; for them the lease is a capital budgeting decision. Cost rates (in percent) to lessees are identical if the outlays, depreciation methods, tax

EXHIBIT 4. OUTLAY COST, PREPAYMENT, MATURITY, COLLATERAL, AND INVESTMENT TAX CREDIT RETENTION BY LEASING FIRM

Company	1	2	3	4	Total Sample
Number of Contracts	125 (24.0%)	278 (53.5%)	104 (20.0%)	13 (2.5%)	520 (100.0%)
Mean Outlay Cost	$15,938	$9,436	$2,817	$16,669	$9,863
Mean Prepayment (prepayment as % of cost)	6.44	11.36	8.45	5.06	9.45
Mean Maturity, months	45	46	40	43	44
Collateral Required (percent of contracts)	25	28	0	100	23
ITC retained by lessor (percent of contracts)	77	77	52	0	70

EXHIBIT 5. OUTLAY COST, PREPAYMENT, MATURITY, COLLATERAL, AND INVESTMENT TAX CREDIT RETENTION BY ASSET CATEGORY

Asset Category	Autos & Trucks	Hospital & Medical	Office	Manufacturing	Construction	Miscellaneous	Total Sample
Number of Contracts	86	59	161	77	30	107	520
Mean Outlay Cost	$11,000	$9,100	$7,100	$8,900	$12,600	$9,400	$9,863
Mean Prepayment (prepayment as % of cost)	7.87	10.92	9.55	10.45	10.59	8.66	9.45
Mean Maturity, months	42	48	44	46	43	44	44
Collateral Required (percent of contracts)	41	14	15	27	33	21	23
ITC retained by lessor (percent of contracts)	73	78	69	78	80	57	70

rates, and salvage values would be the same as for lessors. While it was not possible to calculate cost rates to lessees due to these requirements, cost rates could nevertheless be inferred. For the financial leases in this sample, outlays were the same for lessors as they would have been if the lessees had purchased. Depreciation methods were not necessarily the same, but lessees would have had the same options as lessors. Tax rates were probably not the same for lessors and lessees; for this reason we present results before tax (or zero tax) and for tax rates of 50, 40, and 30 percent. Salvage value estimates were provided by lessors, and we assumed that lessees' estimates would have been identical. The seriousness of this assumption was explored with a sensitivity study on salvage values. In the material which follows, rate of return, cost rate, cost of leasing or implied cost all refer to the same thing, *ex ante* rate of return for the lessor and implied cost to the lessee. (Some lease contracts involved specific out-of-pocket costs to the lessor. These include finders fees or commissions. These costs were intentionally excluded from this study. Accordingly, while r will estimate the implied cost of credit for the lessee, it will overstate the rate of return on investment for lessors. The objective was to estimate the financing related returns and costs to make them comparable with published interest rates.) It was obtained by solving for r in the following model:

$$C = (1 - t) \sum_{i=1}^{n} L_i \left(\frac{1}{1 + r}\right)^i + t \sum_{i=1}^{n} D_i \left(\frac{1}{1 + r}\right)^i + S_n \left(\frac{1}{1 + r}\right)^n + P + ITC$$

where:

n = Life of the lease in months, or number of monthly lease payments required,

C = Original cost of asset, $,

t = Marginal tax rate,

D_i = Depreciation, period i; i = 1, 2, 3, . . . , n, $,

L_i = Lease payment required at end of period i; i = 1, 2, 3, . . . , n, $,

P = Prepayment, time zero, $,

S_n = Salvage value estimate, time n, (no tax; book value = salvage estimate), $,

ITC = Investment tax credit, if retained by lessor, time zero, $,

r = Internal rate of return per month (to annualize, multiply by 12).

If tax is ignored, t is zero in the above equation, and r is a before tax cost rate. If tax rates are included, then the r is an after-tax cost rate. Use of the latter is necessary to account for tax shelters in depreciation and lease payments.

Aggregated Results

Exhibit 6 shows results of calculations of cost rates on the entire sample. The mean before-tax implied costs were just under 25 percent. After-tax these cost rates became 18.69, 20.80, and 22.98 percent per year for tax rates of 50, 40, and 30 percent, respectively.

EXHIBIT 6. AGGREGATE EX ANTE *COST RATES ON 520 LEASE CONTRACTS*

	Per Cent Per Year	
	Mean	Standard Deviation
Before-Tax Rate	24.98	7.27
After-Tax Rate (50%)	18.69	5.98
After-Tax Rate (40%)	20.80	6.35
After-Tax Rate (30%)	22.98	6.81
After-Tax Rate (50%) and Zero Salvage	16.08	5.00
After-Tax Rate (50%) and Twice Expected Salvage	21.25	7.23

As the salvage value is subject to uncertainty, a sensitivity analysis was made on that variable. Using a 50 percent tax rate in each case, the mean cost rate was 18.69 percent using the estimated salvage, 16.08 percent using a zero salvage, and 21.25 percent using twice the estimated salvage. This sensitivity analysis indicated that cost rates were not very sensitive to deviations in the salvage values. Reasons for this are that *ex ante* salvage estimates were rather low (sample mean was 8.52 percent) and that high discount rates (on the order of 20 percent) reduced the impact of deviations in salvage values. Among other things, this infers that moderate deviations between lessors' and lessees' salvage value estimates were not important. The only way substantial differences could exist would be if lessees expected much greater salvage values than indicated by lessors' estimates. If this were the case, cost rates inferred by this study were understated.

Multivariate Analysis of Factors Influencing Cost Rates

A stepwise multiple regression analysis was performed on before- and after-tax interest rates observed on the 520 financial leases. The regression results did not necessarily represent supply or demand functions for leasing. They were descriptive of the contracts in the sample, which were presumably the result of supply and demand interaction.

Exhibit 7 contains the models and results of two stepwise multiple regres-

EXHIBIT 7. REGRESSION ON 520 FINANCIAL LEASES

Cost Rate, % (Dependent Variable)	D.F.	Constant	Regression Coefficients (a)					Regression		
			X_1	X_2	X_3	X_4	X_5	Std. Error	F	R^2
Before-Tax	5/514	22.12	−.00004 (2.00) *	−.17885 (9.789) ***	−1.48906 (2.46) **	1.03888 (13.958) ***	2.54484 (4.866) ***	5.42	84.05 ***	.45
After-Tax (50% tax rate)	5/514	24.84	−.00002 (2.00) *	−.25166 (18.823) ***	−2.5491 (5.756) ***	.55771 (10.239) ***	.83492 (2.181) *	3.96	133.29 ***	.57

(a) t-values in parentheses.
*Significant at less than .05, one-tailed test.
**Significant at less than .01, one-tailed test.
***Significant at less than .001, one-tailed test.

sion runs using as dependent variables the observed before-tax and after-tax (50 percent) cost rates. Independent variables in the equation shown in Exhibit 7 are:

X_1 = Outlay cost of assets; dollars
X_2 = Length of lease period; months
X_3 = Collateral; 0 = no collateral; 1 = Collateralized lease
X_4 = Prepayments; percent of original asset value
X_5 = Investment Tax Credit; 0 = Passed on to lessee; 1 = Retained by lessor.

Both equations indicated that outlay costs and maturity were inversely related to cost rates. However, the correlation coefficient between outlay cost and maturity was .325 (shown in the correlation matrix, Exhibit 8), so it was impossible to determine the independent impact of outlay cost or maturity on cost rates. On a univariate basis, both outlay cost and maturity had strong negative correlations with cost rates.

EXHIBIT 8.   CORRELATION MATRIX ON 520 FINANCIAL LEASES

	Outlay Cost	Contract Period	Collateral	Prepayments	Investment Tax Credit
Cost Rate (before tax)	−.326	−.396	−.223	.507	.167
Cost Rate (after tax, 50%)	−.366	−.642	−.327	.349	.052
Outlay Cost	1.000	.325	.356	−.166	−.029
Contract Period		1.000	.177	−.040	.075
Collateral			1.000	−.054	−.086
Prepayments				1.000	.047
Investment Tax Credit					1.000

Both equations indicated collateralized leases to carry significantly lower cost rates than those not secured by collateral or guarantees. Thus, one must conclude that collateral, when acquired, was considered to be of sufficient quality and quantity to justify a reduction in lease cost rates. However, some of the rate-reducing impact of collateral may have originated with the outlay cost variable. A correlation coefficient of .356 between asset cost and collateral indicated that larger leases were collateralized more frequently than were smaller ones. Recalling the significant rate-reducing impact of increases in outlay cost this possible joint effect should not be disregarded.

Prepayments, as a percentage of outlay cost, had a strong rate-increasing impact. Prepayment requirements were largely negotiable and may be a mechanism for adjusting for the risk class of the lessee.

The investment tax credit variable also provided some explanatory power. The treatment of investment tax credits did significantly influence cost rates on this sample of financial leases. The direction of influence was positive; implicit rates were higher when credits were retained by the lessor than when they were passed on to the lessee. Among the reasons for this outcome could be that the model had missing variables (i.e. credit risk of lessee) or that some lessees were unaware of their options. The investment tax credit variable showed a low, but negative, correlation with outlay cost, indicating that as the size of the contract increased, the more likely was it that the ITC would be passed on to the lessee.

Independent variables were significantly related to lease cost rates on the overall basis, as evidenced by F-statistics (of 84.048 and 133.287, respectively), and all regression coefficients were significant at better than the .05 level. For the first equation, the proportion of variance explained was approximately 45 percent, while on an after-tax interest basis the explained portion of the sum-of-squares reached 56.5 percent. While these were respectable, they were undoubtedly held down by exclusion of variables for which data were not available. There was no way to secure variables which would measure credit risk of lessees.

There was some multicollinearity among independent variables. However, since correlation coefficients were of relatively small magnitudes (from .040 to .356), multicollinearity did not appear to pose a serious problem. The correlation matrix is shown in Exhibit 8.

Stepwise multiple regressions were performed on contracts written by each of the four lessors. The after-tax (50 percent) results appear in Exhibit 9. All four equations had higher R^2 values than the aggregate version, presumably because of greater contract homogeneity within the groupings.

Lessors 1 and 2 wrote leases with cost rates decreasing with outlay cost. Although the opposite appeared true for Lessors 3 and 4, the coefficients were not significant. Further, recall the correlation between outlay cost and maturity, and cost rates were inversely and significantly related to the lease maturity for contracts written by each of the four firms. The existence of collateral beyond the asset leased had a rate reducing impact for leases written by Firm 1 and a small, insignificant effect for those written by Firm 2. Firm 3 did not require extra collateral on any sample contract, while Firm 4 required extra collateral on every sample contract. Prepayments as a percentage of outlay cost had a rate increasing impact on lease costs for contracts written by each of the four firms. The impact, however, was much greater for Firm 2 than for the others. The investment tax credit variable did not appear in the regression for Firm 1. This firm did retain the ITC in most cases, but designed contracts to yield the same rate of return regardless of which party used the credit. Firms 2 and 3 secured significantly higher returns when the investment tax credit was retained than when passed to lessees. Firm 4 passed the ITC to the

EXHIBIT 9. REGRESSIONS ON FINANCIAL LEASES BY LESSOR—
DEPENDENT VARIABLE: COST RATE (AFTER-TAX AT 50 PERCENT)

Lessor Firm	N	D.F.	Mean Cost Rate (%)	Constant	X_1	X_2	X_3	X_4	X_5	Std. Error	F	R^2
											Regression	
1	125	4/120	17.80	19.178	-.00003 (2.47)**	-.16153 (5.28)***	-1.83144 (2.18)*	1.07812 (8.24)***		3.83	65.61 ***	.69
2	278	5/272	17.66	3.41	-.00002 (1.12)	-.32746 (21.19)***	-.20718 (.55)	2.36547 (15.83)***	3.00271 (8.36)***	2.48	126.25 ***	.70
3	104	4/99	23.25	26.15	.00004 (.60)	-.30264 (10.77)***		.98764 (10.24)***	1.33904 (2.49)**	2.63	137.10 ***	.85
4	13	3/9	11.94	9.48	.00001 (.44)	-.08650 (3.45)***		1.19800 (6.42)***		1.03 *	22.23 ***	.88

(a) t-values in parentheses.
*Significant at less than .05, one-tailed test.
**Significant at less than .01, one-tailed test.
***Significant at less than .001, one-tailed test.

X_1 = Outlay cost of assets; dollars
X_2 = Length of lease period; months
X_3 = Collateral; 0 = no collateral; 1 = collateralized lease
X_4 = Prepayments; percent of original asset cost
X_5 = Investment tax credit; 0 = passed on to lessee; 1 = retained by lessor

EXHIBIT 10. REGRESSIONS ON FINANCIAL LEASES BY ASSET CATEGORY— DEPENDENT VARIABLE: COST RATE (AFTER-TAX AT 50 PERCENT)

Asset Category	N	D.F.	Mean Cost Rate (%)	Constant	Regression Coefficients (a)					Regression		
					X_1	X_2	X_3	X_4	X_5	Std. Error	F	R^2
Autos, Trucks	86	4/81	17.20	23.33		-.24028 (6.62)***	-3.52488 (3.47)***	.54261 (4.21)***	1.61949 (1.44)	4.09	28.18 ***	.58
Hospital, Medical	59	5/53	18.58	22.33	.00005 (.71)	-.30328 (6.45)***	.59856 (.36)	.71019 (3.05)**	3.14800 (2.50)**	3.91	15.02 ***	.59
Office	160	5/154	19.68	26.49	-.00003 (1.23)	-.25939 (9.39)***	-2.26339 (2.26)	.55440 (4.94)***	-.13280 (.18)	4.03	39.73 ***	.56
Manufacturing	77	5/71	18.76	23.18	-.00002 (.49)	-.22804 (7.05)***	-1.54120 (1.55)	.47308 (2.96)**	2.19047 (2.20)*	3.56	18.85 ***	.57
Construction	30	5/24	17.78	19.62	.00002 (.41)	-.26481 (4.59)***	.65336 (.51)	.76382 (2.25)*	1.31954 (.93)	3.05	7.49 ***	.61
Misc.	107	5/101	18.74	26.14	-.00003 (.99)	-.26842 (8.42)***	-3.64208 (3.46)***	.59732 (5.13)***	.41135 (.50)	4.04	35.23 ***	.64

(a) t-values in parentheses.

*Significant at less than .05, one-tailed test.
**Significant at less than .01, one-tailed test.
***Significant at less than .001, one-tailed test.

X_1 = Outlay cost of assets; dollars
X_2 = Length of lease period; months
X_3 = Collateral; 0 = no collateral; 1 = collateralized lease
X_4 = Prepayments; percent of original asset cost
X_5 = Investment tax credit; 0 = passed on to lessee; 1 = retained by lessor

279

lessee in every contract, so the variable disappeared from that firm's regression. Mean cost rates ranged from 11.92 percent for Firm 4 to 23.25 percent for Firm 3. Firm 4, however, wrote larger contracts than Firm 3, so this outcome could be as much size as firm related.

The contracts were grouped by asset category, and the regressions were run again. These results are shown in Exhibit 10. As before, the maturity variable was very important. While the outlay cost coefficient did not have consistent signs or significant coefficients, correlation between outlay cost and maturity should again be recalled; maturity may be getting all the credit for a joint relationship. Where the collateral coefficient was significant is showed a substantial rate-reducing impact. The most consistent variable (other than maturity) was the prepayment. In each case the coefficients were positive and significant. The ITC variable was significant for the hospital and manufacturing groups only. Mean cost rates were much more uniform for the asset than for the lessor groupings.

The regressions run by asset grouping were not as strong as those produced by lessor groupings. R^2 and F values were much higher for the latter. The equations were more consistent for the asset than the lessor groupings in that each variable was more uniformly represented in the asset groupings. Average cost rates were also more uniform for asset than lessor groupings. If we assume that these are predominantly supply phenomena, we would assert that the asset user would find greater divergence of terms and conditions from one lessor to another than from one asset category to another.

SUMMARY AND CONCLUSIONS

This paper has presented descriptive and analytical material from a regional sample of 520 financial lease contracts for six different equipment categories. The sample contracts substantially appeared as debt. Leases were noncancellable, had severe remedies in the event of default, and they required down payments and collateral in varying degrees. Lessors provided no services beyond financing.

Implied cost rates were quite high, averaging 24.98 and 18.69 percent on before- and after-tax (50 percent) bases respectively. Whereas one could not, with available data, perform a lease versus purchase analysis on any sample contract, it appears reasonable to speculate that most leases studied would have been rejected under commonly accepted analytic procedures. Results were, therefore, not inconsistent with those of McGugan and Caves [8] and Gudikunst and Roberts [4] which were discussed earlier.

In addition to the generally high costs of leasing implied by contracts in the sample, an important finding was that terms and practices differed substantially from one lessor to another. This means that asset users should be able to secure better leasing terms by being well informed of their options and shopping around. In general, the high costs of leasing, the differences in contract features and terms between lessors, and the treatment of the ITC (higher cost rates when retained by lessors) were suggestive of an imperfect market.

Results cannot necessarily be generalized beyond the region in which the sample was generated. Further, the sample included no contracts larger than $200,000, and results may not extend to larger contracts. The extent to which lease cost rates changed as lessors provide services beyond financing only is unknown. The major limitation of the study was that data on lessees were not available. This meant that the multiple regression models probably should have contained additional explanatory variables, and it also precluded any direct comparison of the cost of leasing with the cost of owning. One must conclude that this study merely broke some new ground in an area deserving of more attention.

REFERENCES

1. *Administrative Management,* "Unscrambling the Claims About Leasing" (May 1966), pp. 28–31.
2. Alan Batkin, "Leasing vs. Buying . . . A Guide for the Perplexed," *Financial Executive* (June 1973), pp. 62–68.
3. Richard S. Bower, "Issues in Lease Financing," *Financial Management* (Winter 1973), pp. 25–34.
4. Arthur C. Gudikunst and Gordon S. Roberts, "Leasing: Analysis of Theoretic-Pragmatic Dilemma," paper presented at the annual meetings of the Financial Management Association, Kansas City, October, 1975.
5. Robert W. Johnson and Wilbur G. Lewellen, "Analysis of the Lease-or-Buy Decision," *Journal of Finance* (September 1974), pp. 815–824.
6. Wilbur G. Lewellen, Michael S. Long and John J. McConnell, "Asset Leasing in Competitive Capital Markets," *The Journal of Finance* (June 1976), pp. 787–798.
7. John P. Matthews, "Equipment Leasing: Before the Cash-Flow Analysis, What Else?" *Journal of Purchasing* (February 1974), pp. 5–11.
8. Vincent J. McGugan and Richard E. Caves, "Integration and Competition in the Equipment Leasing Industry," *The Journal of Business* (July 1974), pp. 382–396.
9. Merton H. Miller and Charles W. Upton, "Leasing, Buying and the Cost of Capital Services," *The Journal of Finance* (June 1976), pp. 761–786.
10. Rick Miniccuci, "Rather Try Than Buy? You Can Do It With Leasing," *Administrative Management* (June 1974), pp. 26–27.
11. Stewart C. Myers, David A. Dill and Alberto J. Bautista, "Valuation of Financial Lease Contracts," *The Journal of Finance* (June 1976), pp. 799–820.

12. Lawrence D. Schall, "The Lease-or-Buy And Asset Acquisition Decisions," *Journal of Finance* (September 1974), pp. 1210–1211.
13. Peter Vanderwicken, "The Powerful Logic of the Leasing Boom," *Fortune* (November 1973), p. 136.

QUESTIONS

1. Why is a prepayment on a lease like a down payment on a loan?
2. Explain why charging a higher prepayment could result in a higher rate of return to the lessor (higher cost rate to the lessee).
3. The average salvage value estimate was 8.52 percent of the original outlay. This seems low for the inflationary period encompassed. If lessors underestimate salvage in calculating the lease payment, what effect will it have on their rate of return (lessees' cost rate)? Explain.
4. The results in Exhibit 6 imply target rates of return for lessor firms. For a lessor firm with a 50 percent tax rate, what is the apparent target rate of return? What things could make their actual realized rate of return lower (higher)?
5. Assume for the moment that a lease contract were signed before discussing which party will keep ITC. Explain how it would influence the cost of leasing, depending upon which party takes the credit.

V | Financial Structure and the Cost of Capital

18

J. Fred Weston and Eugene F. Brigham

The Effect of Capital Structure on Valuation and the Cost of Capital

One of the great issues in the academic finance literature during the 1960s was capital structure and its effect on the cost of capital. The so-called traditional viewpoint was that an optimal balance between long-term debt and equity existed and at this optimal point share price was maximized and cost of capital minimized. The arguments of Modigliani and Miller (MM), published in the latter 1950s, disclaimed the existence of an optimal capital structure. MM employed both a tightly developed argument and some empirical evidence. The debate continued through the 1960s and early 1970s, and it remains an issue today, but not to the degree it had been. In this paper, the authors argue that the modern view on the subject is most appropriately identified as a compromise.

A firm's value is dependent on its expected earnings stream and the rate used to discount this stream, or the cost of capital; therefore, if capital structure is to affect value, it must do so by operating either on expected earnings or on the cost of capital, or on both. Because interest is tax deductible, leverage generally increases expected earnings, at least so long as the firm does not use so much leverage that bankruptcy seriously threatens its continued existence. The effect of leverage on the cost of capital is much less clear; indeed, this issue has been one of the major controversies in finance for the past twenty years, and perhaps more theoretical and empirical work has been done on this subject than on any other in the field. In this article we set forth the major theories relating leverage to the cost of capital.

Source. Adapted from J. Fred Weston and Eugene F. Brigham, *Managerial Finance,* 5th ed. (Hinsdale, Ill.: The Dryden Press, 1975), pp. 636–655. Copyright © 1975 by The Dryden Press, a division of Holt, Rinehart and Winston. Reprinted by permission of Holt, Rinehart and Winston. The paper was coauthored with Professor Abdul Karim Sadik.

THE NET INCOME (NI) AND NET OPERATING INCOME (NOI) APPROACHES

Economists have identified two basic market structures—pure competition and pure monopoly—and they can determine the optimal price = quantity solution for firms in either of these two positions. Most firms in the real world are in the gray area of oligopoly, which lies somewhere between the pure cases, but an understanding of the pure cases is helpful in understanding oligopoly and real-firm behavior.

The situation is similar with respect to leverage—there are two extreme positions corresponding to pure competition and pure monopoly, and a middle ground actually occupied by most, if not all, firms. David Durand, in a key article,[1] identified the two extreme cases:

Net Income Approach (NI).   Under the NI approach to valuation, the interest rate and the cost of equity are independent of the capital structure, but the weighted average or overall cost of capital declines, and the total value (value of stock plus value of debt) rises, with increased use of leverage.

Net Operating Income Approach (NOI).   Under the NOI approach, the cost of equity increases, the weighted average cost of capital remains constant, and the total value of the firm also remains constant as leverage is changed.

Thus, if the NI approach is the correct one, leverage is an important variable, and debt policy decisions have a significant influence on the value of the firm. However, if the NOI approach is correct, then the firm's management need not be too concerned with financial structure, because it simply does not greatly matter.

Basic Assumptions and Definitions

In order to focus on the key elements of the controversy, we begin by making several simplifying assumptions:

1. Only two types of capital are employed: long-term debt and common stock.
2. There is no tax on corporate income. This assumption is later relaxed.
3. The firm's total assets are given, but its capital structure can be changed by selling debt to repurchase stock or selling stock to retire debt.
4. All earnings are paid out as dividends.

[1] See David Durand, "Costs of Debt and Equity Funds for Business: Trends and Problems of Measurement," reprinted in Ezra Solomon, ed., The Management of Corporate Capital (New York: Free Press, 1959), 91–116.

5. All investors have the same subjective probability distributions of expected future operating earnings (*EBIT*) for a given firm; that is, investors have homogeneous expectations.
6. The operating earnings of the firm are not expected to grow; that is, the firm's expected *EBIT* is the same in all future periods.
7. The firm's business risk is constant over time and is independent of its capital structure and financial risk.
8. The firm is expected to continue indefinitely.

In addition to these assumptions, we shall use the following basic definitions and symbols:

S = Total market value of the stock (equity).

B = Total market value of the bonds (debt).

V = Total market value of the firm = $S + B$.

$EBIT$ = Earnings before interest and taxes = net operating income.

I = Interest payments in dollars.

Our next task is to specify and define the key cost of capital and valuation relationships:

1. *Debt*

Cost of debt capital = $k_d = \dfrac{I}{B}$.

Value of debt = $B = \dfrac{I}{k_d}$.

2. *Equity, or Common Stock*

Cost of equity capital = $k_s = \dfrac{D_1}{P_o} + g$.

Here, D_1 is the next dividend, P_o is the current price per share, and g is the expected growth rate. According to assumption 4 above, the percentage of earnings retained, or the retention rate (b), is zero; since $g = br$, where r is the rate of return on equity, $g = br = 0 \times r = 0$; in other words, the growth rate is zero. This is consistent with assumption 6 above. Note also that $D_1 = (1 - b)(E_1)$, and with $b = 0$, $D_1 = (1)(E_1) = E_1$. Thus,

$$k_s = \frac{D_1}{P_o} + g = \frac{E_1}{P_o} + 0 = \frac{E_1}{P_o}.$$

This equation is on a per-share basis; multiplying both the numerator and denominator by the number of shares outstanding (N), we obtain

$$k_s = \frac{E_1(N)}{P_o(N)} = \frac{EBIT - I}{S} = \frac{\text{Net income available to stockholders}}{\text{Total market value of stock}}.$$

Thus, k_s may be defined on a per-share or a total basis.

The value of the stock, or common equity, is equal to earnings divided by the cost of equity,

$$P_o = \frac{E_1}{k_s},$$

or

$$V = \frac{EBIT - I}{k_s} = P_o N.$$

3. *Overall, or Weighted Average, Cost of Capital*

The overall, or weighted average, cost of capital is

$$
\begin{aligned}
k_a &= w_d k_d + w_s k_s \\
&= \left(\frac{B}{V}\right) k_d + \left(\frac{S}{V}\right) k_s \\
&= \left(\frac{B}{B + S}\right) k_d + \left(\frac{S}{B + S}\right) k_s.
\end{aligned}
$$

4. The total value of the firm is thus

$$
\begin{aligned}
V &= B + S \\
&= \frac{I}{k_d} + \frac{EBIT - I}{k_s}.
\end{aligned}
$$

These equations are not controversial—they are simply definitions that apply under either the NI or NOI approaches. However, there are major differences between the NI and NOI theories, as we shall see in the next sections.

The Net Income (NI) Approach

The basic difference between NI and NOI relates to what happens to k_s as the firm's use of debt changes. Under NI, k_s is assumed to be fixed and constant regardless of the firm's degree of financial leverage, while under NOI, k_s is assumed to change. (Both theories assume that k_d, the interest rate on debt, is constant.) To illustrate the NI approach, assume that a firm has $4 million of debt at 7.5 percent, an expected annual net operating earnings (*EBIT*) of $900,000, and an equity capitalization rate (k_s) of 10 percent. With no corporate income taxes, the NI approach gives the value of the firm as follows:

Net operating earnings (*EBIT*)	$900,000
Interest on debt ($4 million × 7.5%)	− 300,000
Available to common	$600,000

Market value of equity = S = $600,000/.10	$ 6,000,000
Market value of bonds = B = $300,000/.075	4,000,000
Total market value of firm = $V = S + B$	$10,000,000

Notice that the component costs of capital under the NI approach are

k_d = 7.5 percent, given as constant, and

k_s = 10 percent, given as constant,

so

$$k_a = 7.5 \left(\frac{4,000,000}{10,000,000} \right) + 10 \left(\frac{6,000,000}{10,000,000} \right)$$

$$= 7.5(4) + 10(6)$$

$$= 3\% + 6\% = 9\%.$$

Now we can examine the effect of a change in financing mix on the firm's cost of capital and market value. Suppose the firm increases its leverage by selling $1 million of debt and using the proceeds to retire stock: What effect will this change have on the value of the firm and its cost of capital? Under the NI approach, it is assumed that the component costs of debt and equity are held constant at 7.5 percent and 10 percent, respectively, so the new situation will be as follows:

Net operating earnings (*EBIT*)	$900,000
Less: Interest on debt ($5 million × 7.5 percent)	− 375,000
Available to common	$525,000

S = $525,000/.10 =	$ 5,250,000
B = $375,000/.075 =	5,000,000
$V = B + S =$	$10,250,000

The overall, or average cost of capital is calculated as follows:

$$k_a = 7.5 \left(\frac{5,000,000}{10,250,000} \right) + 10 \left(\frac{5,250,000}{10,250,000} \right)$$

$$= 7.5 \left(\frac{5}{10.25} \right) + 10 \left(\frac{5.25}{10.25} \right) = 8.78\%.$$

Thus, using additional leverage has caused the total value of the firm to rise and the average cost of capital to fall.

Table 1 shows the firm's overall cost of capital and total market value at different degrees of financial leverage, while the cost of capital figures are plotted in Figure 1. Notice, in the table, that the firm's value rises steadily as the debt ratio increases, and, in both the table and the figure, that the overall, or average, cost of capital declines continuously.

TABLE 1. EFFECT OF CAPITAL STRUCTURE ON VALUE AND COST OF CAPITAL: NI (EBIT = $900,000; OTHER DOLLARS IN MILLIONS)

LEVERAGE RATIO $\left(\frac{B}{V} \right)$	0%	30.77%	65.12%	80.00%	93.62%	100.00%
Value of debt (B)	$ 0	$3.000	$ 7.000	$ 9.000	$11.000	$12.000
Value of equity (S)	$9.000	$6.750	$ 3.750	$ 2.250	$ .750	$ 0
Total value (V)	$9.000	$9.750	$10.750	$11.250	$11.750	$12.000
k_d	7.5%	7.5%	7.5%	7.5%	7.5%	7.5%
k_s	10.0%	10.0%	10.0%	10.0%	10.0%	10.0%
k_a	10.0%	9.2308%	8.3720%	8.000%	7.6595%	7.5000%

The Net Operating Income (NOI) Approach

The second major approach, NOI, is closely identified with the works of Franco Modigliani and Merton Miller (MM), who strongly support NOI on the basis of their theoretical and empirical research.[2] In this section, we set forth the key features of the NOI approach, illustrate the cost of capital and valuation that result under NOI, and summarize Modigliani and Miller's theoretical arguments in support of NOI.

The major assumptions of the NOI approach (in addition to the set of

[2] See F. Modigliani and M. H. Miller, "The Cost of Capital, Corporation Finance and the Theory of Investment," *American Economic Review*, 48 (June 1958), 261–297, and "The Cost of Capital, Corporation Finance and the Theory of Investment: Reply," *American Economic Review*, 49 (September 1958), 655–669; "Taxes and the Cost of Capital: A Correction," *American Economic Review*, 53 (June 1963), 433–443, and "Reply," *American Economic Review*, 55 (June 1965), 524–527.

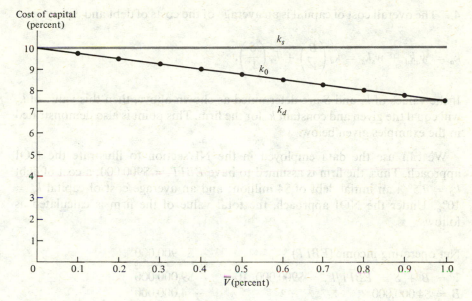

Figure 1. Cost of capital under the NI approach.

assumptions common to both NI and NOI shown in the first section) are as follows.

1.   In a world of no taxes, the total market value of the firm (V) is found by capitalizing net operating income ($EBIT = $ NOI) at the overall cost of capital, k_a, which is a constant. Thus,

$$V = \frac{EBIT}{k_a}.$$

Since k_a is independent of financial mix, as is $EBIT$, V is also a constant and is independent of capital structure.

2.   The value of the equity, or the total value of the stock (S), is found by subtracting the value of the debt (B) from V. Thus, $S = V - B$, which implies that S is a residual obtained by deducting the stated value of the bonds from the total value of the firm, *which was found by capitalizing EBIT or NOI at the constant overall cost of capital.*

3.   The cost of equity was defined earlier as follows:

$$k_s = \frac{EBIT - I}{S}.$$

As we shall see below, *this implies that k_s increases as leverage increases.*

4. The overall cost of capital is an average of the costs of debt and equity:

$$k_a = w_d k_d + w_s k_s = k_d \left(\frac{B}{V}\right) + k_s \left(\frac{S}{V}\right).$$

If the values of k_s and S are determined as shown above, then this value of k_a will equal the given and constant k_a for the firm. This point is also demonstrated in the examples given below.

We can use the data employed in the NI section to illustrate the NOI approach. Thus, the firm is assumed to have $EBIT = \$900,000$; a cost of debt $k_d = 7.5\%$; an initial debt of \$4 million; and an average cost of capital $k_a = 10\%$. Under the NOI approach, the total value of the firm is calculated as follows:

Net operating income ($EBIT$)	$\ 900,000
$V = B + S = EBIT/k_a = \$900,000/.10$	$9,000,000
$B = \$4,000,000$	$-\ 4,000,000
$S = $ a residual $=$	$5,000,000

Given the value of the stock, we can now calculate the cost of equity capital as follows:

$$k_s = \frac{EBIT - I}{S} = \frac{\$900,000 - .075(\$4,000,000)}{\$5,000,000}$$

$$= \$600,000/\$5,000,000 = .12 \text{ or } 12\%.$$

The weighted average cost of capital can now be calculated:

$$k_a = k_d \left(\frac{B}{V}\right) + k_s \left(\frac{S}{V}\right) = 7.5\% \left(\frac{4}{9}\right) + 12\% \left(\frac{5}{9}\right) = 3.33 + 6.67 = 10\%.$$

Thus, the average cost of capital is 10 percent, just as the NOI theory says it should be.

If debt was increased to \$5 million, the value of the firm would remain constant at \$9 million, the value of the stock would drop to \$4 million, and the cost of equity would rise to 13.12 percent:

$$k_s = \frac{\$900,000 - .075(\$5,000,000)}{\$4,000,000} = \frac{\$525,000}{\$4,000,000} = 13.12\%,$$

and

$$k_a = 7.5\% \left(\frac{5}{9}\right) + 13.12 \left(\frac{4}{9}\right) = 4.17 + 5.83 = 10\%.$$

Again, we see that the calculated average cost of capital is a constant.

Values for V, B, S, k_a, and k_s at different debt ratios are shown in Table 2, and a plot of the NOI cost of capital is shown in Figure 2. The key features of these two exhibits are as follows.

1. Both the cost of debt (k_d) and the overall, or average, cost of capital (k_a) are constant.
2. The cost of equity (k_s) increases exponentially with leverage as measured by the ratio (B/V).[3]

---

[3] A firm's leverage can be measured (at market values) by either the debt-to-total-value ratio (B/V), or the debt/equity (B/S) ratio. Under the NOI-MM theory, the cost of equity is an exponential function of the B/V ratio (see Figure 2) but a linear function of the B/S ratio. For a demonstration of this linear relationship, consider the following:

$$k_a = k_d(B/V) + k_s(S/V) \tag{1}$$

or

$$k_s = \frac{k_a - k_d(B/V)}{S/V}. \tag{2}$$

Now note that $V = B + S$, and that the equity ratio S/V may be rewritten as

$$S/V = 1 - \frac{B}{B + S}. \tag{3}$$

We may substitute (2) and (3) into (1), then simplify as follows:

$$k_s = \frac{k_a - k_d \dfrac{B}{B + S}}{1 - \dfrac{B}{B + S}} = \frac{\dfrac{k_a(B + S) - k_d B}{B + S}}{\dfrac{B + S - B}{B + S}}$$

$$= \frac{k_a B + k_a S - k_d B}{S} = k_a + (k_a - k_d)\frac{B}{S}. \tag{4}$$

k_a and k_d are constants, so equation (4) is of the form $y = a + bx$, which is linear. Equation (4) states that the required rate of return on common stock (k_s) is equal to the appropriate capitalization rate for a pure equity stream for that class (k_a) plus a premium for financial risk equal to the spread between that capitalization rate (k_a) and the yield on debt (k_d) times the debt-equity ratio (B/S).

TABLE 2. *EFFECT OF CAPITAL STRUCTURE ON VALUE AND COST OF CAPITAL: NOI (EBIT = $900,000; OTHER DOLLARS IN MILLIONS)*

B/V	0%	22.22%	44.44%	88.89%	100.00%
Debt (B)	$ 0	$2.000	$4.000	$8.000	$9.000
Equity (S)	$9.000	$7.000	$5.000	$1.000	$ 0
Total value (V)	$9.000	$9.000	$9.000	$9.000	$9.000
k_d	7.5%	7.5%	7.5%	7.5%	7.5%
k_s	10.0%	10.71%	12.0%	30.0%	—
k_a	10.0%	10.0%	10.0%	10.0%	10.0%
B/S	0%	28.57%	80.00%	800.00%	—

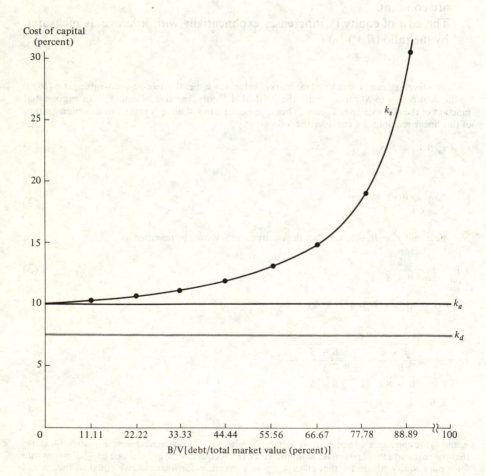

Figure 2. Cost of capital under the NOI approach, no taxes.

Modigliani and Miller's Support for NOI: The Arbitrage Argument

Modigliani and Miller base their support of the NOI hypothesis on arbitrage, arguing that if two companies differ only in the way they are financed and in their total market value, investors will sell shares of the overvalued firm, buy those of the undervalued firm, and continue this process until the companies have the same market value. To illustrate the arbitrage argument, assume that two firms L (for levered) and U (for unlevered) are identical in all respects except financial structure. Firm L has $4 million of 7.5 percent debt; firm U is all equity financed. Both firms have $EBIT = \$900,000$. In the initial situation, before arbitrage, both firms have an equity capitalization rate, $k_s = 10$ percent. Under these conditions, and assuming the NI approach is correct, the following situation will exist.

	Firm U	Firm L
Net operating income ($EBIT$)	$900,000	$900,000
Less interest on debt	0	− 300,000
Available to common (E)	$900,000	$600,000
Value of stock ($S = E/k_s = E/.10$)	$9,000,000	$ 6,000,000
Value of debt (B)	0	4,000,000
Total market value ($V = B + S$)	$9,000,000	$10,000,000

This is the NI solution, and MM argue that it cannot persist.

An investor in firm L can, according to MM, increase his total returns without increasing his financial risk. For example, suppose the investor owns 10 percent of L's stock, so that his investment is $600,000. He can sell his stock in L, borrow an amount equal to 10 percent of L's debt ($400,000), and then buy 10 percent of U's stock for $900,000. Notice that the investor received $1 million from sale of stock plus borrowing, and spent $900,000 on U's stock, so he has $100,000 in uncommitted funds.

Now consider the investor's income position:

Old income: 10% of L's $600,000 =		$60,000
New income: 10% of U's $900,000	$90,000	
Less 7.5% on $400,000 loan	− 30,000	$60,000

Thus, his stock investment income is exactly the same as before, but he has $100,000 left over for investment elsewhere, so his total return will rise. Further, his risk, according to MM, is the same as before—he has simply substituted "homemade" leverage for corporate leverage.

MM argue that this arbitrage process will occur, with sales of L's stock driving its price down and purchases of U's stock driving its prices up, until the market values of the two firms are equal. When this equality is reached the NOI conditions are fulfilled, and the value of the firms and their overall costs of capital are equal; that is, value and k_a are independent of capital structure. However, in reaching this conclusion, MM must make some important assumptions.

1. Their analysis implies that personal and corporate leverage are perfect substitutes. In the case of corporate borrowings, the individual investing in the levered firm has only limited liability. If, however, he engages in arbitrage transactions, there is the possibility that he may lose not only his holdings in the unlevered firm but also his other assets.
2. In the analysis, transaction costs were assumed away, yet such costs may retard the arbitrage process.
3. Corporations and individuals are assumed to borrow at the same rate. The cost of borrowing could be higher for the individual than for the firm.
4. At times, institutional restrictions may retard the arbitrage process. Institutional investors dominate stock markets today, yet most institutional investors are prohibited from engaging in "homemade" leverage.

MM's critics argue that the assumptions of the MM model are invalid, and that, in the real world, firms' values and costs of capital are functions of financial leverage. We shall return to this debate later, after examining the situation when the assumption of no corporate taxes is relaxed.

The Modigliani-Miller View with Taxes

When taxes are introduced, MM's position changes: with corporate taxes, they recognize that the levered firm commands a higher value because interest on debt is a deductible expense. Specifically, MM state that L's value exceeds that of U by an amount equal to L's debt multiplied by the tax rate:

$$V_L = V_U + Bt.$$

Here V_L = value of firm L, V_U = value of firm U, B = amount of debt in L, and t = tax rate. Their proof goes as follows. Consider two firms that are identical in all respects except capital structure. Assume that firm U has no debt in its capital structure, while L employs debt, and that expected operating earnings, $EBIT = X$, is identical for each firm. Under these assumptions, the operating earnings after tax available to investors, X_U and X_L, for firms U and L respectively, are computed as follows:

$$X_U = X(1 - t) \tag{5}$$

and

$$X_U = (X - k_d B)(1 - t) + k_d B \tag{6}$$

where t = tax rate, k_d = interest rate on debt, and B = amount of debt. The first term to the right of the equal sign in Equation (6) is the income available to stockholders; the second term is that available to bondholders.

Since firm U does not employ debt, its value (V_U) may be determined by discounting its annual net income after corporate taxes, $X(1 - t)$, by its capitalization rate, k_s:

$$V_U = \frac{X(1 - t)}{k_s}. \tag{7}$$

The levered firm's after-tax income, X_L, as set forth in Equation (6), can be restated as follows:

$$\begin{aligned}
X_L &= (X - k_d B)(1 - t) + k_d B \\
&= X - k_d B - Xt + k_d Bt + k_d B \\
&= X - Xt + k_d Bt \\
&= X(1 - t) + k_d Bt.
\end{aligned}$$

The first term in the final equation, $X(1 - t)$, is equivalent to U's income, while the second part, $k_d Bt$, represents the tax savings that occur because interest is deductible.

The value of the levered firm is found by capitalizing both parts of its after-tax earnings. MM argue that because L's "regular" earnings stream is precisely as risky as is the income of firm U, it should be capitalized at the same rate (k_s). However, since the debt is assumed to be riskless, interest on the debt must be paid, and the tax saving represents a certain, riskless stream that should be discounted at the riskless rate (k_d). Thus, we obtain equation (8):

$$V_L = \frac{X(1 - t)}{k_s} + \frac{k_d Bt}{k_d} = \frac{X(1 - t)}{k_s} + Bt. \tag{8}$$

However, since

$$V_U = \frac{X(1 - t)}{k_s},$$

we may also express V_L as:

$$V_L = V_U + Bt,$$

which is what we set out to prove.

We may now illustrate the MM valuation and cost of capital hypotheses in a world with corporate taxes.[4] Assume (1) that a firm starts in business with total capital of $5.4 million; (2) that this capital is used to purchase assets costing $5.4 million; (3) that the before-tax rate of return on these assets is 16.67 percent, producing $EBIT = \$900,000$; (4) that the leverage-free equity capitalization rate is $k_s = 10$ percent; and (5) that the corporate income tax rate is 40 percent. We may compute the value of the unlevered firm as follows:

$$V_U = \frac{X(1-t)}{k_s} = \frac{\$900,000(1-.4)}{.10} = \$5,400,000.$$

As debt is added, the total market value of the firm rises by Bt per unit of debt; for example, if $1 million of debt is used, then

$$V_L = V_U + Bt = \$5,400,000 + \$400,000 = \$5,800,000.$$

Note that if we divide $EBIT$ by V, the quotient is the before-tax rate of return on total market value, and this rate of return declines as debt is increased. Values of V and $EBIT/V$, together with several rates of return calculations which are explained below, are shown in Table 3.

The book value and market value of common equity, and the rates of return on these two values, will vary with leverage under the MM tax model. Total corporate assets are $5,400,000 by assumption, and we can establish other items as follows.

1. Net profit after interest and taxes $= (X - I)(1 - t)$.
2. Book value of equity $= \$5,400,000 - B$.
3. Market value of equity $= V - B$.
4. Rate of return on book equity $= [(X - I)(1 - t)]/(\$5,400,000 - B)$.
5. Rate of return on market value of equity $= k_s = [(X - I)(1 - t)]/(V - B) =$ the required rate of return on equity, or the cost of equity capital.
6. Overall cost of capital $= k_a = (B/V)(1 - t)(k_d) + (S/V)(k_s)$.

Using these relationships, and values of V and B as shown in Table 3, we can find the rates of return on book and market equity at different degrees of leverage:

[4] First, it must be recognized that with the introduction of corporate income taxes, either (1) the values of business firms will be lower because of the decline in earnings, or (2) rates of return before taxes ($EBIT$/Assets) will rise to offset the tax revenue; which condition holds depends upon the incidence of corporate income taxes, a long-standing question among economists. We simply note that something must change when taxes are imposed, although in our example we let the rate of return change.

Debt = $0:

Rate of return on book equity $= \dfrac{(\$900,000 - \$0)(.6)}{\$5,400,000 - \$0} = 10.0\%.$

Rate of return on market equity $= k_s = \dfrac{\$540,000}{\$5,400,000} = 10.0\%.$

Average cost of capital $= k_a = (0)(.6)(7.5) + (1.00)(10.0) = 10.0\%.$

Debt = $2 million:

Rate of return on book equity $= \dfrac{(\$900,000 - \$150,000)(.6)}{\$5,400,000 - \$2,000,000}$

$$= \dfrac{\$450,000}{\$3,400,000} = 13.23\%.$$

Rate of return on market equity $= \dfrac{\$450,000}{\$4,200,000} = 10.71\%.$

Average cost of capital $= k_a = (.32)(.6)(7.5) + (.68)(10.71) = 8.72.$

The cost-of-capital situation under the MM assumptions in a world with taxes is graphed in Figure 3. It is interesting to compare Figure 3 and Table 3, and to note the following points:

1. The total value of the firm rises with leverage (Table 3).
2. The rate of return on the book value of equity rises rapidly with leverage, but is meaningless for debt > $5.4 million (Table 3).
3. The rate of return on the market value of equity, which is also the cost of equity capital, rises with leverage, but less rapidly than the rate of return on book values (Table 3 and Figure 3).
4. The before-tax cost of debt is constant (7.5 percent in our example as shown in Figure 3).
5. The overall, or average, cost of capital declines linearly as the debt ratio is increased. However, it would be difficult, if not impossible, for the firm to increase its market value debt ratio to or beyond the point where the book value debt ratio is 100 percent, that is, beyond the point where $B = \$5.4$ million (Table 3 and Figure 3).

Thus, the MM model in a world of taxes leads to the conclusion that the value of a firm will be maximized, and its cost of capital minimized, if it uses only debt in its capital structure. Of course, firms do not engage in 100 percent debt financing, which leads us to question the validity of the MM model and its assumptions.

TABLE 3. *EFFECT OF LEVERAGE ON VALUATION AND THE COST OF CAPITAL: MM ASSUMPTIONS IN A WORLD WITH TAXES (DOLLARS IN MILLIONS)*

DEBT (B)	EQUITY (S)	TOTAL VALUE (V)	B/S	EBIT/V	AFTER-TAX RATE OF RETURN ON EQUITY		AVERAGE COST OF CAPITAL (k_a)
					Book	Market (k_s)	
$0	$5.4	$5.4	0%	16.67%	10.00%	10.00%	10.00%
$2	$4.2	$6.2	47.6%	14.52%	13.23%	10.71%	8.72%
$4	$3.0	$7.0	133.0%	12.86%	17.14%	12.00%	7.77%
$6	$1.8	$7.8	333.3%	11.54%	n.a.	15.00%	6.92%
$8	$0.6	$8.6	1333.3%	10.47%	n.a.	30.00%	6.28%

n.a. = not applicable; implies debt greater than assets ($5,400,000), which would imply a negative accounting net worth, so the rate of return on book equity is not meaningful.

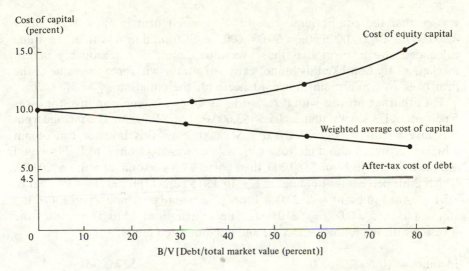

Figure 3.   Cost of capital under the MM assumption with taxes.

The Modigliani-Miller Arbitrage Process in a World with Taxes

With corporate taxes, both the NI and NOI approaches produce higher values for the levered than for the unlevered firms. However, the two ways differ with respect both to the size of this difference and to the manner in which it is generated. To illustrate, we shall use the same data as given previously. The tax rate is 40 percent. Firm L has $4 million of 7.5 percent debt; firm U is all equity financed; and both firms have $EBIT = \$900{,}000$. To begin, assume that both firms have an equity capitalization rate $k_s = 10$ percent. Under these conditions, the NI approach establishes the value of firms U and L as follows:

	Firm U	Firm L
Net operating income (*EBIT*)	$900,000	$900,000
Less: interest on debt	— 0	— 300,000
Taxable income	$900,000	$600,000
Less: taxes at 40 percent	— 360,000	— 240,000
Available to common (*E*)	$540,000	$360,000
Value of stock ($S = E/K_s = E/.10$)	$5,400,000	$3,600,000
Value of debt (*B*)	0	4,000,000
Total market value ($V = B + S$)	$5,400,000	$7,600,000

MM would argue that this NI solution represents a fundamental disequilibrium and therefore cannot persist. Using the MM equations developed above, we see that the equilibrium value of the levered firm is $V_L = V_U + Bt = 4,400,000 + (4,000,000)(.60) = \$6,000,000$, or $1.6 million less than the value calculated above. Firm L is thus overvalued, and, in a reasonably perfect market, a situation like this cannot exist—arbitrage will force the value of the firm back to equilibrium in accordance with the equation $V_L = V_U + Bt$.

The arbitrage process with taxes works as follows. Assume an investor owns 5 percent of L's stocks, that is, $.05 \times \$3,600,000 = \$180,000$. His income from this investment is $.10 \times \$180,000 = \$18,000$. Now this investor can obtain a higher income, without increasing his risk, by moving from L to U. He would sell his holdings in L for $180,000, then borrow on personal account $120,000, which is his percentage holdings in L's stocks (5 percent) times $(1 - t)$—that is, $.05(1 - .4)(\$4 \text{ million}) = \$120,000$. Finally, he would purchase 5 percent of U's stocks $(.05 \times 5,400,000 = \$270,000)$. The switch from L to U provides the investor with the following income and uncommitted funds:

Income $= .10 \times \$270,000$	$27,000
Less: cost of personal debt	
$= 7.5 \text{ percent} \times 120,000$ borrowed capital	9,000
Net income from new investment	$18,000
Total funds: Original capital	$180,000
Borrowed funds	120,000
	$300,000
Total outlay	$270,000
Uncommitted funds	$ 30,000

Through arbitrage and the substitution of personal for corporate leverage, the investor can switch from the levered company into the unlevered one, earn the same total return ($18,000) on his net worth, be exposed to the same leverage as formerly (but on personal rather than corporate account), and have funds left over to invest elsewhere. According to MM, many investors would recognize this arbitrage opportunity, attempt to make the switch, and in the process drive the price of L's stock down to establish an equilibrium where the total market values of the two firms are consistent with the MM equation, that is, $V_U = \$5.4$ million, and $V_L = V_U + Bt = \$5.4$ million $+ \$1.6$ million $= \$7$ million.

CRITICISMS OF THE MODIGLIANI-MILLER POSITION

When MM's work first appeared in 1958, it stimulated a great deal of academic interest. MM's theoretical arguments have borne up quite well, but their assumptions have been questioned extensively, and because of doubts about these assumptions, few authorities today accept the "pure" MM position. Among the arguments used against MM are the following:

1.   *Risk of Ruin.* Business risk is, in a very real sense, a function of the degree of leverage. For one thing, if a firm fails to cover its debt charges during poor periods, it will not survive to attain the fruits of leverage during good periods. Also, bankruptcy has high costs, and the probability of the firm's having to bear these costs rises with leverage.

2.   *Personal versus Corporate Leverage.* It has been argued that investors are not indifferent between personal and corporate leverage. The threat of personal bankruptcy, higher interest rates on individual than corporate debt, and restrictions on margin loans all suggest that corporate leverage may be preferable to personal leverage.

3.   *Empirical Tests of the Leverage Question.* Many empirical studies have tested the effects of leverage on the cost of capital. For the most part, these studies have involved multiple regression models, using an estimate of the cost of capital as the dependent variable and the debt ratio as the principal independent variable. Other independent variables are also included to "hold constant" factors other than financial leverage. Unfortunately, severe problems have been encountered in all these statistical studies, with the primary difficulty being the problem of holding constant factors other than leverage which may affect the cost of capital. Because of these statistical problems, the empirical studies have been unable to resolve the controversy. On balance, however, they seem to offer support for the compromise view discussed in the next section.

The Effect of Leverage on the Cost of Capital: A Summary of Alternative Positions

A careful review of the literature on the leverage question suggests that three alternative positions have, in the past, been advocated: the "traditional" view, the MM view, and what can best be described as a compromise view. Figure 4 gives graphic representations of these three views.

The Traditional View.   Prior to the appearance of the 1958 MM article, most writers dealing with the cost of capital seemed to advocate a position roughly consistent with that shown in Figure 4a. We say "roughly" because, prior to MM's work, academic writers on the subject were not sufficiently rigorous to enable us to pin down their views. At any rate, most academicians who did express views on this subject seemed to go along with the net income approach up to a point—that is, they seemed to feel that the cost of both debt and equity was independent of the debt ratio until some unspecified amount of debt was employed, after which the cost of both equity and debt begin to rise rather sharply. As a result, the average or overall cost of capital in the traditional view declined rather sharply, then rose sharply beyond the optimum debt ratio.

The Modigliani-Miller View.   Figure 4*b* shows the MM view with and without corporate taxes. This figure is similar to Figures 2 and 3.

A Compromise View.   Figure 4*c* shows what might be described as a compromise view of the relationship between debt and the cost of capital. Unlike the traditional view, which has the cost of debt and equity constant when relatively little debt is used, and the MM view, which is that the cost of equity rises at a rate that causes the average cost of capital to be constant (no taxes) or to decline linearly (with taxes), the compromise view holds that the cost of both debt and equity rises with the degree of financial leverage, with the result being a relatively shallow average cost of capital curve.

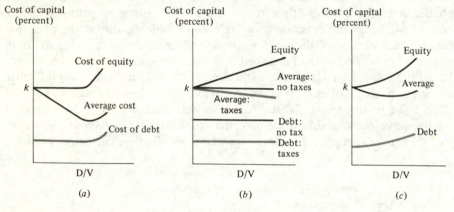

Figure 4.   Alternative views of the relationship between the use of debt and the cost of capital. (*a*) Traditional. (*b*) Modigliani-Miller. (*c*) Compromise.

To summarize, the traditional view suggests that the average cost of capital declines rapidly with debt over a certain range and then begins to rise rapidly. The result is something approximating a V-shaped average cost of capital curve. The average cost of capital, according to MM, is constant in a world with no taxes, but declines continuously with increases in debt when corporate income taxes are considered. Thus, the MM model suggests that a firm that pays no corporate taxes need not worry about its capital structure, while a firm that does pay taxes should take on as much debt as it can get. Under the compromise view—which reflects our own feelings—the average cost of capital curve is U-shaped rather than V-shaped. There is an optimum capital structure, so it pays the financial manager to give careful consideration to his firm's capital structure, but the curve does not have a sharply defined minimum, so the firm is not penalized greatly by departing somewhat from the optimal debt structure. This permits flexibility in financial planning.

Neither theory nor empirical analysis has been able to specify precisely the optimal capital structure for an actual firm, or the precise cost of capital at any given capital structure—capital structure decisions are largely matters of informed judgment. However, *informed* judgment requires that some analysis of the type described in this book be undertaken, and an awareness of the theoretical considerations described here are very useful in such analyses.

QUESTIONS

1. Describe the traditional view regarding the optimal cost of capital; contrast and compare this view with the one identified as "compromise."
2. Explain the position of MM on the issue of an optimal capital structure, ignoring the corporate income tax; show how homemade leverage by the individual investor can replicate the same risk and return as provided by the leveraged corporation. Use a numerical example.
3. Explain the position of MM on the issue of an optimal capital structure, admitting to the existence of the corporate income tax.
4. What assumptions do MM make in developing their theory?
5. Evaluate the reality and importance of each of the assumptions listed in your answer to Question 4.
6. Is the violation of any of the above assumptions important enough to render the MM argument unfounded?

PROBLEMS

1. Companies X and Y are identical in every respect except that X is unlevered, while Y has $10 million of 5 percent bonds outstanding. Assume (1) that all of the MM assumptions are met, (2) that the tax rate is 40 percent, (3) that *EBIT* is $2 million, and (4) that the equity capitalization rate for Company X is 10 percent.
   a. What value would MM estimate for each firm?
   b. Suppose $V_X = 8 million and $V_Y = 18 million. According to MM, do these represent equilibrium values? If not, explain the process by which equilibrium will be restored.
2. Company A and Company B are in the same risk class and are identical in every respect except that Company A is levered, while Company B is not. Company A has $3 million in 5 percent bonds outstanding. Both firms earn 10 percent *before interest and taxes* on their invested capital, or total assets, which amounts to $5 million. Assume perfect capital markets,

rational investors, and so on, a tax rate of 60 percent, and a capitalization rate of 10 percent for an all equity company.

a. Compute the value of Firms A and B using the net income (NI) approach.

b. Compute the value of each firm using the net operating income (NOI) approach.

c. Using the NOI approach, calculate the after-tax weighted average cost of capital, k_a, for Firms A and B. Which of those two firms has an optimal capital structure according to the NOI approach? Why?

d. According to the NOI approach, the values for Firms A and B computed in part a above are not in equilibrium. If a situation like this exists, an investor in the overvalued firm can, through the arbitrage process, secure the same income at lower cost. Assume that you own 1 percent of A's stocks; show the process which will give you the same amount of income but at less cost. At what point would this process stop?

e. Company B (the wholly equity financed firm) wants to change its capital structure by introducing debt. Management believes that the cost of equity to the firm will take the form

$$k_s = R_F + \beta + \theta$$

where

k_s = the cost of equity,

R_F = the after-tax riskless interest rate, currently at about 6 percent,

β = a premium demanded by the firm as a result of its particular business activity, currently estimated to be 4 percent,

θ = a premium demanded as a result of the firm's financial leverage.

Management believes that the premium, θ, can be approximated by taking the firm's *debt-assets* ratio, squaring it, and multiplying by .10 to give the additional percentage points of premium required by the market. Management also feels that the firm's cost of debt is a function of the debt ratio, and estimates that this function is approximately equal to the following schedule:

RATIO: DEBT/ASSETS	AFTER-TAX COST OF DEBT
0%	.05
20%	.05
30%	.06
40%	.07
60%	.12

Is there an optimal capital structure for Firm B? If so, what is this optimal debt-equity ratio? (Use a graphic approach.) Could you say that the value of the firm is strictly in accordance with the equation

$$V_L = V_U + Bt?$$

3. A utility company is supposed to be allowed to charge prices high enough to cover all costs, including its cost of capital. Public service commissions are supposed to take actions to stimulate companies to operate as efficiently as possible in order to keep costs, hence prices, as low as possible. In the mid-1960s, AT&T's debt ratio was about 33 percent. Some people (M. J. Gordon in particular) argued that a higher debt ratio would lower AT&T's cost of capital and permit it to charge lower rates for telephone service. What would be the impact of the NI, NOI, MM, "traditional," and "compromise" theories on this controversy?

19 David F. Scott, Jr.

Evidence on the Importance of Financial Structure

Professor Scott uses the ratio of book value of equity to total assets to measure financial structure, and he finds a greater variance in financial structure among industry groups than within industry groups. This clustering confirms that there are industry norms; it is also consistent with the notion that firms with similar risk characteristics may develop similar "optimal" financial structures.

In financial theory, disagreement has arisen with regard to the effect of financial leverage on the overall cost of capital to the enterprise. The traditional view holds that a firm can substitute debt for equity in lower ranges of debt to equity to lower the firm's cost of capital. Beyond an ill-defined point, however, due to excessive risk, the securities markets will not react favorably to further increases in the degree of leverage used by the firm, and its cost of capital will rise. Thus, there is an optimum financial structure that minimizes cost of capital.

In basic conceptual disagreement are the proponents of the "independence" hypothesis. Modigliani and Miller [5, 6, 7], in particular, argue that, given certain conditions (i.e., no taxes on corporate income and perfect capital markets), cost of capital is not influenced by a firm's financing mix. The favorable effect upon total market value of substituting nominally low-cost debt for high-cost equity in the firm's financial structure will be offset exactly by a decrease in the price that investors are willing to pay for the firm's common stock. A higher common equity yield is imposed by the market in return for being exposed to greater financial risk. Thus the cost of capital is independent of the financial structure of the firm, and financing decisions are of minimal importance.

By strict interpretation, these two theories stand at opposite poles. The principal differences between them disappear, however, in a world where interest expense is tax deductible and market imperfections operate to restrict the amount of fixed-income obligations a firm can issue [9, pp. 39–41]. Both schools of thought do in fact subscribe to the optimum financial structure concept under conditions approximating the actual business environment.

Source. Reprinted by permission from *Financial Management*, Summer 1972, pp. 45–50. The author is professor of finance at Virginia Polytechnic Institute and State University.

Accordingly, it is the objective of this article to present evidence on whether the importance of the financial structure of the firm has in practice been confirmed by corporate decision makers. It is hypothesized that, if the financing decision is critical with respect to the valuation of the firm, then decision makers in various industry groups have recognized this fact and developed financial structures suited to their particular business risk. The approach will be to show that an appropriate range of leverage exists for a particular industry and that firms seek to find this range. In addition, it will be demonstrated that interindustry financial structure differences are persistent over time and are pervasive throughout the industries studied.

PRECEDENTS IN THE LITERATURE

Guthmann and Dougall have pointed out that the similarity in financing patterns by firms in given industries is too prevalent to occur merely by chance [4, p. 235]. Likewise, Solomon in his theoretical treatise has argued that interindustry financial structure differences are likely to be significant [11, pp. 97–98]. Thus, if significant differences could be shown to exist among the financial structures (i.e., all sources of funds to the firm) of a sample of firms classified by industry groups, this evidence would be in support of the optimum financial structure concept. Such an approach is a surrogate for the direct method of testing for the effect of leverage on the cost of capital.

Schwartz and Aronson [10] provided the first empirical work utilizing the surrogate approach. They investigated the effect of one factor, industry, on the proportion of common equity in a firm's financial structure. They tested the hypothesis that financial structures measured by book values do not vary significantly *within* an industry, but do vary significantly *among* industries. The statistical technique employed was the one-way analysis of variance, which used the F-ratio or variance ratio test of statistical significance. Significant results were obtained. Schwartz and Aronson concluded that industries have developed optimum financial structures conditioned by their inherent business risks.

There are shortcomings present in the Schwartz and Aronson study. In particular, four weaknesses in their investigation can be identified and should be resolved.

1. They tested for significantly different equity ratios among only four industries. A stronger case could be made for the existence of optimum ranges of leverage if a wider array of industry groupings were examined and significant results obtained. Grunewald and Nemmers [3, p. 388] also have indicated dissatisfaction with this particular aspect of the Schwartz and Aronson study. The present investigation, therefore, examined the financial structures of 12 industries covering 77 firms.

2.   The four broad classes of firms used by Schwartz and Aronson bias the results in favor of the optimum financial structure concept. Their study is composed of a sample drawn from railroad, electric and gas utility, mining, and industrial companies. The regulation of railroads and utilities makes detailed analysis of their financial structure, in contrast to mining and industrial companies, of doubtful significance. For example, it may be argued that the inclusion of railroads and utilities made the Schwartz and Aronson study simply a test of whether the financial structure pattern of regulated industries differs significantly from that of unregulated industries. The 12 industries used here did not include regulated firms.

3.   Schwartz and Aronson tested for significant differences in financial structures in only two years, 1928 and 1961. They implied later in their paper that significant differences had persisted over time, but presented no statistical test of this assertion. Included in the present study, therefore, is a one-way analysis of variance on equity ratios for the selected sample for each year over a continuous 10-year period, 1959–1968.

4.   The one-way analysis of variance that Schwartz and Aronson performed indicated only that the sample means were not *all* equal. It did not indicate how many of the specific comparisons between industries were significantly different, e.g., whether the difference in mean equity ratios between utilities and railroads was significant. This is a damaging weakness because the rejection of the null hypothesis could be attributed entirely to one industry, such as the utility group. Conclusions asserting that inter-industry financial structure differences are significant based on such data are of uncertain value.

To overcome this weakness a multiple comparison test [13, pp. 690–694] has been employed here to test for significant differences between each pair of sample values. This provides more information about the relationships being examined than the conventional analysis of variance, because it is possible to determine if rejection of the null hypothesis occurs because of the financing behavior of more than one industry group.

ASSUMPTIONS OF THE ANALYSIS

Two underlying assumptions are utilized. First, the financial structures of firms are influenced by the basic business risk to which the firms are exposed. Second, different degrees of business risk can be approximated by different industry groupings. These assumptions are common in the literature of financial structure.

If financial structure is an important consideration in the valuation of the enterprise, then, through trial and error or the method of successive approximation, firms in a given industry should seek an optimum range of leverage. This optimum range will differ significantly among industry groups.

THE SAMPLE

The industries chosen for inclusion in the study meet two criteria. First, to eliminate the influence of regulation, utilities and railroads are not included. Second, for the statistical testing to be meaningful, it is necessary that the industries chosen cover a broad spectrum of business risk. The industries have been chosen on an a priori basis, and not according to any measure of variability. Essentially the same method has been used by Barges [1, pp. 37–39] and Wippern [12, pp. 620–621]. The principal aim is to provide a heterogeneous sample.

The following industries have been used (the number in parentheses following each industry indicates the number of firms representing it in the sample): aircraft manufacturing (5); aluminum (4); automotive parts and accessories (8); chemicals (8); heavy construction and supplies (6); drugs and medicines (8); glass, glassware, and containers (4); machinery (7); mining (7); paper, lumber and wood products (7); department and variety retail stores (8); and steel and iron (5).

From these 12 industries, 77 firms were chosen to make up the sample (a list may be obtained from the author). The procedure was to use *Moody's Industrial Manual* for 1969 [8] and to select at random 20 firms from each of the 12 industries in question. Taking this group of firms, 77 were selected which had been analyzed in the Dominick and Dominick *Corporate Data Service* [2] for 1969. The final sample of 77 firms is large enough to provide a high degree of statistical precision. It can be noted that increasing the sample size from 77 to, say, 200 would result only in a reduction of the F-ratio to be exceeded for significance at the 1% level from 2.54 to 2.35. Further, the financial data are all taken from the same source, ensuring consistency in the treatment of the basic accounting information, a condition vital to this study.

THE STATISTICAL PROCEDURE

For each firm in a given year the percent of common equity in the financial structure was calculated at book value. Arranging the firms by industries permitted mean equity ratios to be derived for each of the 12 industries in the sample. With the data classified in this manner, it was possible to test for significant differences in the mean equity ratios among industry groups. The one-way analysis of variance was the statistical test employed. It tests the null hypothesis that the difference among the population means of the various industrial classes sampled is zero. If the variability of sample means among industry groups is significantly greater than within industry groups, the null hypothesis is rejected.

Such a rejection would imply that the differences in financial structure among the 12 industry groups are deliberate rather than occurring by chance.

EMPIRICAL FINDINGS

The results are summarized in Exhibit 1. The mean common equity ratios for each industry sampled are also presented. With a sample size of 77, and with 12 industry classes, the F-ratio must be greater than 2.54 to be significant at the 1% level.

As the tabulation indicates, the null hypothesis is rejected at the 1% level of significance in each of the 10 years tested. The resulting inference is that the financial structures of firms in the various industry classes investigated *are* significantly different. These findings are compatible with the findings of Schwartz and Aronson [10].

The results are persuasive; in no case is the null hypothesis even close to being accepted at the 1% level. Thus the chances of rejecting the hypothesis when it is, in fact, true are considerably less than 1% throughout the 10 years examined. The findings suggest a conscious policy on the part of financial decision makers to adjust the composition of their sources of funds to the business risk to which the firms are exposed. If this were not the case, the variability of equity ratios *within* industry classes should be much greater. It appears that the financial structures of firms in a given industry do cluster in a definite way, supporting the notion that a central relation between financial structure and the value of the firm is recognized by practicing financial managers. Alternatively, it would be possible to explain the consistently different financial structures among industries by assigning a "follow-the-leader" type of intelligence to the demanders and suppliers of corporate capital. However, in a competitive economy a high degree of such behavior is unlikely. Schwartz and Aronson [10, p. 17] have dealt adequately with this argument.

As a further refinement of the analysis, a multiple comparison test was also performed. This test uses the results of the analysis of variance, provided the result is significant—which was the case here. A pairwise analysis was performed for each of the 10 years studied [13, pp. 690–694].

A significant F-ratio obtained from the overall analysis of variance in any given year does not necessarily indicate that *each* sample mean differs significantly from every other sample mean. A multiple comparison test, however, does make it possible to determine which industries have mean equity ratios that differ significantly from the others in the sample. This test also indicates the depth of the inter-industry differences. The results of two of the tests of differences in sample means are presented in Exhibits 2 and 3. Test results for 1960 and 1968 are displayed for they represent the worst and best years, respectively, as determined by the number of significant comparisons.

EXHIBIT 1. EQUITY AS A PERCENT OF TOTAL CAPITALIZATION, BY INDUSTRY, AND RESULTS OF THE ANALYSIS OF VARIANCE

INDUSTRY

YEAR	x_1 Aircraft	x_2 Aluminum	x_3 Automotive	x_4 Chemical	x_5 Construction	x_6 Drugs	x_7 Glass	x_8 Machinery	x_9 Mining	x_{10} Paper	x_{11} Retail	x_{12} Steel	COMPUTED F-RATIO*
1968	37.9	44.4	48.5	58.7	56.8	67.7	62.0	55.4	78.8	62.9	56.5	64.8	15.69
1967	37.2	45.3	54.6	59.4	61.0	68.5	62.1	59.7	85.0	65.8	57.7	66.5	11.45
1966	41.4	44.4	55.8	59.4	59.4	67.3	62.0	61.6	84.3	68.8	57.8	69.5	9.26
1965	49.3	45.0	58.2	62.4	60.7	68.8	72.4	63.3	84.8	73.6	58.3	68.1	9.52
1964	47.5	45.9	62.3	64.4	58.9	69.5	72.1	65.2	84.7	75.4	61.4	69.6	11.11
1963	41.8	45.9	62.4	65.9	62.7	68.5	70.7	65.6	86.3	76.7	60.0	70.3	10.05
1962	40.7	46.4	62.9	63.5	64.1	67.7	72.1	65.5	85.8	75.5	62.1	70.2	8.21
1961	42.5	44.9	65.1	63.5	64.2	68.7	70.6	67.1	85.6	74.6	60.9	67.8	6.69
1960	44.5	44.8	63.1	63.9	62.6	68.9	70.0	70.3	85.2	73.1	63.9	68.2	5.39
1959	40.5	43.6	59.4	63.6	66.8	67.2	67.4	70.0	84.7	71.0	61.8	68.3	6.56

Source. Computed from Dominick and Dominick [2].

*F-ratio of 2.54 needed for rejection of null hypothesis at the 1% level of significance.

Note: x_j refers to the mean common equity ratio of the jth industry; where $j = 1, \ldots, 12$.

313

EXHIBIT 2. TEST OF DIFFERENCES IN COMMON EQUITY RATIO SAMPLE MEANS, 1960
[In percents]

INDUSTRY	AIRCRAFT	ALUMINUM	AUTOMOTIVE	CHEMICAL	CONSTRUCTION	DRUGS	GLASS	MACHINERY	MINING	PAPER	RETAIL
x_j	$x_j - x_1$	$x_j - x_2$	$x_j - x_3$	$x_j - x_4$	$x_j - x_5$	$x_j - x_6$	$x_j - x_7$	$x_j - x_8$	$x_j - x_9$	$x_j - x_{10}$	$x_j - x_{11}$
x_{12}	23.7*	23.4*	5.1	4.3	5.6	−.7	−1.8	−2.1	−17.0**	−4.9	4.3
x_{11}	19.4*	19.1*	.8	0.0	1.3	−5.0	6.1	−6.4	−21.3*	−9.2	
x_{10}	28.6*	28.3*	10.0	9.2	10.5	4.2	3.1	2.8	−12.1**		
x_9	40.7*	40.4*	22.1*	21.3*	22.6*	16.3*	15.2**	14.9**			
x_8	25.8*	25.5*	7.2	6.4	7.7	1.4	.3				
x_7	25.5*	25.2*	6.9	6.1	7.4	1.1					
x_6	24.4*	24.1*	5.8	5.0	6.3						
x_5	18.1*	17.8**	−.5	−1.3							
x_4	19.4*	19.1*	.8								
x_3	18.6*	18.3*									
x_2	.3										

* Significant at 1% level: 24 of 66 comparisons.
** Significant at 5% level only: 5 of remaining 42 comparisons.

Note: The percentage differences are derived from the appropriate year and industries contained in Exhibit 1. For example, $x_{12} - x_1$ (second column) refers to the mean equity ratio for the steel industry less that of the aircraft manufacturing industry, or 68.2 − 44.5 = 23.7.

314

EXHIBIT 3. TEST OF DIFFERENCES IN COMMON EQUITY RATIO SAMPLE MEANS, 1968

[In percents]

INDUSTRY	AIRCRAFT	ALUMINUM	AUTOMOTIVE	CHEMICAL	CONSTRUCTION	DRUGS	GLASS	MACHINERY	MINING	PAPER	RETAIL
x_j	$x_j - x_1$	$x_j - x_2$	$x_j - x_3$	$x_j - x_4$	$x_j - x_5$	$x_j - x_6$	$x_j - x_7$	$x_j - x_8$	$x_j - x_9$	$x_j - x_{10}$	$x_j - x_{11}$
x_{12}	26.9*	20.4*	16.3*	6.1	8.0	-2.9	2.8	9.4**	-14.0**	1.9	8.3**
x_{11}	18.6*	12.1*	8.0**	-2.2	-.3	-11.2*	-5.5	1.1	-22.3*	-6.4	
x_{10}	25.0*	18.5*	14.4*	4.2	6.1	-4.8	.9	7.5**	-15.9*		
x_9	40.9*	34.4*	30.3*	20.1*	22.0*	11.1*	16.8*	23.4*			
x_8	17.5*	11.0*	6.9**	-3.3	-1.4	-12.3*	-6.6				
x_7	24.1*	17.6*	13.5*	3.3	5.2	-5.7					
x_6	29.8*	23.3*	19.2*	9.0*	10.9*						
x_5	18.9*	12.4*	8.3**	-1.9							
x_4	20.8*	14.3*	10.2*								
x_3	10.6*	4.1									
x_2	6.5										

* Significant at 1% level: 36 of 66 comparisons.

** Significant at 5% level only: 7 of remaining 30 comparisons.

Note: The percentage differences are derived from the appropriate year and industries contained in Exhibit 1. For example, $x_{12} - x_1$ (second column) refers to the mean equity ratio for the steel industry less that of the aircraft manufacturing industry, or 64.8 - 37.9 = 26.9.

315

At the 1% level, the lowest number of comparisons turning out to be statistically significant in any year is 24 out of a total of 66.[1] This low occurred in 1959 (not displayed) and 1960 (Exhibit 2). The greatest number of the 66 comparisons that are significant is 36. This occurred in the latest year tested, 1968 (Exhibit 3). Rejections at the 5% level are noted as well in the tabulations.

These results add weight to the conclusion drawn from the analysis of variance of common equity ratios summarized in Exhibit 1. The rejection of the null hypothesis in the analysis of variance procedure is *not* due to the equity ratios of a single industry sample varying widely from all other industry samples. Were this the case, a maximum of 11 significant differences at either level tested would result. The differences in financial structures are in fact quite pervasive.[2]

CONCLUSION

The evidence presented supports both the independence hypothesis and the traditional position on financial structure, since both acknowledge the (normative) validity of the optimum financial structure concept under realistic capital market conditions. It is clear from the analysis that various industries, subject to various degrees of business risk, have indeed developed characteristically different financial structures. If financial structure were of minimal importance in the ultimate valuation of the firm, then a wide variety of equity ratios should be found within each industry. The findings here indicate instead a definite tendency to cluster, as a matter of practical business policy.

REFERENCES

1. Alexander Barges, *The Effect of Capital Structure on the Cost of Capital*, Englewood Cliffs, New Jersey, Prentice-Hall, Inc., 1963.
2. Dominick and Dominick, *Corporate Data Service*, New York, Dominick and Dominick, 1969.
3. Adolph E. Grunewald and Erwin Esser Nemmers, *Basic Managerial Finance*, New York, Holt, Rinehart and Winston, Inc., 1970.
4. Harry G. Guthmann and Herbert E. Dougall, *Corporate Financial Policy*, 4th ed., Englewood Cliffs, New Jersey, Prentice-Hall, Inc., 1962.
5. Merton H. Miller and Franco Modigliani, "Some Estimates of the Cost of Capital to the Electrical Utility Industry," *American Economic Review* (June 1966), pp. 333–390.

[1] For every choice of an industry, we have 11 other industries to consider, and because the absolute value of the difference between mean equity ratios of any two industries is equal, regardless of the order in which they are considered, we have $(12)(11)/2 = 66$ possible differences.

[2] For example, in 1968 at the 5% level, 65.2% of the differences tested are significant.

6. Franco Modigliani and Merton H. Miller, "The Cost of Capital, Corporation Finance and the Theory of Investment," *American Economic Review* (June 1958), pp. 261–296.

7. Franco Modigliani and Merton H. Miller, "Taxes and the Cost of Capital: A Correction," *American Economic Review* (June 1963), pp. 433–443.

8. Moody's Investors Service, Inc., *Moody's Industrial Manual*, 1969, New York, Robert H. Messner, 1969.

9. Alexander A. Robichek and Stewart C. Myers, *Optimal Financing Decisions*, Englewood Cliffs, New Jersey, Pretnice-Hall, Inc., 1965.

10. Eli Schwartz and J. Richard Aronson, "Some Surrogate Evidence in Support of the Concept of Optimal Financial Structure," *Journal of Finance* (March 1967), pp. 10–18.

11. Ezra Solomon, *The Theory of Financial Management*, New York, Columbia University Press, 1963.

12. Ronald F. Wippern, "Financial Structure and the Value of the Firm," *Journal of Finance* (December 1966), pp. 615–633.

13. Taro Yamane, *Statistics, An Introductory Analysis*, 2nd ed., New York, Harper and Row, Publishers, 1967.

QUESTIONS

1. Regardless of how it came to be established, is there any validity in arguing that an industry norm equity ratio (or debt ratio) becomes a guide for the optimal ratio for a given firm in that industry? Explain.

2. There are obvious reasons for assuming that firms within an industry have similar risk characteristics. Are there reasons for believing that they may not? What are these reasons?

3. Scan Exhibit 1. Select the two industries you suspect to have the most unstable earnings of the group. Should the equity ratio be high or low for these two industries? Are the data consistent with your answer?

4. Select the two industries you believe to have the greatest earnings stability. Should the equity ratio be high or low for these industries? Do the data confirm your answer?

20 Franco Modigliani and Gerald A. Pogue

An Introduction to Risk and Return: Concepts and Evidence, Part I

Risk and return concepts relate to financial management in many ways: portfolio policy for financial assets by financial institutions and individuals and selection of real assets by nonfinancial firms. The latter necessarily requires estimation of the firm's cost of capital. The body of literature which deals formally with risk and return in the portfolio context has not been completely integrated into financial management topics. We feel that it is worthwhile to show what has been done in this field to recognize the more obvious applications in financial management.

1. INTRODUCTION

Portfolio theory deals with the selection of optimal portfolios by rational risk-averse investors: that is, by investors who attempt to maximize their expected portfolio returns consistent with individually acceptable levels of portfolio risk. Capital markets theory deals with the implications for security prices of the decisions made by these investors: that is, what relationship should exist between security returns and risk if investors behave in this optimal fashion. Together, portfolio and capital markets theories provide a framework for the specification and measurement of investment risk, for developing relationships between expected security return and risk, and for measuring the performance of managed portfolios such as mutual funds and pension funds.

The purpose of this article is to present a nontechnical introduction to portfolio and capital markets theories. Our hope is to provide a wide class of readers with an understanding of the foundation upon which the modern

Source. Reprinted by permission from *Financial Analysts Journal*, March–April 1974, pp. 68–80. Franco Modigliani is professor of finance, Sloan School of Management, M.I.T., and Gerald Pogue is professor of finance at Baruch College, City University of New York.

risk and performance measures are based, by presenting the main elements of the theory along with the results of some of the more important empirical tests. We are attempting to present not an exhaustive survey of the theoretical and empirical literature, but rather the main thread of the subject leading the reader from the most basic concepts to the more sophisticated but practically useful results of the theory.

2. INVESTMENT RETURN

Measuring historical rates of return is a relatively straightforward matter. We will begin by showing how investment return during a single interval can be measured, and then present three commonly used measures of average return over a series of such intervals.

The return on an investor's portfolio during a given interval is equal to the change in value of the portfolio plus any distributions received from the portfolio expressed as a fraction of the initial portfolio value. It is important that any capital or income distributions made to the investor be included, or else the measure of return will be deficient. Equivalently, the return can be thought of as the amount (expressed as a fraction of the initial portfolio value) that can be withdrawn at the end of the interval while maintaining the principal intact. The return on the investor's portfolio, designated R_P, is given by

$$R_P = \frac{V_1 - V_0 + D_1}{V_0}, \tag{1a}$$

where

$V_1 =$ the portfolio market value at the end of the interval,

$V_0 =$ the portfolio market value at the beginning of the interval,

$D_1 =$ cash distributions to the investor during the interval.

The calculation assumes that any interest or dividend income received on the portfolio securities and not distributed to the investor is reinvested in the portfolio (and thus reflected in V_1). Furthermore, the calculation assumes that any distributions occur at the end of the interval, or are held in the form of cash until the end of the interval. If the distributions were reinvested prior to the end of the interval, the calculation would have to be modified to consider the gains or losses on the amount reinvested. The formula also assumes no capital inflows during the interval. Otherwise, the calculation would have to be modified to reflect the increased investment base. Capital inflows at the end of the interval, however, can be treated as just the reverse of distributions in the return calculation.

Thus given the beginning and ending portfolio values, plus any contributions from or distributions to the investor (assumed to occur at the end of the interval), we can compute the investor's return using Equation (1a). For example, if the XYZ pension fund had a market value of $100,000 at the end of June, capital contributions of $10,000, benefit payments of $5,000 (both at the end of July), and an end-of-July market value of $95,000, the return for the month is a loss of 10 per cent.

The arithmetic average return is an unweighted average of the returns achieved during a series of such measurement intervals. For example, if the portfolio returns [as measured by Equation (1a)] were −10 per cent, 20 per cent, and 5 per cent in July, August, and September respectively, the average monthly return is 5 per cent. The general formula is

$$R_A = \frac{R_{P1} + R_{P2} + \cdots + R_{PN}}{N}, \tag{1b}$$

where

R_A = the arithmetic average return

R_{PK} = the portfolio return in interval k, $k = 1, \ldots, N$

N = the number of intervals in the performance-evaluation period.

The arithmetic average can be thought of as the mean value of the withdrawals (expressed as a fraction of the initial portfolio value) that can be made at the end of each interval while maintaining the principal intact. In the above example, the investor must add 10 per cent of the principal at the end of the first interval and can withdraw 20 per cent and 5 per cent at the end of the second and third, for a mean withdrawal of 5 per cent of the initial value per period.

The time-weighted return measures the compound rate of growth of the initial portfolio during the performance-evaluation period, assuming that all cash distributions are reinvested in the portfolio. It is also commonly referred to as the "geometric" rate of return. It is computed by taking the geometric average of the portfolio returns computed from Equation (1a). For example, let us assume the portfolio returns were −10 per cent, 20 per cent, and 5 per cent in July, August, and September, as in the example above. The time-weighted rate of return is 4.3 per cent per month. Thus one dollar invested in the portfolio at the end of June would have grown at a rate of 4.3 per cent per month during the three-month period. The general formula is

$$R_T = [(1 + R_{P1})(1 + R_{P2}) \cdots (1 + R_{PN})]^{1/N} - 1, \tag{1c}$$

where

R_T = the time-weighted rate of return,

R_{PK} = the portfolio return during the interval k, $k = 1, \ldots, N$,

N = the number of intervals in the performance-evaluation period.

In general, the arithmetic and time-weighted average returns do not coincide. This is because, in computing the arithmetic average, the amount invested is assumed to be maintained (through additions or withdrawals) at its initial value. The time-weighted return, on the other hand, is the return on a portfolio that varies in size because of the assumption that all proceeds are reinvested. The failure of the two averages to coincide is illustrated in the following example: Consider a portfolio with a $100 market value at the end of 1972, a $200 value at the end of 1973, and a $100 value at the end of 1974. The annual returns are 100 per cent and -50 per cent. The arithmetic and time-weighted average returns are 25 per cent and zero per cent respectively. The arithmetic average return consists of the average of $100 withdrawn at the end of Period 1, and $50 replaced at the end of Period 2. The compound rate of return is clearly zero, the 100 per cent return in the first period being exactly offset by the 50 per cent loss in the second period on the larger asset base. In this example the arithmetic average exceeded the time-weighted average return. This always proves to be true, except in the special situation where the returns in each interval are the same, in which case the averages are identical.

The dollar-weighted return measures the average rate of growth of all funds invested in the portfolio during the performance-evaluation period—that is, the initial value plus any contributions less any distributions. As such, the rate is influenced by the timing and magnitude of the contributions and distributions to and from the portfolio. The measure is also commonly referred to as the "internal rate of return." It is important to corporations, for example, for comparison with the actuarial rates of portfolio growth assumed when funding their employee pension plans.

The dollar-weighted return is computed in exactly the same way that the yield to maturity on a bond is determined. For example, consider a portfolio with market value of $100,000 at the end of 1973 (V_0), capital withdrawals of $5,000 at the end of 1974, 1975, and 1976 (C_1, C_2, and C_3), and a market value of $110,000 at the end of 1976 (V_3). Using compound interest tables, the dollar-weighted rate of return is found by trial and error to be 8.1 per cent per year during the three-year period. Thus each dollar in the fund grew at an average rate of 8.1 per cent per year. The formula used is

$$V_0 = \frac{C_1}{(1 + R_D)} + \frac{C_2}{(1 + R_D)^2} + \frac{C_3}{(1 + R_D)^3} + \frac{V_3}{(1 + R_D)^3}, \tag{1d}$$

where

R_D = the dollar-weighted rate of return.

What is the relationship between the dollar-weighted return (internal rate of return) and the previously defined time-weighted rate of return? It is easy to show that under certain special conditions both rates of return are the same. Consider, for example, a portfolio with initial total value V_0. No further additions or withdrawals occur and all dividends are reinvested. Under these special circumstances all of the C's in Equation (1d) are zero so that

$$V_0 = \frac{V_0(1 + R_{P1})(1 + R_{P2})(1 + R_{P3})}{(1 + R_D)^3},$$

where R_P's are the single-period returns. The numerator of the expression on the right is just the value of the initial investment at the end of the three periods (V_3). Solving for R_D we find

$$R = [(1 + R_{P1})(1 + R_{P2})(1 + R_{P3})]^{1/3} - 1,$$

which is the same as the time-weighted rate of return R_T given by Equation (1c). However, when contributions or withdrawals to the portfolio occur, the two rates of return are not the same. Because the dollar-weighted return (unlike the time-weighted return) is affected by the magnitude and timing of portfolio contributions and distributions (which are typically beyond the portfolio manager's control), it is not useful for measuring the investment performance of the manager. For example, consider two identical portfolios (designated A and B) with year-end 1973 market values of $100,000. During 1974 each portfolio has a 20 per cent return. At the end of 1974, portfolio A has a capital contribution of $50,000 and portfolio B a withdrawal of $50,000. During 1975, both portfolios suffer a 10 per cent loss resulting in year-end market values of $153,000 and $63,000 respectively. Now, both portfolio managers performed equally well, earning 20 per cent in 1974 and −10 per cent in 1975, for a time-weighted average return of 3.9 per cent per year. The dollar-weighted returns are not the same, however, due to the different asset bases for 1975, equaling 1.2 per cent and 8.2 per cent for portfolios A and B respectively. The owners of portfolio B, unlike those of A, made a fortuitous decision to reduce their investment prior to the 1975 decline.

In the remainder of this article, when we mention rate of return, we will generally be referring to the single interval measure given by Equation (1a).

However, from time to time we will refer to the arithmetic and geometric averages of these returns.

3.   PORTFOLIO RISK

The definition of investment risk leads us into much less well explored territory. Not everyone agrees on how to define risk, let alone how to measure it. Nevertheless, there are some attributes of risk which are reasonably well accepted.

If an investor holds a portfolio of treasury bonds, he faces no uncertainty about monetary outcome. The value of the portfolio at maturity of the notes will be identical with the predicted value. In this case the investor bears no monetary risk. However, if he has a portfolio composed of common stocks, it will be impossible to exactly predict the value of the portfolio as of any future date. The best he can do is to make a best guess or most-likely estimate, qualified by statements about the range and likelihood of other values. In this case, the investor does bear risk.

One measure of risk is the extent to which the *future* portfolio values are likely to diverge from the expected or predicted value. More specifically, risk for most investors is related to the chance that future portfolio values will be less than expected. Thus if the investor's portfolio has a current value of $100,000, and an expected value of $110,000 at the end of the next year, he will be concerned about the probability of achieving values less than $110,000.

Before proceeding to the quantification of risk, it is convenient to shift our attention from the terminal value of the portfolio to the portfolio rate of return, R_p, since the increase in portfolio value is directly related to R_p.[1]

A particularly useful way to quantify the uncertainty about the portfolio return is to specify the probability associated with each of the possible future returns. Assume, for example, that an investor has identified five possible outcomes for his portfolio return during the next year. Associated with each return is a subjectively determined probability, or relative chance of occurrence. The five possible outcomes are:

[1] The transformation changes nothing of substance since

$$\tilde{M}_T = (1 + \tilde{R}_p)M_0$$

$$= M_0 + M_0\tilde{R}_p,$$

where

$\tilde{M}_T$ = terminal portfolio value,

$\tilde{R}_p$ = portfolio return.

Since $\tilde{M}_T$ is a linear function of $\tilde{R}_p$, any risk measures developed for the portfolio return will apply equally to the terminal market value.

POSSIBLE RETURN	SUBJECTIVE PROBABILITY
50%	0.1
30%	0.2
10%	0.4
−10%	0.2
−30%	0.1
	1.00

Note that the probabilities sum to 1.00 so that the actual portfolio return is confined to take one of the five possible values. Given this probability distribution, we can measure the expected return and risk for the portfolio.

The expected return is simply the weighted average of possible outcomes, where the weights are the relative chances of occurrence. The expected return on the portfolio is 10 per cent, given by

$$E(R_p) = \sum_{j=1}^{5} P_j R_j$$

$$= 0.1(50.0) + 0.2(30.0) + 0.4(10.0) + 0.2(-10.0) + 0.2(-30.0) \qquad (2)$$

$$= 10\%,$$

where the R_j's are the possible returns and the P_j's the associated probabilities.

If risk is defined as the chance of achieving returns less than expected, it would seem to be logical to measure risk by the dispersion of the possible returns below the expected value. However, risk measures based on below-the-mean variability are difficult to work with and are actually unnecessary as long as the distribution of future return is reasonably symmetric about the expected value.[2] Exhibit 1 shows three probability distributions: the first symmetric, the second skewed to the left, and the third skewed to the right. For a symmetric distribution, the dispersion of returns on one side of the expected return is the same as the dispersion on the other side.

Empirical studies of realized rates of return on diversified portfolios show that skewness is not a significant problem.[3] If future distributions are shaped like historical distributions, then it makes little difference whether we measure variability of returns on one or both sides of the expected return. If the probability distribution is symmetric, measures of the total variability of return will be twice as large as measures of the portfolio's variability below the expected return. Thus if total variability is used as a risk surrogate, the risk rankings for a group of portfolios will be the same as when variability below the expected

---

[2] Risk measures based on below-the-average variation are analytically difficult to deal with. H. Markowitz, in Chapter 9 of [18], develops a semivariance statistic which measures variability below the mean and compares it with the more commonly used variance calculation.

[3] See for example M. E. Blume [2].

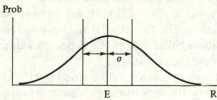

Symmetric probability distribution

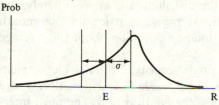

Probability distribution skewed to left

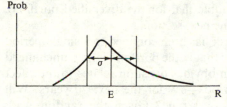

Probability distribution skewed to right

Exhibit 1.   Possible shapes for probability distributions.

return is used. It is for this reason that total variability of returns has been so widely used as a surrogate for risk.

It now remains to choose a specific measure of total variability of returns. The measures most commonly used are the variance and standard deviation of returns.

The variance of return is a weighted sum of the squared deviations from the expected return. Squaring the deviations ensures that deviations above and below the expected value contribute equally to the measure of variability, regardless of sign. The variance, designated σ_p^2 for the portfolio in the previous example is given by

$$\sigma_p^2 = \sum_{j=1}^{5} P_j(R_j - E(R_p))^2$$

$$= 0.1(50.0 - 10.0)^2 + 0.2(30.0 - 10.0)^2 + 0.4(10.0 - 10.0)^2 \qquad (3)$$
$$+ 0.2(-10.0 - 10.0)^2 + 0.1(-30.0 - 10.0)^2$$

$$= 480 \text{ per cent squared.}$$

The standard deviation (σ_p) is defined as the square root of the variance. It is equal to 22 per cent. The larger the variance or standard deviation, the greater the possible dispersion of future realized values around the expected value, and the larger the investor's uncertainty. As a rule of thumb for symmetric distributions, it is often suggested that roughly two-thirds of the possible returns will lie within one standard deviation either side of the expected value, and that 95 per cent will be within two standard deviations.

Exhibit 2 shows the historical return distributions for a diversified portfolio. The portfolio is composed of approximately 100 securities, with each security having equal weight. The month-by-month returns cover the period from January 1945 to June 1970. Note that the distribution is approximately, but not perfectly, symmetric. The arithmetic average return for the 306-month period is 0.91 per cent per month. The standard deviation about this average is 4.45 per cent per month.

Exhibit 3 gives the same data for a single security, National Department Stores. Note that the distribution is highly skewed. The arithmetic average return is 0.81 per cent per month over the 306-month period. The most interesting aspect, however, is the standard deviation of month-by-month returns—9.02 per cent per month, more than double that for the diversified portfolio. This result will be discussed further in the next section.

Thus far our discussion of portfolio risk has been confined to a single-period investment horizon such as the next year; that is, the portfolio is held unchanged and evaluated at the end of the year. An obvious question relates to the effect of holding the portfolio for several periods—say for the next 20 years: Will the one-year risks tend to cancel out over time? Given the random-walk nature of security prices, the answer to this question is no. If the risk level (standard deviation) is maintained during each year, the portfolio risk for longer horizons will increase with the horizon length. The standard deviation of possible terminal portfolio values after N years is equal to $\sqrt{N}$ times the standard deviation after one year.[4] Thus the investor cannot rely on the "long run" to reduce his risk of loss.

---

[4] This result can be illustrated as follows. The portfolio market value after N years, $\tilde{M}_N$, is equal to

$$\tilde{M}_N = M_0[(1 + \tilde{R}_{P1})(1 + \tilde{R}_{P2}) \cdots (1 + \tilde{R}_{PN})],$$

where M_0 is the initial value, and $\tilde{R}_{Pt}(t = 1, \ldots, N)$ is the return during year t [as given by Equation (1a)]. For reasonably small values of the annual returns, the above expression can be approximated by

$$\tilde{M}_N = M_0[1 + \tilde{R}_{P1} + \tilde{R}_{P2} + \cdots + \tilde{R}_{PN}].$$

Now, if the annual returns, $\tilde{R}_{pt}$, are independently and identically distributed with variance σ^2, the variance of $\tilde{M}_N$ will equal $(M_0)^2 N\sigma^2$, or N times the variance after one year. Therefore, the standard deviation of the terminal value will equal $\sqrt{N}$ times the standard deviation after one year. The key assumption of independence of portfolio returns over time is realistic, since security returns appear to follow a random walk through time.

A similar result could be obtained without the restriction on the size of the $\tilde{R}_{pt}$ if we had dealt with continuously, as opposed to annually, compounded rates of return. However, the analysis would be more complicated.

EXHIBIT 2. RATE OF RETURN DISTRIBUTION FOR A PORTFOLIO OF 100 SECURITIES (EQUALLY WEIGHTED)
January 1945–June 1970

	RANGE		FREQ.
1	−13.6210	−12.2685	1
2	−12.2685	−10.9160	2
3	−10.9160	−9.5635	2
4	−9.5635	−8.2110	3
5	−8.2110	−6.8585	8
6	−6.8585	−5.5060	9
7	−5.5060	−4.1535	17
8	−4.1535	−2.8010	18
9	−2.8010	−1.4485	27
10	−1.4485	−0.0960	28
11	−0.0960	1.2565	30
12	1.2565	2.6090	50
13	2.6090	3.9615	35
14	3.9615	5.3140	33
15	5.3140	6.6665	18
16	6.6665	8.0190	14
17	8.0190	9.3715	4
18	9.3715	10.7240	2
19	10.7240	12.0765	2
20	12.0765	13.4290	3

FREQ. axis: 1 | | | 5 | | | 10 | | | 15 | | | 20 | | | 25 | | | 30 | | | 35 | | | 40 | | | 45 | | | 50

SCALING FACTOR = 1
Average Return = 0.91% per month
Standard Deviation = 4.45% per month
Number of Observations = 306

327

EXHIBIT 3. *RATE OF RETURN DISTRIBUTION FOR NATIONAL DEPARTMENT STORES*

January 1945–June 1970

	RANGE		FREQ.	Plot (1 ... 50)
1	−32.3670	−29.4168	1	8
2	−29.4168	−26.4666	0	
3	−26.4666	−23.5163	0	
4	−23.5163	−20.5661	1	8
5	−20.5661	−17.6159	1	8
6	−17.6159	−14.6657	3	8 * *
7	−14.6657	−11.7155	13	8 * * * * * * * * * * * *
8	−11.7155	−8.7653	11	8 * * * * * * * * * *
9	−8.7653	−5.8151	39	8 *
10	−5.8151	−2.8649	47	8 *
11	−2.8649	0.0853	45	8 *
12	0.0853	3.0355	34	8 *
13	3.0355	5.9857	28	8 *
14	5.9857	8.9359	25	8 *
15	8.9359	11.8861	17	8 * * * * * * * * * * * * * * * *
16	11.8861	14.8363	17	8 * * * * * * * * * * * * * * * *
17	14.8363	17.7865	9	8 * * * * * * * *
18	17.7865	20.7366	8	8 * * * * * * *
19	20.7366	23.6868	5	8 * * * *
20	23.6868	26.6370	2	8 *

SCALING FACTOR = 1
Average Return = 0.81% per month
Standard Deviation = 9.02% per month
Number of Observations = 306

A final remark should be made before leaving portfolio risk measures. We have implicitly assumed that investors are risk averse, i.e., that they seek to minimize risk for a given level of return. This assumption appears to be valid for most investors in most situations. The entire theory of portfolio selection and capital asset pricing is based on the belief that investors *on the average* are risk averse.

4. DIVERSIFICATION

When one compares the distribution of historical returns for the 100-stock portfolio (Exhibit 2) with the distribution for National Department Stores (Exhibit 3), he discovers a curious relationship. While the standard deviation of returns for the security is double that of the portfolio, its average return is less. Is the market so imperfect that over a long period of time (25 years) it rewarded substantially higher risk with lower average return?

Not so. As we shall now show, not all of the security's risk is relevant. Much of the total risk (standard deviation of return) of National Department Stores was diversifiable. That is, if it had been combined with other securities, a portion of the variation in its returns could have been smoothed out or cancelled by complementary variation in the other securities. The same portfolio diversification effect accounts for the low standard deviation of return for the 100-stock portfolio. In fact, the portfolio standard deviation was less than that of the typical security in the portfolio. Much of the total risk of the component securities had been eliminated by diversification. Since much of the total risk could be eliminated simply by holding a stock in a portfolio, there was no economic requirement for the return earned to be in line with the total risk. Instead, we should expect realized returns to be related to that portion of security risk which cannot be eliminated by portfolio combination.

Diversification results from combining securities having less than perfect correlation (dependence) among their returns in order to reduce portfolio risk. The portfolio return, being simply a weighted average of the individual security returns, is not diminished by diversification. In general, the lower the correlation among security returns, the greater the impact of diversification. This is true regardless of how risky the securities of the portfolio are when considered in isolation.

Ideally, if we could find sufficient securities with uncorrelated returns, we could completely eliminate portfolio risk. This situation is unfortunately not typical in real securities markets where returns are positively correlated to a considerable degree. Thus while portfolio risk can be substantially reduced by diversification, it cannot be entirely eliminated. This can be demonstrated very clearly by measuring the standard deviations of randomly selected portfolios containing various numbers of securities.

In a study of the impact of portfolio diversification on risk, Wagner and Lau [27] divided a sample of 200 NYSE stocks into six subgroups based on the Standard and Poor's Stock Quality Ratings as of June 1960. The highest quality ratings (A+) formed the first group, the second highest ratings (A) the next group, and so on. Randomly selected portfolios were formed from each of the subgroups, containing from 1 to 20 securities. The month-by-month portfolio returns for the 10-year period through May 1970 were then computed for each portfolio (portfolio composition remaining unchanged). The exercise was repeated ten times to reduce the dependence on single samples, and the values for the ten trials were then averaged.

Table 1 shows the average return and standard deviation for portfolios from the first subgroup (A+ quality stocks). The average return is unrelated to the number of issues in the portfolio. On the other hand, the standard deviation of return declines as the number of holdings increases. On the average, approximately 40 per cent of the single security risk is eliminated by forming randomly selected portfolios of 20 stocks. However, it is also evident that additional diversification yields rapidly diminishing reduction in risk. The improvement is slight when the number of securities held is increased beyond, say, 10. Exhibit 4 shows the results for all six quality groups. The figure shows the rapid decline in total portfolio risk as the portfolios are expanded from 1 to 10 securities.

TABLE 1.   RISK VERSUS DIVERSIFICATION FOR RANDOMLY SELECTED PORTFOLIOS OF A+ QUALITY SECURITIES

June 1960—May 1970

NUMBER OF SECURITIES IN PORTFOLIO	AVERAGE RETURN (%/MONTH)	STD. DEVIATION OF RETURN (%/MONTH)	CORRELATION WITH MARKET	
			R	R^2
1	0.88	7.0	0.54	0.29
2	0.69	5.0	0.63	0.40
3	0.74	4.8	0.75	0.56
4	0.65	4.6	0.77	0.59
5	0.71	4.6	0.79	0.62
10	0.68	4.2	0.85	0.72
15	0.69	4.0	0.88	0.77
20	0.67	3.9	0.89	0.80

Source.   Wagner and Lau [27], Table C, p. 53.

Returning to Table 1, we note from the next to last column in the table that the return on a diversified portfolio follows the market very closely. The degree of association is measured by the correlation coefficient (R) of each portfolio with an unweighted index of all NYSE stocks (perfect positive correlation

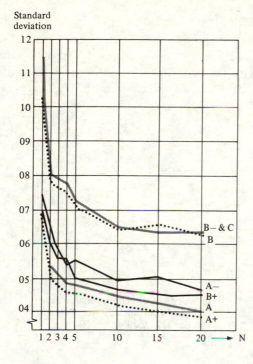

Exhibit 4.   Standard deviation versus number of issues in portfolio. Source: Wagner and Lau (27), Exhibit 1, p. 50.

results in a correlation coefficient of 1.0).[5] The 20-security portfolio has a correlation of 0.89 with the market. The implication is that the risk remaining in the 20-stock portfolio is predominantly a reflection of uncertainty about the performance of the stock market in general. Exhibit 5 shows the results for the six quality groups.

Correlation in Exhibit 5 is represented by the correlation coefficient squared, R^2 (possible values range from 0 to 1.0). The R^2 coefficient has a useful interpretation: it measures the proportion of variability in portfolio return that is attributable to variability in market returns. The remaining variability is risk, which is unique to the portfolio and, as Exhibit 4 shows, can be eliminated by proper diversification of the portfolio. Thus, R^2 measures the degree of portfolio diversification. A poorly diversified portfolio will have a small R^2 (0.30 − 0.40). A well diversified portfolio will have a much higher R^2 (0.85 − 0.95). A perfectly diversified portfolio will have an R^2 of 1.0; that is, all the risk in such a portfolio

[5] Two securities with perfectly correlated return patterns will have a correlation coefficient of 1.0. Conversely, if the return patterns are perfectly negative correlated, the correlation coefficient will equal −1. Two securities with uncorrelated (i.e., statistically unrelated) returns will have a correlation coefficient of zero. The average correlation coefficient between returns for NYSE securities and the S&P 500 Stock Index during the 1945–1970 period was approximately 0.5.

R-square

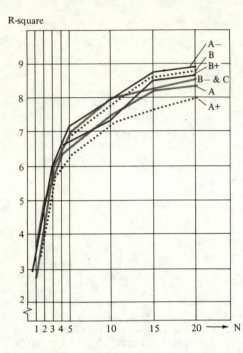

Exhibit 5.   Correlation versus number of issues in portfolio. Source: Wagner and Lau (27), Exhibit 2, p. 50.

is a reflection of market risk. Exhibit 5 shows the rapid gain in diversification as the portfolio is expanded from 1 to 2 securities and up to 10 securities. Beyond 10 securities the gains tend to be smaller. Note that increasing the number of issues tends to be less efficient at achieving diversification for the highest quality A+ issues. Apparently the companies comprising this group are more homogeneous than the companies grouped under the other quality codes.

The results show that while some risks can be eliminated via diversification, others cannot. Thus we are led to distinguish between a security's "unsystematic" risk, which can be washed away by mixing the security with other securities in a diversified portfolio, and its "systematic" risk, which cannot be eliminated by diversification. This proposition is illustrated in Exhibit 6. It shows total portfolio risk declining as the number of holdings increases. Increasing diversification gradually tends to eliminate the unsystematic risk, leaving only systematic, i.e., market-related risk. The remaining variability results from the fact that the return on nearly every security depends to some degree on the overall performance of the market. Consequently, the return on a well diversified portfolio is highly correlated with the market, and its variability or uncertainty is basically the uncertainty of the market as a whole. Investors are exposed to market uncertainty no matter how many stocks they hold.

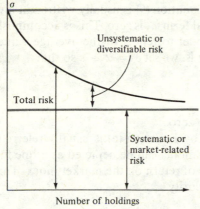

Exhibit 6.   Systematic and unsystematic risk.

5.   THE RISK OF INDIVIDUAL SECURITIES

In the previous section we concluded that the systematic risk of an individual security is that portion of its total risk (standard deviation of return) which cannot be eliminated by combining it with other securities in a well diversified portfolio. We now need a way of quantifying the systematic risk of a security and relating the systematic risk of a portfolio to that of its component securities. This can be accomplished by dividing security return into two parts: one dependent (i.e., perfectly correlated), and a second independent (i.e., uncorrelated) of market return. The first component of return is usually referred to as "systematic," the second as "unsystematic" return. Thus we have

Security Return = Systematic Return + Unsystematic Return.   (4)

Since the systematic return is perfectly correlated with the market return, it can be expressed as a factor, designated beta (β), times the market return, R_m. The beta factor is a market sensitivity index, indicating how sensitive the security return is to changes in the market level. The unsystematic return, which is independent of market returns, is usually represented by a factor epsilon (ε'). Thus the security return, R, may be expressed

$$R = \beta R_m + \varepsilon'.   (5)$$

For example, if a security had a β factor of 2.0 (e.g., an airline stock), then a 10 per cent market return would generate a systematic return for the stock of 20 per cent. The security return for the period would be the 20 per cent plus the unsystematic component. The unsystematic component depends on factors unique to the company, such as labor difficulties, higher than expected sales, etc.

The security returns model given by Equation (5) is usually written in a way such that the average value of the residual term, ε', is zero. This is accomplished by adding a factor, alpha (α), to the model to represent the average value of the unsystematic returns over time. That is, we set $\varepsilon' = \alpha + \varepsilon$ so that

$$R = \alpha + \beta R_m + \varepsilon, \tag{6}$$

where the average ε over time is equal to zero.

The model for security returns given by Equation (6) is usually referred to as the "market model". Graphically, the model can be depicted as a line fitted to a plot of security returns against rates of return on the market index. This is shown in Exhibit 7 for a hypothetical security.

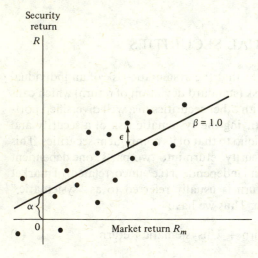

Exhibit 7. The market model for security returns. Beta (β), the market sensitivity index, is the slope of the line. Alpha (α), the average of the residual returns, is the intercept of the line on the security axis. Epsilon (ϵ), the residual returns, are the perpendicular distances of the points from the line.

The beta factor can be thought of as the slope of the line. It gives the expected increase in security return for a one per cent increase in market return. In Exhibit 7, the security has a beta of 1.0. Thus, a ten per cent market return will result, on the average, in a ten per cent security return. The market-weighted average beta for all stocks is 1.0 by definition.

The alpha factor is represented by the intercept of the line on the vertical security return axis. It is equal to the average value over time of the unsystematic returns (ε') on the stock. For most stocks, the alpha factor tends to be small and unstable. (We shall return to alpha later.)

Using the definition of security return given by the market model, the specification of systematic and unsystematic risk is straightforward—they are simply the standard deviations of the two return components.[6]

The systematic risk of a security is equal to β times the standard deviation of the market return:

$$\text{Systematic Risk} = \beta\sigma_m. \tag{7}$$

The unsystematic risk equals the standard deviation of the residual return factor ε:

$$\text{Unsystematic Risk} = \sigma_\varepsilon. \tag{8}$$

Given measures of individual security systematic risk, we can now compute the systematic risk of portfolio. It is equal to the beta factor for the portfolio, β_p, times the risk of the market index, σ_m:

$$\text{Portfolio Systematic Risk} = \beta_p\sigma_m. \tag{9}$$

The portfolio beta factor in turn can be shown to be simply an average of the individual security betas, weighted by the proportion of each security in the portfolio, or

$$\beta_p = \sum_{j=1}^{N} X_j\beta_j, \tag{10}$$

where

X_j = the proportion of portfolio market value represented by security j

N = the number of securities.

[6] The relationship between the risk components is given by

$$\sigma^2 = \beta^2\sigma_m^2 + \sigma_{\varepsilon'}^2.$$

This follows directly from Equation (5) and the assumption of statistical independence of R_m and ε'. The R^2 term previously discussed is the ratio of systematic to total risk (both measured in terms of variance):

$$R^2 = \frac{\beta^2\sigma_m^2}{\sigma^2}.$$

Note also that the R^2 is the square of the correlation coefficient between security and market returns.

Thus the systematic risk of the portfolio is simply a weighted average of the systematic risk of the individual securities. If the portfolio is composed of an equal dollar investment in each stock (as was the case for the 100-security portfolio of Exhibit 2), the β_p is simply an unweighted average of the component security betas.

The unsystematic risk of the portfolio is also a function of the unsystematic security risks, but the form is more complex.[7] The important point is that with increasing diversification this risk can be reduced toward zero.

With these results for portfolio risk, it is useful to return to Exhibit 4. The figure shows the decline in portfolio risk with increasing diversification for each of the six quality groups. However, the portfolio standard deviations for each of the six groups are decreasing toward different limits because the average risks (β) of the groups differ.

Table 2 shows a comparison of the standard deviations for the 20-stock portfolios with the predicted lower limits based on average security systematic risks. The lower limit is equal to the average beta for the quality group ($\bar{\beta}$) times the standard deviation of the market return (σ_m). The standard deviations in all cases are close to the predicted values. These results support the contention that portfolio systematic risk equals the average systematic risks of the component securities.

The main results of this section can be summarized as follows: First, as seen from Exhibit 4, roughly 40 to 50 per cent of total security risk can be eliminated by diversification. Second, the remaining systematic risk is equal to the security β times market risk. Third, portfolio systematic risk is a weighted average of security systematic risks.

The implications of these results are substantial. First, we would expect realized rates of return over substantial periods of time to be related to the systematic as opposed to total risk of securities. Since the unsystematic risk is relatively easily eliminated, we should not expect the market to offer a risk premium for bearing it. Second, since security systematic risk is equal to the security beta times σ_m (which is common to all securities), beta is useful as a

---

[7] Assuming the unsystematic returns (ε_j') of securities to be uncorrelated (reasonably true in practice), the unsystematic portfolio risk is given by

$$\sigma^2(\varepsilon_p') = \sum_{j=1}^{N} X_j^2 \sigma^2(\varepsilon_j),$$

where $\sigma^2(\varepsilon_j')$ is the unsystematic risk for stock j. Assume the portfolio is made up of equal investment in each security and $\bar{\sigma}^2(\varepsilon')$ is the average value of the $\sigma^2(\varepsilon_j')$. Then, $X_j = 1/N$ and

$$\sigma^2(\varepsilon_p') = \frac{1}{N} \bar{\sigma}^2(\varepsilon'),$$

which (assuming $\bar{\sigma}^2(\varepsilon')$ is finite) obviously approaches zero as the number of issues in the portfolio increases.

TABLE 2. STANDARD DEVIATIONS OF 20-STOCK PORTFOLIOS AND
PREDICTED LOWER LIMITS

June 1960—May 1970

(1) STOCK QUALITY GROUP	(2) STANDARD DEVIATION OF 20-STOCK PORTFOLIOS $\sigma \cdot \%/mo$	(3) AVERAGE BETA VALUE FOR QUALITY GROUP $\bar{\beta}$	(4) LOWER LIMIT* $\bar{\beta} \cdot \sigma_m$ $\%/mo$
A+	3.94	0.74	3.51
A	4.17	0.80	3.80
A−	4.52	0.89	4.22
B+	4.45	0.87	4.13
B	6.27	1.24	5.89
B− & C	6.32	1.23	5.84

* $\sigma_m = 4.75\%$ per month.
Source.   Wagner and Lau [27], p. 52, and Table C, p. 53.

relative risk measure. The β gives the systematic risk of a security (or portfolio) relative to the risk of the market index. Thus it is often convenient to speak of systematic risk in relative terms (i.e., in terms of beta rather than beta times σ_m).

REFERENCES

1. Fischer Black, Michael C. Jensen, and Myron S. Scholes, "The Capital Asset Pricing Model: Some Empirical Tests." Published in *Studies in the Theory of Capital Markets*, edited by Michael Jensen. New York, Praeger, 1972, pp. 79–121.

2. Marshall E. Blume, "Portfolio Theory: A Step Toward Its Practical Application." *Journal of Business*, Vol. 43 (April 1970), pp. 152–173.

3. Marshall E. Blume, and Irwin Friend, "A New Look at the Capital Asset Pricing Model." *Journal of Finance*, Vol. XXVIII (March 1973), pp. 19–33.

4. Richard A. Brealey, *An Introduction to Risk and Return from Common Stocks*. Cambridge, Mass., MIT Press, 1969.

5. Eugene F. Fama, "Components of Investment Performance." *The Journal of Finance*, Vol. XXVII (June 1972), pp. 551–567.

6. Eugene F. Fama, and James D. MacBeth, "Risk, Return and Equilibrium: Empirical Tests." Unpublished Working Paper No. 7237, University of Chicago, Graduate School of Business, August 1972.

7. Jack C. Francis, *Investment Analysis and Management*. New York, McGraw-Hill, 1972.

8. Irwin Friend, and Marshall E. Blume, "Risk and the Long Run Rate of Return on NYSE Common Stocks." Working Paper No. 18–72, Wharton School of Commerce and Finance, Rodney L. White Center for Financial Research.

9. Nancy Jacob, "The Measurement of Systematic Risk for Securities and Portfolios: Some Empirical Results." *Journal of Financial and Quantitative Analysis*, Vol. VI (March 1971), pp. 815–834.

10. Michael C. Jensen, "The Performance of Mutual Funds in the Period 1945–1964." *Journal of Finance*, Vol. XXIII (May 1968), pp. 389–416.

11. Michael C. Jensen, "Risk, the Pricing of Capital Assets, and the Evaluation of Investment Portfolios." *Journal of Business*, Vol. 42 (April 1969), pp. 167–247.

12. Michael C. Jensen, "Capital Markets: Theory and Evidence." *The Bell Journal of Economics and Management Science*, Vol. 3 (Autumn 1972), pp. 357–398.

13. Robert A. Levy, "On the Short Term Stationarity of Beta Coefficients." *Financial Analysts Journal*, Vol. 27 (November–December 1971), pp. 55–62.

14. John Lintner, "The Valuation of Risk Assets and the Selection of Risky Investments in Stock Portfolios and Capital Budgets." *Review of Economics and Statistics*, Vol. XLVII (February 1965), pp. 13–37.

15. John Lintner, "Security Prices, Risk, and Maximal Gains from Diversification." *Journal of Finance*, Vol. XX (December 1965), pp. 587–616.

16. Norman E. Mains, "Are Mutual Fund Beta Coefficients Stationary?" Unpublished Working Paper, Investment Company Institute, Washington, D.C., October 1972.

17. Harry M. Markowitz, "Portfolio Selection." *Journal of Finance*, Vol. VII (March 1952), pp. 77–91.

18. Harry M. Markowitz, *Portfolio Selection: Efficient Diversification of Investments*. New York, John Wiley and Sons, 1959.

19. Merton H. Miller, and Myron S. Scholes, "Rates of Returns in Relation to Risk: A Reexamination of Recent Findings." Published in *Studies in the Theory of Capital Markets*, edited by Michael Jensen. New York, Praeger, 1972, pp. 47–78.

20. Franco Modigliani, and Gerald A. Pogue, *A Study of Investment Performance Fees* Lexington, Mass., Heath-Lexington Books, Forthcoming 1974.

21. Gerald A. Pogue, and Walter Conway, "On the Stability of Mutual Fund Beta Values." Unpublished Working Paper, MIT, Sloan School of Management, June 1972.

22. Securities and Exchange Commission, *Institutional Investor Study Report of the Securities and Exchange Commission*, Chapter 4, "Investment Advisory Complexes", pp. 325–347. (Washington, D.C.: U.S. Government Printing Office, 1971.)

23. William F. Sharpe, "Capital Asset Prices: A Theory of Market Equilibrium under Conditions of Risk." *Journal of Finance*, Vol. XIX (September 1964), pp. 425–442.

24. William F. Sharpe, *Portfolio Theory and Capital Markets*. New York, McGraw-Hill, 1970.

25. Jack L. Treynor, "How to Rate the Management of Investment Funds." *Harvard Business Review*, Vol. XLIII (January–February 1965), pp. 63–75.

26. Jack L. Treynor, "The Performance of Mutual Funds in the Period 1945–1964: Discussion." *Journal of Finance*, Vol. XXIII (May 1968), pp. 418–419.

27. Wayne H. Wagner, and Sheila Lau, "The Effect of Diversification on Risk." *Financial Analysts Journal*, Vol. 26 (November–December 1971), pp. 48–53.

QUESTIONS

1. Explain why the authors argue that the dollar weighted rate of return (internal rate of return) is not helpful in *portfolio* related problems.

2. Refer to Table 1. Provide intuitive explanations for the following.
    a. Why the average portfolio return was unrelated to the number of securities in the portfolio.
    b. Why the standard deviation in returns was smaller the greater the number of securities in the portfolio.
    c. Why the returns were more highly correlated with market returns the greater the number of securities in the portfolio.
3. Examine Exhibit 6. Close the page and reproduce the diagram, properly labeled, on a sheet of paper.
4. Define beta, β, and show a diagram of how it is measured for a portfolio or for an individual security.
5. What is meant by unsystematic risk? In a portfolio context, which kind of risk is more important, systematic or unsystematic? Explain.
6. Summarize the main results of this article.

PROBLEMS

1. Assume that returns for four consecutive periods were measured in accordance with Equation (1a). These returns were 15, 10, 5, and -5 percent.
    a. Compute the arithmetic average return.
    b. Compute the geometric average return.
    c. If the answers to a and b are different, explain why.
2. Given the following probability distribution for portfolio returns, compute the mean and variance.

PORTFOLIO RETURN	SUBJECTIVE PROBABILITY
30%	.1
20%	.2
10%	.3
0%	.3
-10%	.1

3. Refer back to the article by Lease, Lewellen, and Schlarbaum and find the average number of securities held by investors in that study. Comment on the extent of portfolio diversification on the average for these investors in context with Exhibit 4 of this paper.

21 | Franco Modigliani and Gerald A. Pogue

An Introduction to Risk and Return: Concepts and Evidence, Part II

In introducing Part I of this series, we noted that the material is applicable to financial management but that much of the spillover or integration remains to be worked out. The capital asset pricing model (CAPM) is a crucial extension of portfolio theory. While some aspects of the CAPM are controversial, beta coefficients are now being published by investor service firms, and the CAPM is being used as one method for estimating the cost of equity for many firms.

6. THE RELATIONSHIP BETWEEN EXPECTED RETURN AND RISK: THE CAPITAL ASSET PRICING MODEL

The first part of this article developed two measures of risk: one is a measure of total risk (standard deviation), the other a relative index of systematic or non-diversifiable risk (beta). The beta measure would appear to be the more relevant for the pricing of securities. Returns expected by investors should logically be related to systematic as opposed to total risk. Securities with higher systematic risk should have higher expected returns.[1]

The question to be considered now is the form of the relationship between risk and return. In this section we describe a relationship called the "Capital Asset Pricing Model" (CAPM), which is based on elementary logic and simple economic principles. The basic postulate underlying finance theory is that assets with the same risk should have the same expected rate of return. That is, the prices of assets in the capital markets should adjust until equivalent risk assets have identical expected returns.

Source. Reprinted by permission from *Financial Analysts Journal*, May–June 1974, pp. 69–86. Franco Modigliani is professor of finance, Sloan School of Management, M.I.T., and Gerald Pogue is professor of finance at Baruch College, City University of New York.

[1] From this point on, systematic risk will be referred to simply as "risk." Total risk will be referred to as "total risk."

To see the implications of this postulate, let us consider an investor who holds a risky portfolio[2] with the same risk as the market portfolio (beta equal to 1.0). What return should he expect? Logically, he should expect the same return as that of the market portfolio.

Let us consider another investor who holds a riskless portfolio (beta equal to zero). The investor in this case should expect to earn the rate of return on riskless assets such as treasury bills. By taking no risk, he earns the riskless rate of return.

Now let us consider the case of an investor who holds a mixture of these two portfolios. Assuming he invests a proportion X of his money in the risky portfolio and $(1 - X)$ in the riskless portfolio, what risk does he bear and what return should he expect? The risk of the composite portfolio is easily computed when we recall that the beta of a portfolio is simply a weighted average of the component security betas, where the weights are the portfolio proportions. Thus the portfolio beta, β_p, is a weighted average of the beta of the market portfolio and the beta of the risk-free rate. However, the market beta is 1.0, and that of the risk-free rate is zero. Therefore

$$\beta_p = (1 - X) \cdot 0 + X \cdot 1,$$
$$= X. \tag{11}$$

Thus β_p is equal to the fraction of his money invested in the risky portfolio. If 100 per cent or less of the investor's funds is invested in the risky portfolio, his portfolio beta will be between zero and 1.0. If he borrows at the risk-free rate and invests the proceeds in the risky portfolio, his portfolio beta will be greater than 1.0.

The expected return of the composite portfolio is also a weighted average of the expected returns on the two-component portfolios; that is,

$$E(R_p) = (1 - X) \cdot R_F + X \cdot E(R_m), \tag{12}$$

where $E(R_p)$, $E(R_m)$, and R_F are the expected returns on the portfolio, the market index, and the risk-free rate. Now, from Equation (11) we know that X is equal to β_p. Substituting into Equation (12), we have

$$E(R_p) = (1 - \beta_p) \cdot R_F + \beta_p \cdot E(R_m),$$

or

$$E(R_p) = R_F + \beta_p \cdot (E(R_m) - R_F). \tag{13}$$

---

[2] We use the term portfolio in a general sense, including the case where the investor holds only one security. Since portfolio return and (systematic) risk are simply weighted averages of security values, risk-return relationships which hold for securities must also be true for portfolios, and vice versa.

Equation (13) is the Capital Asset Pricing Model (CAPM), an extremely important theoretical result. It says that the expected return on a portfolio should exceed the riskless rate of return by an amount which is proportional to the portfolio beta. That is, the relationship between return and risk should be linear.

The model is often stated in "risk-premium" form. Risk premiums are obtained by subtracting the risk-free rate from the rates of return. The expected portfolio and market risk premiums (designated $E(r_p)$ and $E(r_m)$ respectively) are given by

$$E(r_p) = E(R_p) - R_F, \tag{14a}$$

$$E(r_m) = E(R_M) - R_F. \tag{14b}$$

Substituting these risk premiums into Equation (13), we obtain

$$E(r_p) = \beta_P \cdot E(r_m). \tag{15}$$

In this form, the CAPM states that the expected risk premium for the investor's portfolio is equal to its beta value times the expected market risk premium.

We can illustrate the model by assuming that short-term (risk-free) interest rate is 6 per cent and the expected return on the market is 10 per cent. The expected risk premium for holding the market portfolio is just the difference between the 10 per cent and the short-term interest rate of 6 per cent, or 4 per cent. Investors who hold the market portfolio expect to earn 10 per cent, which is 4 per cent greater than they could earn on a short-term market instrument for certain. In order to satisfy Equation (13), the expected return on securities or portfolios with different levels of risk must be:

EXPECTED RETURN FOR
DIFFERENT LEVELS OF
PORTFOLIO BETA

BETA	EXPECTED RETURN
0.0	6%
0.5	8%
1.0	10%
1.5	12%
2.0	14%

The predictions of the model are inherently sensible. For safe investments ($\beta = 0$), the model predicts that investors would expect to earn the risk-free rate of interest. For a risky investment ($\beta > 0$) investors would expect a rate of return proportional to the market sensitivity (β) of the investment. Thus, stocks with lower than average market sensitivities (such as most utilities) would offer expected returns less than the expected market return. Stocks with above average values of beta (such as most airline securities) would offer expected returns in excess of the market.

In our development of CAPM we have made a number of assumptions that are required if the model is to be established on a rigorous basis. These assumptions involve investor behavior and conditions in the capital markets. The following is a set of assumptions that will allow a simple derivation of the model.

a.   The market is composed of risk-averse investors who measure risk in terms of standard deviation of portfolio return. This assumption provides a basis for the use of beta-type risk measures.

b.   All investors have a common time horizon for investment decision making (e.g., one month, one year, etc.). This assumption allows us to measure investor expectations over some common interval, thus making comparisons meaningful.

c.   All investors are assumed to have the same expectations about future security returns and risks. Without this assumption, the analysis would become much more complicated.

d.   Capital markets are perfect in the sense that all assets are completely divisible, there are no transactions costs or differential taxes, and borrowing and lending rates are equal to each other and the same for all investors. Without these conditions, frictional barriers would exist to the equilibrium conditions on which the model is based.

While these assumptions are sufficient to derive the model, it is not clear that all are necessary in their current form. It may well be that several of the assumptions can be substantially relaxed without major change in the form of the model. A good deal of research is currently being conducted toward this end.

While the CAPM is indeed simple and elegant, these qualities do not in themselves guarantee that it will be useful in explaining observed risk-return patterns. In Section 8 we will review the empirical literature on attempts to verify the model.

7.   MEASUREMENT OF SECURITY AND PORTFOLIO BETA VALUES

The basic data for estimating betas are past rates of return earned over a series of relatively short intervals—usually days, weeks, or months. For example, in Tables 3 and 4 we present calculations based on month-by-month rates of return for the periods January 1945 to June 1970 (security betas) and January 1960 to December 1971 (mutual fund betas). The returns were calculated using Equation (1a).

*TABLE 3. REGRESSION STATISTICS FOR 30 RANDOMLY SELECTED SECURITIES**

January 1945–June 1970

SECURITY	(1) NOBS	(2) ALPH	(3) SE.A	(4) BETA	(5) SE.B	(6) SE.R	(7) R**2	(8) ARPJ	(9) SD.R	(10) CRPJ
1 City Investing Co.	306.00	0.30	0.53	1.67	0.14	9.20	31.43	1.45	11.09	0.87
2 Foster Wheeler	306.00	-0.12	0.49	1.57	0.13	8.36	32.98	0.96	10.20	0.46
3 Pennsylvania Dixie	306.00	-0.20	0.47	1.40	0.12	8.15	29.33	0.77	9.67	0.33
4 National Gypsum Co.	306.00	-0.18	0.32	1.38	0.08	5.45	47.29	0.77	7.49	0.50
5 Radio Corp. of America	306.00	0.02	0.38	1.35	0.10	6.60	37.02	0.95	8.30	0.62
6 Fox Film Corp.	306.00	-0.04	0.53	1.31	0.14	9.15	22.35	0.87	10.36	0.38
7 Intercontinental Rubber	306.00	0.69	0.64	1.28	0.17	10.95	16.13	1.58	11.94	0.92
8 National Department	306.00	-0.05	0.45	1.26	0.12	7.73	27.05	0.81	9.04	0.41
9 Phillips Jones Corp.	306.00	0.36	0.44	1.25	0.12	7.54	27.89	1.22	8.86	0.85
10 Chrysler Corp.	306.00	-0.26	0.37	1.21	0.10	6.29	34.12	0.58	7.73	0.28
11 American Hide & Leather	306.00	0.55	0.66	1.16	0.17	11.36	12.78	1.35	12.14	0.67
12 Adams Express	306.00	0.11	0.23	1.16	0.06	3.93	54.87	0.91	5.84	0.75
13 Caterpillar Tractor	306.00	0.43	0.32	1.14	0.08	5.45	38.09	1.22	6.92	0.99
14 Continental Steel Co.	306.00	0.21	0.36	1.12	0.10	6.22	31.31	0.99	7.50	0.72
15 Marland Oil Co.	306.00	0.06	0.29	1.11	0.08	4.99	40.69	0.82	6.47	0.62
16 Air Reduction Co.	306.00	-0.59	0.29	1.08	0.08	4.98	39.73	0.16	6.41	-0.05
17 National Aviation	306.00	0.22	0.39	1.04	0.10	6.71	25.15	0.94	7.74	0.65
18 Na Tomas Co.	306.00	0.28	0.63	1.01	0.17	10.88	10.72	0.98	11.50	0.37
19 NYSE Index	306.00	0.0	0.0	1.00	0.0	0.0	0.0	0.69	3.73	0.62
20 American Ship Building	306.00	0.31	0.52	0.99	0.14	9.01	14.53	0.99	9.73	0.54
21 James Talcott	306.00	0.33	0.42	0.98	0.11	7.23	20.43	1.01	8.09	0.68
22 Jewel Tea Co. Inc.	306.00	0.21	0.32	0.95	0.08	5.42	30.14	0.87	6.47	0.66
23 International Carrier	306.00	0.34	0.26	0.93	0.07	4.39	38.41	0.98	5.58	0.83
24 Keystone Steel & Wire	306.00	0.18	0.30	0.84	0.08	5.19	26.90	0.76	6.05	0.58
25 Swift & Co.	306.00	-0.09	0.30	0.81	0.08	5.08	26.08	0.47	5.89	0.30
26 Southern California	306.00	0.00	0.22	0.77	0.06	3.77	36.60	0.53	4.72	0.42
27 Bayuk Cigars	306.00	-0.04	0.39	0.71	0.10	6.76	13.49	0.45	7.26	0.19
28 First National Store	306.00	-0.08	0.31	0.67	0.08	5.33	18.01	0.38	5.88	0.21
29 National Linen Service	306.00	0.61	0.33	0.63	0.09	5.75	14.50	1.04	6.20	0.86
30 American Snuff	306.00	0.17	0.25	0.54	0.07	4.33	17.74	0.54	4.77	0.43
31 Homestake Mining Co.	306.00	0.16	0.38	0.24	0.10	6.60	1.77	0.33	6.65	0.11
32 Commercial Paper	306.00	0.0	0.0	0.0	0.0	0.0	0.0	0.28	0.17	0.28
··· Mean Sec. Values		0.13	0.39	1.05	0.10	6.76	27.25	0.86	7.88	0.54
··· Standard Deviations	0.0	0.28	0.12	0.31	0.03	2.10	11.85	0.33	2.13	0.26

* Based on monthly data, regression results sorted by beta (column 4).

DESCRIPTION OF COLUMNS IN TABLES 3 AND 4

COLUMN NUMBER	SYMBOL	DESCRIPTION
1	*NOBS*	Number of Monthly Returns
2	*ALPHA*	The Estimated Alpha Value
3	*SE . A*	Standard Error of Alpha
4	*BETA*	Estimated Beta Coefficient
5	*SE . B*	Standard Error of Beta
6	*SE . R*	Standard Error of the Regression—an Estimate of the Unsystematic Risk
7	*R**2*	R^2 Expressed in Percentage Terms
8	*ARPJ*	Arithmetic Average of Monthly Risk Premiums
9	*SD . R*	Standard Deviation of Monthly Risk Premiums
10	*CRPJ*	Geometric (Time-Weighted) Average of Monthly Risk Premiums

It is customary to convert the observed rates of return to risk premiums. Section 6 showed that risk premiums are obtained by subtracting the rates of return that could have been achieved by investing in short-maturity risk-free assets, such as treasury bills or prime commercial paper. This removes a source of "noise" from the data. The noise stems from the fact that observed returns may be higher in some years simply because risk-free rates of interest are higher. Thus, an observed rate of return of eight per cent might be regarded as satisfactory if it occurred in 1960, but as a relatively low rate of return when interest rates were at all-time highs in 1969. Rates of return expressed as risk premiums will be denoted by small r's.

The market model of Equation (6), when expressed in risk-premium form, is the basic equation used to estimate beta. The market model in risk-premium form is given by

$$r = \alpha + \beta r_m + \epsilon. \tag{16a}$$

The use of risk premiums instead of returns as in Equation (6) simply changes the interpretation of alpha, leaving beta unchanged. In the return form, the expected value of alpha as given by the CAPM is $R_F(1 = B_p)$ [compare Equations (6) and (13)]. In the risk-premium form, the expected value of alpha is zero [compare Equations (15) and (16a)]. In the latter case, measured values of alpha different from zero can thus be interpreted as an *excess return* earned by a stock or portfolio beyond the return predicted by the CAPM on the basis of the asset's beta value. (More on the interpretation of alpha in Section 9.)

Beta for a security is calculated by regressing the observed security risk premiums, r, on the observed risk premiums on the market, r_m. By this procedure we are, in effect, estimating the parameters of the market model of Equation (16a). The equation of the fitted line is

$$r = \hat{\alpha} + \hat{\beta} r_m + \hat{\epsilon}, \tag{16b}$$

TABLE 4. REGRESSION STATISTICS FOR 49 MUTUAL FUNDS*

January 1960 – December 1971

SECURITY	(1) NOBS	(2) ALPH	(3) SE.A	(4) BETA	(5) SE.B	(6) SE.R	(7) R**2	(8) ARPJ	(9) SD.R	(10) CRPJ
1 McDonnell Fund	144.00	0.58	0.82	1.50	0.22	9.76	25.18	1.13	11.24	0.67
2 Value Line Spec. Sit.	144.00	0.02	0.40	1.48	0.11	4.78	57.62	0.57	7.32	0.30
3 Keystone S-4	144.00	0.03	0.28	1.43	0.08	3.38	71.77	0.55	6.34	0.35
4 Chase Fund of Boston	144.00	0.11	0.33	1.42	0.09	3.94	64.78	0.63	6.61	0.41
5 Equity Progress	144.00	−0.54	0.41	1.26	0.11	4.85	48.89	−0.08	6.77	−0.31
6 Oppenheimer Fund	144.00	0.42	0.24	1.23	0.06	2.89	72.16	0.88	5.46	0.73
7 Fidelity Trend Fund	144.00	0.79	0.29	1.23	0.08	3.52	63.39	1.24	5.80	1.07
8 Fidelity Capital	144.00	0.41	0.24	1.20	0.06	2.81	72.17	0.85	5.31	0.71
9 Keystone K-2	144.00	0.08	0.22	1.17	0.06	2.63	73.90	0.51	5.13	0.38
10 Delaware Fund	144.00	0.18	0.19	1.15	0.05	2.32	77.62	0.60	4.90	0.48
11 Keystone S-3	144.00	0.18	0.19	1.14	0.05	2.32	77.50	0.60	4.88	0.48
12 Putnam Growth Fund	144.00	0.21	0.19	1.13	0.05	2.25	78.19	0.62	4.80	0.51
13 Scudder Special Fund	144.00	0.39	0.28	1.12	0.07	3.33	61.93	0.80	5.37	0.66
14 Energy Fund	144.00	0.06	0.18	1.10	0.05	2.18	78.39	0.46	4.67	0.35
15 One William Street	144.00	0.13	0.22	1.06	0.06	2.66	69.33	0.52	4.78	0.41
16 The Dreyfus Fund	144.00	0.17	0.14	1.04	0.04	1.69	84.40	0.55	4.26	0.46
17 Mass. Investors Gr. Stk.	144.00	0.15	0.16	1.03	0.04	1.96	79.65	0.52	4.34	0.43
18 Windsor Fund	144.00	0.18	0.16	1.03	0.04	1.95	79.87	0.56	4.33	0.47
19 Axe-Houghton Stock	144.00	0.39	0.30	1.02	0.08	3.62	52.96	0.76	5.26	0.62
20 S & P 500 Stock Index	144.00	0.0	0.0	1.00	0.0	0.0	0.0	0.37	3.76	0.30
21 T. Rowe Price Gr. Stk.	144.00	0.05	0.14	0.98	0.04	1.72	82.08	0.41	4.06	0.32
22 Mass. Investors Trust	144.00	−0.02	0.14	0.97	0.04	1.72	82.07	0.34	4.04	0.26
23 Bullock Fund	144.00	0.09	0.19	0.96	0.05	2.32	71.10	0.44	4.29	0.35
24 Keystone S-2	144.00	0.04	0.12	0.96	0.03	1.45	86.12	0.39	3.89	0.31
25 Eaton & Howard Stock	144.00	−0.05	0.13	0.95	0.03	1.52	84.75	0.30	3.89	0.23

26 The Colonial Fund	144.00	0.06	0.19	0.95	0.05	2.27	71.24	0.41	4.23	0.32
27 Fidelity Fund	144.00	0.15	0.11	0.95	0.03	1.31	88.08	0.50	3.79	0.43
28 Invest. Co. of America	144.00	0.26	0.20	0.95	0.05	2.40	68.79	0.61	4.29	0.51
29 Hamilton Funds—HDA	144.00	−0.12	0.23	0.93	0.06	2.73	62.55	0.22	4.44	0.12
30 Affiliated Fund	144.00	0.08	0.10	0.90	0.03	1.22	88.55	0.41	3.59	0.34
31 Keystone S-1	144.00	0.03	0.10	0.88	0.03	1.21	88.18	0.35	3.51	0.29
32 Axe-Houghton Fund B	144.00	0.01	0.20	0.86	0.05	2.44	63.68	0.32	4.03	0.24
33 American Mutual Fund	144.00	0.20	0.20	0.85	0.05	2.38	64.35	0.51	3.97	0.43
34 Pioneer Fund	144.00	0.24	0.16	0.84	0.04	1.88	73.85	0.55	3.67	0.48
35 Chemical Fund	144.00	0.57	0.25	0.83	0.07	3.03	51.50	0.88	4.33	0.79
36 Stein R & F Balanced Fd.	144.00	0.06	0.10	0.79	0.03	1.21	86.05	0.35	3.22	0.30
37 Puritan Fund	144.00	0.19	0.15	0.78	0.04	1.79	72.89	0.48	3.43	0.42
38 Value Line Income Fd.	144.00	0.07	0.17	0.78	0.04	2.01	67.96	0.36	3.54	0.29
39 Geo. Putnam Fd. Boston	144.00	0.07	0.10	0.77	0.03	1.18	85.75	0.35	3.12	0.30
40 Anchor Income	144.00	−0.03	0.13	0.74	0.04	1.60	75.24	0.24	3.21	0.19
41 Loomis-Sayles Mutual	144.00	0.05	0.10	0.74	0.03	1.22	83.96	0.32	3.04	0.27
42 Wellington Fund	144.00	−0.12	0.13	0.72	0.03	1.54	75.60	0.14	3.11	0.09
43 Massachusetts Fund	144.00	0.04	0.11	0.72	0.03	1.26	82.16	0.30	2.98	0.26
44 Nation-Wide Sec.	144.00	−0.32	0.15	0.67	0.04	1.78	66.45	−0.08	3.07	−0.12
45 Eaton & Howard Bal. Fd.	144.00	−0.07	0.12	0.62	0.03	1.46	71.62	0.16	2.74	0.12
46 American Business Shares	144.00	0.12	0.09	0.53	0.02	1.10	76.96	0.31	2.28	0.29
47 Keystone K-1	144.00	0.01	0.11	0.53	0.03	1.32	69.59	0.21	2.39	0.18
48 Keystone B-4	144.00	0.12	0.13	0.30	0.03	1.51	35.82	0.23	1.88	0.21
49 Keystone B-2	144.00	0.05	0.10	0.16	0.03	1.16	22.03	0.11	1.31	0.10
50 Keystone B-1	144.00	−0.08	0.10	0.07	0.03	1.21	4.43	−0.06	1.23	−0.07
51 30 Day Treasury Bills	144.00	0.0	0.0	0.0	0.0	0.0	0.0	0.34	0.12	0.34
·· Mean Sec. Values	144.00	0.12	0.19	0.93	0.05	2.32	69.25	0.46	4.25	0.36
·· Standard Deviations	0.0	0.22	0.12	0.30	0.03	1.42	17.50	0.27	1.64	0.23

* Based on monthly data, regression results sorted by beta (column 4).

where $\hat{\alpha}$ is the intercept of the fitted line and $\hat{\beta}$ represents the stock's systematic risk. The $\hat{\epsilon}$ term represents variation about the line resulting from the unsystematic component of return. We have put hats ($\hat{}$) over the α, β, and ϵ terms to indicate that these are estimated values. It is important to remember that these estimated values may differ substantially from the true values because of statistical measurement difficulties. However, the extent of possible error can be measured, and we can indicate a range within which the true value is almost certain to lie.

Exhibit 8 shows a risk-premium plot and fitted line for National Department Stores. The market is represented by a weighted index of all NYSE securities. The plot is based on monthly data during the period January 1945 to June 1970.

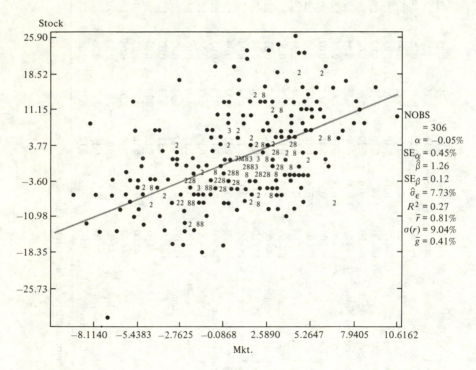

Exhibit 8.   Returns on national department stores versus NYSE index (% per month), January 1945–June 1970.

The estimated beta is 1.26, indicating above average systematic risk. The estimated alpha is −0.05 per cent per month, indicating that the excess return on the security averaged −0.60 per cent per year over the 25-year period. The correlation coefficient is 0.52; thus 27 per cent of the variance of security returns resulted from market movements. The remainder was due to factors unique to the company.

Our interpretation of the estimated alpha and beta values must be conditioned by the degree of possible measurement error. The measurement error is estimated by "standard error" coefficients associated with alpha and beta.

For example, the standard error of beta is 0.12. Thus, the probability is about 66 per cent that the true beta will lie between 1.26 ± 0.12, and about 95 per cent that it will lie between 1.26 ± 0.24 (i.e., plus or minus two times the standard error). Thus we can say with high confidence that National Department Stores has above average risk (i.e., true beta greater than 1.0).

The standard error for alpha is 0.45, which is large compared with the estimated value of -0.05. Thus we cannot conclude that the true alpha is different from zero, since zero lies well within the range of estimated alpha plus or minus one standard error (i.e., -0.05 ± 0.45).

Table 3 presents the same type of regression results for a random collection of 30 NYSE stocks.[3] The table contains the following items: Column (1) gives the number of monthly observations, columns (2) and (3) the estimated alpha ($\hat{\alpha}$) and its standard error, columns (4) and (5) the estimated beta ($\hat{\beta}$) and its standard error, column (6) the unsystematic risk $\hat{\sigma}_e$, column (7) the R^2 in percentage terms, columns (8) and (9) the arithmetic average of monthly risk premiums and the standard deviation, and column (10) the geometric mean risk premium. The results are ranked in terms of descending values of estimated beta. The table includes summary results for the NYSE market index and the prime commercial paper risk-free rate.[4] The last two rows of the table give average values and standard deviations for the sample. The average beta, for example, is 1.05, slightly higher than the average of all NYSE stocks.

The beta value for a portfolio can be estimated in two ways. One method is to compute the beta of all portfolio holdings and weight the results by portfolio representation. However, this method has the disadvantage of requiring beta calculations for each individual portfolio asset. The second method is to use the same computation procedures used for stocks, but to apply them to the portfolio returns. In this way we can obtain estimates of portfolio betas without explicit consideration of the portfolio securities. We have used this approach to compute portfolio and mutual fund beta values.

Exhibit 9 shows the plot of the monthly risk premiums on the 100-stock portfolio against the NYSE index for the same 1945–1970 period. As in the case of National Department Stores, the best-fit line has been put through the points

---

[3] The sample was picked to give the broadest possible range of security beta values. This was accomplished by ranking all NYSE securities with complete data from 1945–70 by their estimated beta values during this period. We then selected every 25th stock from the ordered list. The data was obtained from the University of Chicago CRSP (Center for Research in Security Prices) tape.

[4] The commercial paper results in Table 3 are rates of return, not risk premiums. The risk premiums would equal zero by definition.

using regression analysis. The slope of the line ($\hat{\beta}$) is equal to 1.10, with a standard error of 0.03. Note the substantial reduction in the standard error term compared to the security examples. The estimated alpha is 0.14, with a standard error of 0.10. Again, we cannot conclude that the true alpha is different from zero. Note that the points group much closer to the line than in the National Department Store plot. This results, of course, from the fact that much of the unsystematic risk causing the points to be scattered around the regression line in Exhibit 8 has been eliminated. The reduction is evidenced by the R^2 measure of 0.87 (versus 0.27 for National Department Stores). Thus the market explains more than three times as much of the return variation of the portfolio than for the stock.

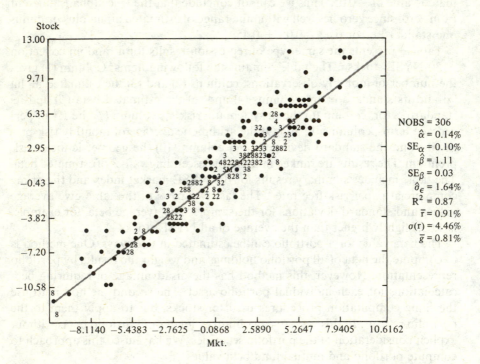

Exhibit 9. Returns on 100 stock portfolio versus NYSE index (% per month), January 1945–June 1970.

Table 4 gives regression results for a sample of 49 mutual funds. The calculations are based on monthly risk premiums for the period January 1960 to December 1971. The market is represented by the Standard & Poor's 500 Stock Index. Average values and standard deviations for the 49 funds in the sample are shown in the last two rows of the table. The average beta value for the group is 0.93—indicating, on the average, that the funds were less risky than the market index. Note the relatively low beta values of the balanced and bond funds, in particular the Keystone B1, B2, and B4 bond funds. This result is due to the low systematic risk of the bond portfolios.

Up to this point we have shown that it is a relatively easy matter to estimate beta values for stocks, portfolios, and mutual funds. Now, if the beta values are to be useful for investment decision making, they must be predictable. Beta values based on historical data should provide considerable information about future beta values if past measures are to be useful. How predictable are the betas estimated for stocks, portfolios of stocks, and mutual funds? Fortunately, we have empirical evidence at each level.

Robert A. Levy [13] has conducted tests of the short-run predictability (also referred to as stationarity) of beta coefficients for securities and unmanaged portfolios of securities. Levy's results are based on weekly returns for 500 NYSE stocks for the period December 30, 1960 through December 18, 1970 (520 weeks). Betas were developed for each security for ten non-overlapping 52-week periods. To measure stationarity, Levy correlated the 500 security betas from each 52-week period (the historical betas) with the 52-week betas in the following period (the future betas). Thus nine correlation studies were performed for the ten periods.

To compare the stationarity of security and portfolio betas, Levy constructed portfolios of 5, 10, 25, and 50 securities and repeated the same correlation analysis for the historical portfolio betas and future beta values for the same portfolios in the subsequent period. The portfolios were constructed by ranking security betas in each period and partitioning the list into portfolios containing 5, 10, 25, and 50 securities. Each portfolio contained an equal investment in each security.

The results of Levy's 52-week correlation studies are presented in Table 5. The average values of the correlation coefficients from the nine trials were 0.486, 0.769, 0.853, 0.939, and 0.972 for portfolios of 1, 5, 10, 25, and 50 stocks, respectively. Correspondingly, the average percentages of the variation in future betas explained by the historical betas are 23.6, 59.1, 72.8, 88.2, and 94.5.

The results show the beta coefficients to be very predictable for large portfolios and progressively less predictable for smaller portfolios and individual securities. These conclusions are not affected by changes in market performance. Of the nine correlation studies, five covered forecast periods during which the market performance was the reverse of the preceding period (61–62, 62–63, 65–66, 66–67, and 68–69). Notably, the betas were approximately as predictable over these five reversal periods as over the remaining four intervals.[5]

---

[5] Correlation studies of this type tend to produce a conservative picture of the degree of beta coefficient stationarity. This results from the fact that it is not possible to correlate the true beta values but only estimates which contain varying degrees of measurement error. Measurement error would reduce the correlation coefficient even though the underlying beta values were unchanged from period to period.

The question of the stability of mutual fund beta values is more complicated. Even if, as seen above, the betas of large unmanaged portfolios are very predictable, there is no *a priori* need for mutual fund betas to be comparatively stable. Indeed, the betas of mutual fund portfolios may change substantially over time by design. For example, a portfolio manager may tend to reduce the risk exposure of his fund prior to an expected market decline and raise it prior to an expected market upswing. However, the range of possible values for beta will tend to be restricted, at least in the longer run, by the fund's investment objective. Thus while one does not expect the same standard of predictability as for large unmanaged portfolios, it may nevertheless be interesting to examine the extent to which fund betas are predictable.

TABLE 5.   CORRELATION OF 52-WEEK BETA FORECASTS
WITH MEASURED VALUES FOR PORTFOLIOS OF N SECURITIES

1962–1970

FORECAST FOR 52 WEEKS ENDED	PRODUCT MOMENT CORRELATIONS: $N =$				
	1	5	10	25	50
12/28/62	.385	.711	.803	.933	.988
12/27/63	.492	.806	.866	.931	.963
12/25/64	.430	.715	.825	.945	.970
12/24/65	.451	.730	.809	.936	.977
12/23/66	.548	.803	.869	.952	.974
12/22/67	.474	.759	.830	.900	.940
12/20/68	.455	.732	.857	.945	.977
12/19/69	.556	.844	.922	.965	.973
12/18/70	.551	.804	.888	.943	.985
Quadratic Mean	.486	.769	.853	.939	.972

Source.   Robert A. Levy [13], Table 2, p. 57.

Pogue and Conway [21] have conducted tests for a sample of 90 mutual funds. The beta values for the period January 1969 through May 1970 were correlated with values from the subsequent period from June 1970 through October 1971. To test the sensitivity of the results to changes in the return measurement interval, the betas for each sub-period were measured for daily, weekly, and monthly returns. The betas were thus based on very different numbers of observations, namely 357, 74, and 17, respectively. The resulting correlation coefficients were 0.915, 0.895, and 0.703 for daily, weekly, and monthly betas. Correspondingly, the average percentages of variation in second-period betas explained by first-period values are 84, 81, and 49, respectively. The results support the contention that historical betas contain useful information about future values. However, the degree of predictability depends on the extent to which measurement errors have been eliminated from beta estimates. In the

Pogue-Conway study, the shift from monthly to daily returns reduced the average standard error of the estimated beta values from 0.11 to 0.03, a 75 per cent reduction. The more accurate daily estimates resulted in a much higher degree of beta predictability, the correlation between sub-period betas increasing from 0.703 to 0.915.[6]

Exhibit 10 shows a Pogue-Conway plot of the first-period versus second-period betas based on daily returns. The figure illustrates the high degree of correlation between first- and second-period betas.

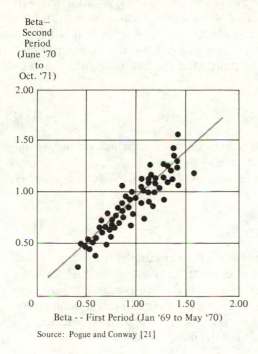

Source: Pogue and Conway [21]

Exhibit 10.   Interperiod beta comparison: daily data for 90 mutual funds.

In summary, we can conclude that estimated individual security betas are not highly predictable. Levy's tests indicated that an average of 24 per cent of the variation in second-period betas is explained by historical values. The betas of his portfolios, on the other hand, were much more predictable, the degree of predictability increasing with portfolio diversification. The results of the Pogue and Conway study and others show that fund betas, not unexpectedly, are not as stable as those for unmanaged portfolios. Nonetheless, two-thirds to three-quarters of the variation in fund betas can be explained by historical values.

[6] These results are consistent with those found by N. Mains in a later study [16]. Mains correlated adjacent calendar-year betas for a sample of 99 funds for the period 1960 through 1971. The betas were based on weekly returns. The average correlation coefficient for 11 tests was 0.788, with individual values ranging from a low of 0.614 to a high of 0.871.

The reader should remember that a significant portion of the measured changes in estimated beta values may not be due to changes in the true values, but rather to measurement errors. This observation is particularly applicable to individual security betas where the standard errors tend to be large.

8. TESTS OF THE CAPITAL ASSET PRICING MODEL*

The major difficulty in testing the CAPM is that the model is stated in terms of investors' expectations and not in terms of realized returns. The fact that expectations are not always realized introduces an error term, which from a statistical point of view should be zero *on the average*, but not necessarily zero for any single stock or single period of time. After the fact, we would expect to observe

$$R_j = R_f + \beta_j(R_m - R_f) + \epsilon_j, \tag{17a}$$

where R_j, R_m, and R_f are the realized returns on stock j, the market index, and the riskless asset; and ϵ_j is the residual term.

If we observe the realized returns over a series of periods, the average security return would be given by

$$\bar{R}_j = \bar{R}_F + \beta_j(\bar{R}_M - \bar{R}_F) + \bar{\epsilon}_j, \tag{17b}$$

where $\bar{R}_j$, $\bar{R}_M$, and $\bar{R}_F$ are the average realized returns on the stock, the market and the risk-free rate. If the CAPM is correct, the average residual term, $\bar{\epsilon}_j$, should approach zero as the number of periods used to compute the average becomes large. To test this hypothesis, we can regress the average returns, R_j, for a series of stocks ($j = 1, \ldots, N$) on the stocks' estimated beta values, $\hat{\beta}_j$, during the period studied. The equation of the fitted line is given by

$$\bar{R}_j = \gamma_0 + \gamma_1 \hat{\beta}_j + \mu_j, \tag{18a}$$

where γ_0 and γ_1 are the intercept and slope of the line, and μ_j is the deviation of stock j from the line. By comparing Equations (17b) and (18a), we infer that if the CAPM hypothesis is valid, μ_j should equal $\bar{\epsilon}_j$ and hence should be small. Furthermore, it should be uncorrelated with $\hat{\beta}_j$, and hence we can also infer that γ_0 and γ_1 should equal $\bar{R}_F$ and $\bar{R}_M - \bar{R}_F$ respectively.

The hypothesis is illustrated in Exhibit 11. Each plotted point represents one stock's realized return versus the stock's beta. The vertical distances of the points

---

* The material in this section was also prepared as an appendix to testimony to be delivered before the Federal Communications Commission by S. C. Myers and G. A. Pogue.

from the CAPM theoretical line (also called the "market line") represent the mean residual returns, $\bar{\epsilon}_j$. Assuming the CAPM to be correct, the $\bar{\epsilon}_j$ should be uncorrelated with the $\hat{\beta}_j$ and thus the regression equation fitted to these points should be (1) linear, (2) upward sloping with slope equal to $\bar{R}_M - \bar{R}_F$, and (3) should pass through the vertical axis at the risk-free rate.

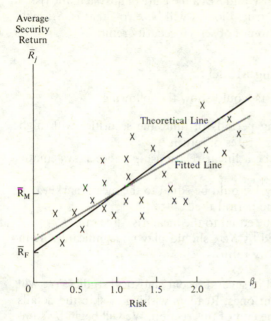

Exhibit 11.   Relationship between average return ($\bar{R}_j$) and security risk (β_j).

Expressed in risk-premium form, the equation of the fitted line is

$$\bar{r}_j = \gamma_0 + \gamma_1 \hat{\beta}_j + \mu_j, \tag{18b}$$

where $\bar{r}_j$ is the average realized risk premium for stock j. Comparing Equation (18b) to the CAPM in risk-premium form [Equation (15)], the predicted values for γ_0 and γ_1 are 0 and $\bar{r}_m$, the mean market risk premium ($\bar{R}_M - \bar{R}_F$). Thus shifting to risk premiums changes the predicted value only for γ_0, but not for γ_1.

Other Measures of Risk

The hypothesis just described is only true if beta is a complete measure of a stock's risk. Various alternative risk measures have been proposed, however. The most common alternative hypothesis states that expected return is related to the standard deviation of return—that is, to a stock's total risk, which includes both systematic and unsystematic components.

Which is more important in explaining average observed returns on securities, systematic or unsystematic risk? The way to find out is to fit an expanded equation to the data:

$$R_j = \gamma_0 + \gamma_1 \hat{\beta}_j + \gamma_2 (S\hat{E}_j) + \mu_j. \tag{19}$$

Here $\hat{\beta}_j$ is a measure of systematic risk and $S\hat{E}_j$ a measure of unsystematic risk.[7] Of course, if the CAPM is exactly true, then γ_2 will be zero—that is, $S\hat{E}_j$ will contribute nothing to the explanation of observed security returns.

Tests of the Capital Asset Pricing Model

If the CAPM is right, empirical tests would show the following:

1. On the average, and over long periods of time, the securities with high systematic risk should have high rates of return.
2. On the average, there should be a linear relationship between systematic risk and return.
3. The slope of the relationship (γ_1) should be equal to the mean market risk premium ($\bar{R}_M - \bar{R}_F$) during the period used.
4. The constant term (γ_0) should be equal to the mean risk-free rate (R_F).
5. Unsystematic risk, as measured by $S\hat{E}_j$, should play no significant role in explaining differences in security returns.

These predictions have been tested in several recent statistical studies. We will review some of the more important ones. Readers wishing to skip the details may proceed to the summary at the end of this section. We will begin by summarizing results from studies based on individual securities, and then we will turn to portfolio results.

Results of Tests Based on Securities

The Jacob Study. The Jacob study [9] deals with the 593 New York Stock Exchange stocks for which there is complete data from 1946 to 1965. Regression analyses were performed for the 1946–55 and 1956–65 periods, using both monthly and annual security returns. The relationship of mean security returns and beta values is shown in Table 6. The last two columns of the table give the theoretical values for the coefficients, as predicted by the CAPM.

The results show a significant positive relationship between realized return and risk during each of the 10-year periods. For example, in 1956–65 there was a 6.7 per cent per year increase in average return for a one-unit increase in beta.

---

[7] SE_j is an estimate of the standard error of the residual term in Equation (17a). Thus it is the estimated value for $\sigma(\epsilon_j)$, the unsystematic risk term defined in Equation (8). See column (6) of Tables 3 and 4 for typical values for securities and mutual funds.

Although the relationships shown in Table 6 are all positive, they are weaker than those predicted by the CAPM. In each period γ_1 is less and γ_0 is greater than the theoretical values.

TABLE 6. RESULTS OF JACOB'S STUDY

$$\bar{r}_j = \gamma_0 + \gamma_1 \hat{\beta}_j + \mu_j$$
Tests Based on 593 Securities

| PERIOD | RETURN INTERVAL | REGRESSION RESULTS[a] | | | THEORETICAL VALUES | |
		$\hat{\gamma}_0$	$\hat{\gamma}_1$	R^2	$\gamma_0 = 0$	$\gamma_1 = \bar{R}_M - \bar{R}_F$
46–55	Monthly	0.80	0.30 (0.07)[b]	0.02	0	1.10
	Yearly	8.9	5.10 (0.53)	0.14	0	14.4
56–65	Monthly	0.70	0.30 (0.06)	0.03	0	0.8
	Yearly	6.7	6.7 (0.53)	0.21	0	10.8

(a) Coefficient units are: monthly data, per cent per month; annual data, per cent per year.
(b) Standard error.
Source.   Jacob [9], Table 3, pp. 827–828.

The Miller-Scholes Study.   The Miller-Scholes research [19] deals with annual returns for 631 stocks during the 1954–63 period. The results of three of their tests are reported in Table 7. The tests are (1) mean return versus beta, (2) mean return versus unsystematic risk, $(S\hat{E}_j)^2$, and (3) mean return versus both beta and unsystematic risk.

TABLE 7. RESULTS OF THE MILLER AND SCHOLES STUDY

$$\bar{R}_m = \gamma_0 + \gamma_1 \hat{\beta}_j + \gamma_2 (S\hat{E}_j)^2 + \mu_j$$
Annual Rates of Return 1954–1963
Tests Based on 631 Securities

| REGRESSION RESULTS[a] | | | | THEORETICAL VALUES | | |
$\hat{\gamma}_0$	$\hat{\gamma}_1$	$\hat{\gamma}_2$	R^2	γ_0	γ_1	γ_2
12.2 (0.7)[b]	7.1 (0.6)		0.19	2.8	8.5	0
16.3 (0.4)		39.3 (2.5)	0.28	2.8	8.5	0
12.7 (0.6)	4.2 (0.6)	31.0 (2.6)	0.33	2.8	8.5	0

(a) Units of Coefficients: per cent per year.
(b) Standard error.
Source.   Miller and Scholes [19], Table 1B, p. 53.

The results for the first test show a significant positive relationship between mean return and beta. A one-unit increase in beta is associated with a 7.1 per cent increase in mean return.

The results for the second test do not agree with the CAPM's predictions. That is, high unsystematic risk is apparently associated with higher realized returns. However, Miller and Scholes show that this correlation may be largely spurious (i.e., it may be due to statistical sampling problems). For example, a substantial positive correlation exists between beta and $(S\hat{E}_j)^2$. Thus unsystematic risk will appear to be significant in tests from which beta has been omitted, even though it may be unimportant to the pricing of securities. This sort of statistical correlation need not imply a causal link between the variables.

Test number (3) includes both beta and $(S\hat{E}_j)^2$ in the regression equation. Both are found to be significantly positively related to mean return. The inclusion of $(S\hat{E}_j)^2$ has somewhat weakened the relationship of return and beta, however. A one-unit increase in beta is now associated with only a 4.2 per cent increase in mean return.

The interpretation of these results is again complicated by the strong positive correlation between beta and $(S\hat{E}_j)^2$, and by other sampling problems.[8] A significant portion of the correlation between mean return and $(S\hat{E}_j)^2$ may well be a spurious result. In any case, the results do show that stocks with high systematic risk tend to have higher rates of return.

Results for Tests Based on Portfolio Returns

Tests based directly on securities clearly show the significant positive correlation between return and systematic risk. Such tests, however, are not the most efficient method of obtaining estimates of the magnitude of the risk-return trade-off. The tests are inefficient for two reasons.

The first problem is well known to economists. It is called "errors in variables bias" and results from the fact that beta, the independent variable in the test, is typically measured with some error. These errors are random in their effect— that is, some stocks' betas are overestimated and some are underestimated. Nevertheless, when these estimated beta values are used in the test, the measurement errors tend to attenuate the relationship between mean return and risk.

By carefully grouping the securities into portfolios, much of this measurement error problem can be eliminated. The errors in individual stocks' betas cancel out so that the portfolio beta can be measured with much greater precision. This in turn means that tests based on portfolio returns will be more efficient than tests based on security returns.

---

[8] For example, skewness in the distributions of stock returns can lead to spurious correlations between mean return and SE_j. See Miller and Scholes [19], pp. 66–71.

The second problem relates to the obscuring effect of residual variation. Realized security returns have a large random component, which typically accounts for about 70 per cent of the variation of return. (This is the diversifiable or unsystematic risk of the stock.) By grouping securities into portfolios, we can eliminate much of this "noise" and thereby get a much clearer view of the relationship between return and systematic risk.

It should be noted that grouping does not distort the underlying risk-return relationship. The relationship that exists for individual securities is exactly the same for portfolios of securities.

Friend and Blume Studies. Professors Friend and Blume [3, 8] have conducted two interrelated risk-return studies. The first examines the relationship between long-run rates of return and various risk measures. The second is a direct test of the CAPM.

In the first study [8], Friend and Blume constructed portfolios of NYSE common stocks at the beginning of three different holding periods. The periods began at the ends of 1929, 1948, and 1956. All stocks for which monthly rate-of-return data could be obtained for at least four years preceding the test period were divided into 10 portfolios. The securities were assigned on the basis of their betas during the preceding four years—the 10 per cent of securities with the lowest betas to the first portfolio, the group with the next lowest betas to the second portfolio, and so on.

After the start of the test periods, the securities were reassigned annually. That is, each stock's estimated beta was recomputed at the end of each successive year, the stocks were ranked again on the basis of their betas, and new portfolios were formed. This procedure kept the portfolio betas reasonably stable over time.

The performance of these portfolios is summarized in Table 8. The table gives the arithmetic mean monthly returns and average beta values for each of the 10 portfolios and for each test period.

For the 1929–69 period, the results indicate a strong positive association between return and beta. For the 1948–69 period, while higher beta portfolios had higher returns than portfolios with lower betas, there was little difference in return among portfolios with betas greater than 1.0. The 1956–69 period results do not show a clear relationship between beta and return. On the basis of these and other tests, the authors conclude that NYSE stocks with above average risk have higher returns than those with below average risk, but that there is little payoff for assuming additional risk within the group of stocks with above average betas.

In their second study [3], Blume and Friend used monthly portfolio returns during the 1955–68 period to test the CAPM. Their tests involved fitting the coefficients of Equation (18a) for three sequential periods: 1955–59, 1960–64,

TABLE 8.   RESULTS OF FRIEND-BLUME STUDY

Returns from a yearly revision policy for
stocks classified by beta for various periods.

| | HOLDING PERIOD | | | | | |
| | 1929–1969 | | 1948–1969 | | 1956–1969 | |
Portfolio No.	Beta	Mean Return %	Beta	Mean Return %	Beta	Mean Return %
1	0.19	0.79	0.45	0.99	0.28	0.95
2	0.49	1.00	0.64	1.01	0.51	0.98
3	0.67	1.10	0.76	1.25	0.66	1.12
4	0.81	1.28	0.85	1.30	0.80	1.18
5	0.92	1.26	0.94	1.35	0.91	1.17
6	1.02	1.34	1.03	1.37	1.03	1.14
7	1.15	1.42	1.12	1.32	1.16	1.10
8	1.29	1.53	1.23	1.33	1.30	1.18
9	1.49	1.55	1.36	1.39	1.48	1.15
10	2.02	1.59	1.67	1.36	1.92	1.10

Monthly arithmetic mean returns.
Source.   Friend and Blume [8], Table 4, p. 10.

and 1965–68. The authors also added a factor to the regression equation to test for the linearity of the risk-return relationship.[9]

The values obtained for γ_0 and γ_1 are not in line with the Capital Asset Pricing Model's predictions, however. In the first two periods, γ_0 is substantially larger than the theoretical value. In the third period, the reverse situation exists, with γ_0 substantially less than predicted. These results imply that γ_1, the slope of the fitted line, is less than predicted in the first two periods and greater in the third.[10] Friend and Blume conclude that "the comparisons as a whole suggest that a linear model is a tenable approximation of the empirical relationship between return and risk for NYSE stocks over the three periods covered."[11]

Black, Jensen, and Scholes.   This study [1] is a careful attempt to reduce measurement errors that would bias the regression results. For each year from 1931 to 1965, the authors grouped all NYSE stocks into 10 portfolios. The number

[9] Their expanded test equation is

$$\bar{R}_j = \gamma_0 + \gamma_1 \hat{\beta}_j + \gamma_2 (\hat{\beta}_j)^2,$$

where, according to the CAPM, the expected value of γ_2 is zero.

[10] Table 1, p. 25, of Blume and Friend [3] presents period-by-period regression results.

[11] Blume and Friend [3], p. 26.

of securities in each portfolio increased over the 35-year period from a low of 58 securities per portfolio in 1931 to a high of 110 in 1965.

Month-by-month returns for the portfolios were computed from January 1931 to December 1965. Average portfolio returns and portfolio betas were computed for the 35-year period and for a variety of subperiods. The results for the complete period are shown in Table 9. The average monthly portfolio returns and beta values for the 10 portfolios are plotted in Exhibit 12. The results indicate that over the complete 35-year period, average return increased by approximately 1.08 per cent per month (13 per cent per year) for a one-unit increase in beta. This is about three-quarters of the amount predicted by the CAPM. As Exhibit 12 shows, there appears to be little reason to question the linearity of the relationship over the 35-year period.

TABLE 9.   RESULTS OF BLACK-JENSEN-SCHOLES
STUDY

$$R_p = \gamma_0 + \gamma_1 \hat{\beta}_p + \mu_p$$
1931–1965
Tests Based on 10 Portfolios
(Averaging 75 Stocks per Portfolio)

REGRESSION RESULTS[a]			THEORETICAL VALUES	
$\hat{\gamma}_0$	$\hat{\gamma}_1$	R^2	$\gamma_0 = \bar{R}_F$	$\gamma_1 = \bar{R}_M - \bar{R}_F$
0.519	1.08	0.90	0.16	1.42
(0.05)[b]	(0.05)			

(a) Units of Coefficients: per cent per month.
(b) Standard error.
Source.   Black, Jensen, and Scholes [1], Table 4, p. 98, and Figure 7, p. 104.

Black, Jensen, and Scholes also estimated the risk-return tradeoff for a number of subperiods.[12] The slopes of the regression lines tend in most periods to understate the theoretical values, but are generally of the correct sign. Also, the subperiod relationships appear to be linear.

This paper provides substantial support for the hypothesis that realized returns are a linear function of systematic risk values. Moreover, it shows that the relationship is significantly positive over long periods of time.

Fama and MacBeth.   Fama and MacBeth [6] have extended the Black-Jensen-Scholes tests to include two additional factors. The first is an average of the β_j^2 for all individual securities in portfolio p, designated $\hat{\beta}_p^2$. The second is a similar

---

[12] Figure 6 of Black, Jensen, and Scholes [1], pp. 101–103, shows average monthly returns versus systematic risk for 17 nonoverlapping 2-year periods from 1932 to 1965.

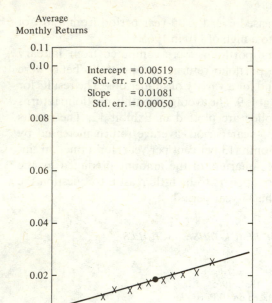

Average Monthly Returns

Intercept = 0.00519
Std. err. = 0.00053
Slope = 0.01081
Std. err. = 0.00050

Systematic Risk

Average monthly returns versus systematic risk for the 35-year period 1931-1965 for ten portfolios and the market portfolio.

Source: Black, Jensen, and Scholes [1], Figure 7, p. 104.

Exhibit 12. Results of Black, Jensen, and Scholes study, 1931–1965. Average monthly returns versus systematic risk for the 35-year period 1931–1965 for 10 portfolios and the market portfolio.
Source: Black, Jensen, and Scholes (1), Fig. 7, p. 104.

average of the residual standard deviations $(S\hat{E}_j)$ for all stocks in portfolio p, designated $S\hat{E}_p$. The first term tests for nonlinearities in the risk-return relationship, the second for the impact of residual variation.

The equation of the fitted line for the Fama-MacBeth study is given by

$$\bar{R}_p = \gamma_0 + \gamma_1\hat{\beta}_p + \gamma_2\hat{\beta}_p^2 + \gamma_3 S\hat{E}_p + \mu_p, \tag{20}$$

where, according to the CAPM, we should expect γ_2 and γ_3 to have zero values.

The results of the Fama-MacBeth tests show that while estimated values of γ_2 and γ_3 are not equal to zero for each interval examined, their average values tend to be insignificantly different from zero. Fama and MacBeth also confirm the Black-Jensen-Scholes result that the realized values of γ_0 are not equal to $\bar{R}_f$, as predicted by the CAPM.

Summary of Test Results

We will briefly summarize the major results of the empirical tests.

1. The evidence shows a significant positive relationship between realized returns and systematic risk. However, the slope of the relationship (γ_1) is usually less than predicted by the CAPM.
2. The relationship between risk and return appears to be linear. The studies give no evidence of significant curvature in the risk-return relationship.
3. Tests that attempt to discriminate between the effects of systematic and unsystematic risk do not yield definitive results. Both kinds of risk appear to be positively related to security returns. However, there is substantial support for the proposition that the relationship between return and unsystematic risk is at least partly spurious—that is, it partly reflects statistical problems rather than the true nature of capital markets.

Obviously, we cannot claim that the CAPM is absolutely right. On the other hand, the empirical tests do support the view that beta is a useful risk measure and that high beta stocks tend to be priced so as to yield correspondingly high rates of return.

9.   MEASUREMENT OF INVESTMENT PERFORMANCE

The basic concept underlying investment performance measurement follows directly from the risk-return theory. The return on managed portfolios, such as mutual funds, can be judged relative to the returns on unmanaged portfolios at the same degree of investment risk. If the return exceeds the standard, the portfolio manager has performed in a superior way, and vice versa. Given this, it remains to select a set of "benchmark" portfolios against which the performance of managed portfolios can be evaluated.

Performance Measures Developed from the Capital Asset Pricing Model

The CAPM provides a convenient and familiar standard for performance measurement; the benchmark portfolios are simply combinations of the riskless asset and the market index. The return standard for a mutual fund, for example, with beta equal to β_P, is equal to the risk-free rate ($\bar{R}_F$) plus β_P times the average realized risk premium on the market ($\bar{R}_M - \bar{R}_F$). Thus the return on the performance standard ($\bar{R}_S$) is given by

$$\bar{R}_S = \bar{R}_F + \beta_P(\bar{R}_M - \bar{R}_F), \tag{21}$$

where $\bar{R}_M$ and $\bar{R}_F$ are the arithmetic average returns on the market index and riskless asset during the evaluation period. The performance measure, designated α_p, is equal to the difference in average returns between the fund and its standard; that is,

$$\alpha_p = \bar{R}_P - \bar{R}_S, \tag{22}$$

where $\bar{R}_P$ is the arithmetic average return on the fund. Under the CAPM assumption, the expected values of $\bar{R}_P$ and $\bar{R}_S$ are the same; therefore the expected value for the performance measure $\hat{\alpha}_p$ is zero. Managed portfolios with positive estimated values for α_p have thus outperformed the standard, and vice versa. Estimated values of alpha $(\hat{\alpha}_p)$ are determined by regressing the portfolio risk premiums on the corresponding market risk premiums.

The intepretation of the estimated alpha must take into consideration possible statistical measurement errors. As we discussed in Section 7, the standard error of alpha (SE_α) is an indication of the extent of the possible measurement error. The larger the standard error, the less certain we can be that measured alpha is a close approximation of the true value.[13]

A measure of the degree of statistical significance of the estimated alpha value is given by the ratio of the estimated alpha to its standard error. The ratio, designated as t_α, is given by

$$t_\alpha = \hat{\alpha}_p/SE_\alpha. \tag{23}$$

The statistic t_α gives a measure of the extent to which the true value of alpha can be considered to be different from zero. If the absolute value of t_α is large, then we have more confidence that the true value of alpha is different from zero. Absolute values of t_α in excess of 2.0 indicate a probability of less than about 2.5 per cent that the true value of alpha is zero.

These methods of performance measurement were originally devised by Michael Jensen [10, 11] and have been widely used in many studies of investment performance, including that of the recent SEC Institutional Investor Study [21].

A performance measure closely related to the Jensen alpha measure was developed by Jack L. Treynor [24]. The Treynor performance measure (designated TI)[14] is given by

$$\text{TI} = \alpha/\beta. \tag{24}$$

---

[13] See columns 2 and 3 of Table 4 for typical mutual fund $\hat{\alpha}$ and SE_α values.

[14] Treynor's work preceded that of Jensen. In a discussion of Jensen's performance measure [26], Treynor showed that his measure (as originally presented in [25]) was equivalent to

$$\text{TI} = R_F - \alpha/\beta.$$

Since R_F is a constant, the TI index for ranking purposes is equivalent to that given in Equation (24).

The difference between the α and TI performance measures is simply that the fund alpha value has been divided by its estimated beta. The effect, however, is significant, eliminating a so-called "leverage bias" from the Jensen alpha measures. This is illustrated in Exhibit 13.

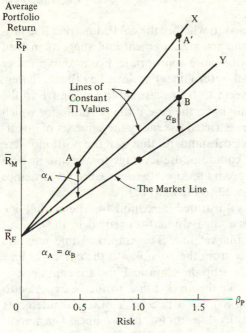

Symbols: $\bar{R}_M$ = Return on Market Index
$\bar{R}_F$ = Risk-free Rate of Interest
A, B = Managed Portfolios
A' = Portfolio A Levered to Same Beta as Portfolio B

Exhibit 13. Relationship between the Jensen and Treynor measures of investment performance. Symbols: R_M = return on market index; R_F = riskfree rate of interest; A, B = managed portfolios; A' = portfolio A levered to same beta as portfolio B.

Funds A and B in Exhibit 13 have the same alpha values. (The alphas are equal to the vertical distance on the diagram between the funds and the market line.) By combining portfolio B with the riskless rate (that is, by borrowing or lending at R_F), any return-risk combination along line Y can be obtained. But such points are clearly dominated by combinations along line X—attainable by borrowing or lending combined with fund A. As Exhibit 13 shows, the alpha for fund A, when levered to the same beta as fund B (Point A'), dominates the latter's alpha value.

The Treynor measure eliminates this leverage effect. All funds which lie along a line (such as X or Y) have the same TI value; therefore borrowing or lending combined with any fund outcome will not increase (or decrease) its performance measure. The Treynor measure thus permits direct performance comparisons among funds with differing beta values.

Problems with the Market Line Standard

The tests of the CAPM summarized in Section 8 indicate that the average returns over time on securities and portfolios tend to deviate from the predictions of the model. Though the observed risk-return relationships seem to be linear, they are generally flatter than predicted by the CAPM, implying that the tradeoff of risk for return is less than predicted.

This evidence raises some question as to whether the CAPM market line provides the best benchmark for performance measurement and suggests instead that other benchmark portfolios may be more appropriate. For example, under certain conditions, the "empirical" risk-return lines developed by Black, Jensen, and Scholes [1] and others would seem to be a reasonable alternative to the CAPM market line standard. This might be the case if the portfolio for which performance is being measured were restricted to exactly the same set of investment options used to create the empirical standard, that is, if the portfolio were fully invested in common stock and could not use leverage to increase its beta value. For such a portfolio it would seem appropriate to measure performance relative to the empirical line, as opposed to the market line.

A comparison of these standards is illustrated in Exhibit 14. The market line performance measure (designated as α_1 in Exhibit 14) is equal to the vertical distance from the portfolio to the market line. The empirical line measure (designated α_2) is the vertical distance from the portfolio to the empirical line. Since ideally all the stocks used to develop the empirical line are contained in the market index, the empirical line, like the market line, would be expected to have a return equal to market return, $\bar{R}_M$, for beta equal to 1.0. The intercepts on the return axis, however, are typically different for the two lines. The market line intercept, by definition, is equal to the average risk-free rate. The empirical line intersects the return axis at a point different from $\bar{R}_F$, and typically above it. This intercept equals the average return on a portfolio with "zero beta," designated $\bar{R}_Z$. The existence of a long-run average return on the zero beta portfolio that differs from the riskless rate is a clear violation of the predictions of the CAPM. As of this time, there is no clear theoretical understanding of the reason for this difference.

To summarize, empirically based performance standards could, under certain conditions, provide alternatives to those of the CAPM market line standard. However, the design of appropriate empirical standards requires further research. In the interim, the familiar market line benchmarks can provide useful information regarding performance, although the information should not be regarded as being very precise.[15]

---

[15] There are a number of excellent references for further study of portfolio theory. Among these we would recommend books by Richard A. Brealey [4], Jack Clark Francis [7], and William F. Sharpe [24]. For a more technical survey of the theoretical and empirical literature, see Jensen [12].

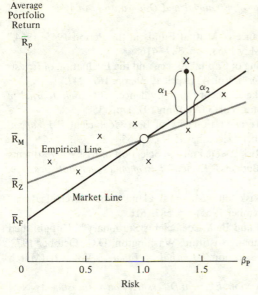

Exhibit 14. Measurement of investment performance: market line versus empirical standard. Symbols: $\bar{R}_M$ = return on market index; $\bar{R}_Z$ = return on zero beta portfolio; $\bar{R}_F$ = riskfree rate of interest; X = investment portfolios; O = market index.

Symbols: $\bar{R}_M$ = Return on Market Index
$\bar{R}_Z$ = Return on Zero Beta Portfolio
$\bar{R}_F$ = Risk-Free Rate of Interest
x = Investment Portfolios
O = Market Index

REFERENCES

1. Fischer Black, Michael C. Jensen, and Myron S. Scholes, "The Capital Asset Pricing Model: Some Empirical Tests." Published in *Studies in the Theory of Capital Markets*, edited by Michael Jensen. New York, Praeger, 1972, pp. 79–121.

2. Marshall E. Blume, "Portfolio Theory: A Step Toward Its Practical Application." *Journal of Business*, Vol. 43 (April 1970), pp. 152–173.

3. Marshall E. Blume, and Irwin Friend, "A New Look at the Capital Asset Pricing Model." *Journal of Finance*, Vol. XXVIII (March 1973), pp. 19–33.

4. Richard A. Brealey, *An Introduction to Risk and Return from Common Stocks*. Cambridge, Mass., MIT Press, 1969.

5. Eugene F. Fama, "Components of Investment Performance." *The Journal of Finance*, Vol. XXVII (June 1972), pp. 551–567.

6. Eugene F. Fama, and James D. MacBeth, "Risk, Return and Equilibrium: Empirical Tests." Unpublished Working Paper No. 7237, University of Chicago, Graduate School of Business, August 1972.

7. Jack C. Francis, *Investment Analysis and Management*. New York, McGraw-Hill, 1972.

8. Irwin Friend, and Marshall E. Blume, "Risk and the Long Run Rate of Return on NYSE Common Stocks." Working Paper No. 18–72, Wharton School of Commerce and Finance, Rodney L. White Center for Financial Research.

9. Nancy Jacob, "The Measurement of Systematic Risk for Securities and Portfolios:

Some Empirical Results." *Journal of Financial and Quantitative Analysis*, Vol. VI (March 1971), pp. 815–834.

10. Michael C. Jensen, "The Performance of Mutual Funds in the Period 1945–1964." *Journal of Finance*, Vol. XXIII (May 1968), pp. 389–416.

11. Michael C. Jensen, "Risk, the Pricing of Capital Assets, and the Evaluation of Investment Portfolios," *Journal of Business*, Vol. 42 (April 1969), pp. 167–247.

12. Michael C. Jensen, "Capital Markets: Theory and Evidence." *The Bell Journal of Economics and Management Science*, Vol. 3 (Autumn 1972), pp. 357–398.

13. Robert A. Levy, "On the Short Term Stationarity of Beta Coefficients." *Financial Analysts Journal*, Vol. 27 (November-December 1971), pp. 55–62.

14. John Lintner, "The Valuation of Risk Assets and the Selection of Risky Investments in Stock Portfolios and Capital Budgets." *Review of Economics and Statistics*, Vol. XLVII (February 1965), pp. 13–37.

15. John Lintner, "Security Prices, Risk, and Maximal Gains from Diversification." *Journal of Finance*, Vol. XX (December 1965), pp. 587–616.

16. Norman E. Mains, "Are Mutual Fund Beta Coefficients Stationary?" Unpublished Working Paper, Investment Company Institute, Washington, D.C., October 1972.

17. Harry M. Markowitz, "Portfolio Selection." *Journal of Finance*, Vol. VII (March 1952). pp. 77–91.

18. Harry M. Markowitz, *Portfolio Selection: Efficient Diversification of Investments*. New York, John Wiley and Sons, 1959.

19. Merton H. Miller, and Myron S. Scholes, "Rates of Returns in Relation to Risk: A Reexamination of Recent Findings." Published in *Studies in the Theory of Capital Markets*, edited by Michael Jensen. (New York: Praeger, 1972), pp. 47–78.

20. Franco Modigliani, and Gerald A. Pogue, *A Study of Investment Performance Fees*. Lexington, Mass., Heath-Lexington Books, Forthcoming 1974.

21. Gerald A. Pogue, and Walter Conway, "On the Stability of Mutual Fund Beta Values." Unpublished Working Paper, MIT, Sloan School of Management, June 1972.

22. Securities and Exchange Commission, *Institutional Investor Study Report of the Securities and Exchange Commission*, Chapter 4. "Investment Advisory Complexes", pp. 325–347. (Washington, D.C.: U.S. Government Printing Office, 1971.)

23. William F. Sharpe, "Capital Asset Prices: A Theory of Market Equilibrium under Conditions of Risk." *Journal of Finance*, Vol. XIX (September 1964), pp. 425–442.

24. William F. Sharpe, *Portfolio Theory and Capital Markets*. New York, McGraw-Hill, 1970.

25. Jack L. Treynor, "How to Rate the Management of Investment Funds." *Harvard Business Review*, Vol. XLIII (January-February 1965), pp. 63–75.

26. Jack L. Treynor, "The Performance of Manual Funds in the Period 1945–1964: Discussion." *Journal of Finance*, Vol. XXIII (May 1968), pp. 418–419.

27. Wayne H. Wagner, and Sheila Lau, "The Effect of Diversification on Risk." *Financial Analysts Journal*, Vol. 26 (November-December 1971), pp. 48–53.

QUESTIONS

1. Summarize the assumptions which allow the theoretical derivation of the CAPM.

2. In the event that empirical testing shows the CAPM to explain relationships among risk, return, and value, is it of any importance whether the assumptions made for deriving the CAPM are indeed realistic? Discuss.
3. If the CAPM is to be useful, why is it necessary that beta values for a firm or mutual fund be predictable (have stationarity)?
4. Comment on the findings of the Levy study that the stationarity of betas was related to the number of securities in the portfolio.
5. Discuss each of the five predictions listed for testing whether the CAPM is appropriate.
6. Summarize the results of the two studies described (the Jacob and the Miller-Scholes studies) which performed tests on individual securities.
7. Explain the two reasons given why CAPM tests on individual securities are less efficient than tests on portfolios.
8. Comment on the general results of the empirical tests on the CAPM.

PROBLEMS

1. Assume that the CAPM is valid and that the betas have stationarity. Use the relationship

$$E(R_p) = R_F + \beta_p(E(R_m) - R_F)$$

to compute $E(R_p)$ for portfolios of one security each. For each calculation, therefore, the $E(R_p)$ is an estimate of the cost of equity for that firm. Perform this calculation for the following firms: Homestake Mining Company, First National Store, American Ship Building, Phillip Jones Corporation, City Investing Company.
   Suggestions:
   a. For your estimate of R_F, look up the current rate on thirty-day treasury bills.
   b. Use the mean security value (times 12) in Table 3, column 10 for your estimate of the risk premium.
   c. Use beta values from Table 3 for each firm indicated.
2. Critically evaluate the potential of this method for estimating the cost of equity for the firm. In your analysis, include a discussion as to what rate is appropriate for the risk-free rate.

22 | James C. Van Horne and John G. McDonald*

Dividend Policy and New Equity Financing

An issue faced by all profitable firms is the appropriate dividend policy. If a high payout is used, the firm may frequently have to rely on new flotations of common stock for its investment program. This will be expensive due to flotation expenses. On the other hand, some firms may opt for a low dividend payout to avoid frequent trips to the capital markets; this policy will produce low current yields, but may result in a greater portion of returns being taxed at the lower capital gains rate. The optimal dividend policy depends on investors' desire for capital gains as opposed to income, their willingness to forego dividends now for future returns, and their perception of the risk associated with postponement of returns.

The purpose of this paper is to investigate the combined effect of dividend policy and new equity financing decisions on the market value of the firm's common stock. Some basic aspects of a conceptual framework are explored, and empirical tests are performed with year-end 1968 cross sections for two industries, using a well-known valuation model. The results must be considered exploratory, but the method of analysis should prove useful in future investigations.

DIVIDENDS, NEW EQUITY ISSUES, AND VALUE

The notion of an optimal dividend policy implies a dividend payout rate which, *ceteris paribus*, maximizes shareholder wealth. Any normative approach to dividend policy intended to be operative under real world conditions should consider the firm's investment opportunities, any preferences that investors have for dividends as opposed to capital gains or vice versa, and differences in "cost"

Source. Reprinted by permission from *Journal of Finance*, May 1971, pp. 507–519. James Van Horne is A. P. Giannini Professor of Finance, and John McDonald is professor of finance, both at Stanford University.

* We are indebted to Michael Kinsman for his programming assistance in the preparation of this paper. This study was supported by the Dean Witter Foundation. The conclusions, opinions, and other statements are those of the authors.

between retained earnings and new equity issues. The extent to which dividends and new issues affect stock price is at this date an unresolved empirical question.

Nearly a decade ago, Modigliani and Miller demonstrated the irrelevance of dividend payout under one set of assumptions as to perfectly competitive financial markets, where the investment decision and total earnings of the firm are given and there exists a frictionless trade-off between dividends and new equity issues.[1] Some key conditions in this analysis include the exogenous investment variable, a constant discount rate applicable to expected future flows, and the absence of taxes, transaction costs, and flotation costs. If these conditions hold, the way in which the current earnings stream is split between dividends and retained earnings (or the extent to which new investment is financed with retained earnings or new equity issues) does not affect the value of the firm to existing stockholders.

As these perfect market assumptions are relaxed, arguments that dividend policy may affect value can be viewed in two categories: (1) investors may have a net preference for dividends relative to capital gains or vice-versa owing to uncertainty resolution, transaction and inconvenience costs, and differential tax rates; (2) costs associated with the sale of new issues of equity securities may make these issues a more "costly" source of equity financing than retained earnings.

Some of the considerations which may be sufficient for a net preference of investors for either dividends or capital gains are briefly reviewed. Gordon has alleged that the required rate of return used by investors to discount dividends expected in future periods increases with time, t.[2] If the level of investment depends on financing from retained earnings, retention for current investment implies that current dividends are foregone in order to increase the future growth of dividends. The implication of Gordon's construct is that the required rate of return, which represents a weighted average of future period required rates, rises with the proportion of earnings retained. As a result, investors would value current dividends over capital gains, ceteris paribus.

The existence of transaction costs and any aversion to the inconvenience of selling shares tends to favor current dividends over capital gains. The irrelevance doctrine implies that investors with a preference for current income above the current dividends can always sell stock to obtain additional income. However, with transaction costs and the inconvenience of selling stock periodically, the

---

[1] See Merton H. Miller and Franco Modigliani. "Dividend Policy, Growth and the Valuation of Shares," *Journal of Business*, XXXIV (October, 1961), pp. 411–33.

[2] See Myron J. Gordon. "Optimal Investment and Financing Policy," *Journal of Finance*, XVIII (May, 1963), pp. 264–72; and "The Savings Investment and Valuation of a Corporation," *Review of Economics and Statistics*, XLIV (February, 1962), pp. 37–51. See also Houng-Yhi Chen, "Valuation Under Uncertainty," *Journal of Finance and Quantitative Analysis*, II (September, 1967), pp. 313–25, and Robert C. Higgins, "Time, Uncertainty and Corporate Dividend Policy," unpublished working paper, University of Washington.

investor with a desire for consumption in excess of current dividends will prefer incremental current dividends to capital gains. Some institutional investors may favor dividends, owing to legal constraints or tax considerations. For example, universities often prefer dividend income to capital gains on endowment investments because of restrictions on expenditures of capital gains. For corporate investors, inter-company dividends are taxed at rates below that applicable to capital gains. However, the more favorable tax rate on capital gains relative to that on dividends for most investors creates a powerful bias in favor of the retention of earnings.[3] Thus, the first three factors suggest a preference for current dividends as opposed to capital gains while the tax effect favors the latter. Whether there is a net preference among investors for current dividends as opposed to capital gains or vice versa depends on the combined influence of these factors.

Flotation costs and the necessity to "underprice" a stock issue are factors tending to favor earnings retention rather than dividend payout and concurrent new equity financing, *ceteris paribus*. Under the assumption that the investment decision and capital structure of the firm are given, dividend payments must be offset exactly by new equity issues when desired investment exceeds internally generated funds. Flotation costs may be significant if the equity financing alternative is chosen. In addition, the firm may face a downward sloping demand curve for new shares when it appeals to existing investors to increase their holdings or tries to attract new investors. Lintner contends that with divergent investor expectations, the equilibrium price of shares will decline as the firm sells additional shares to offset current dividends.[4] With underpricing of this sort, there will be additional dilution of earnings, which, in turn, will result in a lower share value than would obtain in the absence of such underpricing. In sum, any net preference among investors for current dividends, as opposed to the capital gains associated with retention of earnings, is subject to the countervailing influence of flotation costs and underpricing which make new security issues a more expensive form of equity financing than retained earnings.

If there existed a net preference among investors for capital gains as opposed to dividends, then the firm's dividend policy would be a residual decision determined by the profitability of its investments. If we invoke the assumption of an investment decision which is exogenously given, then only if the firm has earnings remaining after financing all "acceptable" investment opportunities would it distribute dividends to stockholders.

Justification for paying a dividend in excess of unused earnings requires a net preference among investors for current dividends as opposed to capital gains,

[3] For an empirical test dealing with this notion, see Edwin J. Elton and Martin J. Gruber, "Marginal Stockholder Tax Rates and the Clientele Effect," *Review of Economics and Statistics*, LII (February, 1970), pp. 68–74.

[4] John Linter, "Dividends, Earnings, Leverage, Stock Prices and the Supply of Capital to Corporations," *Review of Economics and Statistics*, XLIV (August, 1962), pp. 256–59.

and this net preference must more than offset the difference in "cost" between retained earnings and new equity financing. For example, consider a firm which has a capital structure consisting entirely of equity and has acceptable investment opportunities exactly sufficient to exhaust its earnings. If dividends are irrelevant, representing only the distribution of unused funds after all investment opportunities were financed, the firm obviously would pay no dividend. If it did pay a dividend, the payment would have to be financed with new equity at a "cost" disadvantage relative to retained earnings.

Contrarily, if there exists among investors a net preference for current dividends as opposed to capital gains which more than offsets the "cost" disadvantage of new equity financing, share price could be raised at least initially by increasing the dividend payout ratio. This phenomenon would be due to investors placing considerable importance at first on the resolution of uncertainty and other factors favoring current dividends relative to the differential tax treatment of dividends and capital gains. If, as the payout ratio increases, the importance of the former factors diminishes relative to the tax disadvantage of current dividends, the tax disadvantage might cause a change in the net preference of investors toward capital gains as opposed to current dividends, implying an optimal dividend policy. If the firm had earnings remaining after commitments to all acceptable investment projects, it would distribute a greater portion of its earnings than in the case above.

EMPIRICAL TEST METHODOLOGY

In this paper, we specify a cross-section regression model and suggest a method for treating inter-company differences in new equity financing.[5] The valuation of firms which both pay dividends and engage in new equity financing is compared with that of other companies in an industry sample. We hypothesize that the value of the first set of companies is greater than the second, other factors being equal, if investors have a systematic net preference for current dividends relative to capital gains and this net preference more than offsets the "cost" disadvantage of new equity financing relative to the retention of earnings. In lieu of new equity financing, the first set of companies could reduce or eliminate cash dividends, thereby retaining a greater portion of earnings. Instead, these companies behave in a manner that is consistent with the belief that there is a net preference of investors for current dividends as opposed to capital gains and that this net preference exceeds the difference in "cost" described above. In

[5] As an alternative to a cross-section approach, Fischer Black and Myron Scholes, "Dividend Yields and Common Stock Returns: A New Methodology," Working Paper, Sloan School of Management, MIT, September, 1970, employed a time series methodology to test the effect of differential dividend yields on common stock returns. They found that dividend yield was insignificant in explaining security returns.

view of the greater cost of new equity financing, a finding of no essential difference in valuation between the two sets of companies may be considered weak support of the idea of a net preference of investors for current dividends as opposed to capital gains. However, such an inference would require a reasonably well-specified valuation model.

We begin with a traditional share-price model, which represents a solution in price of a capital market equilibrium equation under idealized uncertainty: share price, P_0, equals the present value of a future stream of expected dividends, discounted at a market rate k that depends on the risk-free rate and the riskiness of the security.[6] The share-price model implies that the ratio of current price to earnings, P_0/E_0, is a function of expected growth rate in dividends, g, the dividend payout ratio, D_0/E_0, and a measure of risk of the security, R:

$$P_0/E_0 = f(g, D_0/E_0, R). \tag{1}$$

Models of this general form have been formulated for empirical purposes by Malkiel and Cragg, Bower and Bower, and Brigham and Gordon.[7] We propose to use this model as a point of departure to investigate whether firms which pay dividends and engage in new equity financing have higher price-earning ratios than other firms in an industry sample.

Two samples of firms are employed: the 86 electric utilities in the continental U.S. which are included on the COMPUSTAT utility data tape; and 39 companies in the electronics and electronic components industry as listed on the

---

[6] The equilibrium equation under certainty is as follows:

$$k_t = D_t/P_t + d(\log P_t)/dt.$$

Under conditions of idealized uncertainty, k_t is assumed to be a constant rate of return for all securities of "equivalent risk." A solution of this equation for current market price P_0 is

$$P_0 = \int_0^\infty D_t e^{-kt}\, dt,$$

the familiar formulation of price as the present value of expected future dividends discounted at k. In the special case of "golden age" growth at rate g from the current dividend level D_0, one can divide both sides by current earnings E_0 to obtain

$$P_0/E_0 = (D_0/E_0) \int_0^\infty e^{(g-k)t}\, dt.$$

The implication is that P_0/E_0 varies directly with dividend payout and growth, and inversely with risk, as reflected in the discount rate, k.

[7] See Burton G. Malkiel and John Cragg. "Expectations and the Structure of Share Prices," *American Economic Review*, LX (September, 1970), pp. 601–17; Richard S. Bower and Dorothy H. Bower, "Risk and the Valuation of Common Stock," *Journal of Political Economy*, LXXVII (May–June, 1969), pp. 349–62; and Eugene F. Brigham and Myron J. Gordon, "Leverage, Dividend Policy, and the Cost of Capital," *Journal of Finance*, XXIII (March, 1968), pp. 85–103.

COMPUSTAT industrial data tape. The companies in the two samples are shown in Table 5. The industries were chosen on the basis of frequency of new equity issues and our desire to test both a regulated and an unregulated industry.

TESTS IN THE ELECTRIC UTILITY INDUSTRY

For the electric utility industry, two regression models were tested. The first reflects structural model (1) in the following form:

$$P_0/E_0 = a_0 + a_1(g) + a_2(D_0/E_0) + a_3(\text{Lev}) + u \qquad (2)$$

where

$P_0/E_0 =$ Closing market price in 1968 divided by average earnings per share for 1967 and 1968, adjusted to a consistent "flow through" accounting basis by adding back deferred taxes to reported earnings for each firm.[8]

$g =$ Expected growth rate, measured by the compound annual rate of growth in assets per share for 1960 through 1968, where the first three years and last three years were each normalized and the growth rate computed for the resulting six-year span.

$D_0/E_0 =$ Dividend payout, measured by cash dividends in 1968 divided by earnings in 1968, adjusted to a consistent "flow through" basis by adding back deferred taxes to reported earnings.

$\text{Lev} =$ Financial risk, measured by interest charges divided by the difference of operating revenues and operating expenses.

$u =$ Error term.

A number of alternative historical growth rates were considered as measures of expected future growth in earnings and dividends. The best measure for both industries, in terms of correlation with price-earnings ratios in 1968, was the compound growth rate of assets per share. Capital market theory suggests that an appropriate risk measure is a company parameter, called beta by Sharpe, representing the slope of a regression of returns from a firm's shares on returns

---

[8] Models (2) and (3) were also estimated with average (unadjusted) reported earnings in the denominator of the dependent variable. The resulting R^2 was lower; however, the coefficient estimates were not materially different. Hence, the conclusions of this analysis were the same as those drawn below.

from a market index over comparable holding periods.[9] Recent results by Malkiel,[10] however, suggest that for utility firms a flow measure of leverage is a satisfactory proxy for the over-all risk of the security.[11] Accordingly, we shall use this measure inasmuch as our purpose is not to test for risk but to avoid specification bias. The results of estimation of equation (2) are shown in Table 1. All coefficient estimates have the correct sign and the growth and leverage estimates are significant.[12]

TABLE 1.   REGRESSION ESTIMATES FROM MODEL (2):
ELECTRIC UTILITIES

	CONSTANT	g	D_0/E_0	LEV
Regression coefficient	9.37	114.	7.02	-18.2
Standard error	(3.11)	(17.1)	(3.87)	(7.06)
t-ratio	3.01	6.66	1.82	-2.58
$R^2 = .36$	$F = 15.5(3;82)$			

Dependent variable: P_0/E_0
Sample size: 86 firms

Of the 86 utility firms, 37 had one or more new equity issues during the five-year period, 1964–68. New equity financing is defined here as the sale of common stock or securities convertible into common stock where the proceeds represent new money. All firms in the sample paid a dividend in every year. As a first test of the extent to which firms which both pay dividends and raise new equity differ in value from other firms in the industry, we employed a t-test of the two sets of residuals. The mean residual for firms with new equity issues was larger than that for firms which did not issue stock (.08 versus $-.06$). This difference, however, is not significant, as reflected by a t-ratio of 0.23. Therefore, we are unable to reject the null hypothesis that these two sets of companies come from

[9] William F. Sharpe. "A Simplified Model for Portfolio Analysis," *Management Science*, IX (January, 1963), pp. 122–136.

[10] Burton G. Malkiel. "The Valuation of Public Utility Equities," *Bell Journal of Economics and Management Science*, I (Spring, 1970), pp. 143–160.

[11] An operating risk variable like that used in electronics and electronic components industry regressions was added to equation (2). As the estimated coefficient was quite insignificant and of positive sign, it was excluded in the final run.

[12] The positive sign for the dividend payout variable may be due to spurious correlation. Both the dependent and the independent variable contain earnings per share in the denominator. To the extent that errors of measurement are independent of the numerators, a positive bias in the regression coefficient for the dividend-payout variable would result. However, with a correlation coefficient for the two variables of $-.01$ in the utility sample, spurious correlation is unlikely to be a serious problem. For a discussion of spurious correlation, see Edwin Kuh and John R. Meyer, "Correlation and Regression Estimates When the Data are Ratios," *Econometrica*, XXIII (October, 1955), pp. 400–16.

the same population. As discussed earlier, given the "cost" disadvantage of new equity financing relative to retained earnings, a finding of no essential difference in value between the two sets of companies gives weak support to the idea of a net preference for current dividends as opposed to capital gains.

The prevalence of new issues among public utilities enables us to devise a cardinal measure of new equity financing for firms in this industry. For each firm, "new issue ratio" (NIR) was computed which represents total common shares, including the fully converted equivalent of convertible issues, divided by total shares outstanding at year-end 1968. The firms were grouped in five categories by NIR, as shown in Table 2. This table indicates that the mean dividend payout is slightly higher among those firms in groups D and E—companies which have the highest new issue ratios.

To assess the impact of level of new issue financing on value, we added four dummy variables F_a through F_d corresponding to NIR groups A through D in Table 2. A coefficient for the last group, F_e, cannot be estimated simultaneously with the other four dummy-variable coefficients, as it is a linear function of the other four and would result in singularity. For each firm, the value of the dummy variable representing its NIR group is one and the values of the remaining dummy variables are zero. For example, the value of F_b would be one for a firm whose NIR falls between .001 and .05 (Group B) and the value of the other three variables for this firm would be zero. The resulting valuation model is:

$$P_0/E_0 = a_0 + a_1(g) + a_2(D_0/E_0) + a_3(\text{Lev}) + a_4(F_a)$$
$$+ a_5(F_b) + a_6(F_c) + a_7(F_d) + u$$
$$(3)$$

At high levels of new equity financing, we would expect underpricing effects and flotation costs to be relatively important, resulting in a negative coefficient. The greater the amount of new equity financing, the greater its percentage "cost" is likely to be relative to retained earnings.

TABLE 2.   NEW ISSUE RATIOS (NIR) OF ELECTRIC UTILITY FIRMS

	A	B	C	D	E
NIR: New issues/shares outstanding, 1968	0	.001–.05	.05–.10	.10–.15	greater than .15
Number of firms	49	16	11	6	4
Mean dividend payout, D_0/E_0	.681	.679	.678	.703	.728

Regression results for the estimation of model (3) are shown in Table 3. The estimated coefficients of growth, dividend payout, and leverage are significant and have correct signs. The coefficient estimate for F_b is positive and significant,

TABLE 3. REGRESSION ESTIMATES FROM MODEL (3): ELECTRIC UTILITIES 1968

	CONSTANT	g	D_0/E_0	Lev	DUMMY VARIABLES REPRESENTING LEVEL OF NEW EQUITY FINANCING			
					F_a	F_b	F_c	F_d
Regression coefficient	6.45	115	8.03	−15.3	1.86	3.23	1.26	0.89
Standard error	(3.75)	(17.4)	(3.85)	(7.39)	(1.40)	(1.44)	(1.50)	(1.64)
t-ratio	1.72	6.60	2.08	−2.22	1.33	2.25	0.84	0.54

$R^2 = .42$

$F = 7.04 (8; 77)$

Sample Size: 86 firms

Bi-variate correlation coefficients:

	F_a	F_b	F_c	F_d	F_e
Between growth (g) and	−.32	.15	.16	.14	.06
Between dividend payout (D_0/E_0) and	−.04	−.03	−.02	.05	.12

supporting the notion that at moderate levels of new equity financing, the net preference of investors for dividends more than offsets the "cost" disadvantage of new issues relative to the retention of earnings. Coefficient estimates for the other three dummy variables are positive but not significant. The coefficients decline with increasing employment of new equity financing, from group B to C to D. When we omit any one of the four dummy variables discussed above and add a dummy variable for the last NIR group, E, the estimate of its coefficient is found to be negative. This is consistent with the "cost" disadvantage of new equity financing relative to the retention of earnings widening with high levels of new equity financing.[13]

Two caveats seem obvious. First, the results for one year do not permit us to generalize beyond the present findings for 1968. Secondly, with less than one-half of the total variance explained, we cannot be sure that all factors other than those being investigated are held constant. Criticisms of specification, as to omitted variables, and measurement errors may be applicable to these results.[14]

TESTS IN THE ELECTRONICS AND ELECTRONIC COMPONENTS INDUSTRY

For tests with a sample of firms in the electronics and electronic components industry, the following regression form of structural valuation equation (1) was employed.[15]

$$P_0/E_0 = a_0 + a_1(g) + a_2(D_0/E_0) + a_3(\text{Lev}) + a_4(\text{OR}) + u \qquad (4)$$

[13] It is conceivable that the new issue variable captures an aspect of growth not measured in variable g. As indicated near the bottom of Table 2, the correlation coefficient between the new issue variables for firms that engage in external equity financing (F_b through F_e) and the growth variables are small and positive, ranging from .06 to .15. Except for the four firms in group E, the bi-variate correlations between the new issue variables and dividend payout are consistently small, less than .05.

[14] For a discussion of such biases, see Irwin Friend and Marshall Puckett, "Dividends and Stock Prices," *American Economic Review*, LIV (September, 1964), pp. 656–82.

[15] Because the dependent variable in the regression model is the price/earnings ratio, it was necessary to exclude companies in this sample whose average earnings were negative in 1967 or 1968, or whose earnings were abnormally low during this period of time. The latter was effected by excluding companies whose price/earnings ratios were 60 or above. While the use of 60 is arbitrary, some upper limit was necessary in view of the erratic earnings performance of some of the companies in the electronics and electronic components industry. Also excluded were companies whose average market price per share during 1967 and 1968 was less than $10. Finally, companies whose growth in assets per share was negative were eliminated because, in all three cases, the shrinkage in assets was due to factors that would not be expected to occur in the future. For these firms, historical growth in assets per share would be a poor proxy for the expected growth in the stream of future income available to stockholders. The companies in this sample are shown in Table 5.

where

P_0/E_0 = Average of high and low market price per share in 1968 divided by average earnings per share in 1967 and 1968.

g = Expected growth rate, measured by compound annual rate of growth of assets per share for 1960 through 1968, where the first three years and the last three years were each normalized and the growth rate computed for the resulting six-year span.[16]

D_0/E_0 = Dividend payout, measured by the average of earnings per share in 1967 and 1968 divided by the average of dividends per share in 1967 and 1968.

Lev = Financial risk, measured by long-term debt plus preferred stock divided by net worth as of the end of 1968.

OR = Operating risk, measured by the standard error for the regression of operating earnings per share on time for 1960 through 1968, using a second degree polynomial equation, over average operating earnings per share for nine years.

u = Error term.

In order to test whether companies which both pay dividends and engage in new equity financing differ significantly in value from other companies in the sample, we test the hypothesis that the two sets of residuals come from the same population. The first set consisted of companies which both paid dividends throughout the period 1964–1968 and issued new equity one or more times during the period; the second set comprised all other firms in the sample. New equity financing again included common stock and securities convertible into stock.[17] As only seven companies of the 39 in this industry both paid dividends and issued new equity, it did not seem feasible to develop a cardinal measure, such as the new issue ratio employed with the utility sample. Owing to this small number of companies, only crude insight into the question of the relevance of dividends is possible with this industry sample.

---

[16] For Solitron Devices, the growth in sales per share for the five year period 1964–1968, was employed. As this company was started in 1959, the percentage growth in assets per share from 1960 to 1968 was much larger than could be expected in the future. In addition, the acquisition of a division of another company for stock in 1967 resulted in an extraordinary increase in assets per share. For these reasons, growth in sales per share over the most recent five years was felt to be more representative of expected future growth.

[17] New issue data were obtained from the *Investment Dealers Digest*.

The results using regression equation (4) are shown in Table 4.[18] We see that the variables employed explain about one-half of the variance in the price-earnings ratios. As expected, the growth variable is highly significant and positive. None of the other explanatory variables is significant,[19] and the leverage variable has an unexpected positive sign. The nonparametric Mann-Whitney U test is used to test whether the residuals for the seven companies that paid dividends and engaged in new equity financing were from the same population as the residuals for the other 32 companies in the sample.[20] This test revealed that the bulk of the first set of residuals was higher than the bulk of the second set. However, at the customary .05 level of significance, we are unable to reject the null hypothesis that the two sets of residuals came from the same population.

TABLE 4.   REGRESSION ESTIMATES FROM MODEL (4): ELECTRONICS AND ELECTRONIC COMPONENTS, 1968

	CONSTANT	g	D_0/E_0	Lev	RISK
Regression Coefficient	16.87	56.68	1.08	2.72	−2.31
Standard Error	(2.21)	(10.35)	(4.56)	(8.17)	(2.47)
t-Ratio	7.64	5.47	0.24	0.33	−0.93
$R^2 = .52$	$F = 9.33(4; 34)$				

Dependent variable: P_0/E_0
Sample size: 39 firms

While the evidence does not support the idea that companies which pay dividends and engage in equity financing have a higher value than other companies, *ceteris paribus*, it is not inconsistent with the notion that investors at the margin prefer current dividends to capital gains despite the latter's tax advantage for most investors. Because of the "cost" disadvantage of financing with new equity as opposed to retained earnings, any net preference for current dividends must exceed this "cost" disadvantage in order for the financing of dividend payments with new equity to be a thing of value. Therefore, a finding of a neutral effect with respect to value is consistent with there being a net preference by investors for current dividends as opposed to capital gains.

[18] In general, homoscedasticity for the variance of the error terms prevailed when price-earnings ratios were regressed against the growth variable. Equation (4) was also run in logarithmic form; as the R^2 was somewhat lower, these results are not shown.

[19] As discussed for the utility industry sample, the positive sign for the dividend payout variable may be due to spurious correlation. However, since the correlation coefficient for dividend payout and dependent variables is only 0.01 in this electronics industry sample, it is unlikely that spurious correlation is a serious problem. See footnote 12.

[20] This test is described in Sidney Siegel, *Nonparametric Statistics* (New York: McGraw-Hill, 1956), pp. 116–27.

At best, however, the results in Table 4 offer very weak support for this notion. The proportion of explained variation is not large enough to assure us that the variables other than expected growth are correctly measured or that other relevant variables have not been omitted. The issue of new equity and payment of dividends may be a proxy for other factors affecting value. Moreover, the small number of companies which fell into this classification, namely seven, does not permit us to make broad generalizations. Thus, the insights provided with this industry sample are crude at best.

CONCLUSIONS

The methodology in this study compares the valuation of firms which both pay dividends and engage in new equity financing with other firms in an industry sample. For electric utility firms in 1968, the findings indicate that share value is not adversely affected by new equity financing in the presence of cash dividends, except for those firms in the highest new-issue group. This evidence is consistent with the existence of a net preference for current dividends, despite the differential tax advantage of capital gains for most investors. For electric utilities, except those in the highest new-issue group, this net preference for dividends appears to offset the flotation costs and underpricing effects that make new equity a more costly form of financing than the retention of earnings. The findings indicate that the "cost" disadvantage of new equity issues relative to retained earnings widens as relatively large amounts of new equity are raised, so that the payment of dividends through excessive equity financing reduces share price. For firms in the electronics and electronic components industry, a significant relationship between new equity financing and value was not demonstrated. While the evidence is less than conclusive, the findings are consistent with the existence of a net preference by investors for current dividends as opposed to capital gains, assuming that dividends at the margin are financed with new equity.

The generalizations that can be made from these findings are limited, as tests were undertaken in only two industries for a single year. Moreover, the regression models explained only about one half of the total variance and exhibited other empirical shortcomings. Nevertheless, we feel that the proposed approach of comparing companies that both pay dividends and engage in new equity financing with other companies in a sample offers considerable promise in testing for the relevance of dividends. In a world of market imperfections, it is useful to view separately the net preference of investors for dividends or for capital gains and the fact that new equity financing is more "costly" than the retention of earnings. As additional years are tested and the number of companies investigated is expanded, greater insight into the effect of dividend policy on value may be gained.

TABLE 5. SAMPLES OF COMPANIES

ELECTRIC UTILITY INDUSTRY

Allegheny Power System, Inc.
American Electric Power Co.
Arizona Public Service Co.
Atlantic City Electric Co.
Baltimore Gas & Electric Co.
Boston Edison Co.
Carolina Power & Light Co.
Central Hudson Gas & Electric
Central Illinois Light
Central Illinois Public Service Co.
Central Louisiana Electric
Central Maine Power Co.
Central & Southwest Corp.
Cincinnati Gas & Electric Co.
Cleveland Electric Illuminating Co.
Columbus & Southern Ohio Electric Co.
Commonwealth Edison Co.
Consolidated Edison Co.
Consumers Power Co.
Dayton Power & Light Co.
Delmarva Power & Light Co.
Detroit Edison Co.
Duke Power Co.
Duquesne Light Co.
El Paso Electric Co.
Florida Power Corp.
Florida Power & Light Co.
General Public Utilities Corp.
Gulf States Utilities Co.
Houston Lighting & Power Co.
Idaho Power Co.
Illinois Power Co.
Indianapolis Power & Light
Interstate Power Co.
Iowa-Illinois Gas & Electric
Iowa Power & Light
Iowa Public Service Co.
Kansas City Power & Light Co.
Kansas Gas & Electric
Kentucky Utilities Co.
Long Island Lighting Co.
Louisville Gas & Electric Co.
Middle South Utilities, Inc.

Minnesota Power & Light
Montana-Dakota Utilities
Montana Power Co.
Nevada Power Co.
New England Electric System
New England Gas & Electric
New York State Electric & Gas Co.
Niagara Mohawk Power Corp.
Northeast Utilities
Northern Indiana Public Service Co.
Northern States Power Co. (Minn.)
Ohio Edison Co.
Oklahoma Gas & Electric Co.
Orange & Rockland Utilities
Pacific Gas & Electric Co.
Pacific Power & Light
Pennsylvania Power & Light
Philadelphia Electric Co.
Potomac Electric Power
Public Service Co. of Colorado
Public Service Co. of Indiana, Inc.
Public Service Co. of New Hampshire
Public Service Co. of New Mexico
Public Service Electric & Gas Co.
Puget Sound Power & Light
Rochester Gas & Electric
San Diego Gas & Electric Co.
Sierra Pacific Power Co.
South Carolina Electric & Gas Co.
Southern California Edison Co.
Southern Co.
Southwestern Public Service Co.
Tampa Electric Co.
Texas Utilities Co.
Toledo Edison Co.
Tucson Gas & Electric Co.
Union Electric Co.
United Illuminating Co.
Utah Power & Light
Virginia Electric & Power Co.
Washington Water Power
Wisconsin Electric Power Co.
Wisconsin Public Service

ELECTRONICS AND ELECTRONIC COMPONENTS INDUSTRY

AMP Inc.
Alloys Unlimited
Ambac Industries
Ampex Corp.
Avnet Inc.
Burndy Corp.
Collins R
Conrac Corp.
CTS Corp.
Dynamics Corp. of America
Edo Corp.
Electronic Assistance Corp.
Electronic Engnr. Cal.
General Instrument
General Signal
Genisco Technology
Gulton Industries
Hazeltine Corp.
Hewlett Packard
Hydrometals Inc.

IMC Magnetics
Lear Siegler
P.R. Mallory Co.
Microdot, Inc.
Microwave Associates
Nytronics, Inc.
Oak Electro/netics
Oxford Electric
Pacific Industries
Pepi Inc.
Raytheon Co.
Sanders Associates
Sola Basic
Solitron Devices
Sparton Corp.
Systron-Donner Corp.
Tektronix
Vernitron Corp.
Victoreen Leece Neville

QUESTIONS

1. Explain the probable advantages of a relatively high payout for the firm, although frequent common stock offerings may be necessary.
2. Describe and discuss the advantages of the low dividend payout such that, over time, it is rare for the firm to issue common stock for funds for capital investments.
3. What were the conclusions of this study?
4. Comment on the notion that investors might apply higher discount rates on dividends, the more distant they are in the future.
5. Many large firms pay a stabilized stream of dividends. Do you believe that it would be detrimental to the value of a firm's stock if its dividends were serially unstable? Explain.
6. Do the conclusions of this study carry any implication regarding the cost for a large firm to stabilize dividends? Explain.

23

Samuel S. Stewart, Jr.

Should a Corporation Repurchase Its Own Stock?

Stock repurchase is the opposite of a stock flotation, and it is an alternative to a cash distribution (dividend). It has always been an intriguing issue whether a corporation repurchasing its own stock was a signal that those in the position to know consider this stock to be undervalued. If they do so, and if they are correct, investment in that firm's stock when repurchasing is underway should produce abnormally high returns. Professor Stewart's study indicates that such has been the case when relatively long holding periods were used.

I. INTRODUCTION

During recent years an increasing number of companies have repurchased shares of their own common stock. About ten years ago, Guthart (9) compiled data indicating that by 1963 the volume of shares repurchased by companies listed on the New York Stock Exchange had risen to an annual level of 26 million shares, representing an approximate dollar value of $1.3 billion. Exhibit I presents an update of Guthart's data. Not only has the upward trend continued, but in 1973 the volume of repurchasing rose to the level of 143 million shares, representing a dollar value of $4.9 billion, a figure roughly equal to the $5.5 billion net equity purchases of pension funds.

Although corporate managers frequently state that a major motivation for repurchasing is the divergence of the market price of their firm's stock from its true value,[1] the existence of such price-value divergences and/or the ability to detect and profitably exploit such divergences has frequently been ques-

Source. Reprinted by permission from *Journal of Finance*, June 1976, pp. 911–921. Samuel Stewart is professor of finance at the University of Utah.

[1] In an interview study, Guthart (9) found presumed under-valuation to be an important motivation for repurchase. Other frequently mentioned motives were distribution to shareholders at capital gains tax rates of excessive cash in relation to profitable investment opportunities, reduction of the equity component of the capital structure, avoidance of earnings per share dilution in conjunction with acquisitions, options, convertibles, and warrants, and maintenance of control by elimination of unwanted stockholders.

EXHIBIT I.   REPURCHASING ACTIVITY OF NYSE COMPANIES

Year	Gross Shares Repurchased During Year	Shares Reissued During Year	Net Shares Repurchased During Year
1963	29,277,781	18,386,249	10,891,532
1964	44,031,442	19,697,371	24,334,071
1965	45,155,977	21,518,006	23,637,971
1966	46,112,064	24,196,416	21,915,648
1967	27,272,127	28,996,785	−1,724,658
1968	44,006,311	25,578,137	18,428,174
1969	63,992,471	30,229,298	33,763,173
1970	50,633,213	46,668,340	3,964,873
1971	40,748,500	25,276,156	15,472,344
1972	43,883,724	44,326,532	−442,808
1973	143,780,086	35,551,533	108,228,553
1974	90,379,654	62,742,129	27,637,525

Source.   New York Stock Exchange monthly report of changes in treasury stock.

tioned. Numerous academic studies have presented evidence indicating that securities markets are reasonably efficient, with the result that market prices are approximately reflective of underlying values.[2] If such evidence is correct, the strategic benefits of repurchasing may be diminished. However, there is some indication that corporate insiders possess special abilities in detecting and exploiting price-value divergences.[3] If such abilities can be used in effecting repurchase decisions, repurchasing may be a worthwhile corporate strategy.

Unfortunately, few studies have directly examined the existence and exploitability of price-value divergences of repurchasing companies. The major empirical study [Young (19)] presents data indicating that the stock market performance of firms subsequent to repurchase is roughly equal to the performance of the general market.[4] Unfortunately, Young's study suffers from some methodological weaknesses. In particular, it only examines performance during the year following the announcement of the decision to repurchase via a cash tender offer and the rates of return on the common stock subsequent to repurchases are not adjusted for risk. The purpose of this paper is to correct some of those weaknesses by examining performance subsequent to all types of repurchase (cash tender offers, private buyouts, open market purchases, etc.) over several time periods, thus allowing more time for pos-

[2] A good summary of these studies may be found in Fama, "Efficient Capital Markets: A Review of Theory and Empirical Work," Journal of Finance, May, 1970.

[3] These studies include those of Jaffee (10), Lorie and Niederhoffer (12), Pratt and DeVere (15), and Wu (18).

[4] A more recent study by Nantell and Finnerty (14) presents evidence confirming Young's findings.

sible price-value divergences to be eliminated. Due to funding limitations, no attempt was made to risk-adjust the realized rates of return. However, since this study examines investment performance by creating portfolios of repurchasing companies and since these sample portfolios are rather large (over 500 companies in several cases), it might be argued that the riskiness of such a portfolio would approximate that of the general market and that risk-adjusted rates of return would be approximately equal to the observed rates of return.[5]

II. METHODOLOGY

The data used to examine the effectiveness of repurchase decisions were drawn from the Compustat Annual Industrial Tapes covering the period 1954–1973. The 1973 data, while present on the tapes, were not usable. The 1954 data were discarded as a result of our method for determining the amount of repurchase activity. The repurchase activity for each year was computed by dividing the net number of shares repurchased during the year by the number of shares outstanding at the end of the previous year. In order to filter out "noise" on the tapes, any company repurchasing less than .25% of its shares was deemed to fall in the non-repurchase category. Companies engaging in repurchase were placed into intervals indicating the degree of their activity. Originally, the companies were placed into 5% intervals (i.e., .25%–5.24%, 5.25%–10.24%, etc.); however, these intervals proved to be too wide since more than 95% of the repurchasing companies fell into the first (.25%–5.24%) interval in most years. In the final study, repurchasing companies were put into six 1% intervals (i.e., .25%–1.24%, 1.25%–2.24%, 2.25%–3.24%, 3.25%–4.24%, 4.25%–5.24%, and 5.25%+), which produced a reasonable number of firms within each interval. Exhibit II provides a yearly summary of the companies in each repurchase classification on both a non-cumulative and cumulative basis.

For the companies within each interval, a price index was calculated. The initial value of each price index was computed as the average price at the end of the year during which repurchase occurred (unweighted by number of shares) of the companies within the interval.[6] The value of each index was also

---

[5] It should be mentioned that such portfolios, while large, are not randomly selected. If repurchasing companies were found to have unusual market risk characteristics, not adjusting for risk would bias our performance findings. Specifically, since the 1955–1972 sample period was one of generally rising, though volatile, markets, the results obtained might have been accounted for by repurchasing companies also being high "beta" companies.

[6] This procedure differs from that of previous studies, including Nantell and Finnerty (14) and Young (19), which examine price behavior during the months surrounding the announcement of the intention to repurchase. While necessitated by the format of the Compustat data, our procedure probably more accurately reflects the investment results available to firms, which are constrained to take repurchase "positions" slowly and/or with publicity and generally to hold those positions for an indefinite, but long, time period.

EXHIBIT II. DISTRIBUTION OF REPURCHASING AND NON-REPURCHASING FIRMS

Number of Firms Not Repurchasing During Year			Number of Firms in Each Repurchasing Interval					
			.25–1.24%	1.25–2.24%	2.25–3.24%	3.25–4.24%	4.25–5.24%	5.25%+
1955	272	1955	7	4	3	1	1	4
1956	278	1956	21	3	7	2	0	3
1957	288	1957	42	4	2	0	2	1
1958	298	1958	53	1	2	3	1	5
1959	308	1959	70	3	1	1	1	3
1960	572	1960	89	13	6	0	2	6
1961	634	1961	113	18	7	1	1	5
1962	706	1962	165	22	8	4	8	12
1963	741	1963	215	31	10	6	6	12
1964	768	1964	293	32	16	7	7	15
1965	795	1965	361	25	14	7	3	20
1966	838	1966	432	34	12	11	4	20
1967	873	1967	512	17	5	1	3	14
1968	915	1968	544	17	4	4	4	5
1969	939	1969	566	33	11	11	5	12
1970	946	1970	616	54	21	12	4	21
1971	957	1971	706	36	6	4	3	16
1972	960	1972	704	46	23	11	8	28

	Cumulative Number of Repurchasing Firms					
	.25%+	1.25%+	2.25%+	3.25%+	4.25%+	5.25%+
1955	20	13	9	6	5	4
1956	36	15	12	5	3	3
1957	51	9	5	3	3	1
1958	65	12	11	9	6	5
1959	79	9	6	5	4	3
1960	116	27	14	8	8	6
1961	145	32	14	7	6	5
1962	219	54	32	24	20	12
1963	280	65	34	24	18	12
1964	370	77	45	29	22	15
1965	430	69	44	30	23	20
1966	513	81	47	35	24	20
1967	552	40	23	18	17	14
1968	578	34	17	13	9	5
1969	638	72	39	28	17	12
1970	728	112	58	37	25	21
1971	771	65	29	23	19	16
1972	820	116	70	47	36	28

computed on the basis of closing prices for each subsequent year during the sample period. Finally, each series of index numbers was adjusted to an initial value of 100. Exhibit III provides a sample of the resulting index "triangles."

The index numbers were compared at various time intervals following the repurchase years to determine the effectiveness of various repurchasing

EXHIBIT III.   PERFORMANCE INDEX TRIANGLES

Started		1955	1956	1957	1958	1959	1960	1961	1962	1963
		Index of Companies That Are Not in the Repurchase Group								
Y	1955	100.000								
e	1956	106.985	100.000							
a	1957	84.267	78.846	100.000						
r	1958	126.058	118.373	149.989	100.000					
	1959	145.157	136.353	173.254	115.324	100.000				
	1960	132.737	125.126	159.650	106.798	93.269	100.000			
	1961	159.763	150.951	192.099	128.784	112.375	120.064	100.000		
	1962	129.063	121.857	154.709	103.668	90.211	93.132	76.889	100.000	
	1963	150.984	142.506	181.479	121.533	106.328	107.998	88.879	115.160	100.000
	1964	170.805	160.569	204.190	136.733	118.746	121.320	99.465	129.006	112.329
	1965	213.918	200.918	255.508	171.520	150.181	154.173	126.125	164.705	144.379
	1966	194.039	182.520	231.629	156.072	136.937	141.799	115.675	150.850	131.970
	1967	246.772	233.342	298.129	201.366	177.897	198.297	164.282	218.095	191.940
	1968	271.293	256.179	329.313	222.524	194.987	227.463	191.093	255.697	226.089
	1969	232.413	218.829	280.233	189.408	164.914	179.409	150.795	201.143	177.687
	1970	208.567	196.075	252.322	170.477	147.559	156.254	130.010	172.018	151.557
	1971	240.231	226.274	291.375	197.266	171.507	178.100	149.199	198.118	174.194
	1972	268.930	253.463	325.406	220.026	191.719	194.742	162.521	216.104	189.063

Started		1964	1965	1966	1967	1968	1969	1970	1971	1972
Y	1964	100.000								
e	1965	128.800	100.000							
a	1966	117.831	91.123	100.000						
r	1967	172.628	135.118	150.221	100.000					
	1968	203.949	159.797	179.110	119.795	100.000				
	1969	160.196	125.234	141.178	94.861	79.469	100.000			
	1970	136.269	106.588	119.283	79.530	66.468	83.737	100.000		
	1971	157.097	123.206	137.622	92.158	77.580	97.864	117.097	100.000	
	1972	170.540	133.940	149.243	99.819	84.199	106.333	126.976	108.692	100.000

strategies (differentiated by amount of repurchase activity) in contrast to not repurchasing. Some difficulty arose in attempting to assess the statistical significance of such comparisons. The number of securities in each index varied widely (the range was from 1 to 704—see Exhibit II), many samples being too small to compute sample characteristics, such as variances, with any hope of reliability. Since we made no attempt to adjust for risk, it does not seem likely that these sample variances could be presumed to be equal. Further, controversy still exists as to the exact nature of large sample stock price distributions. For these reasons we turned to a non-parametric test to assess the significance of the observed comparisons. The particular test chosen was the Wilcoxon Matched-Pairs Signed-Ranks Test, which requires only that the sample data be measurable on an ordinal scale. While it is likely that some information has been lost by reverting to a non-parametric test, the

EXHIBIT III (continued)

Started		1955	1956	1957	1958	1959	1960	1961	1962	1963
		Index of Repurchases Greater Than .25 Percent								
Y	1955	100.000								
e	1956	106.728	100.000							
a	1957	93.239	84.086	100.000						
r	1958	128.666	120.754	143.614	100.000					
	1959	153.974	142.060	163.687	114.266	100.000				
	1960	164.335	153.465	169.318	118.942	102.058	100.000			
	1961	215.328	205.290	226.661	159.875	136.778	132.973	100.000		
	1962	177.563	163.689	181.151	128.277	108.735	106.273	80.885	100.000	
	1963	192.166	182.670	201.294	141.961	120.876	119.906	93.261	114.148	100.000
	1964	209.126	208.490	230.675	166.294	140.172	139.154	107.388	131.986	114.199
	1965	254.826	255.610	279.609	201.853	172.802	170.907	132.477	164.850	143.434
	1966	217.563	225.379	243.896	174.777	149.108	147.550	115.442	144.399	127.143
	1967	325.664	336.611	380.031	265.955	228.757	224.160	172.819	217.171	191.649
	1968	379.907	390.819	434.232	300.072	261.325	260.066	201.135	254.657	224.060
	1969	305.886	334.318	351.105	242.093	209.162	204.321	159.717	196.050	170.952
	1970	285.424	314.632	317.372	220.731	187.591	187.124	145.248	177.115	155.044
	1971	320.630	379.500	377.195	259.457	217.560	213.375	165.764	204.047	181.090
	1972	339.927	420.155	413.947	277.772	228.374	230.259	180.954	224.867	199.438

Started		1964	1965	1966	1967	1968	1969	1970	1971	1972
Y	1964	100.000								
e	1965	126.103	100.000							
a	1966	112.896	89.423	100.000						
r	1967	172.061	135.099	150.692	100.000					
	1968	199.711	159.926	181.335	120.603	100.000				
	1969	153.651	123.158	138.261	91.753	76.098	100.000			
	1970	136.825	111.333	125.361	83.108	68.715	90.738	100.000		
	1971	159.034	128.511	145.599	96.043	78.877	104.144	115.025	100.000	
	1972	172.961	139.775	156.575	103.180	84.893	111.633	122.469	106.272	100.000

data did not seem adequate to justify the use of more rigorous parametric methods.

The test was applied by comparing the values of price indexes for non-repurchasing companies with the index values for alternative levels of activity for repurchasing companies. The comparisons were made at various dates subsequent to repurchase. For example, in order to compare non-repurchasing companies with companies repurchasing more than .25% of their stock during a year, the price index at the end of 1956 for companies not repurchasing during 1955 was compared to the 1956 index for companies repurchasing more than .25% of their stock during 1955, the indexes at the end of 1957 for companies not repurchasing or repurchasing during 1956, and so on until 1972 indexes for companies not repurchasing or repurchasing during 1971. The Wilcoxon test provides techniques for assessing the significance of the resulting 17 comparisons measuring the effectiveness of repurchase one year later. Of course, for every additional year of lag (i.e. examining the effectiveness of repurchase two years later), one comparison would be lost. Thus, a test for the effectiveness of repurchase ten years later would only involve eight comparisons. Such tests were conducted for various repurchase strategies at differing time intervals following repurchase. The following section presents and analyzes the results of these tests.

III. FINDINGS

Exhibit IV presents two graphs summarizing the performance of repurchased shares. In the first graph an "index of indexes" for repurchasing firms is plotted against a similar index for non-repurchasing firms. These indexes are

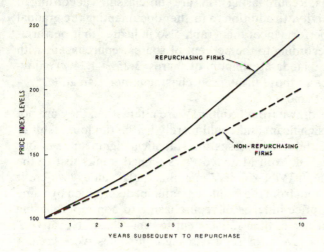

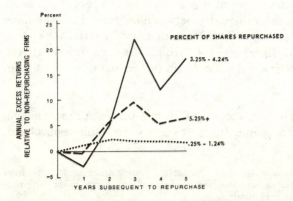

Exhibit IV.   Performance of repurchased shares.

computed by averaging the individual price indexes for one, two, three, etc. years subsequent to repurchase. For example, the one year index for repurchasing companies is an average of 17 individual price indexes and is thus reflective of the performance of 5,591 repurchasing firms.[7] The similar index for non-repurchasing is reflective of the performance of 11,128 firms. As the first graph indicates, the stock market performance of repurchasing firms is generally superior to that of non-repurchasing firms. However, clear superiority does not emerge until several years after repurchase. Thus, these results are not necessarily inconsistent with those of Young (19) who found no significant difference between repurchasing firms and the general market during the year following the announcement of the intention to repurchase via a cash tender offer. He did not examine longer periods.

The second graph in Exhibit IV amplifies the information presented in the first. This graph plots the annual excess returns of repurchasing firms relative to non-repurchasing firms. Repurchasing firms are sub-classified according to degree of repurchase activity. In addition to further documenting the gradual emergence of superior performance, this graph also indicates that performance differences exist according to the percent of shares repurchased, with those firms repurchasing a moderate amount of shares (3.25%–4.24%) enjoying superior performance to those firms repurchasing either a small (.25%–1.24%) or large (5.25%+) amount.

While these inferences drawn from Exhibit IV are interesting, they are not necessarily statistically significant and could merely be the random result of this particular sample. Exhibit V assesses the statistical significance of our findings by applying the Wilcoxon Matched-Pairs Signed-Ranks test to the raw data underlying Exhibit IV. Exhibit V contains the T values (which, it should be noted, are different from the familiar t statistic) determined by using this test to compare the price indexes of repurchasing to non-repurchasing companies at various periods of time subsequent to repurchase. Negative T values indicate that index levels for repurchasing companies were greater than comparable index for non-repurchasing companies; in general, smaller absolute T values indicate greater disparity between indexes. The statistical significance of the T values is indicated by the number of asterisks.

Examination of the T values presented in Exhibit V seems to indicate the existence of two general patterns which confirm our casual inferences from the graphs in Exhibit IV:

1. There is little statistically significant difference between repurchasing and non-repurchasing companies until several years after repurchase.

---

[7] Obviously, this large number reflects a degree of double counting since some firms have repurchased in more than one year and are thus included in more than one index. The non-repurchasing index also reflects double counting.

EXHIBIT V.   CUMULATIVE INDEXES, T VALUES

		1	2	3	4	5	. . . .	10
				Years Following Repurchase				
Degree of Repurchase	.25+	−57	−34	−11.5**	−12.5**	−12**		0***
	1.25+	−61	−22.5**	−15***	−6***	−3***		−2.5*
	2.25+	−51	−25*	−16***	−13***	−5.5***		−1**
	3.25+	−62.5	−42	−22*	−11***	−18.5		−4*
	4.25+	−72.5	−41.5	−18**	−79*	−20.5		−4.5
	5.25+	−78	−47	−26.5	−22	−12*		−7

NON-CUMULATIVE INDEXES, T VALUES

		1	2	3	4	5	. . . .	10
				Years Following Repurchase				
Degree of Repurchase	.25–1.24	−49	−46	−42	−26	−22		0***
	1.25–2.24	−32*	−22*	−15***	−18*	−11**		−8
	2.25–3.24	−34.5	−17***	−16***	−10***	−8.5**		−3
	3.25–4.24	−47.5	−39	−28	−22.5	−10		−2
	4.25–5.24	−68.5	−33	− 9***	−10.5**	−20		−6
	5.25+	−78	−47	−26.5	−22	−12*		−7

*Significant at the .025 level
**Significant at the .01 level
***Significant at the .005 level

At that point, repurchasing companies significantly outperform non-repurchasing companies.

2. The level of repurchase activity and subsequent performance seem to have a *"U"* shaped relationship, with the companies doing a moderate level of repurchasing having the best performance.

Is there any economic rationale for these findings? It might be hypothesized that the gradual superiority of repurchasing stems from the frequently defensive nature of repurchase decisions. When the market assigns such a low value to a company that management feels the need to repurchase shares to express its incredulity, the market is not likely to be easily impressed by the gestures of management. Only after a period of several years, during which management has numerous opportunities to prove its mettle, will the confidence of investors be restored and management's judgement concerning the undervaluation of the stock be confirmed.

The second pattern, the *"U"* shaped relationship between repurchase activity and subsequent performance, may require two explanations. Companies repurchasing only small amounts of their shares (.25%–1.24%), probably repurchase in conjunction with stock options, convertibles, and warrants to avoid the expense and dilution of issuing new shares. Since such repurchases are not motivated by the presumed undervaluation of the firm's stock, it is not particularly surprising that little difference exists between the subsequent market performance of such companies and non-repurchasers. On the other hand, companies repurchasing large amounts of their shares (more than 5.25%) tend to be involved in a major reorganization. Since such reorganization is often in response to severe difficulties, it is not surprising that the subsequent performance of these companies is inferior to that of companies whose undervaluation stems from more ephemeral problems.

IV. SUMMARY AND CONCLUSIONS

This paper has presented an attempt to answer the question, should a corporation repurchase its own stock? The question seems important since the volume of repurchased shares has grown rapidly in spite of a body of theoretical reasoning and empirical evidence questioning the efficacy of repurchasing as a corporate strategy. This study presents evidence similar to that of insider trading studies indicating the ability of corporate managers to detect and profitably exploit price-value divergences existing in the stock market.

The primary contribution of this paper has been to focus on the relatively long "work out" of repurchase decisions. Empirical examination of several thousand repurchase decisions indicates that the success of such decisions requires several years to be reflected with statistical significance in the stock market performance of repurchasing firms. Perhaps the best explanation of this empirical evidence is the frequently defensive nature of repurchase decisions; that is, repurchase is usually considered either when the stock price of a company seems abnormally low or when a company has an excess of cash relative to profitable investment opportunities. It is not too surprising that a period of several years seems to be required to correct such situations.

In attempting to determine the merits of a repurchasing strategy, this empirical evidence should not be used to infer cause and effect relationships. The data presented in the paper will not substantiate the conclusion that repurchasing leads to superior stock market performance. Without a complete theory of valuation, it is impossible to infer causation from the statistical correlation of two variables.

REFERENCES

1.   Douglas V. Austin. "Treasury Stock Reacquisition by American Corporations: 1961–67," *Financial Executive*, May, 1969.

2. Harold Bierman, Jr. and Richard West. "The Acquisition of Common Stock By The Corporate Issuer," *Journal of Finance*, December, 1966.
3. Eugene F. Brigham. "The Profitability of a Firm's Purchase of Its Own Common Stock," *California Management Review*, Winter, 1964.
4. J. G. Cragg and Burton G. Malkiel. "The Consensus and Accuracy of Some Predictions of the Growth of Corporate Earnings," *Journal of Finance*, March, 1968.
5. Charles D. Ellis and Allan E. Young. *The Repurchase of Common Stock*, The Ronald Press Company, New York, 1971.
6. ————. "Repurchase Stock to Revitalize Equity," *Harvard Business Review*, July-August, 1965.
7. Edwin Elton and Martin Gruber. "The Effect of Share Repurchase on the Value of the Firm," *Journal of Finance*, March, 1968.
8. Leo A. Guthart. "Why Companies Are Buying Back Their Own Stock," *Financial Analysts Journal*, March-April, 1967.
9. ————. "More Companies Are Buying Back Their Stock," *Harvard Business Review*, March-April, 1965.
10. Jeffrey F. Jaffe. "Special Information and Insider Trading," *The Journal of Business*, July 1974.
11. I. M. D. Little. "Higgledy Piggledy Growth," *Oxford University Institute of Statistics*, November, 1962.
12. James H. Lorie and Victor Niederhoffer. "Predictive and Statistical Properties of Insider Trading," *Journal of Law and Economics*, April, 1968.
13. J. E. Murphy. "Relative Growth of Earnings Per Share—Past and Future," *Financial Analysts Journal*, November-December, 1966.
14. Timothy J. Nantell and Joseph E. Finnerty. "Effect of Stock Repurchase on Price Performance," Paper presented at the Annual Meeting of the Financial Management Association, San Diego, California, October 25, 1974.
15. Shannon P. Pratt and Charles W. DeVere. "Relationship Between Insider Trading and Rates of Return for NYSE Common Stocks, 1960–66," *Modern Developments in Investment Management*, Unpublished paper presented to the Seminar on the Analysis of Security Prices, May, 1968.
16. Herbert Weinraub and Douglas V. Austin. "Treasury Stock Reacquisition: 1971–1973," *Financial Executive*, August, 1974.
17. Donald H. Woods and Eugene F. Brigham. "Stockholder Distribution Decisions: Share Repurchases or Dividends?," *Journal of Financial and Quantitative Analysis*, March, 1966.
18. Hsiu-Kwang Wu. "Corporate Insider Trading Profits and the Ability to Forecast Stock Prices," *Elements of Investment*, 1963.
19. Allan Edward Young. "Managerial, Market and Investor Problems Associated with the Cash Tender Offers of Corporations for their Own Common Stock," Ph.D. dissertation, Graduate School of Business Administration, Columbia University, 1967.
20. ————. "The Performance of Common Stocks Subsequent to Repurchase," *Financial Analysts Journal*, Sept.-Oct., 1967.
21. Allan Young and Wayne Marshall. "Controlling Shareholder Servicing Costs," *Harvard Business Review*, January-February, 1971.

22. —— and ——. "A Mathematical Model for Re-acquisition of Small Shareholdings," *Journal of Financial and Quantitative Analysis,* December, 1968.

QUESTIONS

1. Suppose the management and directors of a firm embark upon a share repurchase program. Would you expect the stock of that firm to perform well or poorly in the market place in the short run and long run? Explain.
2. Explain why it could be possible for the relative performance of a stock to be related to the relative number of shares repurchased.
3. Discuss the merits or demerits of stock repurchase in contrast to cash dividend payments.
4. Explain why, in an efficient market, the performance of stocks for which repurchase was underway would be no different than that of other stocks.

VI | Integrated Topics in Financial Management

24

Jack Clark Francis and Dexter R. Rowell

A Simultaneous Equation Model of the Firm for Financial Analysis and Planning

At this point in the course, most topics have been covered. Each of these topics may now be examined in an overall context. This article is specifically oriented toward making good forecasts for the purpose of financial planning. In a general sense, however, this article shows how ten sectors are considered to fit together in an interdependent model. Relationships are specified for each sector, and the model's results are generated via a simultaneous equation approach.

Forecasting and planning are essential to good decision making. As a result, financial managers are frequently asked for *pro forma* financial statements. The Securities and Exchange Commission [18] allows the use of published forecasts by publicly owned firms to supplement their required history-oriented financial statements. Such possibilities leave little room for question about whether or not a financial manager is (or at least should be) interested in generating financial forecasts. The important question is how to prepare good forecasts. This paper suggests a simultaneous equation model of moderate size to forecast the future path of a single firm's financial statements.

DESCRIPTION OF THE FRANCIS-ROWELL (FR) MODEL

The model presented below extends the simultaneous linear equation models of the firm developed by Warren and Shelton [19] (hereafter WS) and Pindyck and Rubinfeld [14, Section 12.3]. The objective of this model is to generate *pro*

Source. Reprinted by permission from *Financial Management*, Spring 1978, pp. 29–44. Jack Clark Francis is professor of finance and economics at Baruch College. Dexter R. Rowell is assistant professor of finance and economics at Villanova University.

forma financial statements that describe the future financial condition of the firm for any assumed pattern of sales. Parameters of various equations in the system can be changed to answer "what if" questions, perform sensitivity analysis, and explore various paths toward some goal or goals which may or may not be optimal.

The FR model is an initial effort to capture the complex interaction among objectives in management decisions.[1] Capital expansion and financing decisions affect the risk character of the firm, which in turn affects the firm's equity valuation. Equity valuation feeds back to the financing and expansion decisions. Likewise, the production decision must be viewed in its relationship to the sales forecast, subject to existing finished goods inventories and capacity utilization. If, for instance, an optimistic sales forecast indicated a sharp upturn in future company sales, production need not turn upward in direct proportion to the sales upturn. The production upturn would probably be lower than sales if substantial finished goods inventories existed. As a consequence, cause and effect are not simply unilateral. Therefore, to realistically capture such interdependence, any model must be highly interdependent, or *simultaneous*. It need not be large, but it must be sufficiently complex to allow disaggregation of sales forecast, production, pricing, asset expansion, and financing decisions.

The FR model is composed of ten sectors with a total of 36 equations. (Variables are defined in Appendix A and equations listed in Appendix B.) This is a large enough model to allow substantial *disaggregation,* as well as to capture some of the simultaneity of business operations. The FR model has several other important features besides its simultaneity and disaggregation.

The model incorporates an explicit treatment of *risk* by allowing for stochastic variability in industry sales forecasts. The exogenous input of sales variance is transformed (through simplified linear relations in the model) to coefficients of variation for earnings before interest and taxes (EBIT) and net income after taxes (NIAT).[2] These are used in risk-return functions which determine costs of new financing.

The model also incorporates some variables external to the firm that are important from a financial planning viewpoint. These *industry or economy-wide variables* are introduced in every sector to enable the financial planner to explore their influence on plans. They include: market share, an industry capacity utilization index, the tax rate, and a GNP component price index for explicit analysis of the effects of inflation.

---

[1] The suggested model includes ten main sectors with 34 endogenous variables and 30 exogenous variables which are listed in Appendix A. These variables are interrelated through 36 linear equations shown in Appendix B. This equation system is simultaneous in the usual econometric sense; concurrent interrelationships and feedback loops are involved in the solution for each period. However, the model also contains recursive equations so that all the equations are not solved simultaneously in the mathematical sense (that is, a matrix is not inverted).

[2] The mathematical statistics showing the risk transformations are shown in Appendix C.

The FR model explicitly allows for divergence between planned (or potential) and actual levels of both sales and production. That is, sales forecasts and production potential are compared to determine the existence of slack or idle capacity and company expansion possibilities. Any positive difference between potential or forecasted company sales and actual company sales is decomposed into the portion attributable to idle capacity and the portion requiring expanded production facilities. As a result, a forecasted sales increase need not lead to investment in new capital. Likewise, a forecasted sales downturn would not lead to a divestiture of capital. An advantage of this disaggregation is that it allows for greater realism—that is, it permits both a lagged production response to sales upturns and downturns, as well as lags and asymmetry in new investment decisions.

The FR model offers a disaggregation of the sales equation into separate market share, production, and pricing equations, which has several distinct advantages. It offers the opportunity to treat sales forecasts in physical units that can be compared to technical production capabilities in physical units for both potential and actual levels of sales and production. Such disaggregation also allows distinction between physical units of sales and production and dollar units. Therefore, the pricing decision can be treated separately.

Another aspect of the FR financial forecasting model is the econometrics. The FR model's risk-return function and its production function are estimated econometrically. Also, standard econometric techniques to evaluate goodness-of-fit and predictive power of a simultaneous equation system are reported.

In the remaining sections of the paper, the FR model is explained in its general form. Then the coefficients of the equations are set equal to the values which characterize the operations of an existing company, and then the active operations of a well-known firm are simulated to test the model empirically as a financial tool.

THE FR MODEL SPECIFICATION

The FR model is composed of ten sectors: 1) industry sales, 2) production sector, 3) fixed capital stock requirements, 4) pricing, 5) production costs, 6) income, 7) new financing required, 8) risk, 9) costs of financing, and 10) common stock valuation. These sectors are illustrated in the flow chart shown in Exhibit 1.

The flow chart conveniently illustrates the simultaneity discussed above. All ten sectors are portrayed, labeled, and outlined by dot-dash borders with arrows displaying their interaction. This is summarized for sectors one through ten in the interdependence table, Exhibit 2. An "X" is placed in the table to represent the direction of an arrow (from explaining to explained) on the flow chart.

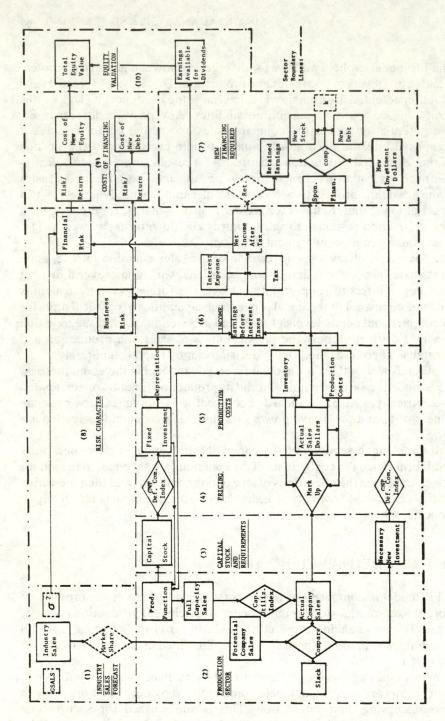

Exhibit 1.   Model flow chart.

402

EXHIBIT 2. SECTOR INDEPENDENCE

					Explaining Sector					
		1	2	3	4	5	6	7	8	9	10
Explained	1										
Sector	2	X									
	3		X								
	4			X							
	5				X						
	6					X					
	7				X		X			X	
	8	X	X	X	X	X	X	X			
	9								X		
	10							X		X	

The pattern of "Xs" demonstrates something interesting about the FR model. Recall that simultaneous means instantaneous interdependence among sectors and equations. Each equation and sector in this model describes a different relationship among a set of variables. However, all the sectors and equations are assumed to hold at once. Furthermore, a simultaneous model must be solved simultaneously—all equations are solved at the same time.

While a model can be simultaneous in the sense that all sectors or equations are assumed to hold at once, the solution could occur *recursively* (that is, not all at once). For instance, the solution of one equation leads to the solution of the next and so on, until the entire model is solved in a time sequence of solutions. If a model were recursive, such an interdependence table would show entries only in the lower triangle of the table. The simplest recursive model—such as a model which uses a fixed percentage of sales to obtain all other amounts—would be characterized in the interdependence table by entries only in column one.

Looking more deeply reveals that the FR model is, to a large extent (but not entirely), recursive between sectors. All entries of the sector interdependence table, with the exception of one (between sectors seven and nine), are below the diagonal. It has been structured in this manner for the specific purpose of ease of exposition and computation. The simultaneity of the FR model is primarily within each sector's equations. For example, this is illustrated for sector seven in the flow chart for that sector, shown as Exhibit 3, and also in the variable interdependence table for sector seven, shown as Exhibit 4.

SECTOR ONE: INDUSTRY SALES

The primary importance of the industry sales forecast sector is highlighted by its upper left position on the flow chart in Exhibit 1. It influences directly the risk sector and production sector and indirectly every sector of the model.

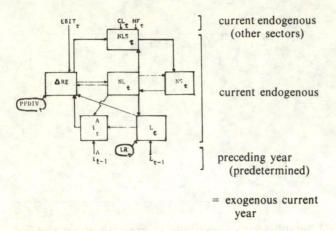

current endogenous
(other sectors)

current endogenous

preceding year
(predetermined)

= exogenous current
year

Exhibit 3. Sector seven flow chart.

The industry sales sector can be any size and is abbreviated here to merely a single equation; see Equation (1). The industry sales equation shows that an industry sales forecast must be made by some means over a pre-defined forecast period and given as an exogenous input to the FR model.

Although sales remain the driving force for the FR model, it is industry instead of company sales which drive the model, since forecasting experience indicates that industry sales are usually more accurately forecasted than company sales. In addition, two parameters of the industry sales forecast are employed, the mean and standard deviation. The mean enters the model in the conventional way, whereas the standard deviation is mathematically transformed to obtain the standard deviations of its derivative quantities, the company's net income after taxes (NIAT) and earnings before interest and taxes (EBIT).[3]

SECTOR TWO: COMPANY SALES AND PRODUCTION

Company sales are obtained through a market share assumption which is typically a more stable parameter than a company's dollar sales level. Poten-

[3] The FR model could easily be linked to a macroeconomic forecasting model to obtain the sales forecast for the industry and the firm. This expanded macroeconomic and microeconomic model could provide detailed forecasts of the economy, the firm's industry, the firm itself, and the firm's equity returns. Francis has also developed a small simultaneous equation model to explain a single firm's changes in earnings per share and stock price per share [5]. This model is driven by macroeconomic factors with some forces from within the firm treated as unexplained residuals (called unsystematic risk). If the Francis quarterly equity returns model were provided with exogenous input data about aggregate profits and a stock market index, it could be modified to operate with the FR model and provide detailed analysis of period-by-period equity returns.

EXHIBIT 4.   VARIABLE INTERDEPENDENCE WITHIN SECTOR SEVEN

		RE_t	L_t	NL_t	NS_t	i_t^A	NLS_t
				Explaining Variables			
	RE_t		X	X		X	
Explained	L_t		X				
Variables	NL_t		X		X		
	NS_t			X			X
	i_t^A		X	X			
	NLS_t	X		X			

tial company sales is obtained from forecasted industry sales through this market share assumption. Equation (4) shows the relationship explicitly.

The FR model distinguishes between potential and actual sales levels, which allows a realistic treatment of slack or idle capacity in the firm. Because of the possibility of under-utilized assets, every sales upturn need not be translated directly into an increase in the asset base. Some or all of the sales upturn can be absorbed by more complete utilization of available resources.

Company production potential is obtained from a production function that defines full capacity company production. This is determined by previous-period full capacity sales, inventory, and fixed assets (see Equation (2) in Appendix B for the exact specification). Actual company production is derived from full capacity production by a capacity utilization index in Equation (3).

The production function allows explicit definition of the company's full capacity production levels. It serves the useful purpose of relaxing the assumption used in many models that whatever is produced is sold. Full capacity production is typically adjusted gradually, or dynamically, over the long run to upward changes in potential sales and is often not responsive to downturns. The non-proportionality and asymmetry discussed earlier with respect to the distinction between actual and potential sales also applies to the distinctions between potential full capacity and actual production. For instance, slack (that is, idle capacity) may be decreased to meet a sales upturn without increasing the firm's investment in manufacturing machinery.

SECTOR THREE: FIXED CAPITAL STOCK REQUIREMENTS

Necessary new investment is not linked directly to company sales in the FR model, but instead results from comparison between potential and actual company sales. Equation (7) measures the company expansion possibility by the difference between potential company sales (itself influenced by management's industry sales forecast and company market share assumption) and full capacity sales. The units of required new capital are derived from this difference in Equation (9), shown in Appendix B.

Through this specification the FR model recognizes the asymmetrical response of the asset base to changes in sales levels. A strict ratio between sales and asset levels, such as used in other *pro forma* models [14, 19], presumes a proportionate and symmetrical response of asset levels to both sales upturns and downturns. The FR distinction between actual and potential sales and the concept of slack allows a realistic nonproportionality and asymmetry in the simulation. (For instance, a sales downturn need not and usually does not lead to a reduction in asset levels; instead it typically causes a decrease in capacity utilization.)

A capacity utilization index for the simulated company and industry translates full capacity output (from the production function) into actual company sales, just as a market share assumption is used to translate potential industry sales into potential company sales. Any positive difference between potential company sales and actual company sales is decomposed into the contribution due to idle capacity and the contribution due to company expansion possibility, as shown mathematically in Equation (5).

SECTOR FOUR: PRICING

The pricing sector of the model plays a key role by relating the real or units sectors to the nominal or dollar sectors. The real sectors of industry sales, company sales and production, and fixed capital stock requirements are all denominated in physical units of output. However, the nominal sectors of production costs, income, financing required, and valuation are all dollar-denominated. The real sectors and the nominal sectors are connected by the pricing sector.

This sector separation allows explicit treatment of the product pricing decision apart from the sales and production decisions. Also, it maintains the important distinction between real and nominal quantities and thus permits an analysis of inflation's impact on the firm (as suggested by the Securities and Exchange Commission [18]).

Equation (13) is a simple formula that generates product price by relating it through a markup to the ratio of previous period gross operating profit to inventory. Real units of company sales are priced out in Equation (12). Required new capital units are priced out using the average unit capital cost specified in Equation (11).

SECTOR FIVE: PRODUCTION COSTS

The production cost sector is similar to previous models; production cost and inventory are related directly to actual company sales dollars. Also, depreciation is linked directly to existing fixed investment.

SECTOR SIX: INCOME

As in the production cost sector, the income sector equations tie inventory, earnings before interest and taxes, and net income after taxes directly to actual company sales dollars. This simplicity is preserved here to create a linearly-determined income statement that produces EBIT as a function of actual company sales (given a few simplifying assumptions). The NIAT is derived from EBIT after deduction of interest expense (also linearly-related to actual sales levels) and taxes.

SECTOR SEVEN: NEW FINANCING REQUIRED

The new financing required sector is composed primarily of accounting relationships that determine the dollar amount of external financing required from the new capital requirements (sector three) and internal financing capability (sector six). Equation (21) obtains this external financing requirement. The retained income portion of internal financing is derived from Equation (23).

Finally, the breakdown of new external financing into new equity and new debt occurs in Equation (25), where the notion of optimal capital structure is exploited. The weighted average cost of debt, Equation (24), consists of a weighted sum of new debt costs and the cost of existing debt. The cost of new debt is not exogenous in this model; it is estimated in a simplified risk-return trade-off from sector nine.

SECTOR EIGHT: RISK

The linear derivation of both EBIT and NIAT in the income sector is used (with simplifying assumptions) in the risk sector to obtain the standard deviation of each income measure. The derivation (presented in Appendix C) demonstrates how management's judgment as to the variability (that is, standard deviation) of forecasted industry sales affects the risk character (of both the business and financial risk) of the company. This risk character influences the costs of financing new stock and debt in risk-return trade-off equations of sector nine. In this way, risk is explicitly accounted for as the principal determinant of financing costs, and financing costs are made endogenous to the model. In addition, the risk relationship (shown in Appendix C) demonstrates a positive cause and effect relationship from the ratio of fixed to variable costs (an operating leverage measure) to the standard deviation of EBIT. The debt-to-equity ratio (a financial leverage ratio) also positively influences the NIAT standard deviation. Thus, the leverage structure of the firm endogenously influences the costs of financing in a realistic way.

SECTOR NINE: COSTS OF FINANCING

Market factors enter into the determination of financing costs through the slope (β_1 and β_2) and intercept (α_1 and α_2) coefficients of the two risk-return trade-off functions—namely Equations (29) and (31). At the present time, all four coefficients must be exogenously provided by management. However, this is not a difficult task. Historical coefficients can be estimated empirically using simple linear regression. The regression coefficients would establish a plausible range of values that might be used by management to determine the present or future coefficient values.

SECTOR TEN: COMMON STOCK VALUATION

The valuation model used finds the present value of dividends which are presumed to grow perpetually at a constant rate. This venerable model can be traced from Williams [22] through more recent analysts. Algebraically reduced to its simplest form, the single-share valuation model is shown below.

$$\text{share price} = \frac{\text{(cash dividend per year)}}{\left(\begin{array}{c}\text{equity capitalization}\\ \text{rate, } i_t^s\end{array}\right) - \left(\begin{array}{c}\text{growth rate,}\\ g_t^a\end{array}\right)}$$

Equation (33) differs slightly from the per share valuation model above because it values the firm's total equity outstanding. This change was accomplished merely by multiplying both sides of the valuation equation shown above by the number of shares outstanding. The remaining equations of this sector are then accounting statements.

FULL MODEL SIMULATION

The degree of simultaneity in the model is useful since it represents an approximation of the true complexity in management decision making. For instance, management decisions affect and are affected by costs of new financing. Likewise, the average debt interest rate both affects and is affected by management decisions. These simultaneous interactions occur dynamically (that is, over time) as well as in current time periods. Since previous decisions influence current decisions, a brief history of previous decisions is incorporated into the model through lagged variables. This occurs in the production function as well as in the product pricing and debt cost equations. The appropriate variables were lagged one year in all cases. In the production function, the lag was thought essential since the existing asset structure of the firm as well as previous sales levels determines current full capacity sales levels. This relationship demonstrates the long-term structural character of the firm—a structure that cannot be drastically altered in the short run.

Practically speaking, the final test of a model is its workability in specific applications. For the proposed model, the company selected for simulation must be a member of an identifiable industry, whose sales and industry sales are available in units as well as dollars. Although there are many companies from several industries that could have been used, the Anheuser-Busch Company was selected for discussion here.

There follows an actual application of the model over a recent historical period for Anheuser-Busch. Several different simulation experiments are reported. Appendix D contains a performance comparison between the proposed model and the most comparable other financial model [19].[4]

The proposed model was simulated over an eight-year sample period.[5] *Ex post* simulation is a useful technique for quantifying the "sample period" performance of the model as a predictor. Several forecast errors are measured for each of the endogenous variables—bias, average absolute error (AAE), and root mean squared error (RMSE).[6] The model should perform "well" as a predictor over the sample period if the specification is valid and the necessary simplifying assumptions do not destroy predictive performances.

Anheuser-Busch Company annual reports provided all the necessary company data for the ten years from 1966 to 1975. A total of ten years of data was needed to provide two years of historical exogenous data to initialize the model plus eight more years of data for the simulation. Industry sales (measured in barrels of beer) were available in the *Brewer's Almanac*. The capacity utilization index, γ_t, was obtained from the Wharton Economic Forecasting Associates capacity utilization series. The price of capital, P_{kt}, was approximated by the Bureau of Economic Analysis GNP deflator component index for capital goods. All the necessary coefficients were obtained by making the appropriate divisions of annual data. The production and risk trade-off func-

---

[4] The FR model is similar to the financial planning models of Pindyck and Rubinfeld [14, Section 12.3] and Warren and Shelton [19]. However, the FR model is completely different from several econometric models which have been developed to relate the U.S. macroeconomic environment to various elements of the business firm (namely, Elliot [4] and Salzman [16]). The FR model also abstracts from regulatory sectors (unlike Davis *et al.* [3]) and marketing (in particular, advertising) campaign variables. However, it would be straightforward to link the FR model to a larger macroeconomic model if the firm needed to be analyzed within its larger economic environment.

[5] The authors have also tested the FR and the WS [19] models with other companies. Details of the tests using Ford Motor Company and Republic Steel data are available from the authors on request. All the test results were not presented here to save space.

[6] The forecast error measurements called bias, average absolute error (AAE), and root mean squared error (RMSE) are well-known econometric measures for evaluating the performance of simultaneous equation models. These measures are defined and discussed on pages 314 to 320 of Pindyck and Rubinfeld [14] and in numerous other econometrics textbooks.

tion coefficients were derived by ordinary least squares regressions over the entire sample period.

The model is solved simultaneously for each period over the 1968–1975 sample period by initializing the right-hand side (RHS) variables in every equation with their actual historical values and then solving for the dependent or left-hand side (LHS) variables. The nature of simultaneous equations is such that the solved LHS variable values are used as RHS values in the next iteration. Each sector is solved separately. Then the entire system of sectors is solved in a sector-step procedure. This same procedure is followed for each of the eight years of the sample period.[7]

EXPERIMENTATION AND EVALUATION

Several simultaion experiments were employed to isolate those sectors in the model that contribute greatly to forecast error: the first order sensitivity experiment and the "what if" type of simulation. Appendix D compares the model's performance with that of Warren and Shelton [19] in successive one-period simulations over the sample period. This comparison demonstrates the benefits made possible by the refinements introduced in the FR model.[8]

FIRST ORDER SENSITIVITY EXPERIMENT (FOSE)

The FOSE experiment is designed to locate and measure the source of a model's forecast error. This is achieved by exogenizing equations or whole sectors so that the dependent variables involved take on their actual historical values in solution. The procedure essentially eliminates these exogenized equations or sectors as sources of error. Consequently, a comparison of the

---

[7] A FORTRAN computer program was used to solve the system of equations. Matrix inversion is not used so that the matrix need not be square; the Gauss-Seidel algorithm is used instead. All equations and sectors in the system must first be ordered so that they are as nearly recursive as possible. If the system cannot converge on a solution, it can be re-ordered and tried again. It is mathematically possible to have non-convergent systems, but this problem is rare in empirical applications. The first period's solution is obtained by initializing the equations with their actual historical values and then solving for the unknown dependent variables. Each sector is solved separately with a maximum of 100 iterations per sector allowed for a converged solution. A specified tolerance of .001 is used to determine when the convergence is tolerably close. After all sectors are solved, a sector-step procedure is employed to solve the entire system. This sector-step procedure is repeated up to a maximum of 30 times until a convergence which satisfies the tolerance criterion over all system dependent variables is obtained for the period. Then, in a similar fashion, the program proceeds to solve the system for the next period's values.

[8] Detailed performance comparisons between the FR and the WS [19] model results are not reported here. They will be made available to interested readers upon request. However, Appendix D shows one prediction comparison for the FR model and the WS model. See footnotes 4, 5, and 6 for references about comparing predictions from competing econometric models and different companies' financial statements.

forecast error of the exogenous simulation with that of the entire model simulation will indicate the portion of forecast error attributable to this sector or equation alone. This is useful information for error tracing and respecification.

Several whole sectors were exogenized separately at their actual historical values to measure their influence. The forecast error for each experiment is recorded in Exhibits 6 and 7. A comparison of the forecast errors of the following exhibits with those of Exhibit 5, the full model solutions, indicates the location and magnitude of the errors.

The historical simulation results (Exhibit 5) indicate high root mean squared error (RMSE) for the dollar values from the industry sales, pricing, production cost, and EBIT sectors that passes on into the new financing required sector. This causes high RMSE error in the external financing requirement variables, NS, NL, and NLS. To explore the magnitude of these attributable errors, both the price and EBIT sectors are made individually exogenous. The model is solved around each, producing the solution series recorded in Exhibits 6 and 7.

The price sector exogenous simulation (Exhibit 6) demonstrates a significant 43% reduction in RMSE of EBIT. Some error remains because the interest rate of new debt issues has been endogenized in this model—the risk-return functions have some simulation error since the α and β coefficients used in Equations (29) and (31) are the actual regression coefficients for the entire sample period. Nevertheless, an exogenous price sector results in a simulation error reduction of 24% for ΔRE, 15% for NL and 2% reduction for NS. Consequently, the price sector alone accounts for 2 to 24% of the simulation error reported in the full model simulation shown in Exhibit 5.

The EBIT sector exogenous simulation shows, as expected, zero forecast error for NIAT and EBIT, and causes a 51% reduction in the RMSE of ΔRE. However, the simulation errors of the external financing variables, NS and NL, revert to their previous magnitudes in the full model simulation. Consequently, the price sector, not the EBIT sector, influences the simulation error in the new financing required sector. However, the EBIT sector influences most of the other model variables.

These two simulations have shown the pricing equations to be critical in influencing new financing required sector error, explaining approximately one-quarter to one-half of that sector's error. On the other hand, the EBIT sector controls the NIAT, EBIT, and RE errors.

SIMULATION OF CHANGES

Second order simulation experiments (SOSE) were conducted to evaluate the probable effects of changes on the firm. These experiments involve changing the exogenous input parameters in order to answer "what if" questions.

EXHIBIT 5. FULL MODEL SIMULATION RESULTS FOR ANHEUSER-BUSCH, INC.

Variable and Code*		1968	1969	1970	1971	1972	1973	1974	1975	Bias	AAE	RMSE
$S_t	A	652.7	666.6	792.78	902.45	977.50	1109.71	1413.09	1644.98			
	S	597.72	712.87	786.69	899.06	1015.91	1097.24	1389.15	1661.11	−0.01	25.21	30.98
	D	−54.98	46.27	−6.09	−3.39	38.41	−12.47	−23.94	16.13			
EBIT	A	100.32	100.34	127.88	142.65	152.93	131.53	133.39	187.90			
	S	88.98	106.25	125.46	143.45	162.14	130.17	122.70	197.83	0.04	6.46	7.66
	D	−11.34	5.91	−2.42	0.80	9.21	−1.36	−10.69	9.93			
I_t^A	A	.05	.06	.06	.06	.06	.06	.06	.07			
	S	.05	.05	.06	.06	.06	.06	.06	.06	0.00	0.00	0.00
	D	.00	−.01	.00	.00	.00	.00	.00	−.01			
NL_t	A	0.0	0.0	0.0	0.0	0.0	0.0	100.0	150.00			
	S	13.65	13.27	2.55	13.93	4.23	0.0	13.40	36.83	24.97	30.93	51.11
	D	13.65	13.27	2.55	13.93	4.23	0.0	−86.60	−113.17			
S_t	A	91.72	93.05	93.85	101.50	103.30	103.57	103.57	103.57			
	S	91.72	91.72	91.71	91.72	91.72	91.71	91.72	91.72	−7.45	−7.45	8.93
	D	0.0	−1.33	−2.13	−9.78	−11.58	−11.58	−11.58	−11.58			
NIAT	A	44.63	45.31	62.55	71.64	76.40	65.58	64.02	84.72			
	S	39.37	47.31	59.78	70.94	79.98	63.71	60.88	92.92	0.04	3.44	4.08
	D	−5.26	2.00	−2.77	−0.70	3.58	−1.87	−3.14	8.20			
ΔRE	A	28.51	27.47	43.56	47.85	46.20	38.54	36.98	55.88			
	S	25.15	28.71	42.00	47.58	47.81	37.37	35.07	61.35	0.05	2.07	2.57
	D	−3.36	1.24	−1.56	−0.27	1.61	−1.17	−1.91	5.47			
NLS_t	A	1.45	1.33	.80	7.65	1.80	.27	100.0	150.0			
	S	13.65	13.27	15.90	13.93	10.49	7.51	13.40	36.83	−17.29	32.65	51.23
	D	12.20	11.94	15.10	6.28	8.69	7.24	−86.6	−113.17			
L_t	A	142.72	134.93	128.08	116.57	99.11	93.41	193.24	342.17			
	S	107.76	148.20	143.98	130.50	109.60	100.93	106.64	229.01	−21.70	36.98	52.82
	D	−34.96	13.27	15.90	13.93	10.49	7.52	−86.60	−113.16			
NS_t	A	1.45	1.33	.80	7.65	1.80	.27	0.0	0.0			
	S	0.0	0.0	0.0	0.0	0.0	0.0	0.0	0.0	−1.66	−1.66	2.88
	D	−1.45	−1.33	−0.80	−7.65	−1.80	−0.27	0.0	0.0			

A = Actual   S = Solved   D = Deviation   *See Appendix A for definitions of all variables.

EXHIBIT 6. SIMULATION WITH PRICE SECTOR EXOGENOUS

Variable and Code*		1968	1969	1970	1971	1972	1973	1974	1975	Bias	AAE	RMSE
$\$S_t$	S	652.7	666.60	792.78	902.45	977.50	1109.71	1413.09	1644.98	0.0	0.0	0.0
	D	0.0	0.0	0.0	0.0	0.0	0.0	0.0	0.0			
$EBIT_t$	S	97.91	99.99	126.85	144.39	156.40	133.16	127.17	197.39	.7918	3.2946	4.3814
	D	-2.41	-0.35	-1.03	1.74	3.47	1.63	-6.21	9.49			
I_t^A	S	.05	.05	.06	.06	.06	.06	.06	.06	-0.0011	0.0031	0.0042
	D	0.00	-.01	0.00	0.00	0.00	0.00	0.00	-.01			
NL_t	S	25.70	20.11	17.36	16.12	14.68	14.71	33.65	57.54	-6.27	33.44	43.27
	D	25.70	20.11	17.36	16.12	14.68	14.71	-66.36	-92.46			
S_t	S	114.83	112.38	99.19	110.75	126.61	142.12	160.23	141.45	26.68	26.68	23.75
	D	23.11	19.33	5.34	9.25	23.31	38.55	56.66	37.88			
NIAT	S	44.19	44.94	61.25	72.11	77.64	65.83	63.38	92.86	.9219	1.6058	2.9710
	D	-.43	-.37	-1.30	0.47	1.24	0.25	-0.64	8.15			
NLS	S	48.81	39.44	22.70	25.37	37.99	53.26	90.31	95.42	18.75	34.82	38.21
	D	47.36	38.11	21.90	17.72	36.19	52.99	-9.69	-54.58			
L_t	S	119.80	155.02	145.43	132.69	113.78	108.11	126.86	249.68	-12.3563	33.092	43.1313
	D	-22.92	20.09	17.35	16.12	14.67	14.70	-66.38	-92.00			
NS_t	S	1.40	0.0	0.0	0.0	0.0	0.0	0.0	0.0	-1.49	-1.49	2.83
	D	-.05	-1.33	-0.80	-7.65	-1.80	-0.27	0.0	0.0			
ΔRE	S	28.29	27.42	42.88	48.31	46.58	38.84	36.76	61.29	.6733	.9680	1.9470
	D	-0.22	-0.05	-0.68	0.46	0.38	0.30	-0.21	541			

*See Appendix A for the definitions of all variables.
(Simulated value) – (Actual value) = S – D = A
(Deviation from actual) = S – A

413

EXHIBIT 7. *SIMULATION WITH EBIT SECTOR EXOGENOUS*

Variable and Code*	1968	1969	1970	1971	1972	1973	1974	1975	Bias	AAE	RMSE
S_t A											
S_t S					(same as full model solution)						
S_t D											
EBIT A											
EBIT S					(exogenous)						
EBIT D											
I_t^A A											
I_t^A S					(same as full model solution)						
I_t^A D											
NL_t A	0.0	0.0	0.0	0.0	0.0	0.0	100.0	150.0			
NL_t S	14.65	11.91	15.59	13.38	9.58	7.31	14.05	33.99			
NL_t D	14.65	11.91	15.59	13.38	9.58	7.31	−85.95	−116.00	−16.19	34.30	52.16
S_t A											
S_t S					(same as full model solution)						
S_t D											
NIAT A											
NIAT S					(exogenous)						
NIAT D											
NLS_t A	1.45	1.33	.80	7.65	1.80	.27	100.00	150.00			
NLS_t S	14.65	11.91	15.59	13.38	9.58	7.31	14.05	33.99			
NLS_t D	13.20	10.58	14.79	5.73	7.78	7.04	−85.95	−116.01	−17.86	32.64	51.83
L_t A	142.72	134.93	128.08	116.57	99.11	93.41	193.24	342.17			
L_t S	108.76	146.84	143.67	129.95	108.69	100.73	107.29	226.17			
L_t D	−33.96	11.91	15.59	13.37	9.58	7.32	−85.95	−116.00	−22.27	36.71	34.03
NS_t A											
NS_t S					(same as full model solution)						
NS_t D											
$ΔRE$ A	28.51	27.47	43.56	47.85	46.20	38.54	36.98	55.88			
$ΔRE$ S	29.30	27.71	43.31	47.78	45.62	38.49	39.03	58.62			
$ΔRE$ D	0.78	0.24	−0.25	−0.02	−0.58	−0.05	2.05	2.74	0.62	.85	1.26

*See Appendix A for definitions of all variables.

414

The outcome of the full model simulation indicated that the *ex post* simulation could not accurately explain the aggessive external financing plan of the Anheuser-Busch management in 1974–1975. The full model simulation (Exhibit 5) produces a RMSE for new debt issues (NL) of 51.11, for new stock issues (NS) of 2.88, and for combined external financing (NLS) of 51.23. However, these simulation results were the result of known industry sales growth rates and known Anheuser-Busch market share. But, the relevant influence in the formulation of capital expansion plans and external financing is expected (that is, *ex ante* rather than actual) levels of industry sales growth and company market share. So, changes to improve this portion of the forecast were simulated.

Several exogenous parameters were changed for the sample period simulation in an attempt to find a better explanation for Anheuser-Busch's external financing (namely, debt issues) in 1974 and 1975. Neither market share nor industry sales growth parameter changes, however, alone or in combination, appeared to offer a reduced simulation error for the new financing required variables (NL, NS). The results shown in Exhibit 8 demonstrate the use of the model when the market share is assumed to climb steadily from an actual value of 17% in 1968 to 25% in 1975. In fact, market share actually climbs from 17% to 21% over this period. The income variables (NIAT and EBIT) and contribution to retained earnings variable (RE) were not thrown into great error by the change. However, NS shows no change from full model simulation, and the new debt issue variable NL shows no better time pattern of debt issue than in the full model case.

This was typical of the results of all the hypothetical simulations performed. These results suggest that more exogenous information could be helpful and that a different specification may be needed to more fully explain Anheuser-Busch's external financing decisions over the 1968–1975 sample period. The model's lack of a perfect fit is not unusual or a cause for concern, however. Fitting an econometric model to a specific application is like fitting a suit of clothes—perfect fits are rare. Most people are willing to settle for a very good fit rather than pay the high cost of endless alterations as they seek that elusive "perfect fit everywhere." In the final analysis, we are convinced that this model has superior explanatory power over a wide range of applications. (See footnote 3.)

SUMMARY AND CONCLUSION

Forecasting is a difficult exercise. The use of a model such as the FR model allows the financial manager insight into what is required for forecasts. Financial managers who must prepare *pro forma* financial statements, project financial needs, and answer "what if" questions about the effects of differing

EXHIBIT 8. HYPOTHETICAL INDUSTRY SALES GROWTH RATE

Variable and Code*		1968	1969	1970	1971	1972	1973	1974	1975	Bias	AAE	RMSE
$S_t	S	625.07	740.22	814.04	926.41	1043.26	1124.59	1416.50	1688.46	27.34	34.25	41.32
	D	-27.63	73.62	21.26	23.96	65.76	14.88	3.41	43.48			
EBIT	S	93.76	111.03	130.25	148.23	166.92	134.95	127.48	202.61	4.78	7.90	9.03
	D	-6.56	10.69	2.37	5.57	13.99	3.42	-5.91	14.71			
I_t^A	S	.05	.05	.06	.06	.06	.06	.06	.06	0.00	0.00	0.00
	D	0.00	-.01	0.00	0.00	0.00	0.00	0.00	-0.01			
NL_t	S	21.06	13.27	15.89	13.92	10.49	7.51	13.40	36.83	-14.70	35.24	51.89
	D	21.06	13.27	15.89	13.92	10.49	7.51	-86.60	-113.17			
S_t	S	106.70	106.70	106.70	106.70	106.70	106.70	106.70	106.70	7.43	7.43	8.97
	D	14.98	13.65	12.85	5.20	3.40	3.13	3.13	3.13			
NIAT	S	42.38	50.61	63.08	74.24	83.27	67.01	64.18	96.22	3.27	3.83	5.27
	D	-2.25	5.29	0.53	2.59	6.87	1.43	0.16	11.50			
NLS_t	S	36.04	13.27	15.89	13.92	10.49	7.51	13.40	36.83	-75.92	75.92	88.73
	D	34.59	11.94	15.09	6.27	8.69	7.24	-86.6	-113.17			
L_t	S	115.16	148.20	143.98	130.49	109.60	100.93	106.64	229.01	-20.78	36.05	52.27
	D	-27.56	13.27	15.89	13.92	10.49	7.52	-86.59	-113.16			
NS_t	S	0.0	0.0	0.0	0.0	0.0	0.0	0.0	0.0	-1.66	-1.66	2.88
	D	-1.45	-1.33	-0.80	-7.65	-1.80	-0.27	0.0	0.0			
ΔRE_t	S	27.13	30.87	44.16	49.74	49.97	39.53	37.22	63.51	2.14	2.49	3.37
	D	-1.38	3.40	0.59	1.89	3.76	0.99	0.25	7.63			

S − A = D
*See Appendix A for definitions of all variables.

416

rates of inflation and/or other proposed changes should find the model helpful. It provides sufficient detail through disaggregation into unit sales, unit production, capacity utilization, and unit pricing sectors to be of considerable use to management for both forecasting and simulation. Disaggregation is carried to the point where economic, technical, and behavioral relationships can be treated explicitly, although not to the point that would cause the model to be unmanageable.

Disaggregation provides the benefit of explicit treatment of the relevant market share assumptions and the behavioral determinants of financing costs which adds considerably to the model's explanatory power. A technical production function relationship allows disaggregation from dollar-denominated quantities to units of output and thus facilitates the analysis of price changes in input factors and/or the firm's own products. In addition, the model's determination of the firm's full capacity production capability as a function of the company's past performance is essential in the development of a realistic analysis of expansion and contraction within the firm.

The model is dynamic, as any model that attempts to simulate asset expansion should be, since previous decisions influence current decisions. A brief history of previous decisions is incorporated into the model through lagged variables. This occurs in the production function as well as in pricing and debt cost equations.

Additionally, the FR model takes explicit account of risk and of the influence that both the operating and financial leverage of the company have on risk. Furthermore, risk is fed back to simultaneously determine capital costs, in turn affecting the financing decision. This is an example of simultaneity in the model among financial decisions, company risk, and financing costs. One decision cannot be made without affecting others.

REFERENCES

1. W. T. Carleton, "An Analytical Model for Long-Range Financial Planning," *Journal of Finance* (May 1970), pp. 291–315.
2. E. Eugene Carter, "A Simultaneous Equation Approach To Financial Planning: A Comment," *Journal of Finance* (September 1973), pp. 1035–38.
3. B. E. Davis, G. J. Caccapplo, and M. A. Chandry, "An Econometric Planning Model for American Telephone and Telegraph Company," *The Bell Journal of Economics and Management Science* (Spring 1973), pp. 29–56.
4. J. Walter Elliot, "Forecasting and Analysis of Corporate Financial Performance With An Econometric Model of The Firm," *Journal of Financial and Quantitative Analysis* (March 1972), pp. 1499–1526.
5. Jack Clark Francis, "Analysis of Equity Returns: A Survey With Extensions," *Journal of Economics and Business* (Spring/Summer 1977), pp. 181–92.
6. G. W. Gershefski, "Building a Corporate Financial Model," *Harvard Business Review* (July/August 1969), pp. 61–72.

7. ———. "Corporate Models: The State of the Art," *Managerial Planning* (November/December 1969), pp. 1–6.
8. T. Haavelmo, "The Statistical Implications of a System of Simultaneous Equations," *Econometrica* (January 1943), pp. 1–12.
9. L. R. Klein, "Estimation of Interdependent Systems in Macroeconometrics," *Econometrica* (April 1969), pp. 171–92.
10. ———. *A Textbook in Econometrics*, 2nd ed., Englewood Cliffs, N.J., Prentice-Hall, Inc., 1974.
11. E. Lerner and W. T. Carleton, "The Integration of Capital Budgeting and Stock Valuation," *American Economic Review* (September 1964), pp. 683–702.
12. R. Mattessich, "Budgeting Models and System Simulation," *Accounting Review* (July 1961), pp. 384–97.
13. S. C. Myers and G. A. Pogue, "A Programming Approach to Corporate Financial Management," *Journal of Finance* (May 1974), pp. 579–99.
14. Robert S. Pindyck and Daniel L. Rubinfeld, *Econometric Models and Economic Forecasts*, New York, McGraw-Hill Book Co., 1976.
15. A. A. Robichek and S. C. Myers, *Optimal Financing Decisions*, Englewood Cliffs, N.J., Prentice-Hall, Inc., 1965.
16. S. Salzman, "An Econometric Model of A Firm," *Review of Economics and Statistics* (August 1967), pp. 332–42.
17. Securities and Exchange Commission, Release No. 5695, "Notice of Adoption of Amendments to Regulations S-X Requiring Disclosure of Certain Replacement Cost Data," March 23, 1976.
18. Securities and Exchange Commission, Release No. 33-5699, April 23, 1976.
19. J. M. Warren and John P. Shelton, "A Simultaneous Equation Approach To Financial Planning," *Journal of Finance* (December 1971), pp. 1123–42.
20. ———. "A Simultaneous Equation Approach to Financial Planning: Reply," *Journal of Finance* (September 1973), pp. 1039–42.
21. H. M. Weingartner, *Mathematical Programming and the Analysis of Capital Budgeting Problems*, Chicago, Markham Publishing Co., 1967.
22. John Burr Williams, *The Theory of Investment Value*, Cambridge, Harvard University Press, 1938.

Appendix A. LIST OF VARIABLES

Endogenous

Sales_t^P	Potential industry sales (units)
S_t^{FC}	Full capacity unit output (company)
S_t^a	Actual company unit output
S_t^P	Potential company unit output
γ_{it}	Measure of necessary new investment (based on units)
γ_{2t}	Measure of *slack* due to underutilization of existing resources
K_t	Units of capital stock
NK_t	Desired new capital (capital units)

FA_t	Fixed assets (current $)
NF_t	Desired new investment (current $)
P_{ts}	Output price
$\$S_t$	Sales dollars (current $)
COG_t	Cost of goods (current $)
OC_t	Overhead, selling, cost of goods, depreciation, and interest expense (current $)
$OC2_t$	Non-operating income (current $)
D_t	Depreciation expense (current $)
INV_t	Inventory (current $)
L_t	Long term debt
i_t^L	Cost of new debt (%)
NL_t	New long term debt needed ($)
NS_t	New common stock (equity) needed ($)
$NIAT_t$	Net income after tax (current $)
RE_t	Retained earnings
$EBIT_t$	Earnings before interest and taxes
i_t^A	Weighted average cost of long term debt
υ_{EBIT}	Coefficient of variation of EBIT
i_t^s	Cost of new stock issue
υ_{NIAT}	Coefficient of variation of NIAT
TEV_t	Total equity value
g_t^a	Growth rate in $\$S_t$
$EAFCD_t$	Earnings available for common dividend
$CMDIV_t$	Common dividend
ΔRE_t	Contributions to RE made in the tth period
GOP_t	Gross operating profit (current $)

Exogenous

$GSALS_t$	Growth rate in potential industry sales
$Sales_{t-1}^P$	Previous period potential industry sales (units)
S_{t-1}^{FC}	Previous period company full capacity unit output
INV_{t-1}	Previous period company finished good inventory
FA_{t-1}	Previous period company fixed asset base ($)
γ_t	Capacity utilization index
c_t	Desired market share
θ	Proportionality coefficient of S_t^{FC} to K_t
P_{kt}	GNP component index for capital equipment
P	Percentage markup of output price over ratio of GOP_t/INV_t
δ_2	Proportionality coefficient of OC_t to $\$S_t$
ϕ	Proportionality coefficient of D_t to FA_t
N	Proportionality coefficient of INV_t to $\$S_t$
LR_t	Repayment of long-term debt

T_t	Corporate tax rate
b_t	Retention rate
U_t^L	Underwriting cost of new debt
$PFDIV_t$	Preferred dividend
i_{t-1}^A	Previous period weighted average cost of long-term debt
L_{t-1}	Previous period long-term debt
k	Optimal capital structure assumption
α_L, β_L	Coefficients in risk-return tradeoff for new debt
α_s, β_s	Coefficients in risk-return tradeoff for new stock
GOP_{t-1}	Gross operating profit of previous period
δ_1	Ratio of COG_t to actual net sales
δ_3	Ratio of OC2 to net sales
$\alpha_1, \alpha_2, \alpha_3$	Production function coefficients
Σ_1	Ratio of CA_t to net sales
Σ_2	Ratio of CL_t to net sales
$\sigma_{Sales_t^p}^2$	Standard deviation of industry sales

Appendix B. LIST OF EQUATIONS

1. Industry Sales
    (1) $Sales_t^p = Sales_{t-1}^p (1 + GSALS_t)$
2. Company Production Sector
    (2) $S_t^{FC} = \alpha_1 S_{t-1}^{FC} + \alpha_2 INV_{t-1} + \alpha_3 FA_{t-1}$
    (3) $\frac{S_t^a}{S_t^{FC}} = \gamma_t \to S_t^a = \gamma_t S_t^{FC}$
    (4) $S_t^p = c_t Sales_t^p$
3. Capital Stock Requirements Sector
    (5) $S_t^p - S_t^a = (S_t^{FC} - S_t^a) + (S_t^p - S_t^{FC})$
    (6) $S_t^{FC} - S_t^a = \gamma_{2t}$
    (7) $S_t^p - S_t^{FC} = \gamma_{1t} \quad 0 \le \gamma_{1t}$
    (8) $K_t = \theta S_t^{FC}$
    (9) $NK_t = \theta \gamma_{1t}$
4. Pricing Sector
    (10) $P_{Kt} \cdot K_t = FA_t, FA_t/K_t = P_{Kt}$
    (11) $P_{Kt} \cdot NK_t = NF_t$
    (12) $P_{st} \cdot S_t^a = \$S_t^a$
    (13) $P_{ts} = p (GOP_{t-1}/ INV_{t-1})$

5. **Production Cost Sector**

   (14) $OC_t = \delta_2(\$S_t^a)$

   (15) $COG_t = \delta_1(\$S_t^a)$

   (16) $GOP_t = \$S_t^a - COG_t$

   (17) $OC2_t = \delta_3(\$S_t^a)$

6. **Income Sector**

   (18) $INV_t = N(\$S_t^a)$

   (19) $EBIT_t = \$S_t^a - OC_t + OC2_t$

   (20) $NIAT_t = (EBIT_2 - i_t^A L_t)(1 - T)$

   (20') $CL_t = \Sigma_2(\$S_t^a)$

7. **New Financing Required Sector**

   (21) $NF_t + b_t \{(1 - T)[i_t^L NL_t + U_t^L NL_t]\} = $
   $$NLS_t + \Delta RE_t + (CL_t - CL_{t-1})$$

   (22) $NLS_t = NS_t + NL_t$

   (23) $\Delta RE_t = b_t \{(1 - T)[EBIT_t - i_t^A L_t - U_t^L NL_t] - PFDIV_t\}$

   (24) $i_t^A = i_{t-1}^A \left[\dfrac{L_{t-1} - LR_t}{L_t} \right] + i_t^L \dfrac{NL_t}{L_t}$

   (25) $\dfrac{NL_t}{NS_t + \Delta RE_t} = k$

   (26) $L_t = L_{t-1} - LR_t + NL_t$

8. **Risk Sector**

   (27) $\sigma_{ebit}^2 = \Theta_1^2 \cdot \Theta_2^2 \cdot \sigma_{sales_t^p}^2$

   (28) $\sigma_{niat}^2 = \Theta_5^2 \cdot \Theta_6^2 \cdot \Theta_2^2 \cdot \sigma_{sales_t^p}^2$

9. **Costs of Financing Sector**

   (29) $i_t^L = \alpha_L + \beta_L v_{EBIT}$

   (30) $v_{EBIT} = \dfrac{\sigma_{EBIT}}{\overline{R}_{EBIT}}$

   (31) $i_t^s = \alpha_s + \beta_s v_{NIAT}$

   (32) $v_{NIAT} = \dfrac{\sigma_{NIAT}}{\overline{R}_{NIAT}}$

10. **Valuation of Equity Sector**

   (33) $TEV_t = \dfrac{CMDIV_t}{i_t^s - g_t^a}$

   (34) $EAFCD_t = (1 - T_t)[EBIT_t - i_t^A L_t - U_t^L NL_t] - PFDIV_t$

   (35) $CMDIV_t = (1 - b_t) EAFCD_t$

   (36) $g_t^a = \dfrac{\$S_t - \$S_{t-1}}{\$S_{t-1}}$

Appendix C. TRANSFORMATION OF INDUSTRY SALES MOMENTS TO COMPANY NIAT AND EBIT MOMENTS

EBIT

$$
\begin{aligned}
\text{EBIT}_t &= \$S_t^a - OC_t - D_t \\
&= \$S_t^a - \delta_2 \$S_t^a - \phi FA_t \\
&= \$S_t^a - \delta_2 \$S_t^a - \phi P_{kt} \, \Theta \cdot \frac{1}{\gamma_t} \cdot \frac{\$S_t^a}{P_{st}} \\
&= \left\{ 1 - \sigma_2 - \phi \left[\left(\frac{P_{kt}}{P_{ts}} \right) \cdot \Theta \left(\frac{1}{\gamma_t} \right) \right] \right\} \$S_t^a \\
&= \Theta_1 \$S_t
\end{aligned}
$$

If $S_t^p = S_t^{FC}$ then $S_t^{FC} = c_t \text{ Sales}_t^p$

$\therefore S_t^p = c_t \text{ Sales}_t^p$

Since: $S_t^a = \gamma_t S_t^{FC} = \gamma_t [c_t \text{ Sales}_t^p]$

so: $P_{ts} S_t^a = \$S_t = P_{ts} \gamma_t [c_t \text{ Sales}_t^p]$

and: $\$S_t^a = \Theta_2 \text{ Sales}_t^p$

Hence: $\text{EBIT}_t = \Theta_i \cdot \Theta_2 \cdot \text{ Sales}_t^p$

then: $\sigma_{\text{EBIT}}^2 = \Theta_1^2 \cdot \Theta_2^2 \, \sigma_{\text{sales}_t^p}^2$

NIAT

$\text{NIAT}_t = [1 - T] [\text{EBIT}_t - i^A L_t - U^L NL_t]$

if $U^L = 0$

also:

$$
L_t = \frac{\left[\Sigma_1 + \dfrac{P_k \Theta_t}{\gamma_t P_{ts}} - \Sigma_2 \right]}{[1 + \dfrac{1}{k}]} \$S_t^a
$$

$$
\begin{aligned}
&= \Theta_4 \$S_t \\
\text{NIAT} &= [1 - T] [\Theta_1 \cdot \$S_t^a - i_t^A \Theta_4 \cdot \$S_t^a] \\
&= [1 - T] [\Theta_1 - i_t^A \Theta_4] \$S_t^a \\
&= [1 - T] [\Theta_1 - i_t^A \Theta_4] \Theta_2 \text{ Sales}_t^p \\
&= \Theta_5 \cdot \Theta_6 \cdot \Theta_2 \text{ Sales}_t^p \\
\text{NIAT}_t &= \Theta_5 \cdot \Theta_6 \cdot \Theta_2 \text{ Sales}_t^p
\end{aligned}
$$

then:

$\sigma_{\text{NIAT}}^2 = \Theta_5^2 \cdot \Theta_6^2 \cdot \Theta_2^2 \cdot \sigma_{\text{sales}^p}^2$

where:

$$\Theta_1 = \left[1 - \delta_2 - \phi \left(\frac{P_k}{P_{ts}} \right) \cdot \Theta \left(\frac{1}{\gamma_t} \right) \right]$$

$$\Theta_2 = P_{ts}\, \gamma_t\, c_t$$

$$\Theta_4 = \left\{ \frac{\left[\Sigma_1 + \dfrac{\Theta_k\, P_k}{\gamma_t\, P_{ts}} - \Sigma_2 \right]}{\left[1 + \dfrac{1}{k} \right]} \right\}$$

$$\Theta_5 = [1 - T_t]$$
$$\Theta_6 = [\Theta_1 - i_t^A\, \Theta_4]$$
and:
$$\mathcal{C}A_t = \Sigma_1 \cdot \$S_t^a$$
$$D_t = \phi FA_t.$$

Also, parameters δ_2, Θ, γ_t, Σ_2, are defined in the List of Equations (Appendix A).

Appendix D. FRANCIS-ROWELL PREDICTIONS COMPARED TO WARREN-SHELTON [19] PREDICTIONS

This Appendix compares the *ex post* simulation results of the FR model with the most similar (and perhaps the best known) other model. In contrast to the FR model, the WS [19] model is exact if the coefficients are allowed to take their actual values during each time period and if the company dollar sales data are accurate. However, if the sales data are erroneous, then every dependent variable is predicted incorrectly (since all are tied directly to company sales). Asset requirements are linked directly to the same period's sales without allowance for slack. This suggests the unlikely short-run result that in a normal business cycle as sales decline, the company will divest capital, and as sales move upward toward previous levels, new assets are acquired. Furthermore, no distinction is made between company sales growth attributable to either price increases or output volume increases. Asset expansion will occur for either type of company sales increase. Because the WS model is based on a percentage of sales specification, error in the exogenous company sales input will be transmitted to all accounts. To demonstrate this, as well as to put both models on a comparable sales basis, the solved sales data from the FR model were employed as the exogenous input to the WS model.

EXHIBIT 9. WARREN & SHELTON MODEL RESULTS

Variable and Code*		1968	1969	1970	1971	1972	1973	1974	1975	Bias	AAE	RMSE
$S_t	S					(exogenous)						
	D											
EBIT_t	S	96.01	111.48	131.30	146.35	163.26	133.24	133.76	192.97	3.93	5.01	6.16
	D	-4.30	11.14	3.42	3.70	10.33	1.71	0.36	5.07			
I^A_t	S	.05	.06	.06	.06	.06	.06	.07	.07	.005	.005	.006
	D	.00	.00	.00	.00	.00	.00	.01	.00			
NL_t	S	70.77	95.27	65.03	57.32	83.26	78.67	72.78	140.65	51.72	60.86	66.66
	D	70.77	95.27	65.03	57.32	83.26	78.67	-27.22	-9.35			
S_t	S	90.27	91.72	93.05	93.85	101.5	103.3	203.57	253.57	29.59	32.91	63.80
	D	-1.45	-1.33	-0.80	-7.65	-1.8	-0.27	100.00	150.00			
NIAT	S	42.66	50.61	64.23	73.92	81.85	66.31	62.33	82.93	1.25	2.61	3.09
	D	-1.97	5.30	1.68	2.28	5.45	0.73	-1.69	-1.79			
NLS_t	S	71.77	96.72	66.36	58.12	90.91	80.47	173.05	190.65	70.61	70.61	72.68
	D	70.32	95.39	65.66	50.47	89.11	80.20	73.05	40.65			
L_t	S	142.58	136.55	129.76	114.73	97.54	95.50	230.89	433.72	16.38	17.27	35.03
	D	-0.13	1.62	1.67	-1.84	-1.57	2.09	37.66	91.55			
NS_t	S	1.0	1.45	1.33	.80	7.65	1.80	100.27	50.00	18.88	20.70	39.76
	D	-0.45	0.12	.53	-6.85	5.85	1.53	100.27	50.00			
ΔRE	S	28.51	30.94	41.54	48.52	47.05	36.41	38.45	56.41	0.36	1.39	1.74
	D	0.0	3.47	-2.02	0.67	0.85	-2.13	1.47	.053			

S = Solved
D = Deviation
*See Appendix A for definitions of all variables.

424

This shows the transmission of error and allows a direct comparison of RMSE of both models (see footnote six about RMSE).

Exhibit 9 presents the results of the WS model simulated on Anheuser-Busch data over the 1968–1975 sample period. These results should be compared with the FR full model simulation results shown in Exhibit 5. The WS model performs comparatively well for EBIT, NIAT, and RE, showing a lower RMSE in all cases than the FR model. This is due to the endogenized cost of new debt (i_t^* of the FR model). This cost, as explained earlier, must be simulated with error because the historically fit risk-tradeoff function coefficients were used without any changes. However, the difference in errors is not great. The most pronounced difference in the models' performances occurs in the new financing-required sector variables. In the case of NS (new stock financing), the RMSE difference is 93%, whereas NL (new debt financing) shows a RMSE difference of 23%. The RMSE differences of the WS model results are considerably larger. Consequently, the asymmetrical-non-proportionality specification of the FR model appears to explain more accurately the variability in external financing required. Furthermore, if the errors introduced by the cost of financing and pricing sectors are eliminated, the difference between FR and WS models would be negligible in the case of the income variables but huge (in favor of the FR model) over the external financing variables.

The results for Anheuser-Busch reported above suggest that the advantages inherent in the comparable WS model were not lost in extending it to develop the FR model. However, it appears that refinements added in the FR model will result in improved predictive performance.

QUESTIONS

1. Contrast the meaning of simultaneous and recursive.
2. Describe the importance of the industry sales forecast to the FR model.
3. In the FR model, how are industry sales used to predict firm sales and production?
4. Explain how fixed capital stock (plant, equipment, and permanent working capital) is assumed to be related to sales.
5. How is price related to cost in this model?
6. How is NIAT related to sales in the model?
7. Explain how new financing is determined.
8. In the FR model, what is used to represent risk? How does this compare with risk in the Modigliani-Pogue articles?
9. What determines the cost of financing?
10. Describe the common stock valuation formula. What assumptions are consistent with this formula?

25 | Michael C. Jensen and William H. Meckling

Can the Corporation Survive?

The authors present a disturbing analysis of trends regarding government and business in the United States. While this article may not be strictly classified as financial management, it most assuredly has to do with the environment in which financial managers must operate. Certainly, the success of the corporation in America is related to how well financial managers respond to the challenges presented.

A. THE GROWTH OF GOVERNMENT AND ITS IMPACT ON THE CORPORATION

The corporate executive's power to make decisions affecting owners, employees, and consumers, is becoming more constrained every day. He must answer to various governmental authorities for his personnel policies—hiring, firing, promotion, wages, pensions and other compensation, unionization, etc. His financial reporting must meet the requirements of the Securities and Exchange Commission and the Federal Trade Commission. The Internal Revenue Service dictates how he must keep his accounts for their purposes. The Justice Department and Federal Trade Commission must be consulted on acquisitions and mergers. He must meet the requirements of the Occupational Safety and Health Act in his plants or places of business. His advertising and sales practices are scrutinized by the Federal Trade Commission. He must comply with an imposing array of environmental regulations (federal, state, and local) dealing both with his products and his operations. He is restricted in his use of land. Sales of some products such as DDT, cyclamates, and red number 2 food coloring have been banned, TV sets must have UHF tuners, automobiles must embody a long list of safety and anti-pollution devices, new drugs can be marketed only with permission of the FDA. The list of regulations confronted by a businessman today is almost endless.

Source. Reprinted by permission from *Financial Analysts Journal*, January–February 1978, pp. 31–37. This version is slightly different because the authors requested that we use an unedited version, which we did. Michael Jensen is associate professor and William Meckling is dean, both at the Graduate School of Management, University of Rochester.

Though it is only a tiny portion of the costs of regulation, the paper work required to meet the demands of the cognizant regulatory agencies is alone almost overwhelming. Some recent estimates[1] indicate that the twenty major oil companies spend approximately $60 million per year just to meet government report requirements. Indiana Standard, for example, files 24,000 pages of reports per year with federal agencies, plus another 225,000 pages of supplementary computer output to FEA per year.

"What else is new?" you say. The growth of government—as measured either by its expenditures or by its propensity to regulate, traces back almost to the ratification of the Constitution. During the last 200 years we've managed to achieve the most spectacular growth in human welfare in history. Why can't we expect the same kind of economic growth in the future? Indeed, won't the pendulum swing back toward a reduction in the role of government? Aren't there signs of concern on the part of the public with government's size and the extent of its interventions in private affairs, which will turn things around in the future?

Our answers to those questions are all negative. We see no forces which are likely to curb the gradual encroachment of government. Moreover, we believe the era of dramatic economic growth is over; not because of new resource or technological constraints; not because we are running short of energy, we are not; not because we are confronted with environmental or ecological disaster, we are not; *but because government is destroying the individual incentives which are the well-springs of economic growth*. We see the large private corporation as one of the casualties of this process. The corporate form of organization is likely to disappear completely, but even if it survives in some form, the larger corporations as we know them are destined to be destroyed. Indeed, in a few industries we believe their demise is imminent!

Assets of these firms will not instantaneously disappear. Some firms will simply go out of business, selling off those assets which have value in other uses and abandoning those that don't. Other firms will take different organizational forms. Some will be nationalized, some will become labor managed, and many more companies (in the early stages at least) will be subjected to increased governmental control through the appointment of more "public representatives" on their boards of directors.

We raise the question of the survivability of the corporate form not because we are particularly concerned with the welfare of current stockholders, but because we believe the process which is endangering corporate survival will in the aggregate reduce human welfare and lead to a society in which the right of individuals to decide their own fate is substantially reduced.

---

[1] James Carberry, "Red Tape Entangles Big Petroleum Firms in Complying With Federal Regulations," *Wall Street Journal*, September 3, 1975, p. 32.

B. "SOCIAL RESPONSIBILITY"
AND THE ATTACK ON CORPORATIONS

Large corporations today are being forced by law and by threat of law (euphemistically called social responsibility) to serve as a vehicle for effecting almost any social reform which happens to take someone's fancy—discrimination, poverty, training, safety, pollution, etc. These demands generally amount to nothing more than a requirement that the corporation bestow benefits on one group of individuals at the expense of another group.

People are often led to believe by the press, politicians, social activists, etc. that benefits or costs can be granted or imposed on "corporations". This is a brilliant fallacy, useful in championing many causes. A moment's thought, however, will convince almost anyone that since the corporation is not human (in fact, it is only a legal fiction which serves as a nexus for a very complex set of contracts between individuals), to speak of imposing costs or benefits on it is just as sensible as speaking about imposing costs or benefits on a rock or a machine. The costs and benefits which are often characterized as being imposed on the corporation are in fact imposed on the human parties to the contracts (explicit and implicit) effected through the corporation. These individuals are the owners of the corporation (stock and bond holders), consumers, and labor.

In almost all cases, part of the wealth transfer implied by the various "socially responsible" actions demanded of corporations is from the owners of the corporation to the beneficiaries of the actions—women, Blacks, consumers of a clean environment, etc. Whether one judges these wealth transfers to be good or bad, desirable or undesirable, is a matter of personal value judgment which as economists and scientists, we can say nothing about. However, we can, as economists, analyze the impact such changes will have on individuals and on the corporation as an organizational form.

Corporations can, in the long run, behave in a "socially responsible" way only to a very limited extent. When it becomes clear that "socially responsible" behavior is abrogating the rights of the owners, the values of corporate ownership claims will fall (as they have) and corporations will be unable to raise new capital, or will be able to raise it only at very high costs. The costs imposed on the owners of corporations through the implementation of the notion of corporate responsibility (often accomplished through procedures which are only thinly disguised blackmail) is generally equivalent to the imposition of special taxes on those owners. At some point when the expected future cash flows to the owners are sufficiently small and sufficiently uncertain, those ownership claims will become worthless (like the value of many rent controlled apartment buildings in New York City which continue to be abandoned by their owners at record rates). In these circumstances, the corporation will be able to remain in business only to the extent that it can finance its operations out of internally generated cash flows or through financing or subsidies from the public sector. If such subsidies are forthcoming, of course they will be accompanied by additional constraints, controls and guidelines, and the end result will be either government takeover or destruction. The Penn Central Railroad is an example of the terminal stages of this process, and we discuss it in more detail below.

C. THE INCONSISTENCY BETWEEN DEMOCRACY AND THE MARKET SYSTEM

The threat to the continued existence of the large corporation is only part of a much more pervasive issue which affects most aspects of every individual's life. This issue is the fundamental conflict between our form of political democracy and the market system. We are convinced that these two systems are incompatible with each other, and it seems only a matter of time before the political sector succeeds in eliminating much of the private sector of the economy. We readily acknowledge that this incompatibility is inconsistent with the notion with which we have all been indoctrinated, that government is the agency which *protects* the rights of individuals, *enforces* contracts, etc.

In fact, of course, the government plays two very different roles. It does have responsibility for protecting rights, but it also has the power through legislation and through court decisions to alter individual rights. The use of this power by politicians, bureaucrats, and various special interest groups to increase their own welfare at the expense of others is the basic source of the inconsistency between a political democracy as we know it, and the market system.

D. THE ROLE OF CONTRACTING RIGHTS AND RIGHTS IN PROPERTY

While property rights and contracting rights play a crucial role in all our lives, we tend to take them for granted. Even economists in their analyses of the forces which determine the prices of various goods and services, often overlook the fact that what is really bought and sold in markets is not simply physical objects, but sets of rights in those objects—the right to take physical possession, the right to resell, the right to consume, the right to change the form of the object, the right to transport it, etc. It is not the price of a bushel of wheat as a physical object that is determined by the forces of supply and demand; it is the price of the set of rights which goes with "title" to wheat, i.e., the right to resell it, to grind it into flour, to take physical possession, to transport it, etc. If the bundle of rights which goes with owning wheat is changed, the value of the "wheat" changes. The same comments hold for land, (e.g., does it include mineral rights?, how is it zoned?), for buildings, for capital equipment, for radio frequencies, for money, even for the value of the services which we perform with our minds and muscle. The value of all goods is determined by the rights individuals possess in those goods.

By now, it should be clear what we mean by rights. We do not use that term in any moral or ethical sense, but simply to refer to actions which the law allows *specific* individuals (owners) to take, including writing contracts with others.

Consideration of the role of rights is particularly important in the case of financial instruments—stocks, bonds, notes, even money. Financial instruments are simply contracts. Their value depends on the rights which they confer on the owners. Generally, shares of stock give the owner a "residual" claim on the assets of the corporation—a claim on what remains after all other claimants are paid off. Bond and note holders hold claims on the assets of the corporation which are usually fixed in dollar amounts. One of the reasons the corporation is particularly vulnerable is that its very existence depends on the viability of this system of financial claims.

E. THE ROLE OF GOVERNMENT AND THE REVOCATION AND ABROGATION OF RIGHTS

Government plays two distinct roles in the operation of the property rights system. On the one hand it establishes the rules of the game; that is, it prescribes rules that determine which individuals have what rights. On the other hand, it acts as umpire or referee; it adjudicates disputes over which specific individuals have what rights, and it has a responsibility to see that the rules are followed.

It is the first of these roles, the capacity of governments to change the rules, that lies at the heart of the problem which concerns us here. As the rule maker, government can and does frequently *revoke* rights, i.e., it decrees that henceforth it will not be legal for individuals to use their property, or to enter into contracts in ways which heretofore had been sanctioned. When the government decrees that new automobiles sold in the United States must meet certain safety, antipollution, and fuel consumption requirements, they are revoking certain rights to use assets held in the name of the owners of firms and the rights of consumers to purchase products without these devices. Price controls revoke rights in the use of money, and thereby reduce the value of money (ironically, under the guise of preventing devaluation of the money).

In addition to taking actions which revoke general classes of rights, however, the government also uses its powers to *abrogate* specific contracts between individuals. Abrogation occurs when governmental authority is used to deny without compensation the rights of individuals who are party to a contract which has been created as a consideration in an exchange. This is what the government did to the bondholders of the New York Port Authority, New York City, and the Penn Central Railroad.

F. RECENT HISTORY OF REVOCATION OF RIGHTS

In recent times we seem to have witnessed a major upsurge in the revocation of rights. Examples abound and we mention only a few to illustrate the form and scope of the problem.

1. The first peacetime imposition of wage and price controls in the United States in August of 1971.
2. Environmental Protection Programs:
   a) Section 110A of the 1970 Clean Air Act limits the rights of landowners to develop such projects as major new shopping centers. The Act requires that such projects must file environmental impact statements and meet the requirements of regional planning boards before implementation.
   b) EPA standards which banned the use of high sulfur coal in many areas, and forced many utilities to convert from coal to oil, followed by Federal Energy Agency rulings which forced many of these same utilities to reconvert from oil to coal.
3. Land use planning and control:
   a) The outright prohibition of further development of the California Seashore for several years, and the current stringent limitations on building which have replaced that ban.
   b) Stringent new restrictions limiting the use of lakes and land owned by individuals in the Adirondack State Park in New York.
   c) The enactment of a law in Minnesota in 1973 placing all contained water in the State (lakes, potholes, marshes, and even puddles) under public ownership and control.
4. The spread of rent controls in metropolitan areas such as Washington, D.C., and Boston.
5. The provisions of the Occupational Safety and Health Act (OSHA) which limit the freedom of individuals to contract with employers to work under more hazardous conditions in return for higher pay.
6. Various Affirmative Action Programs of the Department of Health, Education and Welfare, which limit the employment policies of organizations.
7. The recent Federal pension reform act (ERISA) which limits the type of pension programs which firms may offer to their employees.
8. The regulation of the oil industry by the Federal Energy Administration which fixes the prices of output, and imposes production controls.

9.   Finally, we have the Woodcock-Leontief National Planning Proposal
     which is a clever first step on the road to even more widespread gov-
     ernmental control of the production and purchasing decisions of indi-
     vidual businesses and consumers. We can be sure that the proposed
     "advisory plans" will not long remain advisory when business and indi-
     viduals refuse to conform.

All of these rights have been revoked without compensation to any of the
parties who are forced to bear the costs, whether they be owners of the land,
utilities, water, rental property, etc.; employees in the industries involved; or
consumers of the product. Revocation has not been treated as an eminent
domain proceeding under which the state is required to compensate the
property owners.

G. ABROGATIONS OF CONTRACTS IN
THE FINANCIAL SECTOR

Abrogation of rights like revocation is becoming more and more common, and
the Penn Central Railroad provides one of the more prominent examples. The
story of bankruptcy of the Penn Central Railroad is interesting for two reasons: 1) because of the role which government regulatory policies have played
in bringing about the bankruptcy, and 2) because of the abrogation of the
creditors' rights which occurred following the bankruptcy.

Government policies, especially those that limited the rights of the management to hire, fire, and fix the compensation and terms of service of labor, to
abandon uneconomic lines and services, and to establish an economic tariff
structure, are the major reasons for the difficulties faced by the rail system.
Despite competition from other forms of transportation, there is no doubt that
there exists some set of rail lines and services which the owners could provide
at prices which would cover costs. Regulation, however, has prevented the
rail companies, and Penn Central in particular, from adopting this structure.

Having forced the Penn Central into bankruptcy, the government then
simply abrogated the contractual rights of bondholders and other claimants.
The creditors of the Penn Central were prevented by the federal government
from seizing the assets of the firm; a right which they clearly had under the
provisions of the indenture agreements and bankruptcy law. Meanwhile,
during the period the assets were withheld from the creditors, the firm was
operated by court appointed trustees who significantly eroded the value of the
assets—some argue to the extent of a billion dollars or more.

Furthermore, under the plan proposed and implemented by the U.S. Rail-
way Association (established by Congress in 1973 to develop a "rescue plan"
for the Penn Central and other Eastern railroads) those assets have been

transferred to Conrail in return for Conrail common and junior preferred stock, and USRA "certificates of value" (and not a cent in cash). It is unlikely that the Conrail common and junior preferred stock will ever have value (imagine the value of residual claims on the Post Office). The USRA "certificates of value" which are similar to debentures maturing in 12 years (or earlier, at the option of USRA) carry an 8% interest rate, but the base value of the certificates was set at approximately $450 million. The final payment on the certificates will be reduced from $450 million by the actual value of the Conrail common and junior preferred stock at the time of the certificates' redemption. This is the total compensation offered Penn Central's creditors whose claims amounted to $3.5 billion.

The trustees for the creditors assert that the assets of the Penn Central are worth $7.5 billion. The approximate valuation of $450 million placed on those assets in the government's takeover was arrived at by a procedure which can only be described as ludicrous. First, the assets were valued at their dismantled scrap value ($3.6 billion). It was then assumed that conversion to scrap would take place over 25 years. 50% of the estimated scrap value was deducted for the cost of the liquidation. Another $1 billion was subtracted for the time delay in the receipt of such proceeds, and another deduction was made for payment for the Northeastern corridor, which will go to Amtrak. The $450 million figure was what was left.

Meanwhile, the Department of Transportation stopped the trustees from paying debt service due on equipment obligations despite the special exemption provision in Section 77j of the Bankruptcy Act passed by Congress which provides that these obligations shall be enforced despite bankruptcy proceedings.[2] The important point in all of this is that these changes in the contractual rights have been made by the Congress and the courts without consent of the Penn Central creditors, and in violation of the agreement which they had effected with the Penn Central when the loans were made.

We predict that the implications of these actions taken by the government in the Penn Central case will be the nationalization of much of the rest of the transportation industry (including the airlines). The public utility and oil industries will not be far behind.

Why do we make these predictions? Given what is happening to financial contracts, we believe that a mortgage on a Commonwealth Edison plant is not worth much more than the paper it is printed on. In the event of bankruptcy, the political authorities will never allow the creditors to take over those assets. Furthermore, utilities are facing a serious cost-price squeeze. The costs of fuel, of dealing with regulators, of meeting environmental standards are all rising while at the same time, political resistance to price increases is

---

[2] Richard Dicker, "U.S. Officials Blunder in Treating Creditors of Rails Adversely," *Money Manager*, February 9, 1976.

becoming more intense. The combination of these forces has substantially increased the probability of bankruptcy for many of these firms.

The increased likelihood that the bond indenture agreements will not be enforced in the event of bankruptcy and the increased probability of that event, has crippled the utilities' efforts to raise capital in the private capital market, and what little they have been able to raise has been very costly. The combination of these forces will eventually produce a decline in the quality and quantity of service offered by the utilities. When blackouts and other service failures become common, consumers will be irate. The politicians and the news media will seize on this opportunity to manufacture another of their crises—this time over the failure of privately owned regulated utilities to "properly serve" the public. The result will be public financing of some form coupled eventually with a public takeover of the assets and operations of the utilities.

H. THE NEW YORK CITY "CRISIS" AND THE ABROGATION OF CONTRACTS

Abrogation of contracts has been a major factor in the so-called New York City crisis. In June of 1975 the New York State Legislature enacted a law establishing the Municipal Assistance Corporation ("Big MAC"). This act arbitrarily, after the fact, and without compensation, abrogated the bond indenture covenants providing that the bond and note holders of New York City had first claim on the tax revenues of the City in the event of default. As reported in the Annual Report of the Controller of the City of New York 1974-75, Section 25.00 of the Local Finance Law specifies that revenue anticipation notes ". . . are issued in anticipation of the receipt of such revenues as State aid for education, local non-property taxes, etc. When these revenues are received, they must be used only for the payment of these notes as they become due." Under the law establishing "Big MAC", these revenues are now to be used first to pay for "essential services" and not as specified by the Local Finance Law.

The "moratorium" on the payment of interest on $1.6 billion of City notes maturing from December 1975 through March 1976 is another example of abrogation of New York City contracts. Note holders were offered 8% "Big MAC" bonds maturing in July 1986 in exchange. In evaluating this offer, it is interesting to note that the formal 66 page Exchange Offer says:[3]

---

[3] As quoted by Thornton L. O'Glove and Robert A. Olstein, "Out of the Frying Pan," *Barrons*, December 15, 1975, p. 11.

"The (MAC) Corporation has no taxing power. The bonds do not constitute an enforceable obligation, or a debt, of either the State or the City, and neither the State nor the City is liable thereon. Neither the faith and credit nor the taxing power of the City is pledged to the payment of the principal or of interest on the bonds."

It is unclear to us just what the noteholders of New York City were offered which might conceivably have value.

President Ford and the Congress, however, have no trouble understanding this problem of priorities from their standpoint. Their "bailout" plan provides that first claim on city revenues goes to the Federal government. This provision was also enacted without permission of the creditors of New York City.

On a more general scale, the proposed revision of the bankruptcy laws now in Congress, which, if enacted will apply to all municipalities, involves similar abrogations of the contracts of municipal bondholders throughout the entire country. The effect of the Ford bankruptcy plan will be to:

a. give the court trustee the right to issue prior claim bonds without approval of the current bondholders;
b. give the court trustee the right to decide municipal expenditures without bondholder approval;
c. finally, it will reduce the position of bondholders to one of "equity holders" in the bankrupt city with no rights to control the city's management or spending or taxing policies. They are allowed to hope that there will be something left over to pay their claims.

Contrary to the hysterical predictions by city, state, and federal political authorities and echoed by most of the news media, the mere default of New York City on its bonds would not have caused much difficulty in other cities across the country. However, if the proposed revisions to the bankruptcy law are enacted, all municipalities will face a much more hostile capital market. New York State's casual treatment of its contractual obligations will not go unnoticed in the capital markets. We cannot expect investors to be willing to hold municipal securities in the future at the same interest rates as in the past.

Unfortunately, these are not isolated instances of government abrogation of contracts. On June 15, 1975, the New York and New Jersey State Legislatures repealed the Port Authority Covenant passed by both State Legislatures in 1962 and included in all Port Authority bonds since then. This covenant forbade the Port Authority from ever financing deficit ridden mass transit systems, and it was abrogated by the two State Legislatures even though the bonds were still outstanding. Furthermore, there was no compensation made to these bondholders, and (as could be expected) the market prices of the bonds fell significantly upon repeal of the covenant.

On the purely private contracting side, we have the case of Westinghouse Electric Corporation, which has over the years made a practice of contracting with the purchasers of its nuclear plants to supply nuclear fuel. Though those contracts contained price escalator clauses, they did not allow for increases large enough to offset the dramatic increase in the cost of nuclear fuel that has occurred in the last few years. The reaction of Westinghouse was to announce that fulfilling the contracts was "commercially impracticable," and that "it is therefore legally excused from a portion of its obligations to deliver uranium."[4] It remains to be seen whether the courts will permit Westinghouse to abrogate these contracts without awarding damages to the firms which purchased reactors.

I. THE IMPACT OF REVOCATION AND ABROGATION ON THE VALUE OF RIGHTS AND PRODUCTIVE ACTIVITY

Individuals have displayed surprising ingenuity in adjusting to changes in the rules of the game in the past. Indeed, individual ingenuity lies behind the resiliency which the market place has exhibited in achieving the incredible economic progress mentioned earlier in the face of the disincentives and constraints thrown up by the political sector. But it is that same ingenuity which we believe will in the end be the undoing of the corporation. Individuals in deciding both how much wealth they will hold and the form in which they will hold it, will take into account potential returns and risk, and the same is true for trustees of pension funds, endowments, insurance funds, banks, etc. Neither individuals nor agents responsible for investment on behalf of individuals will voluntarily hold wealth in forms which promise highly uncertain and yet modest rates of return.

The value of a right to an individual depends on how transitory (or alternatively, how permanent) that right is believed to be. Tenuous rights, rights which are likely to be revoked on short notice, or abrogated when the owner attempts to enforce them, will be of little value. When potential investors become convinced that the rights of managers to use the assets of corporations in the interest of stockholders and creditors is very tenuous, or when they become convinced that the contractual rights represented by their shares, bonds, or other financial instruments are likely to be abrogated, they will simply stop investing in corporations. Mr. Richard Dicker, Vice President and General Counsel of the Equitable Life Assurance Society of the United

---

[4] "Sanctity of Contract?", *Barrons,* September 15, 1975, p. 7.

States, put the problem very well.[5] Referring to the abrogation of creditors' rights under Section 77j of the Bankruptcy Law that the Department of Transportation had perpetrated in the Penn Central case, he said:

> This is another example of why I have found it necessary to advise our investment people that in considering new capital investments in equipment obligations they can no longer rely on the Bankruptcy Act exemption provided for such obligations, so long as the Federal Government and specifically the DOT is asserting its present proposition on this matter.
>
> Not only does this deter knowledgeable investors from making new investments in railroad rolling stock, but it also has the same effect upon the similar Bankruptcy Act exemption for aviation equipment. If a Federal court can be importuned by the DOT to restrain enforcement in one case, it can be done in another.

The "rule of law" or common law devotion to precedent which introduced substantial stability into the structure of rights is being abandoned by the courts and overridden by legislative action in the passing of statutory law. We are much less certain that any contract we enter into now, or investment we might make, or property we might buy, will be subject to the same rules and regulations in the future.

Uncertainty in the structure of rights or in the "rules of the game" substantially changes both people's behavior and the use of resources. In particular, it significantly reduces private investment in the kind of long term projects which have played such an important role in determining our standard of living. It is very difficult to observe these effects because they primarily involve actions not taken, that is projects not undertaken, buildings not built, etc., and are not the stuff of which newspaper headlines are made. Nevertheless we believe their impact is substantial. The low standard of living in South America and other underdeveloped countries is due we believe in large part to the uncertainties in contract and property rights induced by the tremendous instabilities of the political system—uncertainties and instabilities brought on by revolutions, nationalizations, imposition of exchange controls, wage and price controls, etc.

We believe that the remarkably poor performance of the stock market over the past decade is due in substantial part to the fact that the concentration of wealth in large publicly held corporations is particularly susceptible to expropriation through changes in the legal, political, and regulatory climate. The total real return on the S & P 500 (adjusted for inflation) over the period 1965–1975 was −20%. For the decade 1964–1974 it was −31%. Since 1926, no

---

[5] In *Money Manager*, Vol. 5, No. 6 (February 9, 1976).

other 10-year period has shown such low returns as these two, even including those of the great depression and market crash in the 1930's. The real rate of return on all common stocks on the NYSE from 1926 to 1965 was about 7.2% per year. If stocks had risen in price enough in the period 1965–1975 to provide investors with this same average inflation adjusted return, the Dow Jones Index would have ended 1975 at a level of about 2,400 instead of 900. A. F. Ehrbar reported recently[6] that the inflation adjusted total market value of publicly held companies in the U.S. fell by $388 billion over the 10-year period 1965–1975 or almost 50% of its value. These facts are difficult to explain, because unlike the 1930's we did not experience a major collapse in the economy during this period.

We expect the effect of the erosion of private rights to show up first as a reduction in the capitalized values of the claims on assets of firms. The decline in capital values reflects investors' anticipations of reduced cash flows and increased risk. What has happened to equity values in the last decade is thus consistent with the hypothesis that private rights are deteriorating at an increasing rate. The fact that the prices of assets which are far less susceptible to "theft" by the political sector (such as gold, silver, other precious metals, and art) have increased substantially over the same period provides additional evidence consistent with our hypothesis.

J. HUMAN RIGHTS VS. PROPERTY RIGHTS AND WHY GOVERNMENT AUTHORITIES ATTACK THE PRIVATE RIGHTS SYSTEM

Understanding the nature of private rights and the role of government in the system of rights is crucial to understanding why private rights are being gradually whittled away, and why we see no stabilization or reversal of that trend. In this connection, it is worth pointing out another brilliant fallacy, namely, the false distinction between so-called "human rights" and "property rights." *All rights* are, of course, human rights; there can be no other kind. Those who use this distinction are simply resorting to a clever semantic ploy. They are fabricating a conflict between one kind of rights ("human") which are "good" and another kind of rights ("property") which are "bad". Since all rights are human rights, the only possible conflict is between individuals, i.e., conflict over which individual will have what rights.

Moreover, participants in the government sector, politicians, and bureaucrats, are as individuals no different from the rest of us. They prefer more rights to less; and they have the same incentive as the rest of us to expand the

---

[6] *Fortune Magazine* (February, 1976), p. 59.

set of rights from which they benefit. It is the latter fact that lies at the bottom of the conflict between political democracy and the market system.

As individuals, of course, government authorities cannot literally acquire title to assets like those of the Penn Central, even if the government takes over the assets. But it is not necessary for them to have full title to assets in order to capture for themselves some of the benefits derived from the use of those assets. The more readily they can control the use of the assets, the more opportunity they have to ensure that they get some benefits, and the benefits need not come to them directly. Bureaucrats and politicians can and do use their positions in government to bestow benefits on others, but they do so in exchange for votes, for campaign funds, for favors, for job offers, etc., all of which yield benefits indirectly.

Individuals who have rights benefit from stability in those rights. The more confident owners are that they will be able to retain rights, the more valuable those rights will be. If it is easy for government officials to alter rights, or if the government structure itself is very unstable, as it has been in many countries, rights will have little value.

If one looks at the other side of that coin, however, stability in private rights is by its very nature a constraint on what government (i.e., bureaucrats and politicians) can do! The more difficult it is to enact laws, issue administrative rules and regulations, or make court decisions which revoke or abrogate individual rights, the more restricted is the domain of the bureaucrat and politician. To the extent that government's power to revoke or abrogate rights is limited, the market for the services of individuals in government is limited.

Revocation and abrogation of rights is the currency in which politicians and bureaucrats deal. Like all of us, they are constantly searching for ways to expand the market for their services. To do so, they must effectively break down the system of private rights because it limits their market. Our individual interest in having rights which are immutable, is in direct conflict with the interest of bureaucrats and politicians who want to be able to alter rights at will.

K. WHY THE POLITICAL SECTOR WILL BE THE ULTIMATE VICTOR

There are two sorts of constraints that potentially could limit the efforts of government authorities to dismember the private rights system. One of these is simply the Constitution. The original framers of the Constitution clearly understood the temptation which always confronts those who exercise the power to change the rules of the game. They tried very hard to limit what government authorities could do to private rights. In Section 10 of Article I, for example, they provided that, "No State shall make any law impairing the obligation of contracts," and in Article V they provided that, "No person shall be deprived of life, liberty or property without due process of law, nor shall private property be taken for public use, without just compensation."

Whatever the Constitution says, however, the evidence suggests it is useless to rely on the courts to check either the abrogation or revocation erosion process. While a final judgement cannot be rendered yet, the courts have done nothing to deter any of the abrogations discussed above. The mere fact that the legislatures of New York and New Jersey have openly enacted laws which clearly violate the provisions of Section 10, Article I of the Constitution says something about what the legislatures think the courts will do, and therefore what we can expect from the courts on this front.

The picture is, if anything, much worse when it comes to revocation of rights. The courts have consistently upheld the power of Congress, the Administration, and regulatory authorities to promulgate almost any regulation they happen to fancy, no matter what the consequences in terms of revocation of private rights. Indeed, the courts have in recent years often taken the lead in making new laws which consistently have *revoked* previously extant private rights, especially, in the so-called "Civil Rights" arena (another semantic ploy). The truth is there is little, if any, remaining Constitutional protection of private rights against governmental attack.

In the absence of Constitutional constraints, Congress, the administration, regulatory bodies, the bureaucracy, state legislatures, etc., are constrained only by the electorate itself. We are left with the question of whether it is possible to elect a set of public officials who will not succumb to the temptation to enlarge the market for their services at the expense of private rights. We believe that this is impossible.

The basic problem is that as individuals we can all make ourselves better off in two major ways:

1. By expending time and other resources operating in the private sector to produce goods and services (be they art, automobiles, film, or education) which other people wish to buy, and
2. By expending time and other resources operating in the political sector to get the rulemaker (i.e., the government) to change the rules of the game to reallocate wealth from others in society to ourselves.

In our production activities, we generally make other people better off (otherwise they wouldn't engage in voluntary exchange with us). In our political or rule changing activities, we generally make other people worse off and for two reasons:

1. The direct effects of the wealth transfers, and
2. The indirect effects caused by the reduced incentive to produce; income

taxes, production restrictions such as are common in agriculture, licensing restrictions which prevent entry into various professions and markets, and the attenuation of property rights caused by significantly increased uncertainty over what the future rules of the game will be are some examples.

These latter effects, the effects on production, are by far the most important source of reductions in our welfare and in the long run they amount to killing the goose that laid the golden egg.

Even if we all recognize that we are in the long run making ourselves worse off as a society by appealing to the political system for individual largess, we cannot stop the process. The reason is, we cannot as an electorate, effectively agree among ourselves not to appeal to government for individual favors. It always pays some of us to form special interest groups in order to get favorable consideration. This in turn plays directly into the hands of public officials anxious to enhance their roles in society. Once some special interest groups succeed in their efforts, other groups inevitably are formed to press the cause of their members.

L. POLITICIANS AS ENTREPRENEURS

It is important to understand that politicians do not act as passive bystanders in all of this. Successful politicians are entrepreneurs, just like successful businessmen, and successful academics. They are constantly at work marketing their product. One of the most effective tactics they can use is to manufacture and promote various crises and then magnanimously come to our rescue. This is why they engage in the rhetoric of crisis—the energy crisis, the environmental crisis, the food crisis, the New York City crisis, the population crisis, the consumerism crisis, the multi-national corporation crisis, the unemployment crisis, etc., etc.

The creation of crises is, of course, an old political strategem. 180 years ago, James Madison described it as: "The old trick of turning every contingency into a resource for accumulating force in the government." In their marketing campaigns designed to create crises, politicians and bureaucrats have an enormous advantage because of their access to the press and the media. Furthermore, the fact that crises sell newspapers and attract TV viewers results in a natural alliance between the political sector and the mass media which does not exist for the corporate sector.

Corporations are a particularly vulnerable target for the marketing campaigns of politicians, and this is not simply a matter of identifying the behavior of corporate executives with self-interest and exploitation in contrast to the asserted "public interest" motivation of politicians. Corporations represent large visible blocks of wealth. Corporate stockholders and creditors are a widely dispersed and incohesive group. The financial claims on the assets of corporations are often held by intermediaries—banks, insurance companies, pension funds, college endowments, etc.—so that many of the beneficiaries (depositors, insured individuals, students, etc.) are not even aware that they are the beneficiaries. Moreover, the market for these claims is both volatile and complex, so that even if the "owners" are aware of their ownership, they cannot easily identify any decline in the value of their claims with the actions of government. Only a naive view of the behavior of politicians would lead anyone to believe that they would pass up this obvious opportunity to use the corporation as a pawn in expanding their own power.

In the early 1930's the famous economist Henry Simons correctly foresaw the trend toward organized interest groups and its implications for the future. The trade union movement of the 1930's provided the motivating force for his concerns. Speaking about this trend he said:

> "The petty warfare of competition within groups can be kept on such a level that it protects and actually promotes the general welfare. The warfare among organized economic groups, on the other hand, is unlikely to be more controllable or less destructive than warfare among nations. Indeed, democratic governments would have hardly so good a chance of arbitrating these conflicts tolerably as have the League of Nations and the World Court in their field.
>
> "Suppression of the competitive struggle within economic groups, and their organization into collective fighting units, will create conditions such that only ruthless dictatorship can maintain the degree of order necessary to survival of the population in an economy of intricate division of labor. Under these circumstances the distribution of power among nations is likely, by the way, to be altered drastically in favor of those people best disciplined to submission and least contaminated with dangerous notions about the rights of man. . . .
>
> "It seems nowise fantastic, indeed, to suggest that present developments point toward a historic era which will bear close resemblance at many points to the early Middle Ages. . . . With the disappearance of free trade within national areas will come endless, destructive conflict among organized economic groups—which should suffice, without assistance from international wars, for the destruction of Western civilization and its institutional heritage."[7]

[7] Henry Simons, "A Positive Program for Laissez Faire: Some Positive Proposals for a Liberal Economic Society," in *Economic Policy for a Free Society* (University of Chicago Press: Chicago, Illinois, 1948).

M. THE PITFALLS OF EVALUATION OF INDIVIDUAL PROGRAMS

By now it will surely have occurred to the critical reader that we have not addressed the question of whether some of these government regulatory activities or programs are on balance desirable. Don't any of them do more good than harm? Our neglect of that issue is not accidental. We believe that focusing on costs and benefits of government in the small is a pitfall. It prevents us from seeing the forest for the trees.

Government officials neither advocate nor use the net benefits criterion as a basis for their decisions. There is no survival test in the political arena which induces politicians and bureaucrats to enact only those programs or take only those actions for which the benefits exceed the costs. It is in their interest to expand the demand for their services through expanding their power in any way they can, and we cannot expect them to limit that expansion only to acts which yield net benefits to society.

To assess the consequences of government one must look at the total picture in the context of how the political system actually functions, rather than at individual programs in the context of some hypothetical or wishful notion about how the political system might operate. It is our judgment that regulatory programs which confer benefits in excess of costs are few and far between; indeed, we know of no major program for which a strong case could be made. Furthermore, when we look at the total of such activity, the case appears to us to be overwhelmingly negative. If the total effect is negative, and if that result is inherent in our political system, it is not much consolation to know that sometimes individual programs may on balance yield benefits.

One cost which gets neglected when we focus on individual decisions or individual regulatory programs rather than on the total impact of all such programs is the cost of the threat to property rights and contract rights induced by the revocations and abrogations which accompany every governmental program. Individuals, in deciding how they will invest their wealth, and how they will allocate their labor will form expectations about the likelihood of expropriation based on what they observe happening to others throughout the system. As revocation and abrogation become more common, individuals will forego socially desirable investment opportunities because of the threat to their property rights. These foregone opportunities are difficult to perceive because they take the form of buildings not built, new machines not procured, new products delayed, etc., and therefore they are generally not even considered in evaluating the consequences of government actions.

In this same vein, implementation of the programs mentioned above tends to have a special bias in the wealth transfers it brings about. When new regulatory programs are implemented, it is generally assumed that present right holders should not be compensated for the costs they will incur as a result of the loss of their rights. That is, it is generally assumed that the establishment of the desirability of a particular program (by whatever criterion) is sufficient to justify the expropriation of the wealth of the current right holders. The extreme case is the environmental programs where those who want a pristine California shoreline, untouched wilderness areas, reduced use of pesticides, airports moved elsewhere, etc. are never required to bear the costs of their choices, even if, in fact, they would be willing to pay enough to reimburse those who lose. The bulk of the costs in these cases is usually imposed on property owners who have their rights in land constrained.

The mere fact that individual programs might yield net benefits is not a justification for imposing the costs of such programs on present owners of rights in the affected resources. Indeed, much could be said for the reverse. We are much more likely to restrict government officials to actions which do yield net benefits if the beneficiaries are required to compensate the losers. Such compensation would also eliminate the costs imposed on society at large emanating from the misallocation of resources induced by the revocation and abrogation of rights.

N. THE FUTURE

Given the incentives which government officials have to undermine the private rights system, and given the way representative government functions, we see little reason to believe that the trend toward more and more government will be arrested. In particular, the process cannot be checked by electing the "right" people to office. Only a radical change of some sort in the basic structure of our political institutions could at this point alter the course of events, and it is hard to imagine how such a radical change could ever be brought about.

The private corporation has been an enormously productive social invention, but it is on the way to being destroyed. Large corporations will become more like Conrail, Amtrak, and the Post Office. One scenario seems clear. It begins with the creation of a crisis by the politicians and the media. In some cases the crisis will be blamed on the "bad" things corporations do or might do, e.g., the multinationals. In any case, the remedy will be more and more controls on the corporations (something like what has been happening in the transportation and oil industries). When the controls endanger the financial structure of the corporations they will be subsidized by the public sector at the cost of more controls. When the controls bring the industry to the brink of collapse the government will take over. The details of the scenario will no doubt vary. Moreover, some firms will simply be driven out of business because of regulatory costs and the inability to raise capital.

There will be more "public" directors on the boards of large corporations.

There will be increasing involvement of labor in the control and management of corporations. In West Germany corporations are now required to have labor union representatives on their boards of directors.

Although we believe the probability that our forecasts will be realized is high, it is not one. Indeed, we hope that bringing the problem to the attention of the public will generate a solution. Moreover, even if our predictions are realized, it won't happen tomorrow, and it won't mean the end of humanity. It will only mean that we will be much poorer and much less free.

Humanity has survived in various states of tyranny for thousands of years—one might even say this is the natural state of affairs for man. Future historians may look back and see the period from 1776 to 1976 as a brief 200-year accident in the history of man in which real freedoms existed.